William J. Fay

Resurrection and Discipleship

Interpretive Models, Biblical Reflections,
Theological Consequences

THORWALD LORENZEN

ORBIS BOOKS

Maryknoll, New York 10545

Copyright © 1995 by Thorwald Lorenzen
Published by Orbis Books, Maryknoll, New York 10545, U.S.A.

Manufactured in the United States of America.

Library of Congress Cataloging-in-Publication Data

Lorenzen, Thorwald.
    Resurrection and discipleship :   interpretive models, biblical
reflections, theological consequences / Thorwald Lorenzen.
        p.   cm.
    Includes bibliographical references and indexes.
    ISBN 1-57075-042-4 (alk. paper)
    1. Jesus Christ—Resurrection.   2. Jesus Christ—Resurrection—
History of doctrines—20th century.   I. Title.
BT481.L67   1995
232' .5—dc20   95-31252
                                                            CIP

Jill
Christina, Stephan
Nikolai

and in grateful remembrance
of the students, from many countries of this world,
at the Baptist Theological Seminary in Rüschlikon, Switzerland
1974–1995

Contents

v

Acknowledgments

This book was not simply written in an uninterrupted period of time. It has grown over several years. I have used and tested the material in my regular teaching activities, and also in lecture courses, seminars, pastors' conferences, and continuing theological education conferences in Switzerland, Germany, Portugal, the USA, and Australia. In many of these encounters I have been challenged, and I have learned and profited much.

Some friends and colleagues, notably Dr. Noel Vose, Dr. Yandall Woodfin, Dr. Keith Dyer, and Dr. Paul Fiddes, have read earlier versions of the manuscript or parts thereof. For their critique and encouragement I am grateful.

Student assistants and friends have verified the Scripture and literary references. I have appreciated the help of Dr. James Nogalski, Galina Angelova, Dagmar Gollatz, Jack Porter, Ginny Graylin, Rhoda MacLean and especially Lidija Novakovic.

For abbreviations I have followed Siegfried M. Schwertner, *Abkürzungsverzeichnis*. 2., überarbeitete und erweiterte Auflage. *Theologische Realenzyklopädie* (New York/Berlin: Walter de Gruyter, 1994).

Introduction

When we speak about the resurrection of Jesus Christ we are not dealing with *a* question of faith, but with *the* question of the Christian faith. The resurrection is not merely an object of faith, and it is not merely a credal statement to accept; it is the *origin* and *ground* of faith. Here the *nature* and *content* of faith, what Christian faith actually *is*, is decided. It is not merely a historical problem, but we are confronted with the challenge as to what history itself is. We are not merely dealing with one of God's acts in history, we are confronted with God's very nature and how he relates to us and to his creation.

The understanding of the resurrection has always been controversial. Not the resurrection itself, but how we are to grasp it, relate to it, and how it affects and qualifies our situation. We are here confronted with the fundamental hermeneutical question as to how we as human beings can understand and talk about an event which the texts describe as an act of God. More exactly, how can we as sinful human beings understand and talk about the act of a holy God?

How can we understand and how can we talk about such an event in terms of that event itself, and not merely on our own terms? In other words, how can we protect the reality and dignity of such an event against our own interests? Is it possible to perceive such an event without immediately reducing it to our possibilities of understanding; without pressing it into our established thought patterns? We must even ask whether our attempt to understand is not already a subtle expression of our desire to define the event, in order then to rule over it and use it for our own purposes.

Related more closely to our subject of investigation: how can we protect the uniqueness, the identity, and the reality of the resurrection of Jesus Christ? How can we make clear that the resurrection of Jesus Christ is qualitatively different from the resurrection of Lazarus and the many other resurrections reported from the ancient world? How can we maintain the biblical intention that Christ "will never die again", that "death no longer has dominion over him", that now "he lives to God" (Rom 6:9f.)? How can we make sure that we do not reduce this event to an occurrence that is part of a nature and history that are marked and delimited by the reality of death?

The Gospel narratives and some of the Epistles in the New Testament were in part written to protect the reality of the resurrection and defend its message against denials and inadequate explanations. One only has to think of Paul's controversy with the Christians in Corinth (1 Cor 15; 2 Cor 5); or of

1

Matthew's attempt to meet the challenge that the tomb was empty because the disciples had stolen the body of the dead Jesus (Matt 27:62–66, 28:11–15); or of Luke's emphasis that the Lord had "really" risen (24:34), and that this resurrection was not merely a vision or some kind of spiritual happening, but that it was a real event in time and space: they could see him, and handle him, and he ate in their presence (24:36–43).[1]

I think that it cannot be questioned that for the New Testament writings, even where this is not explicitly stated, the resurrection of Jesus Christ is the foundational event for the Christian faith and the Christian church. Without the resurrection of Jesus Christ there would have been no Christian faith and there would have been no Christian church. Luke affirms that "the Lord has really [ὄντως(ontōs)] risen . . ." (24:34); and we all know the passionate assertions of Paul:

> If Christ has not been raised, then our preaching is in vain and your faith is in vain. We are found to be misrepresenting God that he raised Christ, whom he did not raise if it is true that the dead are not raised. . . . If Christ has not been raised, your faith is futile and you are still in your sins. Then those also who have fallen asleep in Christ have perished. (1 Cor 15:14–15.17–18).

We are not asking whether the resurrection is true or false. The answer to that question is not at our disposal as Christian theologians who accept the authority of the biblical message. We are asking, how we can best—i.e., in terms of the event itself—understand, grasp, and respond to the resurrection of the crucified Christ.

Being conscious of the fact that all theological reflection is situational, and that every theologian is in danger of using rather than obeying the biblical texts, I must say a further word about the context from which I am writing. With all good intention to be fair, modest, objective, and to problematize any illegitimate self-interest, there cannot be and there should not be any disinterested theology. The subject under investigation is of existential relevance to me and to the community of faith in the context of which I am teaching, preaching, and writing. I am a member of a theological faculty in an international Baptist Theological Seminary, learning and living together with colleagues and students from all parts of the world. I am a member of a local church, and I try to communicate the riches of our faith through regular preaching and teaching activities. I have participated in a number of ecumenical conversations, dialogues, consultations, and conferences, and I am involved in various denominational

---

1. Luke then has to describe the further event of the ascension in order to elevate Jesus again from the categories of time and space to "the right hand of God" (Luke 24:50–53; Acts 1:3.9).

and ecumenical groups and organizations that are concerned about justice and peace in our world.

My ecclesiastical context explains why I tend to have a more immediate access to the scriptures than it is the case with many other theologians. Yet, in our ecumenical age this may be a virtue. Most churches and most theologians are committed to participate actively in the ecumenical process. In this process there is a definite tendency of most or even all churches to accept the authority of the scriptures as the basis for Christian faith and Christian praxis. The reading of the biblical texts is an important part of the ecumenical process.

This brings me to a comment about the method and procedure. This is not a book about the New Testament understanding of the resurrection; there are many such books and monographs. They study how Paul and Mark and Matthew and John and all the other New Testament authors and their traditions have understood and communicated the resurrection of Jesus. I presuppose such exegetical scholarship, and I am indebted to it. Indeed, since besides the New Testament writings there are no other primary sources about the resurrection of Christ, they are our major point of reference. And yet, there is a difference to the New Testament scholar. I have tried to remain aware of the fact that an event cannot continue to modify history apart from a text or a people or a community that remember it and pass it on. Nevertheless, an event is not identical with the people or the texts that witness to it. We must recognize the essential interrelationship between an event and its witnesses, be they texts or people, but within this interrelationship the priority of the event must be recognized and preserved. An event must not be dissolved into its witnesses. As Christians, we do not believe in Paul's, or Luke's, or John's faith. We also do not feed on our own faith. We do not even believe in Jesus' faith. We believe in Jesus Christ—who lived a certain kind of life, who was opposed and crucified because of it, and whom God raised from the dead. We, the believers, change. We are very different. He, Jesus Christ, remains the same. It is therefore the noble task of theology to try to understand the Christ-event, so that we can know whom we have believed, and then examine our faith and ask whether it is in continuity with Jesus Christ and has not become a projection of our own needs and interests. This in no way underestimates the importance of the "word" (the kerygma) and the need to decide, but it recognizes that the word has content, and, knowing our self-interest, it insists that our faith must constantly be measured against its ground and content. Although we cannot know the resurrection apart from its witnesses, its reality cannot be reduced to or even dissolved into its witnesses. We have therefore tried to "get behind" the texts and ask for the "reality" from which the texts come and to which they witness. Recognizing that words can never adequately "capture" an event, but can only "witness" to and "approximate" it, we have attempted to discern the nature of the event and seek to discern the way of knowing that is appropriate to it.

We are guided by the generally accepted scientific procedure, that the way of knowing must correspond to the object of inquiry. With theologians from Karl Barth,[2] via Jürgen Moltmann,[3] to Wolfhart Pannenberg,[4] we assert and argue for the reality of the resurrection of Christ, even though this reality may be in tension with or even contradict the generally accepted understanding of reality. If God is God, then we cannot merely think him in continuity, but we must also think him in discontinuity with the world and with our own world-view. It is the task of theology to remind the church and the world that God, in his being for and with us, does not cease to be different from us. Indeed: God's being with us and for us must entail his being different from us, because otherwise there would be no basis for a real, life-changing word of hope, conso-lation, and empowerment. We therefore do not approach the object of our inquiry with a predetermined and universally accepted scientific method. Rather, we seek to discover the way of knowing that is appropriate to the object of our study, the resurrection of the crucified Christ. Our theological thinking there-fore does not create reality, but it receives and interprets a given reality. We ask before we answer; we listen before we speak. Our inquiry, as does all scientific inquiry, takes place in a circular relationship between the object of our research and ourselves who are engaged in the research. Yet within that circle, priority must be ascribed to the object of inquiry. In that sense the object of inquiry must also be its determining subject. The interpreter is not master over the text, or the event, or the object, but rather its servant.

This procedure to approximate the reality of the resurrection as much as it is possible, given our human and historical limitations, implies a certain selec-tivity. Some texts, e.g., Romans 6:9f., 1 Corinthians 15, and certain resurrec-tion narratives in the gospels, have acquired more prominence than others. Not only because they speak about the resurrection, but also because they speak of the resurrection in a way which we consider to be closer to the nature of the event, than other texts, in which the situational elements appear to be more prominent. Hopefully, our selection is not arbitrary! We have tried to avoid a biblicism that denigrates the Bible to provide proof texts for certain precon-ceived theological constructs and convictions. Yet, admittedly, an element of subjectivity remains, and we have tried to remain suspicious at this point. Our intention has been to follow christological criteria which we have derived from our study of the biblical message.

The other implication from trying to get as close to the event as possible is the use of the historical-philological method—commonly called the historical-

---

2. Compare the excellent summary of Barth's understanding of reality by Ingolf U. Dalferth, "Theologischer Realismus und realistische Theologie bei Karl Barth," *EvTh* 46 (4–5/1986), pp. 402–422; see pp. 66–71 below.

3. Compare e.g.: *Theology of Hope* (1967), III/6, pp. 172–182; *The Crucified God* (1974), chapt. 5, pp. 160–199; see pp. 91–97 below.

4. Most recently: "Die Auferstehung Jesu—Historie und Theologie," *ZThK* 91 (1994), pp. 318–328; see pp. 17–25 below.

critical method. Although I am aware of the multiplicity of methods that are being used in contemporary biblical scholarship to interpret and understand biblical texts,[5] I am convinced that the historical-philological method must still be foundational for trying to perceive the "word" in and beyond the "words". None of the other methods known to me is equally adequate to distinguish between text and event on the one hand, and to protect the text against the interest of the reader and interpreter on the other. Only when the linguistic and historical work is done, can the text itself call for the aid of other approaches that may help in grasping the reality from which the text comes and to which it witnesses and discerning the consequences for our understanding.[6]

In our approach we have sought to respect the faith-convictions of Christians and the achievements of the theological community. Nevertheless, our primary commitment has been to the authority of the Word of God as it is being witnessed in the biblical traditions and as we have understood it. This primary commitment to the authority of the scriptures implies a constructive-critical relationship to the church. The church, so our conviction, is not identical with Christ, nor is it the continuing incarnation. It is a human and therefore sinful community of believers. It is in need of constant repentance, renewal, and reform. Our claim is that God can say something new to his people and to the world, because he is in his being with and for the world at the same time different

---

5. Compare the survey in Anthony C. Thiselton, *New Horizons in Hermeneutics* (London: Harper Collins Publishers, 1992).

6. The *Pontifical Biblical Commission* has recently examined the different methods and approaches to the biblical texts in order to find the best way to recognize "the riches contained in the biblical texts" (p. 111): *The Interpretation of the Bible in the Church*. With a Preface by Joseph Cardinal Ratzinger (November 1993), in: *Catholic International* (March 1994), pp. 109–147. They assert that the "historical-critical method is the indispensable method for the scientific study of the meaning of ancient texts" (p. 112), because it alone promises to be "as objective as possible" (p. 113). This does not negate the potential significance of "synchronic" approaches, but it does mean, that "synchronic approaches should accept the conclusions of the diachronic, at least according to their main lines" (p. 147). The historical-critical method therefore deserves a procedural priority with respect to other methods. This interesting and important statement is aware of the danger that the biblical texts may be functionalized to serve ecclesiastical interests—"The text of the Bible has authority over the Christian Church at all times . . . The Magisterium of the Church 'is not above the Word of God, but serves it . . .' (*Dei Verbum*, 10)" (p. 142). Nevertheless, by submitting the text to the "control" (p. 131) of the church (p. 119), and by making bishops and the Magisterium, i.e., the official representatives of the church, the "guarantors of the living tradition" and the guardians of the Word of God (p. 136), and by assigning to the Magisterium *alone* the "responsibility for authentically interpreting the Word of God, as transmitted by Scripture and Tradition" (p. 137), one wonders, whether the over-againstness of the biblical message as the Word of God has not in fact been dissolved into what the church is able and willing to understand. Although the Roman Catholic church is remarkably clear and honest at this point, the problem as such is present in all the churches! The constant danger of Christ being dissolved into the self-interest of the church and of the believer makes a hermeneutic of suspicion a necessary part of theological reflection.

from the world. Indeed: by raising the crucified (killed) Jesus from the dead, God *has* said and done something new. It remains our task and privilege trying to hear and understand what he has said and done.

In the first part of this volume we have tried to meet the pedagogical challenge of providing an overview of some major Christian approaches to the resurrection. We have therefore described, analyzed, and evaluated four major approaches to the resurrection: the "traditional" approach, focusing on historical fact and rational perception; the "liberal" approach, shifting the attention from what happened to the dead Jesus, to the consequences of the resurrection for faith and for the community of faith, or to the resurrection as a symbol for the significance of the pre-Easter Jesus; the "evangelical" approach, which seeks to assert the interlocking of the "divine" and the "historical" aspects of the resurrection; and finally, the "liberation" approach, emphasizing the importance and implication of the resurrection for the pursuit of justice and liberation. In the second part we have turned to the primary sources ourselves. This was necessary because there exists no consensus among New Testament scholars as to the interpretation of the resurrection texts. The study of the sources has led to natural divisions: the resurrection as an "act of God", in which we analyze the "novum" character of the resurrection. The resurrection in its foundational relatedness to history, in which we examine the appearances of the risen Christ, the experience of the Holy Spirit, and the "empty tomb" narratives. In that second part we had also planned to examine the ecological and cosmological dimensions of the resurrection. However, this would have meant unnecessary duplications with other sections.[7] In the third part I have asked what kind and what ways of knowing the nature of the resurrection calls for. And finally, in the fourth part, I have sought to outline the implication of the nature and reality of the resurrection for the nature of God, for Christology, for soteriology, and for the nature and mission of the church.

Ultimately, all theological reflection must help the church to clarify its mission in the world. No one who confesses God as the creator, sustainer, redeemer, and final fulfiller of the world and of history, can bypass the cries for justice, the longing for peace, the outstretched hands of the poor and oppressed. While I was writing, the question "What can the resources of Christian faith contribute to the process of justice, peace, and integrity of creation?" has always been present.

With most theologians I believe that theology must serve the church by helping the church to be the church. Theology must therefore be constructive and critical at the same time. If this essay helps a little to make us aware of the rich resources that God seeks to share with the poverty of our human life and with the fragility and need of the world and of nature, and that he invites us to the great privilege of participating in his saving and liberating passion for his creation, then he who raised Jesus from the dead will create ever new faith, hope, and love in our lives.

---

7. Compare pp. 245–247, 267–269, 284–294 below.

Part I

ORIENTATION

Models for Understanding the
Resurrection of Jesus Christ

Introduction to Part I

Our aim is to understand the resurrection of Jesus Christ. In this quest we join a host of people who since New Testament days have attempted the same. This presents us with a dilemma. On the one hand, it is not possible, within the context of this brief presentation, to give a historical survey of the many ways in which the church has understood the resurrection of Jesus Christ. On the other hand, it would not only be presumptuous, but it would be unwise, not to recognize the many approaches to the reality of the resurrection.

We propose to follow a middle way. Rather than describing the approaches of the many individual theologians who have dealt with the resurrection of Jesus Christ, we have grouped their major emphases into different models or approaches. These models will help us to become aware of the theological problems related to the resurrection of Christ, and they will indicate to us how the church has attempted to deal with these problems. In a critical dialogue with these models we shall seek to develop an understanding of the resurrection that is appropriate to its reality and relevant to our time and situation.

This is, of course, a somewhat problematic undertaking. By trying to develop models, rather than understanding individual approaches, we can hardly avoid being unfair to the individual contributions of scholars. We had to be very selective, and those whom we have selected serve mainly to illustrate the various models. It is not their individual contribution that demands our major attention, but we are interested in developing clear parameters of understanding, which should then guide us in our own theological attempt to think of the resurrection in ways that are adequate to its reality. Our emphasis on models also fails to give adequate recognition to the situation in which Christian thinkers have shaped their understanding of the resurrection. And, finally, this emphasis on models tends to play down the fact that most scholars are aware of the criticisms that have been leveled against their position. Fairness would demand a presentation as to how they respond to such criticism. But this again would lead us beyond our intention to present models for our orientation. We shall try to be aware of the difficulties mentioned as we endeavor to grasp the positive and constructive intention of each theological position. Indeed our sense of fairness and our respect for the genuine commitment that Christian scholars bring to the theological task should mean that each approach can become a personal possibility and as such a personal challenge to us.

The need for models that outline in a brief, concise, and clear manner the alternatives of thinking about the resurrection of Christ is apparent to anyone who has tried to understand and communicate this important symbol of our faith. No theological student, no pastor, and certainly no layperson has the time and the energy to read the thousands of pages in order to discover what theologians like Karl Barth, Edward Schillebeeckx, Carl F. H. Henry, Rudolf Bultmann, Wolfhart Pannenberg, or Jürgen Moltmann say about the resurrection.

At the same time, every Christian, and certainly every Christian minister, must seek to *understand* the resurrection. It is the foundational reality of the Christian faith and of the Christian church. It must shape the manifestation of the gospel in our life, in the church, and in the world. Our interest is therefore quite personal, and it concerns our Christian existence in church and world. We do not study these models for their own sake. We study them in order to become aware what Christians before us have thought and what those around us are thinking, in order that we may learn from them and try to avoid what we consider to be theological dangers or even theological errors.

But there is also an inherently theological reason for the use of models. It belongs to the very nature of the resurrection as an "act of God" that we cannot really fathom its reality and depth with our finite minds and with our "fallen" reason. The apostle Paul calls the gospel of Christ a μυστήριον (mystērion) which escapes our finite and self-interested apprehension (1 Cor 1:18-2:16). The most we can do in theological reflection, is to approximate the reality of the resurrection with our understanding, and to fend off false alternatives. Models can serve as images or reflections of a reality whose very essence is not accessible to us. The different models therefore do not necessarily exclude each other. They are different ways of looking at the same subject, and they do so from different situations. They emphasize certain aspects which in their positive impact upon us may lead us to a more adequate vision. Jesus Christ is the person "who fits no formula".[1] The early Christians used many images and titles trying to spell Jesus the Christ into words—Messiah/Christ, Son of God, Son of Man, Servant of God, Lamb of God—but none of these images and titles succeeded in gathering who he really was and is. This means, of course, that also our suggestions will remain fragmentary and can only serve as an invitation to engage, ever anew, in the christological task. Together with most other theologians I have sought to develop an understanding of the resurrection of Christ that faithfully represents the meaning and intention of the biblical message, is understandable, and is meaningful for our situation.

---

1. So the helpful formulation of Eduard Schweizer in *Jesus* (London: SCM, 1971), p. 13.

Chapter 1

The "Traditional" Approach

Fact and Reason

INTRODUCTION

The "traditional" approach argues that the historicity of the resurrection of Jesus is the necessary foundation for the Christian faith and the Christian church.[1] As a historical fact the resurrection of Jesus calls for historical investigation and rational perception. This approach claims to provide a rationally accessible basis for the confession that God has raised Jesus from the dead, or that Jesus has risen from the dead. That which has actually happened in time and space—in a tomb outside of Jerusalem sometime between the death and burial of Jesus, and the visit of the women to the tomb—is the necessary and objective basis for faith and for salvation. There, in that tomb, death has actually been defeated and its estranging power has been broken—once and for all time. It is only the manifestation of this victory which remains to be fulfilled at the end of time when God will be all in all. But this end-time has been foreshadowed concretely with the resurrection of Jesus; and by believing in the risen Christ, the final verification is already being anticipated in the "here and now". Apart from the historical event of the resurrection there would be no Christian faith. Theologians of this persuasion are convinced that for people who genuinely open themselves to the available evidence and who are not caught in a worldview that does not allow for a resurrection, belief in the resurrection becomes a real option. Christians who hold this view lament other explanations of the resurrection because they feel that only this one is rational and therefore communicative to the modern person.

---

1. Compare the brief descriptions of this model in: Francis Schüssler Fiorenza, *Foundational Theology: Jesus and the Church* (New York: Crossroad, 1986), pp. 5–12; Peter Carnley, *The Structure of Resurrection Belief* (Oxford: Clarendon Press, 1987), pp. 29–95.

In order to sustain the case for the resurrection of Jesus Christ from the dead, one or more of the following arguments usually feature prominently:

1. The Old Testament had predicted it: e.g. Psalm 16:9–11; Hosea 6:1f.
2. Jesus had predicted his own resurrection: Mark 8:31 par., 9:31 par., 10:34 par., John 10:17f.
3. The miracles of Jesus can be interpreted as foreshadowing the great miracle of the resurrection.
4. The empty tomb narratives in the four gospels are stressed as historical evidence. They provide the historical proof that the tomb, into which the dead Jesus had been laid, was empty, and that therefore he must have risen bodily from his grave.
5. The resurrection appearances of Jesus after his death and burial proved that he was alive and some witnesses were still alive to verify this fact (1 Cor 15:5–8).
6. As risen Lord, Jesus continued to be active in the church and in the world by creating faith, exorcising demons, and healing the sick.

Thus, it is argued, that the resurrection of Jesus Christ proves that God can and does act in history. With the resurrection of Jesus Christ, God has provided historically accessible proof for the truth of revelation and for the supernatural origin of Christianity.

Up to the Enlightenment (17th and 18th centuries) this understanding was generally accepted in the church. After the Enlightenment it was developed in an apologetic manner against those who questioned it. It is probably the way most Christians understand the resurrection today. At the same time, an intellectual reaction to this understanding has led many people to a denial of the Christian faith.

CONTEXT

Many proponents of this approach presuppose a general agreement as to what history is. They argue that the biblical narratives contain reliable historical information in our sense of the word, and that our view of history is or should be the same as that of the early Christians. They are motivated by a genuine concern to communicate the Christian faith to the modern secular person, and they believe that rationally accessible historical facts are in our time the only credible and convincing basis for faith.

The question is whether in this view the hermeneutical gulf between the world view reflected in the New Testament writings and our own understanding of reality is sufficiently recognized. Many Christians today simply take it for granted that the earliest Christians meant the same thing in their use of the word "history" that we do. For instance, many people do not think about the problem that during the New Testament days it was not questioned that God acted in history and that God could do something new in history. An Israelite could not conceive of and therefore could not produce a secular history.[2] For them God and history were inseparable. God was understood as the creator and sustainer of everything, and he would naturally reveal his will in history.[3] In history, it was generally believed, we "have not merely the working out of human impulses and the chance interplay of natural forces. We have the activity of God in inspiration and revelation, and the evidence of his presence in Nature and history."[4] Yet we must ask, is this what we mean by history today? Is this the understanding of history that we learn in school, college and university? Does this understanding of history govern our every-day life?

ILLUSTRATIONS

We will now illustrate this approach with reference to two prominent contemporary Protestant theologians: the American Carl F. H. Henry and the German Wolfhart Pannenberg. I am not suggesting that Henry and Pannenberg share the same understanding of the resurrection of Jesus Christ. Indeed there are significant differences, and they would probably be surprised (or even annoyed) to be grouped together in this way. But they do place a similar emphasis on the historical fact of the resurrection and on the possibility of its rational perception. It is this emphasis that we wish to highlight with this model.

Carl F. H. Henry

Henry may be called the don of conservative evangelical theology. The long-time editor of *Christianity Today* and author of a six-volume systematic theology[5] never ceases to lament the cognitive vacuum in modern theology.[6] He fears that modern theologians like Barth, Brunner, Bultmann, and Tillich[7] have

---

2. Compare: John L. McKenzie, *A Theology of the Old Testament* (Garden City: Doubleday Image Books, 1974), pp. 139, 143.

3. See for instance: G. Ernest Wright, *God Who Acts. Biblical Theology as Recital.* Studies in Biblical Theology no. 8 (London: SCM, 1952), p. 44.

4. H.H. Rowley, *The Faith of Israel: Aspects of Old Testament Thought* (London: SCM, 1961), p. 59.

5. *God, Revelation and Authority*, vols. 1–6 (Waco, Tex.: Word Books, 1976–1983; = *God*).

6. "The weakness in neo-Protestant theories of revelation stems precisely from this hesitancy to affirm the content of divine disclosure to be cognitive and intelligible." (Henry, *God*, vol. 3 [1979], p. 283).

7. A long list of theologians over against whom Henry develops his theology can be found in Henry, *God*, vol. 3 (1979), p. 248, and in the "Person Index" of the various volumes.

dissolved dogmatic propositions and objective historical events of revelation
into a faith experience which is no longer accessible to neutral, rational, and
objective inquiry. He accuses Karl Barth, for instance, of having "a particular
and idiosyncratic view of revelation which locates its significance for mankind
outside the sphere of rational persuasion,"[8] and in this lack of rational trans-
parency he sees the reason "why theology would have no persuasive message
for the outside world."[9]

Henry's intention is clear and positive. He wants to communicate the gospel
to the unbeliever. He wants to convince the unbeliever that the Christian has
"persuasive reasons . . . for believing."[10] He calls modern theologians "exis-
tentialists", and he names modern theology "existential theology", because he
fears that objective truth and propositional revelation have been dissolved into
personal existential encounters that are as such no longer rationally communicative and verifiable. He insists that "God's revelation is rational communication conveyed in intelligible ideas and meaningful words, that is, in
conceptual-verbal form."[11] He emphasizes the propositional nature of truth and
revelation,[12] and he asserts the inerrancy and infallibility of the Bible.[13] He does
all this with the laudable intention of protecting the godhood of God in his dealing with humanity and to erect an unassailable bastion against atheism, agnosticism, and existentialism, both in their secular and in their Christian
manifestations.

He argues that the centrality of the resurrection for Christian faith can be rationally demonstrated by the historical facts of the empty tomb and the appearances of the risen Christ.

> The rise of the Christian movement can be adequately explained in only
> one way, that Jesus' followers *personally saw the risen Lord* and con-
> sidered his *resurrection from the tomb conclusive evidence* that he was
> truly the Messiah of Old Testament promise.[14]

If we ask what Henry means by "personally saw" and "conclusive evidence",
he does not answer in terms of faith and discipleship, but he speaks about historical reason.

His aim is to prove the resurrection of Jesus in a way acceptable to our rational capacity. Anyone who goes to the New Testament sources with cognitive openness and without a methodological or a philosophical precommitment,

---

8. Henry, *God*, vol. 1 (1976), p. 242.

9. Henry, *God*, vol. 1 (1976), p. 243.

10. Henry, *God*, vol. 1 (1976), p. 213.

11. Henry, *God*, vol. 3 (1979), p. 248; compare the whole section pp. 248–487.

12. Henry, *God*, vol. 3 (1979), pp. 248–487.

13. Henry, *God*, vol. 4 (1979), pp. 129–271.

14. Henry, *God*, vol. 3 (1979), p. 147 (my emphases); see the whole section pp.
147–163.

should become convinced that the resurrection of Jesus actually happened.[15] Henry's presupposition is that the resurrection stories in the gospels are historical records analogous to our understanding of history.

In order to prove the resurrection of Jesus, Henry turns to the testimony of the opponents of Jesus and also of his followers.[16] When Henry argues that the opponents are reliable witnesses because they could have no interest in postulating the resurrection of Jesus, his case is logically convincing. The problem which Henry fails to face, however, is that the New Testament sources to which he refers are pressed into a methodological approach which he has decided upon quite separately from these sources. He expects the sources to fit his hermeneutical scheme. He does not ask: What is the nature of the biblical texts? What is their original purpose and context? Rather, he predetermines the scientific categories to which the biblical texts are supposed to speak. His questions are of a specific historical nature, and he simply takes for granted that the New Testament texts are historical texts that can provide answers to his questions. His approach, which is sensible and logical as such, breaks down, because the sources witness to an event that cannot be captured with our modern historical methods. More so, modern New Testament scholarship considers most of the texts to which Henry refers to be of an apologetic or explanatory nature. They speak to a specific problem, rather than being historical texts in our sense of the word. Therefore, by imposing a methodology on the texts which does not arise from these texts themselves, the author fails to submit to the authority of the text. He remains master over, rather than being servant of the text.

Henry sets out to prove that the tomb was empty. "Without the empty tomb any claim for Jesus' resurrection was meaningless."[17] From texts which are only found in the Gospel of Matthew, and which clearly serve apologetic functions,[18] he postulates that the Jewish Sanhedrin placed "a day-and-night round-the-

---

15. Henry's apologetic thrust to prove the truth of the Christian faith to the forum of reason is well seen from the following quotations: "Few developments have so disadvantaged biblical religion in confronting the world of secular thought as the impression that faith is merely a gratuitous believing, a private conviction about spiritual realities that lacks compelling evidence." (*God*, vol. 3 [1979], p. 272) We are, of course, agreeing that Christian faith is more than "gratuitous believing" and "a private conviction about spiritual realities", but the question is, whether Henry does not reduce faith to historical reason. For him the "compelling evidence" seems to come predominantly from reason (see *God*, vol. 3 [1979], pp. 272–303). He therefore says: "Divine revelation is the source of all truth, the truth of Christianity included; *reason is the instrument for recognizing it*; Scripture is its verifying principle; logical consistency is a negative test for truth and coherence a subordinate test." (*God*, vol. 1 [1976], p. 215 [emphasis mine]).

16. *God*, vol. 3 (1979), pp. 147–154.

17. *God*, vol. 3 (1979), p. 149.

18. The fact which needed to be explained was the discovery of an empty tomb. While the opponents of the church suspected that the disciples had stolen the body, the Christians found this accusation outrageous and felt the need to counteract such

clock watch" of a "military guard" at the tomb into which Jesus had been laid.[19] This was to make sure that the disciples could not steal the body. Then a "sharp earthquake thrust open the tomb and disclosed to the erstwhile slumbering soldiers that Jesus' body was missing (Matt. 28:2)."[20]

Important for Henry is the "primary evidence" that the opponents of Jesus admitted to the emptiness of the tomb.[21] While the authorities claimed that the disciples had stolen the body, the disciples asserted that Jesus had bodily risen from the dead. Henry concludes:

> From the technically qualified representative of the Hebrew Sanhedrin, from the military watch officially surrounding and guarding the grave of the entombed crucified Jesus—from them the God of history in his divine providence elicited the candid, unreserved confession and open acknowledgement that the tomb was empty.[22]

This testimony of the Jewish authorities was later confirmed by the experience of another opponent, a representative of the Jewish Sanhedrin and a persecutor of the Christian churches: Saul of Tarsus. On the basis of his Damascus road experience this opponent of the early Christians "conceded that Jesus is alive in a resurrection body and named him the promised Messiah."[23]

To understand Henry's rational emphasis, we have to note a further point. For him the resurrection was neither an unexpected nor an altogether new event. The disciples and the world should not have been caught by surprise. Both the teaching of the Old Testament and of Jesus provided a long-range and a short-range preparation for the resurrection: ". . . never were the disciples without an intelligible context in which to evaluate the phenomenon of the resurrection of the crucified Jesus."[24] To the question why the disciples did not understand the Old Testament promises and the teaching of Jesus, why they fled, and then later were caught by surprise, Henry answers: "God designed, purposed, willed the disciples' lack of perception."[25]

Before we comment on this attempt to prove the reality of the resurrection let us look at another representative of the "traditional" approach.

---

suspicion. In that situation a narrative took shape in which it was argued that such an attempt would have been quite impossible because the tomb was securely guarded by the leaders of the opposition (Matt 27:62–66). Henry fails to appreciate this hermeneutical and apologetic function of the text.

19. *God*, vol. 3 (1979), p. 148, referring to Matt 27:62–66.
20. *God*, vol. 3 (1979), p. 148.
21. *God*, vol. 3 (1979), p. 148.
22. *God*, vol. 3 (1979), p. 150.
23. *God*, vol. 3 (1979), p. 162.
24. *God*, vol. 3 (1979), p. 159.
25. *God*, vol. 3 (1979), p. 159.

Wolfhart Pannenberg

The most sophisticated modern proponent of this emphasis is Wolfhart Pannenberg.[26] Since Pannenberg is still developing and clarifying his thought, it would be too early to sketch his theology.[27] We need to repeat, therefore, that our main interest is not to present Pannenberg's theological position, but to illustrate the model which we have sketched, with reference to certain emphases in Pannenberg's thinking. These emphases are especially clear in his early writings. In response to criticism, Pannenberg has somewhat modified his position, so that now the importance and significance of rational and historical verification is more cautiously asserted, and as such we could also discuss his understanding of the resurrection in the context of the "evangelical" model.

Pannenberg's theology has an eristic thrust.[28] He wants to formulate a solid and credible basis for Christian faith; a basis that is more reliable than human experience, or the human assertion of an infallible Bible or an infallible dogma; a basis that is more readily accessible than the inherent authority that is claimed for the preaching of the gospel. At the same time he is interested in communicating the gospel to the modern person. To meet this apologetic and hermeneutical challenge he found the theologies of Karl Barth and Rudolf Bultmann to

---

26. Pannenberg's major work on Christology is: *Jesus—God and Man* (Philadelphia: Westminster, 1968 [1964]; = *Jesus*). The approach developed there has recently been summarized and explained in *Systematic Theology*, vol. 2 (Grand Rapids, Mich.: Eerdmans, 1994 [1991]), chaps. 9 and 10. A good summary statement of his understanding of the resurrection of Jesus is: "Did Jesus really rise from the dead?" (1965), in: Richard Batey ed., *New Testament Issues* (London: SCM, 1970), pp. 102–117. Furthermore, his article "Redemptive Event and History," (1959), in: *Basic Questions in Theology: Collected Essays*, vol. 1 (Philadelphia: Fortress Press, 1970), pp. 15–80, is of special interest to our investigation. The difference between his theology and Carl F. H. Henry's becomes clear in the article "Christologie und Theologie," in: *Grundfragen Systematischer Theologie. Gesammelte Aufsätze*, Bd. 2 (Göttingen: Vandenhoeck & Ruprecht, 1980), pp. 129–145 (also in: *KuD* 21 [1975], pp. 159–175).

27. Preliminary but helpful summaries of Pannenberg's theology are: E. Frank Tupper, *The Theology of Wolfhart Pannenberg* (Philadelphia: Westminster, 1973); Stanley J. Grenz, *Reason for Hope. The Systematic Theology of Wolfhart Pannenberg* (New York, Oxford: Oxford University Press, 1990); Krzysztof Gózdz, *Jesus Christus als Sinn der Geschichte bei Wolfhart Pannenberg*. Eichstätter Studien, Neue Folge 25 (Regensburg: Pustet, 1988). Pannenberg's view of the resurrection is well summarized in: Günter Wenz, "Ostern als Urdatum des Christentums. Zu Wolfhart Pannenbergs Theologie der Auferweckung Jesu," in: Ingo Broer/Jürgen Werbick, eds., "Der Herr ist wahrhaft erschienen" (Lk 24,34). *Biblische und systematische Beiträge zur Entstehung des Osterglaubens*. SBS 134 (Stuttgart: Verlag Katholisches Bibelwerk, 1988), pp. 133–157.

28. We use the term "eristic" rather than "apologetic" in order to make clear that Pannenberg's interest is not to justify the assertions of faith before the bar of reason, but to communicate the Christian truth to the modern rational mind. For this shift in terminology see Emil Brunner, *The Christian Doctrine of God. Dogmatics*, vol. 1 (Philadelphia: Westminster, 1950), pp. 98–101.

be wanting. His basic charge against them is that they did not give adequate theological attention to the stage of history and the possibilities of rational verification.

Pannenberg therefore felt the need to develop a theological approach that can be seen as an alternative to the existential approach of Rudolf Bultmann on the one hand, and the supra-historical approach of Karl Barth on the other. Bultmann, he maintains, "dissolves history into the historicity of existence," and with regard to Barthian thinking he alleges that if the content of faith is understood as supra- or prehistorical, then it cannot be relevant to the modern human person.[29]

In an intentional contrast to these dominant theological approaches Pannenberg wants to give a theological status to history.[30] Not merely to our historical experience of faith, or to a history of a special kind (salvation history), but to real history which can be investigated with generally accepted scientific methods. History *can* be the vehicle of divine revelation, and history *must* be the medium of revelation if such revelation is addressed to the human person and is to serve as the basis for a person's faith.

Pannenberg rejects the approaches of Barth and Bultmann because they are not open to rational historical inquiry and scientific verification.[31] He contends that modern science has caused theology to flee into the supposedly safe harbor of supra-historical statements on the one hand and existential assertions on the other.[32]

Such a withdrawal from the stage of history, however, has been fatal for Christian theology and for the credibility of Christian proclamation. Theology and proclamation have withdrawn from the marketplace of human life and escaped into a sectarian existence. They have failed to assume a responsible place in modern society, and therefore they cannot fulfill their mission of giving a credible account for their faith in the categories of the modern world.

He insists that the modern human person cannot disregard the achievements of the Enlightenment and must therefore submit all claims to historical reason. History alone can function as a legitimate authority for all interpretations of reality:

29. Pannenberg, "Redemptive Event and History," (1959), pp. 15f.; compare "Types of Atheism and their Theological Significance," (1960), in: *Basic Questions in Theology: Collected Essays*, vol. 2 (Philadelphia: Fortress Press, 1971, pp. 184–200), p. 199. A good description of the situation in which Pannenberg's emphasis was born is given by James M. Robinson, "Revelation as Word and as History," in: James M. Robinson and John B. Cobb, Jr., eds., *Theology as History. New Frontiers of Theology. Discussion among Continental and American Theologians*, vol. 3 (New York: Harper and Row, 1967), pp. 1–100.

30. Pannenberg, "Redemptive Event and History," (1959), pp. 53–80.

31. Pannenberg, "Redemptive Event and History," (1959), p. 16.

32. Pannenberg, "Redemptive Event and History," (1959), p. 16.

Theology has to learn that after Feuerbach it can no longer mouth the word "God" without offering any explanation; that it can no longer speak as if the meaning of this word were self-evident; that it cannot pursue theology "from above," as Barth says, if it does not want to fall into the hopeless and, what is more, self-inflicted isolation of a higher glossolalia, and lead the whole church into this blind alley. . . . The struggle over the concept of God has to be conducted indeed in the fields of philosophy, the sciences of religion, and anthropology.[33]

He considers Barth's and Bultmann's approaches to be "authoritarian" because they fail to submit themselves to such "critical rationality",[34] and therefore they are not adequate for helping the church to communicate with the modern world.[35]

With these introductory comments we now turn to Pannenberg's understanding of the resurrection of Jesus. Basic to his assertion of the historicity of the resurrection are the appearances of the risen Jesus after his death and burial. These appearances—extraordinary visions, "not an event that was visible to everyone"[36]—were confirmed by the Jerusalem tradition that the tomb was indeed empty.[37] He emphasizes that on the basis of these historical facts the theologian must enquire as to what the resurrection meant for Jesus himself.[38]

He offers four methodological observations to pave the way for his theological conclusions: first, the historian must try to be objective and not approach history with preconceived philosophical commitments: "if the historian approaches his work with the conviction that 'the dead do not rise,' then it has already been decided that Jesus also has not risen (cf. 1 Cor 15:16)."[39] Historians need to be critical, but they must also be self-critical. Their criticism must not

---

33. Pannenberg, "Types of Atheism and their Theological Significance," (1960), pp. 189f., compare p. 195.

34. Pannenberg, "Response to the Discussion," in: James M. Robinson and John B. Cobb, *Theology as History* (New York: Harper and Row, 1967, pp. 221–276), pp. 226f.

35. "The Christian faith manifestly cannot withdraw from every kind of cooperation with rational thought. Some such cooperation is implied in the commissioning of the Christian message to all men, with the task of preaching the message convincingly as the truth which is universally binding." (Pannenberg, "Faith and Reason," [1965], in: *Basic Questions in Theology* 2 [1971, pp. 46–64], p. 46).

36. Pannenberg, *Jesus* (1968), p. 93; in "Dogmatische Erwägungen zur Auferstehung Jesu," (1968), in: *Grundfragen Systematischer Theologie. Gesammelte Aufsätze*, vol. 2 (Göttingen: Vandenhoeck & Ruprecht, 1980, pp. 160–173 [also in *KuD* 14 [1968], pp. 105–118] he calls them "apocalyptic visions", i.e., anticipatory visions of that which is in heaven with God and which will be revealed at the end of time (p. 170); compare further "Did Jesus really rise from the dead?" (1965), pp. 110–113.

37. *Systematic Theology*, vol. 2 (1994), pp. 352–359.

38. Pannenberg, "Dogmatische Erwägungen zur Auferstehung Jesu," (1968), p. 168.

39. Pannenberg, *Jesus* (1968), p. 97; compare: *Systematic Theology*, vol. 2 (1994), p. 362.

blind them to perceive the unique and unexpected in history. They must investigate what they find in history. In their methodology they must not predetermine what can and what cannot be historical.

Secondly, it corresponds to human hopes, and it is therefore a general anthropological fact "that the definition of the essence of man does not come to ultimate fulfilment in the finitude of his earthly life."[40] It belongs to the basic structure of human existence that the human person lives in openness to the world, to the environment, to the future.[41] All reality is characterized by this openness to the future, and therefore a general anticipation of this future and a more specific expectation of a future resurrection of all humankind can be meaningfully argued with the modern secular person.[42]

Thirdly, the resurrection language of the New Testament is drawn from an apocalyptic worldview[43] that locates the resurrection of Jesus in the context of a universal history, including a general resurrection at the end of time. Of this general resurrection the resurrection of Jesus is the historical prolepsis: "Jesus of Nazareth is the final revelation of God because the End of history appeared in him."[44] This revelatory event "before the end of history," and in anticipation of that end, is a manifestation in history and must therefore be open to historical investigation.

Fourthly, no other theological explanation of the biblical witness to the resurrection of Jesus has been convincing to him. If, therefore

> ... an element of truth is to be granted to the apocalyptic expectation with regard to the hope of resurrection, then the historian must also consider this possibility for the reconstruction of the course of events as long as no special circumstances in the tradition suggest another explanation.[45]

Consequently, the only convincing explanation of the New Testament texts is to accept their insistence that the resurrection of Jesus is a historical event.

---

40. Pannenberg, *Jesus* (1968), p. 83.

41. Wolfhart Pannenberg, *What Is Man? Contemporary Anthropology in Theological Perspective* (Philadelphia: Fortress Press, 1970), pp. 1–13; "Did Jesus really rise from the dead?" (1965), pp. 107f.

42. Pannenberg, *Jesus* (1968), pp. 81–88. E.g.: "The expectation of resurrection must already be presupposed as a truth that is given by tradition or anthropologically or is established philosophically when one speaks about Jesus' resurrection." (p. 81). Compare also: Wolfhart Pannenberg, "On Historical and Theological Hermeneutic," (1964), in: *Basic Questions in Theology*, vol. 1 (1971, pp. 137–181), e.g.: "If reference to the future characterizes not only man but all beings, then only in anticipation of their future can one adequately state what something is." (p. 169); *Systematic Theology*, vol. 2 (1994), pp. 351f.

43. Pannenberg, *Jesus* (1968), pp. 78–88.

44. Pannenberg, "The Revelation of God in Jesus of Nazareth," (1965), in: Robinson and Cobb, *Theology as History* (1967, pp. 101–133), p. 125.

45. Pannenberg, *Jesus* (1968), pp. 97f.

For Pannenberg, then, the resurrection of Jesus is a historical event.[46] It is an event in time and space. It took place in a tomb outside of Jerusalem during the time between the burial of the dead Jesus and the visit of the women to the tomb.[47] God proves "his deity in this language of facts,"[48] and this "historical revelation is open to anyone who has eyes to see."[49] He even accuses the conservative theologian Walter Künneth of emphasizing too strongly "the nonhistoricity of the resurrection".[50] Pannenberg refuses to adopt a so-called modern view of history that has no room for the resurrection of Jesus. Instead, he asserts that every event that has happened in time and space "implies logically a claim to historicity."[51] One must therefore reject the postulate that an event is only historical if there are analogies to it. Quite the contrary: "Contingency and individuality are indeed fundamental characteristics of the historical."[52] The transcendent God, who is the ground of all history, "can break into the course of his creation and initiate new events in it in an unpredictable way."[53] God has done this when he raised Jesus from the dead; an event which "has broken through everything we can conceive of."[54] Consequently, history does not just include analogous and homogeneous events, but it must have room for the unique, the unexpected, the individual, the contingent:

It is characteristic of the activity of the transcendent God, whose essence is not adequately expressed in any cosmic order but remains free from every such order, that it constantly gives rise to something new in reality, something never before present. For this reason theology is interested primarily in the individual, particular, and contingent.[55]

He maintains further: "That a reported event bursts analogies with otherwise usual or repeatedly attested events is still no ground for disputing its facticity."[56]

---

46. Pannenberg, *Jesus* (1968), pp. 88–106; "Did Jesus really rise from the dead?" (1965), pp. 102–117; *Systematic Theology*, vol. 2 (1994), pp. 285, 345f.

47. Pannenberg, *Systematic Theology*, vol. 2 (1994), p. 360.

48. "Dogmatic Theses on the Doctrine of Revelation," (1960), in: Wolfhart Pannenberg, ed., *Revelation as History* (London: Macmillan, 1968, pp. 123–158), p. 137.

49. "Dogmatic Theses on the Doctrine of Revelation," (1960), p. 135. Pannenberg explains and modifies this statement in *Systematic Theology*, vol. 1 (1991), pp. 249f.

50. Pannenberg, *Jesus* (1968), p. 113, referring to Walter Künneth, *The Theology of the Resurrection* (London: SCM, 1965).

51. Wolfhart Pannenberg, "Response to the Debate," in: Terry L. Miethe, ed., *Did Jesus Rise From the Dead? The Resurrection Debate* (San Francisco: Harper & Row, 1987, pp. 125–135), p. 126.

52. Pannenberg, "Redemptive Event and History," (1959), p. 72; he finds support for this view also in modern science ("Did Jesus really rise from the dead?" [1965], p. 116).

53. Pannenberg, "Redemptive Event and History," (1959), p. 18, compare p. 48.

54. Pannenberg, "Redemptive Event and History," (1959), p. 37.

55. Pannenberg, "Redemptive Event and History," (1959), p. 48.

56. Pannenberg, "Redemptive Event and History," (1959), pp. 48f.

Thus Pannenberg develops an understanding of history which allows room to include the resurrection of Jesus as a new and unique event; an event that happened at a particular time in a particular place to a particular person.[57]

The resurrection of Jesus is related to his life in that it establishes, validates, and verifies Jesus' claim to divine authority. Quoting Luke 12:8 (". . . I tell you, every one who acknowledges me before men, the Son of man will also acknowledge before the angels of God") Pannenberg argues that the resurrection was necessary to validate Jesus' claim to authority.[58] For this reason, while not wanting to separate the resurrection of Jesus from his life and death, for Pannenberg the resurrection is clearly the decisive and essential event.[59] Only on this basis can the unity of Jesus with the Father be asserted and confessed. For Pannenberg the resurrection therefore does not only serve the noetic function of helping us to know and understand the deity of Christ, but it is the necessary ontological basis for establishing Jesus' unity with the Father.[60]

Since the resurrection is a historical event, it must be open to historical perception and historical inquiry. There "is no other mode of access to a past event than historical research", which indeed means that the burden of proof that God has revealed himself in Jesus falls upon the historian![61] In other words, "the historical revelation is open to anyone who has eyes to see."[62] It would be a departure from biblical religion "into a gnostic knowledge of secrets"[63] if this public, universal, and rational availability of revelation is surrendered.

Faith in Jesus Christ and in the God of Jesus Christ is therefore not merely a supernatural or a psychological experience which is beyond critical discussion

---

57. Pannenberg, *Jesus* (1968), p. 99; "Dogmatische Erwägungen zur Auferstehung Jesu," (1968), pp. 166–168.

58. Pannenberg, *Jesus* (1968), pp. 53–66; e.g.: "To summarize: There is no reason for the assumption that Jesus' claim to authority taken by itself justified faith in him. On the contrary, the pre-Easter Jesus' claim to authority stands from the beginning in relationship to the question of the future verification of his message through the occurrence of the future judgment of the Son of Man according to the attitude taken by men toward Jesus. . . . everything depends upon the connection between Jesus' claim and its confirmation by God." (p. 66); compare also: "Dogmatische Erwägungen zur Auferstehung Jesu," (1968), p. 163; *Systematic Theology*, vol. 2 (1994), pp. 337f., 345f., 363–372.

59. "The Christ event is God's revelation . . . only to the extent that it brings the beginning of the end of all things. Therefore, Jesus' resurrection from the dead, in which the end that stands before all men has happened before its time, is the actual [*eigentliche*] event of revelation. Only because of Jesus' resurrection . . . can one speak of God's self-revelation in Jesus Christ. Without the event of Jesus' resurrection the ground would be pulled out from under theological statements about God's self-revelation in Jesus Christ." (Pannenberg, *Jesus* [1968], p. 129, compare p. 307).

60. *Systematic Theology*, vol. 2 (1994), pp. 345f.

61. Pannenberg, "Redemptive Event and History," (1959), p. 66; *Jesus* (1968), p. 99.

62. Pannenberg, "Dogmatic Theses on the Doctrine of Revelation," (1960), p. 135.

63. Pannenberg, "Dogmatic Theses on the Doctrine of Revelation," (1960), p. 135.

and analysis and which can only be confessed and accepted. No, faith is built on a firm historical foundation, and this historical foundation is the resurrection of Jesus Christ. Faith presupposes historical facts that can be investigated by reason. Not faith but reason ascertains that God has raised Jesus from the dead: "Whether or not a particular event happened two thousand years ago is not made certain by faith but only by historical research. . . ."[64] It is this rationally established historical fact that must be proclaimed from the Christian pulpit because it alone can then serve as a reliable basis for faith in the God who raised Jesus from the dead. Grounded in this historical fact, faith can then develop as trust in the God who raised Christ from the dead.[65] First comes the rational assent to the historical fact of the resurrection, and only then can one trust and obey the God who raised Jesus from the dead.

At the same time, Pannenberg is very concerned to maintain the newness and the uniqueness of the resurrection of Jesus. He asserts its difference from revivification stories that are told in the New Testament and in the ancient world,[66] and he emphasizes that our language is inadequate to capture the reality of the resurrection. Since Jesus' resurrection is a reality "on the other side of death . . . we do not really know . . . what happened to Jesus then nor what kind of reality the Risen One may have in relation to our present life."[67]

In conclusion we may say that for Pannenberg, as was the case with Henry, the resurrection of Jesus is a historical event that was independently established by the appearances of the risen Christ and by the discovery of the empty tomb:

> If the appearance tradition and the grave tradition came into existence independently, then by their mutually complementing each other they let the assertion of the reality of Jesus' resurrection . . . appear as historically very probable, and that always means in historical inquiry that it is to be presupposed until contrary evidence appears.[68]

---

64. *Jesus* (1968), p. 99.

65. "Dogmatic Theses on the Doctrine of Revelation," (1960), pp. 137f. See especially the two essays in which Pannenberg discusses the relationship between faith and knowledge: "Insight and Faith," (1963), and "Faith and Reason," (1965), both in: *Basic Questions in Theology* 2 (1971), pp. 28–45 and pp. 46–64 respectively.

66. "Did Jesus really rise from the dead?" (1965), pp. 105f.

67. Pannenberg, "The Revelation of God in Jesus of Nazareth," (1965), p. 115; compare *Jesus* (1968), pp. 74–77; "Did Jesus really rise from the dead?" (1965), pp. 115f.; "Dogmatische Erwäungen zur Auferstehung Jesu," (1968), pp. 166–169, note also footnote 4 on p. 168 where Pannenberg suggests that metaphorical language alone is not enough to capture the reality of the resurrection. He insists that our linguistic limitations should in no way question the "real event" character of the resurrection (*Systematic Theology*, vol. 2 [1994], pp. 346f.).

68. Pannenberg, *Jesus* (1968), p. 105; Pannenberg has modified this somewhat by emphasizing that the appearances form the basis for the witness to the resurrection while the discovery of the empty tomb serves as a confirmation (*Systematic Theology*, vol. 2 [1994], pp. 353, 356–359).

This emphasis on the historicity of the resurrection is important for Pannenberg because it alone can serve as a reliable foundation for the assertion that death has really been defeated and the new eschatological life has become part of our history.[69]

We had said at the beginning of our summary of Pannenberg's position that we have mentioned him in the context of this first model because of his emphasis on fact and reason. However, his theology contains important modifications that transcend this model, so that Pannenberg could also be discussed in the context of the "evangelical" approach.

There is firstly the fact that Pannenberg refuses to agree to a given understanding of history. He maintains that if the resurrection is a historical event, then we must develop a view of history that is adequate to contain that event. This would also be the emphasis of the theologians that we shall discuss in our third model.

This is related, secondly, to Pannenberg's postulate that historical verification only applies to the fact that the resurrection has occurred. When it is asked what the event of the resurrection has really been and really means, then we must go beyond that which can be historically controlled.[70]

Thirdly, for Pannenberg the resurrection is an open event and its ultimate verification can only happen in the *eschaton*. In the present, before that end-time, all historical verdicts remain hypothetical, awaiting their eschatological verification.[71] The open and anticipatory nature of the resurrection, indeed of all historical events, imposes limitations on historical reason.

Fourthly, Pannenberg admits that our language is inadequate to capture the reality of the resurrection; the resurrection is an event "on the other side of death."[72]

And, finally, for Pannenberg the relationship between reason and faith is more complicated than my presentation may suggest. He insists that "both are

69. Pannenberg, *Systematic Theology*, vol. 2 (1994), pp. 360–363.

70. Pannenberg, "Dogmatische Erwäungen zur Auferstehung Jesu," (1968), p. 168. At this point it is helpful when Pannenberg brings the human engagement for peace and justice into the relationship between God and humanity: "In dem Maße wie die Menschen Frieden und Recht und Liebe üben, verwirklicht sich durch ihr Handeln Gott. . . ." ("Christologie und Theologie," [1975], p. 144, translation: "to the extent that human beings practice peace and law and love, God realizes himself through their activity . . ."); compare also: *Systematic Theology*, vol. 2 (1994), p. 344[57] (the original German text is clearer than the English translation: "Erst mit der Identifikation des in ihnen sich bekundenden Sachverhalts als Auferstehung Jesu ist die im Text behauptete Eindeutigkeit gegeben." [*Systematische Theologie*, Bd. 2 [1991], p. 386[57]]).

71. Compare: Pannenberg, "Introduction," (1960), in: Wolfhart Pannenberg, ed., *Revelation as History* (London: Macmillan, 1968, pp. 1–21), pp. 15f.; Pannenberg, "Christologie und Theologie," (1975), p. 138; *Systematic Theology*, vol. I (1991), p. 250; *Systematic Theology*, vol. 2 (1994), pp. 350f.

72. Pannenberg, "The Revelation of God in Jesus of Nazareth," (1965), p. 115.

bound to each other" and that "faith is not brought into being by an external cause", but the historical "verification of its sources strengthens it."[73]

Nevertheless, Pannenberg's intentional attempt to provide a theological alternative to Karl Barth and Rudolf Bultmann and the fact that this attempt is bound up with his emphasis on the historical facticity of the resurrection of Jesus make it advisable to locate him within the parameters of the "traditional" model.

SUMMARY

With this model we have sought to describe the theological approach that emphasizes the resurrection of Jesus as a historical fact which can be understood and appropriated by human reason. The transcendent God has acted in history by raising the dead Jesus out of the tomb in which he had been buried. This took place in time and space. As such it is open to historical reason. By analyzing the reports about the Easter experiences of the disciples and about the discovery of the empty tomb, reason must come to the conclusion that God has raised Jesus from the dead; or at least, the burden of proof is upon those who would deny that.

This objective reality of the resurrection, established by historical reason, is the necessary basis for faith in the God who raised Jesus from the dead. The fact of the resurrection was there before and apart from faith. It is not the product or postulation of faith, but the presupposition for faith. Whether it happened or not is to be discovered by reason, not by faith. First comes the intellectual assent to the fact of God's revelation in the resurrection of Jesus Christ, and only then, on the basis of that established historical fact, can faith as trust, obedience, and hope be built.

QUESTIONS AND ISSUES

This appears to be an attractive approach, an approach that seems to do full justice to the biblical witness to the resurrection of Jesus Christ as an act of God in history. If God, the creator and sustainer of history, has really acted in history by raising Jesus Christ from the dead, then the promises of God have been fulfilled and the tomb must have been empty. This event is God's supernatural revelation, it proves the truth of the Christian faith, and it must be the criterion for all else in history.

---

73. "Dogmatic Theses on the Doctrine of Revelation," (1960), p. 157[15]; compare also: "Insight and Faith." (1963), p. 44.

Appreciation

It is important to appreciate the concern of these theologians to protect the objective reality of the resurrection event over against any possibility of human distortions. Indeed, the riches of the reality of the resurrection of Jesus should not be dissolved into the poverty of the human experience of faith.

We also commend this approach for asserting the historical thrust of the resurrection. We must never forget that abstract, supernatural, and spiritual assertions lack reality until they become formative in history.

We are, finally, grateful for the eristic and missionary concern which is a major motivation for this approach. Both Carl F. H. Henry and Wolfhart Pannenberg are obviously interested in communicating the Christian message to modern persons in such a way that they can come to faith in Jesus Christ without being asked to make unnecessary intellectual sacrifices.

But we must not forget our question: how can we, in our time and in our situation, best understand, interpret, and appropriate the resurrection as it is witnessed to us in the scriptures. With this hermeneutical concern we must raise a number of issues and questions that need further attention. Our theological commitment to biblical authority demands that we measure this and other models by our perception of the biblical message.

The Meaning of History

This model emphasizes that the resurrection of Jesus is a historical event. For such a statement to be transparent and communicative, it must be clear what is meant by "historical". If this matter is not clarified, then people will operate with different understandings of history, and this will almost certainly lead to confusion, to misunderstanding, and to a lack of meaningful communication.

The basic issue is whether for an event to be called "historical" there need to be analogies to it in our present experience of life and of history. The modern view of history generally held today seems to affirm this,[74] while the theologians who think within the parameters of this model deny it. Pannenberg, for instance, asserts that *all* historical events are new and contingent and as such unique. The resurrection of Jesus is only a "borderline case" of what is true for every historical event.[75]

It seems that we would have to choose one of three possible alternatives.[76] Either we adapt to a so-called modern understanding of history; an understanding

---

74. Compare the summary of Troeltsch's position, pp. 39–42 above.

75. "Dogmatische Erwägungen zur Auferstehung Jesu," (1968), p. 164.

76. This problem is well stated and discussed in: Van A. Harvey, *The Historian and the Believer: The Morality of Historical Knowledge and Christian Belief* (Philadelphia: Westminster, 1966), for instance pp. 98f., 113f.; and: Richard R. Niebuhr, *Resurrection and Historical Reason. A Study of Theological Method* (New York: Charles Scribner's Sons, 1957), for instance pp. 32–34.

that is held "here and now" by the ordinary citizen, which is taught in our schools and universities. Then we would measure, evaluate, and interpret a past event by that understanding. If, for instance, a generally agreed modern understanding of history does not allow for a unique act of God in history, then, in order to maintain the reality of the resurrection of Jesus as a unique act of God, we must find another adjective than "historical". Or at least we must make it absolutely clear and transparent that "historical" does not cover the reality of the resurrection of Jesus Christ. The problem with this alternative would be that we could not communicate the resurrection as a new and unique act of God in commonly used historical terminology.

Or we first try to understand the resurrection of Jesus Christ, and then, in a second step, develop a view of history that is wide enough to contain the resurrection as a "historical" event. Such a view of history would then contain the possibility for a new and unique act of God. In fact this would mean that we adopt the view of history of the early Christians who clothed the resurrection of Jesus in words that reflected their experience and their worldview. The expectation of the Christian today would then be that modern human persons would examine the historical evidence for the resurrection and in the light of such an examination modify their view of history so that the resurrection could be called a historical event. If modern human persons were unwilling to modify their view of history, then we would have to operate with two different views of history. The dangers associated with this view would be twofold. On the one hand, Christians could become isolated, and as such be unable to communicate their faith. On the other hand, Christians themselves may consciously or unconsciously operate with two views of history: a modern one for everyday life (flying in aeroplanes, driving in cars, viewing TV) where history is the unbroken flow of cause and effect, and an ancient one, where in the religious realm God is said to have acted in events of revelation.

A third possibility would be that theologians enter into a dialogue or dispute with scientists and historians for the most adequate interpretation of reality. Pannenberg, for instance, refers to secular historians and scientists who would allow for contingent events both in the realm of history and of nature.[77]

---

77. "Did Jesus Really Rise From The Dead?" (1965), pp. 115f. With reference to the realm of history, the philosopher often referred to is R.G. Collingwood, *The Idea of History* (Oxford: Clarendon Press, 1946). Collingwood distinguishes between the *laws of nature*, that have always been the same, and the realm of the *historical* which differs "so much at different times that no argument from analogy will hold." (p. 239). "History is its own criterion; it does not depend for its validity on something outside itself, it is an autonomous form of thought with its own principles and its own methods." (p. 140, compare p. 243). Theologically, this position is argued by Richard R. Niebuhr, *Resurrection and Historical Reason* (1957).

While Henry tends to opt for the second approach described above, Pannenberg adopts the third. Both would agree in rejecting the first possibility, and they would also not agree to the dangers that I have mentioned. They are of the firm conviction that the neutral and objective enquirer will indeed find the historical evidence for the resurrection of Jesus sufficiently convincing to assert that Jesus has risen from the dead. Consequently, on the basis of the thus asserted historical event of the resurrection, the parameters of history must be defined in such a way as to call the resurrection a historical event.

But the questions of truth and relevance must not be dismissed too easily. We saw that these are also at the heart of Henry's and Pannenberg's theology. As far as relevance is concerned, it must become clear that when we call the resurrection of Jesus Christ a "historical" event we do not mean by "historical" what we normally learn in our schools and universities. Our question to Henry and Pannenberg is whether reason is the most adequate way of understanding the resurrection. Agreeing with their concern that the reality of the resurrection should not be dissolved into our experience of faith, we must be equally concerned that the riches of the resurrection will not be dissolved into the poverty of historical reason!

As far as the question of truth is concerned, we must remember that both Pannenberg and Henry maintain that the resurrection of Jesus Christ is a *divine* event. It is an act of God. If we now claim to perceive it with our rational capacity and historical methodology, do we not thereby make it into a natural event?[78] Do we not then in fact, whether we intend it or not, view the resurrection of Jesus on the same plane as the resurrection of Lazarus, or of the daughter of Jairus, or of the widow's son at Nain, or of any other resuscitation? We saw that Pannenberg himself admits that every historical event has its own individuality and contingency. But how then can we think and verbalize the *eschatological* nature of the resurrection? Do we not surrender the important insistence of Paul that "Christ being raised from the dead will never die again; death no longer has dominion over him" (Rom. 6:9)? Whatever language we use, we must find a way to protect the resurrection of Jesus against being seen as a resuscitation. The resurrection of Jesus has broken the barriers of the realm of death that marks our historical existence.

The question is indeed whether, when pushed, the proponents of this model will not have to admit that the resurrection of Jesus Christ is a new event that created a new reality, of which only some manifestations are observable in history. Such an admission would bring us close to our third model. All we can say at this point is that the resurrection of Jesus Christ touches and affects our history. What this means and how we can know this remains an important issue for further discussion.

---

78. Richard R. Niebuhr says: ". . . the resurrection of Christ does not violate Nature but only death." (*Resurrection and Historical Reason* [1957], p. 177).

૪ *Fact and Reason vs. Gospel and Faith*

Pannenberg and Henry offer an important reminder that no one does justice to the biblical texts about the resurrection of Jesus who does not ask whether something happened to Jesus himself. However, in their attempt to safeguard the New Testament witness to the resurrection of Jesus, they are in danger of reducing the reality of the resurrection to its postulated historicity. Do they not lose sight of the fact that in the New Testament the correlation is not historical fact and rational perception, but the word of the gospel and the obedience of faith? We must therefore ask whether Henry and Pannenberg do not in fact pave the way for a number of distortions of the Christian faith.

Firstly, do they not remove the central role of faith and replace it with reason when they insist that an act of God can be verified with historical reason? If by rational inquiry it can be proven that Jesus rose from the dead, then no faith is needed to confess that Jesus is risen. This does not only stand in contrast to the New Testament insistence that the statement "Jesus is risen!" is a confession of faith made only by believers, but it may indeed signify a fundamental misunderstanding of the reality of the resurrection and the way we can perceive and appropriate it.

At stake is, secondly, the understanding of faith itself. Is faith primarily intellectual assent to a historically established truth? Or is faith merely the trust in a reality that reason has established as being true? Both seem to be inadequate representations of the New Testament understanding of faith.[79]

The emphasis on historical fact may, thirdly, imply a distortion of the nature of the gospel. In the New Testament it is the word of preaching, centered in the foolishness of the cross and brought into the present situation by credible witnesses, that creates faith. In the words of the apostle Paul, both the event of reconciliation and the ministry of reconciliation form a theological unity (2 Cor 5:18-21). The Christ-event includes the resurrection of Jesus, the witness to the resurrection, and the creation of faith. This holistic reality tends to become lost in this approach. The sermon and Christian praxis are attributed secondary significance. The Christ-event is understood to be complete in itself. The sermon only reports about it,[80] and if the hearer has an open mind, he or she will believe that report. The offense of the cross and the foolishness of preaching have become merely a matter of the intellect. The preacher becomes a teacher of history and faith becomes the intellectual assent to divine happenings in the past.

Pannenberg anticipates this objection when he says that the appearances of the risen Christ were not accessible to everyone and that the resurrection could

---

79. Compare Paul Tillich's discussion on the distortions of faith in *Dynamics of Faith* (1957), in: Carl Heinz Ratschow, ed., *Paul Tillich, Main Works/Hauptwerke*, vol. 5 (Berlin/New York: De Gruyter, 1988, pp. 231–290), pp. 245–250.

80. Pannenberg, "Dogmatic Theses on the Doctrine of Revelation" (1960), pp. 154f.

only be captured in the language of eschatological expectation,[81] yet he still insists that the rationally perceived historical event of the resurrection is the necessary presupposition for faith.

We can illustrate this point with the biblical witness to the empty tomb. The empty tomb narratives in the four gospels differ significantly. The most that one can say is that after the burial of Jesus a woman by the name of Mary of Magdala discovered an empty tomb. That is probably the historical kernel which has then been embellished to meet certain theological and kerygmatic needs. But the empty tomb narratives do not carry the weight which has been assigned to them by the theologians that represent this model. Except for John 20:8, the empty tomb narratives do not claim to provide a basis for the origin of faith; and John 20:2–9 is almost certainly a later elaboration to validate the empty tomb tradition by male disciples, and to highlight the authority of the beloved disciple for the Johannine church.

It is interesting that the apologetic use of the empty tomb narrative is found in a gospel which was not accepted into the Christian Canon: the Gospel of Peter.[82] There we read that after the death and burial of Jesus the tomb was carefully sealed with a "great stone" and "seven seals", and guarded by soldiers who "pitched a tent and kept watch" "lest his disciples come and steal him away and the people suppose that he is risen from the dead". Also scribes and elders and crowds from Jerusalem and the surrounding country witness this safety operation. The text then continues:

Now in the night in which the Lord's day dawned, when the soldiers, two by two in every watch, were keeping guard, there rang a loud voice in heaven, and they saw the heavens opened and two men come down from there in a great brightness and draw nigh to the sepulchre. That stone which had been laid against the entrance to the sepulchre started of itself to roll and gave way to the side, and the sepulchre was opened, and both the young men entered in. When now the soldiers saw this, they wakened the centurion and the elders—for they also were there to assist at the watch. And whilst they were relating what they had seen, they saw again three men come down from the sepulchre, and two of them sustaining the other, and a cross following them, and the heads of the two reaching to heaven, but that of him who was led of them by the hand overpassing the heavens.

All of this climaxes in the confession (which in Mark 15:39 is made in face of the Crucified Christ!): "In truth he was the Son of God." Here then, in an

---

81. *Jesus* (1968), pp. 93 and 98.

82. Of the Gospel of Peter only a fragment has been found. It was probably written around 150 C.E. in gnostic circles in Syria. Text and Introduction in: Edgar Hennecke and Wilhelm Schneemelcher, eds., *New Testament Apocrypha*, vol. 1: *Gospels and Related Writings* (Philadelphia: Westminster, 1963 [1959]), pp. 179–187; the text I am referring to is found on pp. 185f.

extracanonical writing, we do have the emphasis that marks the "traditional" approach.

The New Testament stories, however, caution us not to assign to the empty tomb narratives a theological task which runs counter to the intention of the texts. Let us not forget that the apostle Paul develops his theology of the resurrection without explicit reference to the empty tomb.

In this context we should also mention the miracles of Jesus because they are often used as a supporting proof for the reality of the resurrection of Jesus Christ. Again, we do not question that Jesus performed miracles. But we have to realize that in the ancient world miracle workers were not uncommon. Jesus and the early church lived in a religious world in which the divine and the miraculous belonged together. The question is not whether they happened, but what they mean! And in answer to that question we should not overlook the tendencies in the New Testament which are critical of a "miracle" faith.

In the Gospel of John Jesus chides his followers: "Truly, truly, I say to you, you seek me, not because you saw signs, but because you ate your fill of loaves. Do not labor for the food which perishes, but for the food which endures to eternal life, which the Son of man will give to you; for on him has God the Father set his seal" (John 6:26f.). This means that miracles serve their function as signs to invite us to follow Jesus Christ by faith. If this sign character is replaced by reason or historical research then faith becomes superfluous.

The Gospel of Mark follows the same theological intention when the author integrates his miracle sources into the passion story of Jesus, so that the decisive confession to the deity of Christ is not made in response to a miracle, but in view of the Crucified Christ (15:39).

The same theological intention guides Paul in his correspondence with the various opposition groups in the churches. Against those who pride themselves (e.g., his opponents in Corinth or Philippi) that they are of noble birth, that they can speak in tongues and perform miracles, he says that he could also pride himself of those things, but in fact the signs of Christian apostleship are sleepless nights, hunger, thirst, beatings, and imprisonment. The riches of Christ are made manifest to the world, to angels and to humanity in the crucified existence of the apostle.[83]

We may therefore say, in conclusion, that the content of the gospel is the foolishness of the cross; and this gospel does not primarily aim at the human intellect, but at the human conscience and the human will, both of which are captive to self-interest. The proper response to the gospel is primarily not one of theoretical affirmation, but of repentance, faith, and obedience. All of this points to the fact that the proper perception of the resurrection of Jesus is not in the realm of reason but in the realm of discipleship.

---

83. Compare 1 and 2 Corinthians, Philippians, and Galatians, especially 1 Cor 1–2, 4:1–13; 2 Cor 1:3–11, 4:1–12, 6:1–10, 10:1–13:10; Gal 4:12–20, 6:14.17.

The Interlocutor[84]

It is quite evident that for Henry and Pannenberg the main addressees of their concern are unbelievers on the one hand, and Christians who have intellectual difficulties with their faith on the other. That is legitimate and understandable in the secular context of Europe and America. Yet in our time it becomes increasingly problematic, for two reasons.

Firstly, it can easily convey the impression that the main hindrance to faith in God or in Jesus Christ are intellectual problems. For most people this is hardly the case. Following Jesus as the Christ calls for a change of will, and frees us to a new vision of life. Intellectual problems often serve to avoid the challenge to the conscience and to the will.

And secondly, as serious as the challenge of atheism and secularism is to the Christian faith, the greater challenge today is given by the threats to the humane survival of the human race: the ecology crisis, the arms race, denial of justice and of human rights, a mind set locked into militarism and consumerism. What does the resurrection of Jesus Christ say to the injustice in our world and to the despair of people? Does the resurrection of Jesus Christ have any relevance for the human exploitation of nature? Does the "traditional" approach not reflect the rational and academic captivity of much of our theology and as such hinder us from understanding the reality of the resurrection of Jesus Christ as a life and history changing event?[85]

Christian Certainty and Historical Research

A further danger implied in this approach is that Christian certainty may become dependent on historical research and intellectual assent. This would disregard the biblical insistence that the Holy Spirit alone through the word of the gospel can grant faith, and with it certainty in our conscience. Basing Christian certainty on the historian's affirmation of the resurrection can, in light of the widespread historical and theological diversity with regard to this question, only produce grave uncertainty. Historical research is helpful in clarifying and formulating the content of faith, it can even serve as a secondary confirmation of faith, but it cannot grant the certainty of faith. Only God can do that through his Spirit in our conscience.

---

84. Compare: Robert McAfee Brown, *Theology in a New Key: Responding to Liberation Themes* (Philadelphia: Westminster, 1978), pp. 62–64.

85. Pannenberg seems to move also in this direction when, in a critical discussion of his *Jesus*, he speaks of the incarnation as the "self-realization of God" and then binds this self-realization of God to the human activity of love for peace and justice. "The self-realization of the human person and the self-realization of God are therefore identical; they take place in one and the same process." ("Christologie und Theologie," [1975], pp. 142–145, quotations are from p. 142 and p. 144 [my translations]).

⤳ *The Novum of the Resurrection of Jesus Christ*

We have already intimated in our discussion of Pannenberg's position that it is doubtful whether in the context of this model the divine and eschatological character of the resurrection of Jesus Christ can be expressed. Even if one agrees with Pannenberg that modern historians and scientists allow for unique and contingent events, and that they no longer insist that an event is historical only if there are analogies to it in our experience, then the problem is only shifted, but it is not solved. If all historical events are contingent and unique, does this then mean there is no qualitative difference between all historical events and the resurrection of Jesus Christ? The challenge is to find a way to speak of the resurrection of Jesus so that it becomes clear that there is a decisive difference between the resurrection of Lazarus and others that were said to have been raised in the ancient world, and the resurrection of Jesus. Can this model express what Paul says in Romans 6:9: "For we know that Christ being raised from the dead will never die again; death no longer has dominion over him"?

The Predictions

To Henry it must be said that there is an increasing consensus among biblical scholars that Old Testament prophecies were the word of God in and for the particular time in which they were spoken or written. Even if they look beyond their immediate situation, there is no text in the Old Testament which would unambiguously point to the resurrection of Jesus Christ. Only in retrospect, after the event had occurred, has the church searched in their scriptures and found certain texts which in their view predicted the resurrection. But none of the texts are in themselves conclusive at this point.

The resurrection predictions of Jesus are more difficult to understand. In modern New Testament scholarship they are generally considered to be the formulations of the early church, made after the event of the resurrection. In order to understand this procedure we must again remind ourselves that their view of history and reality was different from ours. In the early church they did not make our clear distinctions between the historical Jesus and the risen Christ. We may illustrate this with a reference to the letters to the seven churches in Revelation 2–3. Each of the letters could be attributed to three different authors: to a Christian prophet, i.e., John of Patmos, the earthly author of these letters; to the risen Christ, who appears as the divine author in the introduction of each of the letters, ("the words of him who holds the seven stars in his right hand," etc.); and to the voice of the Holy Spirit, who is referred to in the conclusion of the letters ("let him hear what the Spirit says to the churches"). Modern readers have to appreciate this different understanding of the early Christians before they can understand the New Testament. Only then will it be understood that in the New Testament there are many words which are attributed to Jesus but which in fact the historical Jesus never spoke. They were in fact created by the early church. But the earliest Christians believed that in their words the risen Christ himself continued his ministry on earth. For them these words were the words of Jesus, who, being no longer in their midst, had been exalted "to the right hand of God", and from there was continuing his ministry through the Spirit. They did not make the clear analytical distinctions to which we are accustomed. What was important for them is that what they formulated was in continuity with the vision of reality for which Jesus lived and died and was raised. With the predictions in Mark 8, 9, and 10 the church wanted to emphasize that Jesus Christ can only be understood in the total context of his life, death, and resurrection.

CONCLUSION

We saw that this approach emphasizes the resurrection of Jesus Christ as a historical event. Something happened to the dead Jesus, and the results are accessible to human reason. "Did it really happen?"—was the decisive question. And the unambiguous answer was "yes". The scientific proof for this "yes" is open to anyone who with an open mind and without philosophical precommitments examines the sources about the appearances of the risen Christ and about the empty tomb. The eristic interest to make the reality of the resurrection of Jesus acceptable and accessible to human reason is the hermeneutical key to this approach.

The question is, however, whether this approach is able to capture the New Testament witness to and the meaning of the resurrection. The danger with this approach is that the rich reality of the resurrection of Jesus Christ becomes reduced to the poverty of historical reason which is supposed to prove the supernatural origin of our faith. This emphasis cannot be sustained on New Testament grounds.[86]

We must recognize, however, that Pannenberg and Henry do in our situation what different New Testament traditions have done in theirs. One only has to recall the Lukan emphasis that Jesus had "really" risen from the dead (Luke 24:34); or that Paul argues vehemently in I Corinthians 15 that the resurrection of Jesus is not the result, but the ground and cause for our faith. For the same reason the Matthean resurrection narratives include the story about the special guard who was placed at the tomb and who was supposed to make it impossible for the disciples to steal the body (Matt 27:62–66). Also the Lukan and Johannine stories which portray the risen Lord as eating and drinking with his disciples may be mentioned here (Luke 24:36–43; John 21:9–13). All of

---

86. Peter Carnley comments: ". . . the very methodological commitment to scientific historiography tends to lead in the direction of a fundamental misunderstanding of the very nature of the Easter event." (*The Structure of Resurrection Belief* [Oxford: Clarendon Press, 1987], p. 185).

these are the legitimate and necessary attempts to safeguard the reality of the resurrection against existential, rational, or spiritual reductions, and against explanations that serve human interests.

But it would be a misunderstanding of the New Testament message to think that with our reason we can understand and appropriate God and his work in the world. This model places the emphasis on reason, while the New Testament speaks about the obedience of faith as the proper human response to the resurrection. We may therefore say that the emphases of this model are neither appropriate to the nature of the event itself, nor to the New Testament sources witnessing to it.

The important positive emphasis from this approach is that we must guard the *extra nos* of our faith, and that our confession to the resurrection of Jesus Christ must have historical consequences. Our faith does not create the resurrection, but the risen Lord creates our faith.

Chapter 2

The "Liberal" Approach

Word and Faith

INTRODUCTION

With this approach we refer to those theologians who are convinced that the reality of the resurrection of Jesus Christ can and must be expressed within the parameters set by modern science.[1] Behind this insistence there is, as we saw also with Henry and Pannenberg, the genuine concern to address the gospel to the modern person; and the modern person, so it is said, cannot believe that a transcendent God would suspend the laws of nature and history in order to resurrect a dead person. "It is impossible to use electric light and the wireless and to avail ourselves of modern medical and surgical discoveries, and at the same time to believe in the New Testament world of spirits and miracles."[2]

One would suspect that this seemingly high regard for science would be linked with an apologetic interest to make the message of the resurrection acceptable to human reason. And indeed, this tendency can be discerned within that group of theologians who focus their interest not on the risen Christ, but on the historical Jesus. We shall discuss this emphasis as one expression of this model.

However, the more prominent theologians, like Rudolf Bultmann and John Knox, whom I had in mind when I chose as the subtitle for this model "word

---

1. For a brief description of this approach see: David Tracy, *Blessed Rage for Order: The New Pluralism in Theology.* A Crossroad Book (New York: Seabury, 1975), pp. 25–27; Langdon Gilkey, *Naming the Whirlwind: The Renewal of God-Language* (Indianapolis/New York: Bobbs-Merrill, 1969), pp. 73–80, 185f.; Peter Carnley, *The Structure of Resurrection Belief* (1987), pp. 96–182.

2. Rudolf Bultmann, "New Testament and Mythology," (1941) in: Hans Werner Bartsch, ed., *Kerygma and Myth: A Theological Debate* (New York: Harper & Row, 1961, pp. 1–44), p. 5, compare pp. 3–8.

36

and faith", plead a shift of emphasis for theological reasons. They fear that with the emphasis on fact and reason, or on dogma and reason—as in the "traditional" model—the true stumbling block of the Christian gospel could become blurred or even surrendered. They maintain that the "stumbling block to Jews" and the "folly to the Gentiles" (1 Cor 1:23) is not related to the intellect, but to the conscience and the will. The challenge for the Christian is not to make the Christian message acceptable to intellect and reason, but to make it understandable, so that the decision for or against Christ is made in view of the proper content of the gospel.[3] The decisive question is whether the addressees of the gospel discover that they are sinners who are in need of salvation. It is feared that this fundamental thrust of the gospel is lost when the stumbling block is located at the point of scientific acceptability. When people are forced to make their decision in the area of science, they are not confronted with the real challenge of the gospel. The stumbling block inherent to the Christian gospel is not related to the intellect, but to the will; the offense of the gospel does not aim at our reason, but at our selfishness; the problem is not rational perception, but the obedience of faith. The ultimate challenge is not whether I can believe in the resurrection with my reason, but whether I let the risen Lord determine my life. The correlative is therefore not fact and reason, but the word of the gospel and the obedience of faith.

This theological interest, centered on the nature of faith and salvation, is further underlined by the insistence that the resurrection of Jesus Christ, however it may be understood, includes the faith of the believer and the faith of the believing community. But before we elaborate on this shift of emphasis over against the "traditional" model, we must become aware of the major philosophical influences that have been significant in the shaping of this approach.

CONTEXT

In order to understand the various expressions of the "liberal" model we must recall the importance of the Enlightenment for Christology, and we must try to understand the so-called modern view of history.

---

3. Rudolf Bultmann says for instance: "Christian preaching, in so far as it is preaching of the Word of God by God's command and in His name, does not offer a doctrine which can be accepted either by reason or by a sacrificium intellectus. Christian preaching is kerygma, that is, a proclamation addressed not to the theoretical reason, but to the hearer as a self. . . . De-mythologizing will make clear this function of preaching as a personal message, and in doing so it will eliminate a false stumbling-block and bring into sharp focus the real stumbling-block, the word of the cross." (*Jesus Christ and Mythology* [New York: Scribner's Sons, 1958], p. 36).

The Enlightenment and Christology

During the European Enlightenment of the 17th and 18th centuries the traditional way of doing theology was questioned.[4] Intellectuals asserted, for instance, that human beings have "inherent" rights; rights that were not conferred by human institutions, and that therefore cannot be taken away by them. These rights were claimed over against the traditional authorities of crown, state, and church.

Truth was seen as being located within the human person or in nature or in God, but the decisive factor was the claim that this truth can be discovered by human reason. Authorities that were traditionally unquestioned, like church, dogma, and the Bible, now had to justify their claims before the forum of reason, and reason was informed by the new scientific discoveries and the emerging new understanding of history.

In a summary fashion we may say that the Enlightenment ushered in the triumph of reason. This went hand in hand with an important shift of emphasis: to locate reality no longer in transcendence but in history. Reality became historicized. Human beings wanted to take destiny into their own hands, and people began to feel that this could be done.[5] Traditional authorities were challenged, and human reason became the decisive forum to discern and judge all reality.[6]

Important Christian convictions about original sin, about the lostness of humanity, about the necessity of salvation, and about miracles, including the resurrection of Jesus Christ, were considered to be irrational. Dearly held beliefs about supernatural miracles and supernatural revelation clashed with scientific discoveries and were therefore viewed with suspicion. Jesus' deity and uniqueness was explained in terms of moral excellence. He was understood in terms of being a good teacher and a moral example rather than a divine savior. The way he differed from humanity was seen as a matter of degree rather than of kind. Christian faith was understood in terms of following Christ's teachings and his moral example. In this way it was felt that humanity would discover the way to freedom and happiness unaided by a power from outside itself.

---

4. Compare: Alister E. McGrath, *The Making of Modern German Christology: From the Enlightenment to Pannenberg* (Oxford: Blackwell, 1986), pp. 9–31; Alasdair I. C. Heron, *A Century of Protestant Theology* (Guildford: Lutterworth, 1980), pp. 1–21.

5. McGrath says: "The rationalism of the *Aufklärung* is probably best summarized in three propositions: (1) reality is rational; (2) man has the necessary epistemological capacities to uncover the rational *Ordnung* of reality; (3) man is capable of acting upon his cognition of reality in order to achieve his rational destiny by acting morally." (*The Making of Modern German Christology* [1986], p. 11).

6. McGrath says about the German Enlightenment: ". . . unlike its French counterpart, the *Aufklärung* cannot be regarded as a specifically anti-religious or anti-Christian movement. Rather, [they] . . . were concerned to reformulate Christian doctrines upon the basis of premises more justifiable upon rational grounds, either by reducing them, reinterpreting them or eliminating them." (*The Making of Modern German Christology* [1986], p. 10).

The Modern View of History

In order to further appreciate this approach we must understand that "liberal" theologians are not only concerned with developing their theology within the parameters set by a modern scientific view of history, but at the same time they also display a profound scepticism when it comes to making any soteriological claims for events that are verified by historical reason. We may learn to appreciate their approach when we recall the emphases of a modern scientific view of history that has been influential for these theologians. Such a view has been well summarized by Ernst Troeltsch (1865–1923).[7]

He says, first of all, "that every historical structure and moment can be understood only in relation to others and ultimately to the total context. . . ."[8] He speaks of

> . . . the interaction of all phenomena in the history of civilization. This concept implies that there can be no change at any one point without some preceding and consequent change elsewhere, so that all historical happening is knit together in a permanent relationship of correlation, inevitably forming a current in which everything is interconnected and each single event is related to all others.[9]

In such a view there would be no room for the resurrection of Jesus Christ as a new act of God. Bultmann observes that this closed unity of cause and effect

> . . . means that the continuum of historical happenings cannot be rent by the interference of supernatural, transcendent powers and that therefore there is no 'miracle' in this sense of the word. Such a miracle would be an event whose cause did not lie within history.[10]

Since all events are interrelated, this implies, secondly, "the similarity (in principle) of all historical events". This in turn means that the historicity of an

---

7. Ernst Troeltsch, "Historical and Dogmatic Method in Theology," (1898), in: *Religion in History*. Fortress Texts in Modern Theology (Minneapolis: Fortress, 1991), pp. 11–32; compare: Van Austin Harvey, *The Historian and the Believer: The Morality of Historical Knowledge and Christian Belief* (Philadelphia: Westminster, 1966), pp. 3–33.

8. Troeltsch, "Historical and Dogmatic Method in Theology," (1898), p. 18, compare p. 22. Similarly Rudolf Bultmann: ". . . history is a unity in the sense of a closed continuum of effects in which individual events are connected by the succession of cause and effect." ("Is Exegesis without Presuppositions Possible?" [1957], in: Schubert M. Ogden, ed. and trans., *Existence and Faith: Shorter Writings of Rudolf Bultmann* [London: Hodder and Stoughton, 1961, pp. 289–296], p. 291).

9. Troeltsch, "Historical and Dogmatic Method in Theology," (1898), p. 14.

10. Bultmann, "Is Exegesis without Presuppositions Possible?" (1957), p. 292.

event can only be deemed reliable if we in our own experience have known or can expect similar events. Troeltsch speaks of the "omnipotence of analogy".[11] This reminds us of the words of the Preacher:

> Is there a thing of which it is said,
>   "See, this is new"?
> It has been already,
>   in the ages before us.
>
>   . . . there is nothing new under the sun.
>   (Eccl 1:10.9b)

Troeltsch thus presupposes that on the basis of experience the human person can grasp all of reality and consequently decide what is a historical fact and what is not.

This would mean for instance that we can affirm the death of Jesus as a historical event, because we know that he was opposed by religious and political forces, we know that others in his time were crucified as criminals, and we ourselves have seen people being executed. But for the modern person there seem to be no analogies for a person being raised from the dead by God. Thus within this framework of understanding the resurrection of Jesus Christ cannot be counted as a historical event.

Thirdly, Troeltsch insists "that in the realm of history there are only judgements of probability."[12] This means that a historical inquiry is never completed. It can only produce a greater or lesser degree of probability. It must remain open for revision. It is obvious that with such an understanding of historical judgments the results of historical research can never function as a reliable basis for faith.[13]

Finally, it is a dominant modern scientific conviction that the only actor on the historical stage and the only subject of the historical process is not God but the human person. The human person alone! This claim does not overlook the fact that natural forces like the earthquakes in Lisbon and San Francisco, or the Russian winter that helped to defeat the armies of Napoleon and Hitler, can influence the history of humankind. It simply wants to emphasize that the human being is the only consciously acting subject in the historical process. Troeltsch does not deny that God exists, nor does he suggest that the process of history is a nihilistic chaos.[14] Indeed, he specifically denies historical relativism and

---

11. Troeltsch, "Historical and Dogmatic Method in Theology," (1898), p. 14.

12. Troeltsch, "Historical and Dogmatic Method in Theology," (1898), p. 13.

13. Troeltsch, "Historical and Dogmatic Method in Theology," (1898), p. 17: " . . . historical criticism brings a measure of uncertainty to every single fact and shows that certainty attaches only to its affects upon the present;" it is therefore "impossible to base religious faith on any single fact."

14. Troeltsch, "Historical and Dogmatic Method in Theology," (1898), p. 19.

affirms "history as a disclosure of the divine reason."[15] But he insists that God would not interrupt the unity of history with unique and supernatural acts.

Before we proceed to show how this view of history has influenced theological thought, let us register a few questions that immediately come to mind.

Firstly, we notice the tendency to absolutize present experience and the present understanding of reality. These are, in addition, limited to a certain geographical region and culture. Is it justifiable to make our present ("North Atlantic") experience and our present ("North Atlantic") worldview the final criteria for what could have happened in the past and what can happen in the future? We recall, for instance, that in the 1960s the widespread feeling of the absence of God, linked with the optimism of civil rights successes, and the unsolved dilemma of "Auschwitz", gave rise to a "God is dead!" theology. Autobiographical experiences, successes, failures, and problems were thereby claimed to have universal and ontological dignity. Is this justified in light of many and various human experiences that reflect quite a different view of history?

Secondly, we must ask whether the dimensions of transcendence that we experience in manifold ways cannot and should not shed light on our understanding of history. Is a "closed" and "immanent" view of history really an adequate expression of the experience of humanity?

Thirdly, we should be hesitant to dismiss the fact that in the Jewish and Christian religions, as well as in many others, the concept of "new" events plays an important role. Indeed, does not any meaningful use of the word "God" imply a qualitative difference between God and humanity, and therefore the necessary claim that knowledge of God and his acts always entails continuity as well as discontinuity with our present experience? Any and every experience with God includes a dimension of the "new".

Finally, it is simply not correct when Troeltsch argues that all historical events can only have the character of probability. This is true as far as the details surrounding an event are concerned. It is also true with regard to the interpretations of an event. But the actual occurrence of an event—for instance that Jesus lived, that Jesus died, that Luther, Calvin and Zwingli were reformers in the 16th century, that Hitler came to power in 1933, and that the second World War ended in 1945, etc.—can be established with certainty.[16] We shall have to ask, however, whether such historical verdicts can be derived from the narratives about the resurrection of Jesus Christ, and what role such historical verdicts play for the reality of faith. But we must reject any methodological precommitment that would say that one cannot establish any event with certainty.

---

15. Troeltsch, "Historical and Dogmatic Method in Theology," (1898), p. 27, compare p. 26.

16. Compare: Peter Carnley, *The Structure of Resurrection Belief* (1987), pp. 133–147; Peter Carnley, "The Poverty of Historical Scepticism," in: S.W. Sykes and J.P. Clayton, eds., *Christ, Faith and History* (Cambridge: Cambridge University Press, 1972), pp. 165–189.

The "modern" understanding of history that we have tried to sketch leaves the Christian in a dilemma. On one hand we are people of our age. We cannot and we do not want to divorce ourselves from the time and the situation in which we are placed. We want to be responsible citizens; responsible participants in the shaping of humanity's future. As such we face a prevalent historical methodology and a popular understanding of history that by definition leaves no room for a new and unique act of God. Consequently, within the framework of this historical understanding it is difficult to believe in the resurrection of Jesus Christ as a historical event. On the other hand as Christians we have experienced the reality of God in our own lives and we are part of a worldwide community that has through the ages confessed that God raised Jesus from the dead. Indeed our hope in the future of humanity is focused in the sustaining and providing activity of God, that he will help us to bridle our self-interest and deal creatively with the problems that threaten our health and our survival. Through the Christian tradition the resurrection of Jesus Christ has become part of human experience, and we therefore feel that the so-called modern view of history has suppressed an important event in the history of humankind and an important reality in the historical process.

We need to return to this dilemma. At the moment, however, in trying to illustrate the "liberal" model, we need to ask what happened when this "modern" view of history became an important hermeneutical principle for understanding the resurrection of Jesus Christ.

TRANSITION: TWO BRANCHES OF THE "LIBERAL" MODEL

Theology has responded to the "modern" understanding of history in several ways. Two of these shall receive our attention in this model of interpreting the resurrection of Jesus Christ. What these two have in common is that they shift their attention away from what happened to Jesus after his crucifixion and burial. One approach shifts the attention to the effects of the resurrection in the lives of the believer and in the life of the church. The other approach shifts the attention to the historical Jesus. In the first approach, then, the resurrection is a symbol to mark the reality and significance of the event of faith and the creation of the community of faith, while in the second approach the resurrection serves as a symbol to highlight the significance of the historical Jesus.

"WORD AND FAITH"

According to one branch of "liberal" theologians faith is created and sustained through the word of preaching, not through the investigation and results of historical reason. This is what distinguishes these representatives of the "liberal" model from the "traditional" approach. Based on the philosophical dictum that all historical verdicts can only be expressed in terms of greater or lesser

probability, and taking for granted the historical scepticism of the form-criti-
cal school, these theologians want to dismiss any possibility of making faith
dependent on the results of historical investigation. These theologians therefore make the philosophical dictum that all historical verdicts can only have a
provisional character into a theological virtue. Historical research is theologically qualified as a "human work", while faith lives from grace alone, not from
human works.

These theologians would question therefore whether 1 Corinthians 15:1–11
can be used to provide historical proof for the event of the resurrection; that the
empty tomb narratives can carry the historical weight of providing proof for the
physical resurrection of Jesus; and that the appearance stories are objectively
convincing reports that the disciples really saw Jesus as the risen Christ.

On the contrary, these theologians would see no theological need for such
historical proofs. They are convinced that the word of the gospel, in which the
risen Christ is present, carries its own authentication. Beyond this authentication, contained in the event of word and faith, faith needs no further support.
Indeed, it is felt that any search for a reference point outside the reality contained in the event of word and faith can only result in objectifications, and
through objectification an eschatological event becomes dissolved into a historical or a natural event.[17] Thus for the sake of protecting the nature of the resurrection of Jesus Christ as an eschatological event, any objectification of this
event is resisted.

There seems to be ample New Testament support for such an emphasis on
"word and faith": ". . . faith comes from what is heard, and what is heard comes
by the preaching of Christ" (Rom 10:17). In the Gospel of John, Christ underlines the soteriological and eschatological significance of the encounter of word
and faith: "Truly, truly, I say to you, he who hears my word and believes him
who sent me, has eternal life; he does not come into judgement, but has passed
from death to life" (John 5:24).

Therefore it is not what happened to the (dead) Jesus of history, but the effect of his risen life on the disciples, the believers, and the believing community that is of central significance to this approach. If the effect of his risen life
is authentic and authenticates itself, then beyond this self-authentication one

---

17. Behind Bultmann's program of demythologizing there lies the theological aim to
retrieve the eschatological character of the events of redemption from their mythological objectifications. "It may be said that myths give to the transcendent reality an immanent, this-worldly objectivity. Myths give worldly objectivity to that which is
unworldly." (Rudolf Bultmann, *Jesus Christ and Mythology* [1958], p. 19). Therefore,
in order to discover the truth of the gospel, the biblical texts need to be demythologized.
They need to be interpreted in such a way that modern human persons are not expected
to believe in an ancient world view, but that they are confronted with the possibility of
a transition from an inauthentic (sinful) to an authentic existence made possible by an
act of God coming to the believer in the word of preaching. (Rudolf Bultmann, "New
Testament and Mythology," [1941], in: *Kerygma and Myth. A Theological Debate* [1961,
pp. 1–44], pp. 19–33).

does not need any further historical verification for the reality and effectiveness of faith in Jesus Christ. The believer walks by faith, not by sight. Therefore this approach emphasizes the significance of faith for the individual (Rudolf Bultmann) and for the community of faith (John Knox).

Rudolf Bultmann: The Presence of Christ in the Kerygma[18]

Rudolf Bultmann (1884–1976) agrees with the "modern" understanding of history and says that a "historical fact which involves a resurrection from the dead is utterly inconceivable!"[19] This does not mean, however, that the resurrection of Jesus Christ is of no or only of marginal theological importance. Quite the contrary. According to Bultmann one can only understand the real and central significance of the resurrection if one is liberated from seeking a historical verification for one's faith. As long as we are concerned with objective historical questions, we tend to subject the resurrection event to our categories of science and understanding. We demand of God that he speak on our terms. Instead, we need to realize that we are the ones who are being questioned by the word of God; we are being asked "whether we will believe the word or reject it."[20]

The study of literary forms in the gospels had convinced Bultmann that the New Testament is not primarily interested in what happened to Jesus himself, but rather in what happened to the early Christians through the ministry of Jesus. Form analysis is interested in the life of the earliest communities and in the literary forms that they produced, but it withholds judgment as to the historical nature and validity of the content of the events to which the earliest Christian literature points.

The New Testament—and especially Paul and John—emphasizes that faith alone can bring us to a knowledge of God and his acts. Bultmann therefore has theological reasons for his disinterest in the historical quest:

> Yes indeed: the resurrection of Jesus cannot be a miraculous proof by which the sceptic might be compelled to believe in Christ. The difficulty is not simply the incredibility of a mythical event like the resuscitation of a dead person. . . . Nor is it merely the impossibility of establishing

---

18. The following primary sources are important: Rudolf Bultmann, "New Testament and Mythology," (1941), in: *Kerygma and Myth. A Theological Debate* (New York: Harper & Row, 1961, pp. 1–44), especially pp. 33–44; in the same volume see also: "A Reply to the Theses of J. Schniewind," (pp. 102–132), pp. 111–113, and: "Bultmann Replies to His Critics," (pp. 191–211), pp. 196–211; Rudolf Bultmann, *Jesus Christ and Mythology* (New York: Scribner's Sons, 1958); Rudolf Bultmann, "The Primitive Christian Kerygma and the Historical Jesus," (1959), in: Carl E. Braaten and Roy A. Harrisville, eds., *The Historical Jesus and the Kerygmatic Christ: Essays on the New Quest of the Historical Jesus* (New York/Nashville: Abingdon, 1964), pp. 15–42.

19. "New Testament and Mythology," (1941), p. 39.

20. "New Testament and Mythology," (1941), p. 41.

the objective historicity of the resurrection. . . . No; the real difficulty is that the resurrection is itself an article[21] of faith, and you cannot establish one article of faith by invoking another. You cannot prove the redemptive efficacy of the cross by invoking the resurrection. For the resurrection is an article of faith because it is far more than the resuscitation of a corpse— it is the eschatological event. And so it cannot be a miraculous proof. For . . . the bare miracle tells us nothing about the eschatological fact of the destruction of death.[22]

The resurrection of Jesus Christ, then, is not a tangible historical event. It is for Bultmann "the eschatological event par excellence",[23] an event in which God aims at renewing human existence. Bultmann in no way questions the reality of God outside the event of faith.[24] Rather, he presupposes the reality of God, and he wants to examine it at the point where it affects human existence. The risen Lord meets persons in the word of preaching and aims to change their existence from inauthenticity to authenticity. "Christ meets us in the preaching as one crucified and risen. He meets us in the word of preaching and nowhere else. The faith of Easter is just this—faith in the word of preaching."[25] The "kerygma itself is an eschatological event, and it expresses the fact that Jesus is really present in the kerygma, that it is his word which involves the hearer in the kerygma."[26]

If the risen Christ really meets us in the kerygma, then, according to Bultmann, it is inappropriate to ask the historical question as to what happened to the dead Jesus.[27] Indeed, such a question would be a sign of unbelief, because it would give the impression that one seeks historical verification for the

---

21. The word "article" is an inappropriate translation for the German *Gegenstand*. It would be better translated "object." Bultmann does not want to say here that the resurrection of Jesus Christ is a product of faith; he wants to say that its reality can only be comprehended by faith. In *Jesus Christ and Mythology* (1958) this becomes clear: ". . . what we call facts of redemption are themselves objects of faith and are apprehended as such only by the eye of faith" (p. 72). Bultmann therefore calls both cross and resurrection "mythological" and "eschatological" events ("New Testament and Mythology," [1941], pp. 35–38). They are "divine" events and this "divine" reality is only accessible to faith. Faith does not create the resurrection; the risen Lord, present in the Word of preaching, creates faith. The important issue is: while the eschatological event of the cross is essentially linked to the historical event of the crucifixion of Jesus, the eschatological event of the resurrection seems to have no further historical reference point beyond the crucifixion of Jesus and the Easter-faith of the earliest Christians.

22. "New Testament and Mythology," (1941), pp. 39f.

23. "New Testament and Mythology," (1941), p. 40.

24. "New Testament and Mythology," (1941), pp. 22–33; "Bultmann Replies to his Critics," (1961), pp. 199–201; *Jesus Christ and Mythology* (1958), pp. 70f.

25. "New Testament and Mythology," (1941), p. 41.

26. Bultmann, "The Primitive Christian Kerygma and the Historical Jesus," (1959), p. 42.

27. In the above quotation Bultmann continues: "If that is the case, then all speculation concerning the modes of being of the risen Jesus, all the narratives of the empty tomb

authenticity of one's present experience of faith. The certainty of faith would then be made dependent on historical research. This would be contrary to the aim of the word of preaching which is to deliver us from the limitations of sight and reason, and from the prison of the past.

When it comes to the concrete content and meaning of the resurrection, Bultmann points us into two directions: to the cross of Christ and to Christian existence. Affirming the "inseparable unity" between the cross and resurrection,[28] he says that "faith in the resurrection is really the same thing as faith in the saving efficacy of the cross . . .".[29] When one asks what that concretely means, Bultmann points to the existence of the believer: "To believe in the cross of Christ does not mean to concern ourselves with a mythical process wrought outside of us and our world, . . . but rather to make the cross of Christ our own, to undergo crucifixion with him."[30] As "eschatological events" the cross and the resurrection are ever-present realities in the life of the Christian.[31] The resurrection, then, is not an act of God with its own identity. Rather, it is the continuing witness to the saving significance of the cross, and, at the same time, it is the symbol for the faith that lives from that saving significance. It can therefore be said that for Bultmann the "resurrection of Christ" stands for the saving significance of the cross and for the arrival of that saving significance in the life of the believer.

With Bultmann, then, we notice a definite shift in emphasis from the historical to the existential plane; from what happened to Jesus to what happened to the disciples and what can happen to us. This shift of emphasis is due to three things: firstly, the conviction that the modern view of history does not allow for a historical resurrection of Jesus from the dead. Beyond the assertion that Christ is present in the kerygma, Bultmann refuses to give objective christological content to the resurrection. He fears that this would mythologize the faith and demand an intellectual sacrifice from the potential believer. Secondly, Bultmann is convinced that the existential interpretation of the Christ event is demanded by the major traditions of the New Testament. Thirdly, Protestant, and among them mainly Lutheran, theologians resist attempts to divert attention from the Reformation insight that the believer is saved by faith alone (*sola gratia, sola fide*). Grounding one's faith in an objectively verifiable historical fact means that faith would remain dependent on historical research, and that in turn would imply a salvation by works: "There is no difference between security based on

---

and all the Easter legends, whatever elements of historical fact they may contain, and as true as they may be in their symbolic form, are of no consequence. To believe in the Christ present in the kerygma is the meaning of the Easter faith." ("The Primitive Christian Kerygma and the Historical Jesus," [1959], p. 42).

28. ". . . the cross and the resurrection form a single, indivisible cosmic event." ("New Testament and Mythology," [1941], p. 38).

29. "New Testament and Mythology," (1941), p. 41.

30. "New Testament and Mythology," (1941), p. 36, compare pp. 35–38.

31. "New Testament and Mythology," (1941), pp. 37, 38, 40.

good works and security built on objectifying knowledge."[32] Only he "who abandons every form of security shall find the true security."[33]

John Knox: The Presence of Christ in the Living Memory of the Church.

If one could say that for Bultmann, Jesus Christ has risen into and is ever present in the kerygma,[34] for the American Protestant theologian John Knox (1900-) one could say that Christ, through the ministry of the Holy Spirit, has risen into the living and self-conscious memory of the church.[35]

For Knox the resurrection of Jesus "is a fact of the objective order, both indubitable and essential."[36] By "fact", however, he does not mean an isolated occurrence in past history which could be perceived and investigated by historical reason. The resurrection is "more than the merely formal, external fact . . . at a given time and place."[37] The reality of the resurrection includes both the occurrence and the responses to it. Jesus and the church together form the Christ-event.[38] The event cannot be separated from those on whom it has an effect. Therefore only faith can grasp the event of the resurrection.[39] With this

---

32. Rudolf Bultmann, *Jesus Christ and Mythology* (1958), p. 84; compare: "New Testament and Mythology," (1941), pp. 3f.

33. Rudolf Bultmann, *Jesus Christ and Mythology* (1958), p. 84.

34. Bultmann has accepted this characterization: "The Primitive Christian Kerygma and the Historical Jesus," (1959), p. 42.

35. I only mention the following of Knox's manifold works: *Jesus: Lord and Christ: A Trilogy Comprising "The Man Christ Jesus,"* (1941) *"Christ the Lord,"* (1945) *"On the Meaning of Christ,"* (1947) (New York: Harper & Brothers, 1958), see especially pp. 117–139, 214–224, 242–246 (= *Jesus*); *The Church and the Reality of Christ* (New York: Harper & Row, 1962), see especially pp. 37–77 (= *Church*); *The Humanity and Divinity of Christ: A Study of Pattern in Christology* (Cambridge: University Press, 1967), see especially pp. 77f. fn 2 (= *Humanity and Divinity*); *Criticism and Faith* (New York, Nashville: Abingdon—Cokesbury, 1952) (= *Criticism*). A bibliography of Knox's writings and a discussion of his theology can be found in: W. R. Farmer, C. F. D. Moule, R. R. Niebuhr, eds., *Christian History and Interpretation: Studies Presented to John Knox* (Cambridge: University Press, 1967). For a discussion of Knox's Christology see: Robert E. Cushman, "Christology or Ecclesiology? A Critical Examination of the Christology of John Knox," *RelLife* 27 (Autumn 1958, No. 4), pp. 515–526; Peter Carnley, *The Structure of Resurrection Belief* (1987), pp. 268–296; Richard R. Niebuhr, *Resurrection and Historical Reason* (1957), pp. 62–71, 94–102.

36. *Church* (1962), p. 76. *Jesus: "Christ the Lord"* (1945), p. 118: "I have spoken of the resurrection as a fact, not as a belief;. . . . The resurrection is a part of the concrete empirical meaning of Jesus, not the result of mere reflection upon that meaning. Beliefs were based upon the resurrection; it was not itself a belief. It was something given. It was a reality grasped in faith."

37. *Jesus: "Christ the Lord"* (1945), p. 119; *Humanity and Divinity* (1967), pp. 77f., fn. 2.

38. *Jesus: "On the Meaning of Christ"* (1947), pp. 214–224.

39. *Jesus: "Christ the Lord"* (1945), pp. 121–126. Although Knox does not doubt the historical occurrence of the resurrection appearances, for him they are theologically not

assertion we could also discuss Knox in the context of our third model. However, as we saw with Bultmann, Knox is not concerned with what happened to the dead Jesus. His theological interest is focused on the presence of the risen Christ in the experience of faith. In contrast to Bultmann, however, faith is understood primarily as a communal rather than an individual reality.

The resurrection of Jesus Christ, then, for Knox is not a historical occurrence in the sense of an "observable incident"[40] which everyone who has eyes to see could see. Rather, it is a historical event insofar as the church holds the risen Lord in its living memory. This implies that only within the church can the risen Lord be known: "Outside the Church, the evidence cannot be seen; inside the Church, the argument is not needed."[41] Consequently, to "share in the substance of the Church's life is to know the concrete meaning of the Resurrection. To affirm the Resurrection is to affirm the distinctive character of the Church's own existence."[42] "It took more than twenty years for me to reach the point of seeing that in having the Church we have everything."[43] Theologically speaking, the resurrection of Christ, the coming of the Holy Spirit, and the self-awareness of the church are one and the same event, or at least, they can no longer be clearly distinguished: "We sometimes speak of the Event as culminating in the Resurrection; but we are just as likely to speak of it as culminating in the coming of the Spirit or in the full self-conscious emergence of the Church."[44] Neither the empty tomb nor even the resurrection appearances to the disciples can or need to serve as proofs for the resurrection of Jesus Christ.

> The Church was born of the Spirit; and that Spirit was from the beginning recognized to be the presence and power of the living Jesus. It is in that fact (not in any appearances, merely as such) that the resurrection faith was securely based.[45]

Only the Holy Spirit who ministers in and through the church can make us sure of the resurrection of Jesus Christ.

---

necessary to affirm the reality of the resurrection. "For if our faith in the resurrection has any vitality or validity, it is nothing less than the conviction that there is even now present and knowable within the Christian fellowship through 'the Holy Spirit, which is given unto us,' the full concrete personal meaning of 'Jesus Christ and him crucified.'" (Ibid., p. 125). The risen Christ is present in the Spirit and is known through the Spirit in the Christian community.

40. *Church* (1962), p. 69.

41. *Church* (1962), p. 66.

42. *Church* (1962), p. 66, compare p. 46. Note that Knox spells "Church" always with a capital *C*.

43. *Church* (1962), p. 10.

44. *Church* (1962), p. 70.

45. *Jesus: "Christ the Lord"* (1945), p. 125.

When asked about the content of the resurrection faith, Knox distinguishes between the church's memory of Jesus, which is an essential aspect of Christian faith, and historical knowledge of facts about Jesus. The latter can be found in the gospels, and historical reason needs to search for them. But their relevance for faith is auxiliary rather than essential. Like Bultmann, who emphasized the central fact that Jesus lived and died, and who considered it to be of no theological significance what Jesus thought and how he lived, Knox is very hesitant to give content to the church's memory of Jesus.[46] He speaks of Jesus' moral goodness and the quality of his love,[47] but that leaves the content of the resurrection faith fairly colourless. As with Bultmann one has a strong sense that the community's faith can easily become more formative of the resurrection faith than Jesus himself.

With Bultmann, Knox shifts the emphasis of the reality of the resurrection of Jesus Christ from what happened to Jesus to what happened to those who confess him as the Christ. He goes beyond Bultmann by emphasizing the communal aspect of faith. Christ is present as Lord not merely in the encounter of word and faith in the life of the individual believer, but especially in the living memory of the church.

2) FOCUS ON THE PRE-EASTER JESUS[48]

We saw that it was characteristic of "liberal" theologians to understand the resurrection of Jesus Christ within the parameters set by modern historical science. This made it very difficult, if not impossible, to speak meaningfully of the physical resurrection of the dead Jesus. The emphasis therefore shifted away from what happened to the dead Jesus. With Bultmann and Knox it shifted from what happened to Jesus to what happened to the disciples and to the community of faith. With the theologians whom we shall refer to now the emphasis did not shift forward to the faith of the disciples, but backward to the pre-Easter Jesus.

---

46. We saw that Bultmann maintains that for Christian faith it is only essential that Jesus lived and died. Knox's emphasis is very similar: " . . . I am referring, not to any fact about Jesus, not even to his 'historicity,' but to the person himself as, living and dying, he is remembered in the church." (*Criticism* [1952], p. 37); " . . . in affirming that a memory of Jesus exists in the Church, I am not suggesting that it contains a single specific datum concerning the circumstances or incidents of Jesus' career or a single sentence from his lips. . . . When I say, then, that the Church remembers Jesus, I do not mean that it remembers *facts about him*." (*Church* [1962], p. 50; compare: *Jesus: "Christ the Lord"* [1945], pp. 114–116).

47. *Humanity and Divinity* (1967), p. 45; *Church* (1962), pp. 52–57.

48. Compare: Francis Schüssler Fiorenza, *Foundational Theology* (1986), pp. 18–28, discussing the views of Rudolf Pesch and Edward Schillebeeckx; Peter Carnley, *The Structure of Resurrection Belief* (1987), pp. 148–182; under the heading "The Resurrection as a Non-Event" Carnley analyzes the positions of David Friedrich Strauss, Ernest Renan, Willi Marxsen, and Don Cupitt.

In this view the resurrection serves as a symbol of faith to highlight the significance of the historical Jesus.[49] The origin of Christian faith is not seen in the activity of the risen Christ, but rather in the ministry of the historical Jesus. The
confession that God raised Jesus from the dead is therefore not the presupposition for faith, but it is the consequence and the product of faith. Faith in Jesus
as the Christ uses the symbol of the resurrection to interpret itself. To pave the
way for this understanding in contemporary theology we need to recall briefly
how the modern understanding of history began to influence theology.

Jesus Did Not Really Rise from the Dead (David Friedrich Strauss)

David Friedrich Strauss (1808–1874), a 19th century German Protestant theologian, stated in his major theological work that our "modern world, . . . after
many centuries of tedious research, has attained a conviction, that all things are
linked together by a chain of causes and effects, which suffers no interruption."[50]
Consequently, the Christian faith could only be maintained in our "modern"
times if the miraculous element is eliminated. Reason cannot and therefore must
not be contradicted by revelation. Since the resurrection of Jesus is reported to
be a "supernatural" event, it cannot be historical. The resulting alternative is
clearly stated: ". . . the cultivated intellect of the present day has very decid-
edly stated the following dilemma: *either Jesus was not really dead, or he did
not really rise again.*"[51]
Strauss opted for the latter. How then did the faith in the risen Christ origi-
nate? To answer this question Strauss, first of all, analyzes the situation of the
disciples after the death of Jesus. Their fundamental existential challenge was
to reconcile the fact that they believed in Jesus as Messiah with the fact of his
death. A second element was, that after "the first shock" of Jesus' death was
over,[52] there began to grow within them the continuing "impression of the sub-
lime personality of Jesus."[53] As a third element, the study of the scriptures helped
them to understand that a person who takes God seriously must expect his death,

---

49. It is interesting that a similar shift of emphasis has been attempted within the
Anglican context of Incarnational (Logos) Christology. Not the incarnate Logos, so it
is said there, but the historical Jesus is the proper object of faith: compare the essays in:
John Hick, ed., *The Myth of God Incarnate* (London: SCM, 1977). If we were to respond to that debate from the perspective developed in this essay, I would say that neither the incarnate Logos, nor the historical Jesus, but the crucified and risen Christ is
the subject and the object of our faith. This does not negate the importance of the incarnation nor of the historical Jesus, but it views both of them in light of the resurrection of the crucified Christ; compare further: Ingolf U. Dalferth, "Der Mythos vom
inkarnierten Gott und das Thema der Christologie," *ZThK* 84 (1987), pp. 320–344.
50. *The Life of Jesus Critically Examined*, (4th ed. 1840) (Philadelphia: Fortress,
1972), p. 78.
51. *The Life of Jesus Critically Examined* (1840), p. 736 (emphasis mine).
52. *The Life of Jesus Critically Examined* (1840), p. 742.
53. *The Life of Jesus Critically Examined* (1840), p. 741.

but he will, as a reward for his faithfulness, be taken into the glory of God. This, fourthly, led to the question: " . . . how could he fail, out of this glory . . . to give tidings of himself to his followers?"[54]

This constellation of their own theological and existential difficulties, mixed with the continuing memory of the impressive personality of Jesus, their instructive study of the scriptures, and their own theological hopes and speculations, resulted in inner subjective visionary experiences which convinced the disciples that Jesus had risen from the dead. Since all this happened while they were in Galilee, the dead body of Jesus could not contradict their visions, and by the time they came to Jerusalem to proclaim the resurrection, the body could no longer be viewed.[55]

The obvious conclusion is that according to modern scientific canons Jesus could not have risen, and therefore in fact he did not rise from the dead. In his last major work Strauss says: ". . . looking at it historically, as an outward event, the resurrection of Jesus had not the very slightest foundation."[56]

Christian faith, then, does not arise from the risen Christ, but from the historical Jesus who "came to life again" in and through a complex psychological experience of emotional needs, rational reflections, and theological speculations, all of which were focused on the impressive personality of the historical Jesus. Christian faith has therefore created the "resurrection" in order to verbalize that faith in Jesus lives on after his death.[57]

Jesus Was Not Really Dead (Heinrich Eberhard Gottlob Paulus)

The other alternative that Strauss had suggested was adopted by the German Protestant theologian Heinrich Eberhard Gottlob Paulus (1761–1851). He reasoned that on the cross Jesus fell into a "deathlike trance" from which, through a providential conflation of circumstances, he was brought back to consciousness. Albert Schweitzer summarizes Paulus's view of Jesus' "resurrection" as follows:

> The lance-thrust, which we are to think of rather as a mere surface wound, served the purpose of a phlebotomy. The cool grave and the aromatic

---

54. *The Life of Jesus Critically Examined* (1840), p. 742.

55. *The Life of Jesus Critically Examined* (1840), pp. 741–743.

56. David Friedrich Strauss, *The Old Faith and the New: A Confession* (New York: Henry Holt & Co., 1873), p. 82.

57. This understanding of the resurrection has recently been renewed in the somewhat controversial book by Gerd Lüdemann, *Die Auferstehung Jesu. Historie, Erfahrung, Theologie* (Göttingen: Vandenhoeck & Ruprecht, 1994). Following a careful exegesis of all relevant New Testament texts, Lüdemann concludes that primal "appearances" occurred only to Peter and Paul, while all other reported "appearances" are dependent ones (p.124). The "appearances" are then interpreted in terms of depth psychology (pp. 106–112, 124–129). For Saul (pp. 106–112, 124–126), his encounters with Christians left unresolved problems on the emotional and subconscious level (p. 110) which

unguents continued the process of resuscitation, until finally the storm
and earthquake aroused Jesus to full consciousness. Fortunately the
earthquake also had the effect of rolling away the stone from the mouth
of the grave. The Lord stripped off the grave-clothes and put on a gardener's dress. . . . Through the women, He sends a message to His disciples bidding them meet Him in Galilee, and Himself sets out to go
thither.[58]

So, in a very natural way, after his death, Jesus was again among them providing the leadership they needed.

The Resurrection as a Symbol for the Eschatological Significance of Jesus (Rudolf Pesch)

In recent years the German Roman Catholic New Testament Scholar Rudolf
Pesch has suggested the interpretation of the resurrection as a symbol for the
significance of the Jesus of history for the faith of the earliest Christians.[59]
Like Pannenberg and Bultmann, Pesch is concerned that this central symbol
of the Christian faith can be communicated in an effective manner. If our faith
cannot be made rationally transparent and scientifically credible, so his argument runs, then in fact "the believer postulates himself as the basis of faith."[60]
Such a subjective fideism could be avoided, however, if faith is grounded in the
historical Jesus; and Jesus' life and death is accessible by historical reason.

---

intensified into a subconscious "Christuskomplex" (p.111), which then in turn released
itself into hallucinations on the road to Damascus (p.111). In Peter's case (pp. 124–129),
it was his ambivalent and dependent relation to Jesus on the one hand, and his guilt feel-
ings (pp.124, 213) for having denied Jesus on the other, which hindered the grief process
after the sudden death of Jesus. This intensified into a vision in which he experienced
Jesus' word of forgiveness once again (pp. 126, 128). These visions and hallucinations
led to the conclusion that God had raised Jesus from the dead (p. 42). Thus, nothing new
happened at "Easter". "Easter" meant the intensification and strengthening of the disciples' experience with the historical Jesus (pp. 218f.). For us today this means that
Jesus, the pre-Easter historical Jesus, is the objective ground of our faith (pp. 219f.).

58. Albert Schweitzer, *The Quest of the Historical Jesus: A Critical Study of Its Progress
from Reimarus to Wrede* (London: Adam & Charles Black, 1948 [1906]), p. 54.

59. Rudolf Pesch, "Zur Entstehung des Glaubens an die Auferstehung Jesu. Ein
Vorschlag zur Diskussion," *ThQ* 153 (1973), pp. 201–228. Pesch's view is summarized
in English in: John P. Galvin, "Resurrection as *Theologia crucis Jesu:* The Foundational
Christology of Rudolf Pesch," *TS* 38 (1977), pp. 513–525. Since his first proposal, Pesch
has considerably modified his position. We have neglected this change since it is not
our intention to present the Christology of Rudolf Pesch as such, but simply to use his
essay to illustrate a theological model. The modification of Pesch's view is described
in John P. Galvin, "The Origin of Faith in the Resurrection of Jesus: Two Recent
Perspectives," *TS* 49 (1988), pp. 25–44.

60. "Zur Entstehung des Glaubens an die Auferstehung Jesu," *ThQ* 153 (1973), p. 202
(my translation).

Building on the research of Klaus Berger[61] and Ulrich Wilckens[62] Pesch suggests that the confession of the resurrection of Jesus is the disciples' way of saying that Jesus' life and death are part of being the legitimate messenger of God, and that their faith in him did not cease with his crucifixion, but it continued to be alive. The argument proceeds as follows.

With many scholars, Pesch rejects the idea that the resurrection is a supernatural miracle to prove the deity of Jesus.[63] He also notes that in the New Testament the empty tomb narratives nowhere provide the basis for faith.[64] The reports about the appearances of the risen Christ to Peter and to others are to be understood as *Legitimationsformeln* (formulas of validation) that serve to validate the authority of Peter and the other leaders in the early church.[65] The appearance formulas are therefore not statements about Jesus' resurrection and his appearance, but their theological function is to reinforce the authority of Peter and the other leaders in the early church. The "appearances" therefore did not cause faith in the risen Christ, rather they "presuppose" faith in the resurrection.[66]

Pesch then addresses the traditional theory that apart from the resurrection of Jesus the radical change in the disciples from despondency and fear to hope and courage could find no satisfactory explanation. Based on the research of Klaus Berger he maintains that during the time of Jesus it was known, believed, and expected that an eschatological messenger of God would rise again after his violent death.[67] Jesus himself was convinced to be such an eschatological messenger and he shared that conviction with his disciples. The expectation of John the Baptist's resurrection in Mark 6:14–16 showed that such a view was not uncommon during Jesus' day. Indeed the followers of John the

---

61. Compare for instance: Klaus Berger, *Die Auferstehung des Propheten und die Erhöhung des Menschensohnes. Traditionsgeschichtliche Untersuchungen zur Deutung des Geschickes Jesu in frühchristlichen Texten.* StUNT, 13 (Göttingen: Vandenhoeck & Ruprecht, 1976).

62. Ulrich Wilckens, "Der Ursprung der Überlieferung der Erscheinungen des Auferstandenen. Zur traditionsgeschichtlichen Analyse von 1 Kor. 15,1–11," in: Wilfried Joest and Wolfhart Pannenberg, eds., *Dogma und Denkstrukturen* (Göttingen: Vandenhoeck & Ruprecht, 1963), pp. 56–95; Ulrich Wilckens, "The Tradition-history of the Resurrection of Jesus," (1966), in: C.F.D. Moule, ed., *The Significance of the Message of the Resurrection for Faith in Jesus Christ.* Studies in Biblical Theology, Second Series 8 (London: SCM, 1968), pp. 51–76; Ulrich Wilckens, *Resurrection. Biblical Testimony to the Resurrection, An Historical Examination and Explanation* (Atlanta: John Knox, 1978).

63. "Zur Entstehung des Glaubens an die Auferstehung Jesu," *ThQ* 153 (1973), pp. 202f.

64. "Zur Entstehung des Glaubens an die Auferstehung Jesu," *ThQ* 153 (1973), pp. 204–208.

65. "Zur Entstehung des Glaubens an die Auferstehung Jesu," *ThQ* 153 (1973), pp. 209–218.

66. "Zur Entstehung des Glaubens an die Auferstehung Jesu," *ThQ* 153 (1973), pp. 216f.

67. "Zur Entstehung des Glaubens an die Auferstehung Jesu," *ThQ* 153 (1973), pp. 222–226. It is at this point where Pesch later modified his view. He now affirms the necessity of the appearances in order to overcome the crisis of faith in the disciples, and

Baptist identified John with such a messianic prophet, and therefore at least some of his followers went on believing in him after his death (Acts 19:1–7). This expectation then provided the material to interpret Jesus' death as an event of salvation, and to proclaim him as the risen savior.

Since the disciples' faith in Jesus did not fail with the events surrounding the crucifixion, it therefore did not need to be renewed or recreated. They believed in Jesus as the Christ before Easter, and since they expected the eschatological messenger to be killed, their faith was sustained throughout the events of the cross.[68] With their confession to the resurrection of Jesus they verbalized their conviction that Jesus was indeed the Christ, and that their faith, not only in his message, but in his person, was sustained through the death of this eschatological messenger of God.

> He is risen. With these words they asserted the validation of his mission, his legitimate eschatological authority. . . . Not Enoch, not Elijah, and also not Moses, not John the Baptist—but Jesus . . . is the Son of Man, the Messiah, the Kyrios and the Son of God. To test the credibility of this claim, the rational dimension of faith is not pointed to the "appearances", but to Jesus of Nazareth himself.[69]

To speak of the resurrection of Jesus Christ is therefore the believers' way to confess the "eschatological significance of Jesus. . . ."[70]

The Resurrection as Optional for the Christian Faith (David Griffin)

The approach of David R. Griffin is similar in emphasis. He develops his christology within the context of process theology.[71] Griffin's apologetic interest consists in wanting to bring together a "formal commitment to rationality" and the Christian claim that in Jesus God has decisively revealed himself.[72] He believes that process philosophy can help to achieve that aim:

---

he now argues that the appearances are visions of the Son of Man who is none other than the crucified Christ who has been exalted to the right hand of God. (See: John P. Galvin, "The Origin of Faith in the Resurrection of Jesus: Two Recent Perspectives," *TS* 49 [1988], pp. 25–35).

68. Rudolf Pesch, "Zur Entstehung des Glaubens an die Auferstehung Jesu," *ThQ* 153 (1973), p. 227: "For the disciples of Jesus the dispute concerning his Messiahship was decided before Easter: in their faith which was initiated by and grounded in Jesus." (My translation).

69. "Zur Entstehung des Glaubens an die Auferstehung Jesu," *ThQ* 153 (1973), p. 225 (my translation).

70. "Zur Entstehung des Glaubens an die Auferstehung Jesu," *ThQ* 153 (1973), p. 226 (my translation).

71. Griffin, *A Process Christology* (Philadelphia: Westminster, 1973).

72. Griffin, *A Process Christology* (1973) pp. 10f.

It is the formal thesis of the present essay that Whitehead's metaphysics provides us with a conceptuality never before equaled in its combination of appropriateness to the Christian faith and intrinsic excellence as measured by the normal rational and empirical criteria.[73]

With the help of process categories Griffin therefore speaks of Jesus as a supreme act of God "without implying the interruption of the normal course of natural causation."[74]

Jesus of Nazareth was not only a "special act of God", but he was "God's supreme act".[75] All human beings are in some sense unique and special. But Jesus differed from other human beings in that God had a special aim for him, and that Jesus through a free and voluntary decision and obedience actualized that aim in a "unsurpassable degree"[76]: "The aims given to Jesus and actualized by him during his active ministry were such that the basic vision of reality contained in his message of word and deed was the supreme expression of God's eternal character and purpose."[77]

This ministry and message of Jesus has saving significance for us in that its cognitive content is communicated to us, and as such influences "the volitional and affective sides of our being."[78]

In this scenario the resurrection has no place. Griffin admits:

> . . . Christian faith (as I understand it) is possible apart from belief in Jesus' resurrection in particular and life beyond bodily death in general, and because of the widespread skepticism regarding these traditional beliefs, they should be presented as optional. . . .[79]

SUMMARY

Let us pause to recall the shift of emphasis that has taken place with this model. The interest in the historical question and the turn to the priority of reason had made all doctrinal statements and theological assertions problematic that deviated from accepted scientific parameters. In addition, critical New Testament studies had shown the intricate interwovenness of theological and historical statements in the Bible. Finally, Protestant theologians in particular wanted to protect the reformation emphasis on *sola gratia* and *sola fide* in all realms of theology.

---

73. Griffin, *A Process Christology* (1973), p. 165, compare pp. 167–192.
74. Griffin, *A Process Christology* (1973), p. 207.
75. Griffin, *A Process Christology* (1973), p. 216.
76. Griffin, *A Process Christology* (1973), p. 216, also pp. 217f.
77. Griffin, *A Process Christology* (1973), p. 218.
78. Griffin, *A Process Christology* (1973), p. 17, compare p. 15.
79. *A Process Christology* (1973), p. 12.

These factors led to a shift of emphasis: from what was thought to be speculative to that which reason could accept as historical, without surrendering the importance of faith and the importance of Jesus for faith. Concretely speaking: the emphasis on what happened to the dead Jesus in the tomb and the supporting historical evidence for the empty tomb was replaced by what was historically more accessible and more credible: the appearance experiences to Peter and others, and the pre-Easter Jesus. This meant a shift of emphasis from the resurrection of Jesus to its consequences in the lives of the disciples, or to that which is historically accessible of Jesus, namely his life and death.

Although there are fundamental theological differences between Bultmann and Knox on the one hand, and Pesch and Griffin on the other, they agree in their high regard for modern historical science, and therefore in their attempt to verbalize the reality of the resurrection of Jesus Christ in a way that makes it acceptable to the modern human person.

QUESTIONS AND ISSUES: "WORD AND FAITH"

We have outlined some representative theological positions that attempt to verbalize the doctrine of the resurrection of Christ within the parameters of a view of history that tends to leave no room for a historical resurrection of Jesus by God from the dead. Such theologians either denied that Jesus was really dead (Paulus); or they affirmed his real death, but denied his resurrection, and then gave other explanations for the Easter narratives (Strauss, Pesch, Griffin); or they shifted the interest from what happened to Jesus to what happened to the disciples and what may happen to us (Bultmann); or they tended to dissolve the resurrection into the living memory of the church (Knox).

Without going into a detailed criticism of the above positions we shall try to locate those areas where this approach is controversial and may need correction. For the sake of clarity, we shall deal firstly with questions and issues related to the approaches of Bultmann and Knox ("Word and Faith") and then turn to questions and issues related to those who focus their attention on the pre-Easter Jesus.

Appreciation

The emphasis on "word and faith" as the foundation of Christian experience is thoroughly biblical: ". . . faith comes from what is heard, and what is heard comes by the preaching of Christ." (Rom 10:17; compare Gal 3:2.5; Col 3:16). In the Johannine church the risen and exalted Christ comes to his people in and through the word of preaching: "Truly, truly, I say to you, he who hears my word and believes him who sent me, has eternal life . . ." (John 5:24). This biblical emphasis has been correctly featured by Bultmann and Knox, and from this emphasis we must not retreat. Faith is the gift of God that comes to the believer in and through the hearing of the word. This word is not information about Jesus the Christ, but it is the word in which Christ is present in the power of the Spirit.

Bultmann and Knox therefore provide a helpful corrective to Pannenberg and Henry who tended to freeze the event of revelation into the past and thereby defined preaching as information about an event that had happened long ago. Information calls for the response of reason, while according to New Testament Christianity preaching calls for and creates the response of repentance and faith. Bultmann and Knox therefore provide important theological resources for our attempt to find an understanding of the resurrection of Christ that is appropriate to its reality. Yet there are some problems associated with this approach that need to be addressed.

Historical Scepticism

Both Bultmann and Knox make the philosophical assertion that historical verdicts can only have a greater or lesser probability into a theological virtue. They maintain that this understanding of history is indeed helpful to theologians. It reminds them never to ground soteriological certainty in a historical event, and never to make faith dependent on the results of historical research. Faith, they say, is anchored in God, not in history, and God comes to us in the word of preaching, not in the information about an event of history.

This seemingly logical and biblical conclusion becomes problematic at the point where Christians confess that God has revealed himself in the particular historical person Jesus of Nazareth. That particular historical event, Christians claim, is essential for Christian faith. Apart from Jesus of Nazareth there would be no Christian faith, no Christian church, and no Christian religion. So far, Bultmann and Knox would still agree. They both affirm that the historical Jesus is essential for faith.

However, their historical scepticism led them to emphasize only the mere historical fact (the "that") of Jesus' life and death. While for them the "how" of his life, the details surrounding his death, and the "what" of his vision of reality, may be of historical interest, they are of no theological importance. They affirmed that the mere fact of his historical life and death (the "that") is essential for Christian faith at all times and in all situations. But for them the "how" and "what" are bound to the particular time and situation of first-century Palestine and have therefore no theological relevance beyond that time.

It is at this point where our criticism must come in. We must assert, firstly, that it is not possible to separate the mere fact of Jesus' life and death (the "that") from "how" he lived and "what" he died for. The Jesus who is essential for Christian faith includes not only the fact "that" he lived and died, but also "how" he lived and "what" he died for. We will have to ask, of course, how we can appropriately access the "how" and "what" of Jesus' life and death. But without giving discernible content to the "that" of Jesus' existence we would be in danger of developing a docetic Christology.

It needs to be asserted, secondly, that faith centered in Jesus Christ must have content, and this content can only come from his life, death, and resurrection. If that is not firmly established, then the content of faith will derive from somewhere else, and that will most likely be our personal, religious, cultural, economic, or political self-interest.

Our criticism of Bultmann and Knox so far then leaves us with two questions that need to be kept in mind as we develop our own approach. Firstly, what is the place of historical knowledge in the event of faith? How can we maintain the important theological emphasis that faith is created by the word, and at the same time insist, that this faith has as its content Jesus Christ. We will have to distinguish between the grounding of faith in the word and the content of faith deriving from the Christ-event.

We will have to ask, secondly, in which way the resurrection of Christ is a historical event. We saw that Pannenberg's and Henry's approach tended to objectify the resurrection and thereby freeze it into the past, while Bultmann's and Knox's approach tended to subjectify the resurrection of Christ into the ever-present experience of faith. Is there a way beyond this alternative? A way that is more able to capture the New Testament witness to the resurrection of Christ?

It is important to recognize that modern critical scholarship has helped us to see that it is no longer appropriate to make a methodological precommitment to historical scepticism, both in its philosophical and its theological form. Peter Carnley, for instance, has convincingly argued that a methodological precommitment to historical scepticism "is logically erroneous."[80] Moreover, with regard to the New Testament, recent critical commentaries on the gospels and scholarly monographs about Jesus of Nazareth have uncovered many historical details that can merge into an understanding of Jesus of Nazareth which is more concrete than asserting the mere historical fact that Jesus lived and died. We shall have to carefully investigate what in the texts and narratives that speak of Christ's resurrection is of a historical nature, what is meant by their reference to history, and what can and what cannot be captured in historical categories.

Christology

Bultmann and Knox have helped us to understand that no approach can do justice to the scriptural testimony of the resurrection of Christ that does not clearly spell out the effect Christ has on the life of the believer and on the life of the community of faith. This is an important emphasis. But this emphasis contains the danger that the resurrection of Christ (christology) is dissolved

---

80. Peter Carnley, *The Structure of Resurrection Belief* (1987), p. 133, see especially pp. 103–147; also: Peter Carnley, "The Poverty of Historical Scepticism," in: S.W. Sykes and J.P. Clayton, eds., *Christ, Faith and History* (1972), pp. 165–189.

into the experience of faith (soteriology) or into the faith of the community (ecclesiology). If that should be the case then the over-againstness of Christ, the Lordship of Christ as the ground and measure of faith and of the life and praxis of the church, can easily be lost. Today, as it was in New Testament times, it needs to become clear that "Jesus Christ" is not identical with Christian experience or with the memory of the community. If this concrete otherness and over-againstness is lost, then the call to repentance, the prayer for renewal, and the hope for liberation lose their ultimate source, their distinctive content, and hence their relevance.

We shall therefore have to ask whether the effect that Christ has on the believer and on the believing community is not in fact a psychological illusion, if it is not also asserted that the dead Jesus was raised from the dead, that he was exalted to the right hand of God, and that from there he has been given back to the world in the power of the Spirit. Is this ontological ground not a necessary presupposition for the reality of the effect Christ has?

There can be no doubt that both Bultmann and Knox wanted to escape the danger of psychologyzing faith. They wanted to resist the possibility of understanding faith as a psychological phenomenon, and they therefore emphasized the external cause of faith. Faith, they maintained, does not create itself. It is created by the Word and the Spirit. Yet it has remained unclear whether the "resurrection of Jesus Christ" is only a symbol for the kerygma, or whether it is the necessary ontological ground of the kerygma.

A further christological problem is raised by the fact that not only in their description of the resurrection, but also in their understanding of the life and death of Jesus, Bultmann and Knox are hesitant to ascribe theological importance to the historical details that made up Jesus' life and led to his death. Is this not a form of docetism? Do we not lose sight of the concrete reality of Jesus' life, that he was a friend of publicans and sinners, that the religious and political establishment opposed him, and that he was condemned and crucified as a direct consequence of his life? Can we properly understand the cross and the resurrection if we do not ask why he was crucified, and who exactly this person was whom God raised from the dead?

If then the concrete historical "event" character of Jesus' life, death, and resurrection is so clearly shifted from Jesus to Christian existence or to the Christian community, from the "then" to the "now," how shall the christological content of our faith and the christological commission of our community be defined and safeguarded? In other words, a primarily existential or ecclesiological focus can blind us to the Lordship of Christ and to our responsibility in the world. This brings us to a final point.

Justice

The scriptural witness to the resurrection of Christ makes quite clear that by raising his Son from the dead, God has affirmed and validated the particular life of Jesus, and with the resurrection of Jesus God has begun to win the world, his creation, back to himself. It would therefore mean a reduction of the reality of the resurrection if with Bultmann and Knox we limit its effect to the believer and to the church. The effect of the resurrection of Christ includes the world, nature, and the future. Jesus did not only forgive sins and create a community of disciples, but he also brought hope, liberation, and healing to the poor and oppressed. We must therefore be careful that our interest in the believer and in the church does not lead us to a disinterest in the world and its problems, in history and its future. The reality of the resurrection must be related to the social ethical problems of our world and to the question of how it can stimulate hope in face of an uncertain future.

Caution must of course be taken that faith is not dissolved into morality, and that the dynamic presence of God in the world (the "kingdom of God") is not identified with human ideologies or with historical schemes and institutions. But it must be remembered that the God who raised Jesus from the dead is the creator of heaven and earth who has, with the resurrection of Jesus Christ, begun to win his world back to himself.

QUESTIONS AND ISSUES: FOCUS ON THE PRE-EASTER JESUS

What we have intimated above must be repeated here: the position that the resurrection of Jesus Christ has no reality in itself or that it is not central to the Christian faith is not an alternative for those whose theological thinking is bound to the message and authority of the New Testament. There are, of course, various theological traditions in the New Testament, but there can be no doubt that the resurrection of Jesus Christ stands at the heart of and forms the basis for New Testament thinking. It is the foundational event for Christian faith and for the Christian church. This does not mean that the resurrection is only a statement about Jesus. It certainly includes the faith and the changed lives of the first disciples; it certainly includes the shaping of the Christian church; it certainly includes a new understanding of history; it certainly includes a new vision of our life, our world, and our future. But all of these are aspects and consequences of the resurrection of Jesus Christ. They lose their ontological foundation if the resurrection of Christ as a real event is denied.

We shall now mention some problems related to the positions that we have associated with the names of Strauss, Paulus, Pesch, and Griffin. Their theological approaches to the resurrection are very different. What they have in common is their focus on the pre-Easter Jesus.

Appreciation

The early Christians confessed that it was the crucified Christ whom God raised from the dead. They therefore formulated that the risen Lord showed his identity by pointing to the marks of his crucifixion (Luke 24:39; John 20:20.25.27), and they interpreted their Christian discipleship as the presence of the crucified and risen Christ in their own existence (e.g., 2 Cor 1:3–7, 4:7–15, 10:1–13:10; Gal 2:20, 6:17; Phil 3:2–4:1). It must also be remembered that Peter and the disciples recognized that it was Jesus who appeared to them as the risen Christ.

We therefore need to be constantly reminded that our understanding of the resurrection of Christ must clearly spell out that it was Jesus who was raised from the dead, and we must recognize the theological consequences of this affirmation. Where this does not become transparent, christology becomes docetic. Yet we must equally insist that a christology that does not consider the resurrection to be essential for understanding Jesus Christ falls into the opposite heresy of ebionitism. It is therefore important to locate the problems with the approach that focuses the attention on the historical Jesus.

The Subjective-Vision Hypothesis

The "rational" explanation of Paulus does not stand up to a critical reading of the New Testament texts and it is therefore rejected by New Testament scholars today.

Strauss's subjective-vision hypothesis on the other hand still enjoys some attraction; but its problems are greater than its promises. If the strong personality of Jesus, the disciples' knowledge of the scriptures, and their expectation that a godly man may have to suffer, did not hinder the disciples from forsaking Jesus at his arrest, why should this knowledge and experience be strong enough a few days later to create subjective visions within them? The New Testament texts do not support any of the psychological speculations that according to Strauss led to those visionary experiences. Strauss can also not explain the fact that the New Testament texts distinguish clearly between the Easter experiences and other visionary experiences. Furthermore, it is at least possible that a number of different people at different times at different places experienced encounters with the risen Lord. Also the fact cannot be overlooked that according to the New Testament in the resurrection something happened to Jesus himself!

Nevertheless, it may be affirmed that, given the fact that the disciples experienced the risen Christ, then in their theological reflection and interpretation of that experience, the memory of Jesus and their knowledge of the Scriptures would of course have helped them to give content and shape to their newly experienced faith.

The same would have to be said about the position that Rudolf Pesch proposed in the article mentioned. Even if the historical evidence would support the suggestion that during the time of Jesus it was a common expectation that an eschatological messenger of God could expect to be killed but would then be raised from the dead,[81] it would still not explain why the disciples fled when

---

81. There are many scholars who doubt that the historical evidence is adequate for Pesch's thesis, e.g.: Peter Stuhlmacher (in direct response to Pesch's essay), "Kritischer müssten mir die Historisch-Kritischen sein!" *TQ* 153 (1973), pp. 244–251; Martin

Jesus was captured and why later they returned with new vigor from Galilee to Jerusalem. Pesch's thesis therefore requires further modifications of the passion story and the Easter events, such as denying that the disciples' faith in Jesus ever came into a crisis or that they fled after Jesus' arrest. We shall see that such constructions are questionable interpretations of the available texts.[82]

Historical Reductionism

By concentrating theological attention on the pre-Easter Jesus (Pesch, Griffin), or on the existence of the believer (Bultmann), or on the church (Knox), the great theological danger is that the spiritual foundation for faith and for the church remains unrecognized. Although revelation necessarily includes the historical Jesus, when it becomes limited to the historical Jesus, living faith easily changes into sterile morality. Just as in dialogue with Bultmann and Knox we have to insist on the christological content that comes to faith from the Christ event, so in dialogue with those who place the emphasis on the historical Jesus we have to insist that such a focus leads to morality and legalism if it is not part of a liberating experience that can only come from the reality of the resurrection of Christ.

It is therefore imperative that we retrieve the New Testament emphasis that the risen Christ comes to the believers in the Spirit and liberates them to worship God, to love their neighbor, and to be responsible partners of creation. It is this soteriological depth which reference to the historical Jesus alone cannot sustain.

The Totality of the Christ-Event

The position of Pesch and Griffin is right in placing emphasis on the historical Jesus, but their explanation of the resurrection language lacks concrete textual and historical evidence, and it underestimates the theological content and importance of the appearance formulas and appearance narratives in the New Testament. It is not possible to reduce the "appearance" formulas to formulas of validation, and it is not possible to say that all resurrection narratives and the empty tomb stories are merely apologetic and kerygmatic legends. That is most

Hengel (in direct response to Pesch's essay), "Ist der Osterglaube noch zu retten?" *TQ* 153 (1973), pp. 252–269; Johannes M. Nützel (in a careful analysis of the major texts that Pesch mentions), "Zum Schicksal der eschatologischen Propheten," *BZ* 20 (1976), pp. 59–94; Eduard Schweizer (in a review of Klaus Berger's book, *Die Auferstehung des Propheten und die Erhöhung des Menschensohnes* [1976]), *ThLZ* 103 (1978) pp. 876–878; more cautious is the verdict of Anton Vögtle in "Wie kam es zum Osterglauben?" in: Anton Vögtle/Rudolf Pesch, *Wie kam es zum Osterglauben?* (Düsseldorf: Patmos Verlag, 1975, pp. 9–131), pp. 27–37, 44–51, 69–85, 105f., 127–131.
82. Compare pp. 119–122 below.

probably true in some cases, but it cannot be assumed. It must be established with the exegesis of the respective texts. We may say, however, that given the fact that Jesus was raised from the dead, then in response to that fact many stories evolved to communicate that fact and to guard its reality against various distortions. And given the fact that the risen Christ appeared to Peter and others, then in consequence of this life-changing encounter, those to whom he appeared could interpret this appearance as a divine call and verbalize it in formulas of validation.

Nevertheless, the continuity between the historical Jesus and the Christian church is not found merely in the faith and the memory of the disciples. Nor is it necessary to deny the disciples' crisis of faith and their flight to Galilee. In fact, God himself, by raising Jesus from the dead, provided the continuity from Jesus to Christian faith and to the Christian church.

CONCLUSION

While the "traditional" approach is primarily interested in questions related to what happened to Jesus after his death and burial, the "liberal" approach, under the imperative of another view of history, changes this emphasis.

When the question is asked whether anything happened to Jesus after his death and burial, the answer is negative or agnostic. We don't know, they respond, and the New Testament does not authorize us to make that question the hermeneutical key for understanding the resurrection.

Accepting the parameters of modern historical science, the reality of the resurrection of Jesus Christ is interpreted as highlighting the significance of the pre-Easter Jesus, or as creating the faith of the believer and the church. Consequently, the emphasis shifts from what happened to Jesus after his death, to who he was and what he did before his death, or to what happened to the disciples and the church after his death.

These explanations have left us somewhat dissatisfied. We therefore need to continue our search for interpreting the resurrection of Jesus Christ in such a way that it does not distort the New Testament emphases, and is at the same time meaningful to present experience and relevant to the world in which we live.

Chapter 3

The "Evangelical" Approach

Fact and Faith

INTRODUCTION

A third group of theologians states confidently that the resurrection of Jesus is a real, tangible, objective, and historical event. With an intentional commitment to the authority of the New Testament message they claim that, following Jesus' death and burial, God raised Jesus from the dead, that consequently the tomb was empty, and that the risen Christ appeared to the apostles. He could be seen, heard, and touched. He again lived among the disciples; he spoke and ate with them. The reality of the resurrection is therefore firmly related to history, and some of its manifestations—the "appearances" and the "empty tomb"—are also open to historical investigation. Nevertheless, the resurrection as such, its very essence, is not accessible to historical reason. It is open only to the eyes of faith. This approach distinguishes between events that are real and historical in a theological sense, and events that are historical in an immanent and secular sense. The resurrection of Christ, for these theologians, is a real and an objective event—but is not objectifiable![1]

---

1. A general description of this approach may be found in: Peter Carnley, *The Structure of Resurrection Belief* (Oxford: Clarendon Press, 1987), chapter III, pp. 96–147; Langdon Gilkey, *Naming the Whirlwind. The Renewal of God-Language* (Indianapolis: Bobbs-Merrill, 1969), pp. 80–104; David Tracy, *Blessed Rage for Order: The New Pluralism in Theology.* A Crossroad Book (New York: Seabury, 1975), pp. 27–31. The dialectic of "objective" but "not objectifiable" events is reflected in the terminology of "evangelical" theologians. Karl Barth calls the resurrection a prehistorical event with a tiny historical margin (see below). Walter Künneth speaks of a metahistorical *Urwunder* (primal miracle) (see below), and George Eldon Ladd refers to the resurrection as a supra-historical event ("The Resurrection of Jesus Christ," in: Carl F. H. Henry, ed., *Christian Faith and Modern Theology. Contemporary Evangelical Thought* [New York:

Within this third model the affirmation of the objective nature of the resurrection is not the rational statement of the historian or the philosopher; it is the confession of the theologian as a believer in Jesus Christ. This confession is not considered to be irrational or antirational, but it challenges the autonomy of secular reason. It wants to locate reason within the parameters of revelation and faith: *fides quaerens intellectum.*[2]

This approach tries to retain the positive emphases of the "traditional" and the "liberal" models and then correlate them with each other. With the "liberal" approach of Bultmann and Knox, "evangelical" theologians emphasize that *faith* is the proper mode to know and to respond to the resurrection of Jesus Christ. But faith receives someone! Having come to faith in the risen Christ, they are not satisfied to emphasize merely the "that" of his life and death. Rather, within the circle of faith, they now retrieve the objective and historical content of the resurrection event that was emphasized by the "traditional" model.

CONTEXT

With this approach we meet theologians who are developing their thinking often in deliberate opposition to and dialogue with the "liberal" and/or the "traditional" approaches. With the "traditional" approach they want to remain faithful to the scriptures, and they do not want to surrender the historical nature of the resurrection. They fear, however, that in the "traditional" approach the New Testament emphasis on faith is not sufficiently recognized. They claim that both the New Testament sources and our Christian experience affirm that not historical reason but faith is the adequate way to discern and verify that God has raised Jesus from the dead.

Therefore, as the "liberal" approach they recognize that faith is the proper way to respond to God's acts. They fear, however, that the "liberal" theologians have sold out the specific biblical understanding of reality to a modern worldview. "Evangelical" theologians are also concerned with communicating the message to the modern world. They believe, however, that a primary commitment to the biblical message is necessary so that the church has something to say to the world that the world cannot discover by its own resources.

Their main orientation is therefore on the biblical message. They want to be interpreters of the biblical texts. Whether an event to which the Bible witnesses

---

Channel Press, 1964, pp. 263–284], p. 279; compare: George Eldon Ladd, *I Believe in the Resurrection of Jesus* [London: Hodder and Stoughton, 1975]).

2. Under this title Karl Barth published in 1931 a book that provided the methodological groundwork for his *Church Dogmatics.* George Hunsinger comments on Barth's location of reason: ". . . the rationalism peculiar to Barth's theology, being internal and not external to faith, might . . . be described as 'reason within the limits of revelation alone.'" (*How to Read Karl Barth. The Shape of His Theology* [New York/Oxford: Oxford University Press, 1991], p. 49).

is historical or not, must not be decided by the interpreter, but by the text itself. Karl Barth is representative of this approach when he insists that the theologian must ask

> ... what the texts say ... in their attestation of this event, without measuring them by an imported picture of the world and history, without reading them through these alien spectacles, without prejudice as to what is possible or impossible, good or less good, without prescribing what they have to say and what they cannot say, without imposing questions which they themselves do not ask, but entering into their own questions and remaining open to their own replies which, if our thinking is to be genuinely 'historical,' must have precedence over our own attitude. . . .[3]

Consequently, these theologians are critical of a modern understanding of history, which, in their view, leaves no room for the resurrection as it is testified in the scriptures:

> If in modern scholarship 'historical ground' means the outline of an event as it can be seen in its 'How' independently of the standpoint of the onlooker, as it can be presented in this way, as it can be proved in itself and in its general and more specific context and in relation to the analogies of other events, as it can be established as having certainly taken place, the New Testament itself does not enable us to state that we are on 'historical ground' in relation to the event here recorded.[4]

If, however, the theologian affirms the authority of the Bible, then together with the biblical texts, he or she has to speak of the resurrection as a real and historical event. For the theologian the authority of the text must be more compelling than any commitment to a "modern" scientific view of history. The implication is, of course, that the biblical text will also be determinative for the theologian's understanding of what history is.

KARL BARTH: A PREHISTORICAL EVENT WITH A HISTORICAL MARGIN

The most prominent modern representative of this approach is the Swiss Protestant theologian Karl Barth (1886–1968).[5] He consciously argues as a believer who is committed to the authority of the Bible, and as such he maintains

---

3. *CD* IV/2 (1958), p. 150.
4. *CD* IV/1 (1956), p. 335.
5. The following texts are of special relevance for our discussion: *Church Dogmatics*, vol. III: The Doctrine of Creation, Part 2 (Edinburgh: T. & T. Clark, 1960), pp. 441–493

that the resurrection of Jesus Christ is a God-given reality that includes a concrete historical margin, although it is not identical with that historical manifestation. He calls the resurrection a "pre-historical" event.[6] What does this mean as far as the theological content is concerned? For Barth, the resurrection of Jesus Christ is related to his historical existence in terms of "being" and the "revelation" of that being. The "being of Jesus Christ" as Savior and Son of God is complete and fulfilled in the life and death of Jesus. Nothing needs to be added. It is the event of salvation, even if there were no resurrection.[7] But this "being of Jesus Christ", which is our salvation and the salvation of the world, calls for revelation, so that it can be known what God has done.

> For when the New Testament speaks of these events (resurrection and ascension), or rather this one event, it speaks of the perfect being of Jesus Christ, and His accomplished reconciliation of the world with God, in its character as *revelation*. And that is how we must speak of it. The resurrection and ascension of Jesus Christ are the event of His *self-declaration*.[8]

Since revelation aims at being known, it must be historical. Not in the sense of immanent and secular historical reason, but in the sense that it may be known by human beings. But it must be known for what it is. It must be known as an act of God.

(= *CD* III/2); *Church Dogmatics*, vol. IV: The Doctrine of Reconciliation, Part 1 (New York: Scribner's Sons, 1956), pp. 297–357 (= *CD* IV/1); *Church Dogmatics*, vol. IV: The Doctrine of Reconciliation, Part 2 (Edinburgh: T. & T. Clark, 1958), pp. 131–154 (= *CD* IV/2); *Church Dogmatics*, vol. IV: The Doctrine of Reconciliation, Part 3, 1st half (Edinburgh: T. & T. Clark, 1961), pp. 281–324 (= *CD* IV/3,1). We do not here address the question whether Barth has changed his mind in his interpretation of the resurrection—compare Van Austin Harvey, *The Historian and the Believer* (1966), pp. 153–159—rather, we relate the position of the "later" Barth as it can be portrayed from the above mentioned texts. In the *Church Dogmatics* Barth ascribed much more theological significance to the biblical statements about the life of the risen Christ, while in the earlier writings—e.g., *The Epistle to the Romans* (London: Oxford University Press, 1933 [6th ed. 1928]) and *The Resurrection of the Dead* (London: Hodder & Stoughton, 1933 [1924])—he considered the historical manifestations of the resurrection to be theologically unimportant.

6. *CD* IV/1 (1956), p. 336.

7. "The being of Jesus Christ was and is perfect and complete in itself in His history as the true Son of God and Son of Man. It does not need to be transcended or augmented by new qualities or further developments. The humiliation of God and the exaltation of man as they took place in Him are the *completed* fulfilment of the covenant, the *completed* reconciliation of the world with God. His being as such . . . was and is the end of the old and the beginning of the new form of this world even *without* His resurrection and ascension. He did not and does not lack anything in Himself." (*CD* IV/2 [1958], pp. 132f.; emphases are in the original German text: *KD* IV/2 [1955], p. 148).

8. *CD* IV/2 (1958), p. 133; emphases are in the original German text: *KD* IV/2 (1955), p. 149; compare *CD* IV/4 (1969), pp. 24f.

For Barth, then, the resurrection is, first of all, a new, free, liberating, and unique act of God.[9] In contrast to other historical events, "it does not have in the very least this component of human willing and activity."[10] God alone is the subject of the resurrection of Jesus. Since the element of human decision and human action is missing, we are dealing here with a "historical sphere of a different kind."[11] Consequently the real content of the resurrection—". . . the appearance of this terminated existence in its participation in the sovereign life of God, in its endowment with eternity, in the transcendence, incorruptibility and immortality. . . ."[12]—"cannot be verified by historico-critical methods."[13] But this in no way implies that it has not really happened. Indeed it is a real event—it is a historical event in a "higher sense."[14] The newness of the resurrection does not consist in adding anything to the soteriological work of Christ, or in transfiguring Christ into a different existence, or in transporting him to a different plane. New is that now, on the basis of the resurrection, he acts as savior and liberator in the world, that he is recognized for what he is, and that he can be worshipped and obeyed as such.

Barth would therefore agree with Bultmann and Knox that the appropriate response to an act of God is not reason but faith. Yet, in contrast to Bultmann and Knox, Barth insists that faith is in Jesus Christ, and "Jesus Christ" cannot be reduced to the mere assertion that he lived and died. Faith is created by the risen Christ through the Spirit and it receives and confesses the whole story of Jesus, his life and death, as it is portrayed in the New Testament. Faith is therefore not merely a decision, but it also has an objective content. That brings us to the next point.

The resurrection, this historical event in a "higher sense" and "of a different kind", has, secondly, "a tiny 'historical' margin."[15] This means in fact that the

---

9. *CD* IV/1 (1956), pp. 300–309, 338; *CD* IV/2 (1958), p. 147; *CD* IV/3,1 (1961), pp. 296–301. The liberating dimension of the resurrection in Barth's doctrine of reconciliation has been convincingly demonstrated by Bertold Klappert, "Die Rechts-, Freiheits- und Befreiungsgeschichte Gottes mit den Menschen. Erwägungen zum Verständnis der Auferstehung in Karl Barths Versöhnungslehre (KD IV/1–3)," *EvTh* 49 (1989), pp. 460–478.

10. *CD* IV/1 (1956), p. 300.

11. *CD* IV/1 (1956), p. 334. Barth makes a theoretical distinction between historical events that are caused by human beings and are as such open to historical reason ("Historie"), and historical events that are caused by God; they are also real, but they escape recognition by historical reason ("Geschichte"). Yet Barth immediately relativizes this theoretical distinction by insisting that all of history is part of God's continuing creation and therefore is graced by God's providing and sustaining activity. In any case, given the theoretical distinction between "Historie" and "Geschichte", the resurrection of Jesus Christ and the Creation of the world are the prime examples of the latter. (*CD* III/1 [1958], pp. 78–81; *CD* III/2 [1960], p. 446 [criticizing Bultmann]).

12. *CD* IV/3,1 (1961), p. 312.

13. *CD* IV/3,1 (1961), p. 310; compare *CD* IV/1 (1956), p. 336.

14. *CD* III/2 (1960), p. 446.

15. *CD* III/2 (1960), p. 446.

resurrection is a concrete event that happened in time and space. Barth criticizes Bultmann for refusing to list the resurrection together with other historical events like the death of Jesus, the coming to faith of the disciples, the forming of the church, the proclamation activities of the early Christians, the sacraments, and the Christian life. All of these events have a divine and a historical dimension.[16] While Bultmann excludes the resurrection of Jesus in his listing of events, Barth includes it. For him the resurrection of Jesus is an objective historical event, even though only "a tiny historical margin" is accessible to reason and its methods. To illustrate Barth's emphasis on the objective character of the risen Christ, we shall cite a few telling texts from different volumes of the *Church Dogmatics*:

> The Resurrected is the man Jesus, who now came and went among them · as such, whom they saw and touched and heard, who ate and drank with them, and who, as I believe, was still before them as true man, *vere homo*.[17]

> The resurrection of Jesus Christ . . . has happened in the same sense as His crucifixion and His death, in the human sphere and human time, as an actual event within the world with an objective content.[18]

> It is an event which involves a definite seeing with the eyes and hearing with the ears and handling with the hands. . . . It involves real eating and drinking, speaking and answering, reasoning . . . and doubting and then believing.[19]

> . . . in the Easter records we have to do with the concrete, visible, audible, tangible new presence of the man Jesus who was crucified, dead and buried.[20]

> The One who had come before, who had been crucified, dead and buried, who had perished like all flesh, came again among His disciples and participated in the existence of men who were still moving forward to death, of perishing creation in all its corruptibility, of world-occurrence in its spatio-temporal contingency and limitation.[21]

---

16. *CD* III/2 (1960), p. 444.

17. *CD* III/2 (1960), p. 448.

18. *CD* IV/1 (1956), p. 333, see the whole section pp. 333–342; compare *CD* III/2 (1960), p. 442: ". . . it is essential to grasp that when the New Testament speaks of the event of Easter it really means the Easter *history* and Easter *time*. We are here in the sphere of history and time no less than in the case of the words and acts and even the death of Jesus." (The emphasis is in the original German text: *KD* III/2 [1948], p. 530). We need to recall, however, that for Barth the resurrection differs from Jesus' death in that human willing and acting had no part in it, and that therefore it was a historical event of a special kind (*CD* IV/1 [1956], pp. 300, 334f.).

19. *CD* IV/2 (1958), p. 143.

20. *CD* IV/3,1 (1961), p. 311.

21. *CD* IV/3, 1 (1961), p. 311, compare p. 312.

These quotations show that for Barth the resurrection of Jesus is a real "event within the world, in time and space."[22] It happened at a definite time and at a definite place. After his resurrection, Jesus, "in the psycho-physical totality of His temporal existence familiar from His first coming",[23] lived and moved among the disciples for forty days.[24] And the accompanying "indispensable" signs and consequences[25]—the empty tomb and the appearances—can be investigated with our historical methodology, although their real meaning escapes historical reason.[26]

Barth interprets his emphasis that it was the human person Jesus (*vere homo*) who was as risen Lord among them, by saying that Jesus was among them "in the mode of God."[27] It was God, really God, who in and through the resurrection revealed that in Christ he has reconciled the world with himself.

This brings us to a third point that is important for understanding Barth's view of the resurrection. Barth speaks of the historical nature of the resurrection mainly in the context of his *Doctrine of Reconciliation*.[28] The insistence on the historical nature of the resurrection has the purpose of ensuring that the human being as a historical being can perceive it, that Christ can become real to the believer, that God's revelation in Jesus Christ is indeed God's concrete "Yes" to humanity and God's real and liberating answer to human need.[29] Only if the resurrection has really occurred and as such was historical, can we, who are part of history, become sure that we are saved, and that it was really Jesus Christ who saved us. The resurrection of Jesus Christ is the "Verdict of the Father" who with this event ratifies, validates, proclaims, reveals, and puts into effect the salvation that he has accomplished in the life and death of Jesus Christ.[30] Therefore Barth's insistence on the resurrection as an historical event in time and space is

> ... not in order to explain the resurrection of Jesus Christ as a historically indisputable fact. Certainly not to create for faith in the Resurrected a ground in terms of this world which we can demonstrate and therefore control. Certainly not to destroy its character as faith. . . .[31]

---

22. *CD* IV/2 (1958), p. 143.

23. *CD* IV/3, 1 (1961), p. 312.

24. *CD* III/2 (1960), p. 450.

25. *CD* III/2 (1960), p. 453; *CD* IV/1 (1956), p. 341.

26. In Barth's christology the Virgin Birth and the Empty Tomb serve a similar theological purpose. They are "indispensable signs" whose function it is to guard the objective reality of the incarnation (Virgin Birth) and the resurrection (Empty Tomb). (*CD* I/2 [1956], pp. 147, 179, 182; *CD* III/2 [1960], pp. 452f.). Yet with all the emphasis on objectivity, Barth also distinguishes between the events and their signs. The latter have "noetic" rather than "ontic" significance (*CD* I/2 [1956], p. 202).

27. *CD* III/2 (1960), p. 448.

28. *CD* IV/1–3 (1956–1969).

29. *CD* IV/1 (1956), pp. 348f.; *CD* IV/3, 1 (1961), pp. 314f.

30. *CD* IV/1 (1956), § 59,3 carries the heading "The Verdict of the Father"; compare specifically pp. 318, 334.

31. *CD* IV/1 (1956), p. 351.

Rather, the concrete objectivity of the resurrection is essential in order

... to hear in Him the Yes which has been spoken in and with and under the No of His death and ours, to find ourselves addressed in Him as those who are liberated from judgment and death, as those who are set in fellowship and peace with God, as those who are adopted as the children of God.[32]

The belief in the historical nature of the resurrection is therefore inseparable from Barth's understanding of revelation and of salvation. If the resurrection "were a supernatural or even supersensual event which as such would not be experienced or attested by men,... it would not be an event of revelation."[33]

Barth therefore suggests a way which is distinct from the "traditional" and the "liberal" approaches. Over against the "liberal" approach he maintains the objective, factual, and historical nature of the particular person Jesus. He, Jesus, is the presupposition for and content of the disciples' faith. The risen Lord is there apart from the faith of the disciples, although it is the aim of the resurrection to convey the reality of salvation to the believer. Over against the "traditional" approach he asserts that the real content of the resurrection is not open to the instruments of historical and modern scientific reason, but only to the eyes of faith. The resurrection is an objective and historical event, but modern scientific reason does not have the tools to know the resurrection on its own terms.

WALTER KÜNNETH: A METAHISTORICAL *URWUNDER*

The German Lutheran theologian Walter Künneth (1901-) is another well-known representative of this position.[34] Künneth battles vehemently against any attempt to remove the historical reality and the concrete, factual event charac-

---

32. *CD* IV/1 (1956), p. 351, compare p. 347; also *CD* III/2 (1960), pp. 450f.

33. *CD* IV/2 (1958), p. 143. Compare the excellent discussion in Bertold Klappert, *Die Auferweckung des Gekreuzigten. Der Ansatz der Christologie Karl Barths im Zusammenhang der Christologie der Gegenwart* (Neukirchen-Vluyn: Neukirchener Verlag, 1971), pp. 325–347.

34. I mention three of Künneth's writings that deal with our topic: *The Theology of the Resurrection* (St. Louis, Missouri: Concordia, 1965 [1933, 1951]); Ernst Fuchs, Walter Künneth, *Die Auferstehung Jesu Christi von den Toten. Dokumentation eines Streitgesprächs*. Nach einer Tonbandaufzeichnung hg. von Christian Möller (Neukirchen-Vluyn: Neukirchener Verlag, 1973); *Entscheidung heute. Jesu Auferstehung—Brennpunkt der theologischen Diskussion* (Hamburg: Friedrich Wittig Verlag, 1966). Since *Entscheidung heute* is the most recent of the three (the "Streitgespräch" took place in 1964), most references are to that book; all translations are mine.

ter of the resurrection of Jesus. He accuses modern theologians—and mentions
specifically Rudolf Bultmann, Willi Marxsen, Gerhard Ebeling, Ernst Fuchs,
and Herbert Braun—of forcing the resurrection into the straitjacket of a modern understanding of history that is not able to contain the reality of the resurrection. He charges that with their philosophical disposition and their historical
critical methodologies these theologians are unable to understand the resurrection.

Künneth suggests that the resurrection of Jesus must be seen as a "self-revelation of reality" ("Selbsterschliessung der Wirklichkeit").[35] Consequently, it
inaugurates a new understanding of history and of reality.[36]

For Künneth, the decisive question is whether theologians are prepared to
correct their understanding of history in light of the resurrection of Jesus, or
whether they will press the resurrection of Jesus into their given view of history. The resurrection, according to Künneth, "demands a fundamental re-
thinking, an intellectual logical *metanoia* (repentance) which alone will make
a real understanding possible."[37] If theologians refuse to submit to this intellectual *metanoia*, they will remain under the "spell of the laws of death" (im
"Bannkreis der Todesgesetze") and as such they will not be able to perceive the
reality of the resurrection.[38]

What then constitutes the reality of the resurrection according to Künneth?
The resurrection of Jesus is "a reality, created, effected, and revealed by God"
("eine von Gott gesetzte, bewirkte und offenbar gemachte Wirklichkeit")[39]
which contains historical and metahistorical elements.[40]

The resurrection manifests itself as a historical fact in three historical events:
First, Jesus appeared in his new spiritual body to the apostles and was seen by
them.[41] It is decisive, secondly, that the tomb into which the dead Jesus had been
laid was empty after Jesus had been raised from the dead. Here theologians will
have "to show their theological cards."[42] Künneth argues that the tomb is "the
historical place in which the resurrection of Jesus in its effect on history takes
place as a fact."[43] In the tomb God changed the mortal earthly body of the dead
Jesus into the spiritual body of his new existence. Thus the tomb must have
been empty.[44] We have, thirdly, the authentic eye and ear witness reports of the
apostles who saw the risen Lord. Their proclamation that Jesus had been raised
from the dead was a total "novum in history".[45] This novum can only be

---

35. Künneth, *Entscheidung heute* (1966), p. 34.
36. Künneth, *Entscheidung heute* (1966), pp. 33–40.
37. Künneth, *Entscheidung heute* (1966), p. 18.
38. Künneth, *Entscheidung heute* (1966), p. 18.
39. Künneth, *Entscheidung heute* (1966), p. 34.
40. Künneth, *Entscheidung heute* (1966), pp. 33–40.
41. Künneth, *Entscheidung heute* (1966), pp. 51–59.
42. Künneth, *Entscheidung heute* (1966), p. 62.
43. Künneth, *Entscheidung heute* (1966), p. 64.
44. Künneth, *Entscheidung heute* (1966), pp. 60–66.
45. Künneth, *Entscheidung heute* (1966), p. 67.

explained by the fact that God himself had acted after the crisis of the cross, and this act of God in raising Jesus from the dead included the call to apostleship and mission.[46]

These historical events, however, do not contain the whole reality of the resurrection, and therefore they do not suffice to prove the reality of the resurrection to secular reason: "The report of the empty tomb no more proves the resurrection than do the appearances of the Risen One."[47] The resurrection is more than what can be discerned by historical reason. It is a historical event and at the same time a metahistorical reality,[48] and the metahistorical reality of the resurrection is open only to the eyes of faith.[49]

Therefore, to know and understand the resurrection itself, one needs spiritual perception. Only when theologians give up a "rational—historicizing—psychological—existential approach" and become part of the "circle of spiritual understanding" ("pneumatischer Erkenntnisring"), can they begin to understand the resurrection in its historical and metahistorical reality.[50]

This reality is further explained in that the resurrection of Jesus is, firstly, a new act of the transcendent God.[51] Into the "'fallen world' marked by the reality of death" God has acted in a new and unique way.[52] This act has no analogies and parallels in our understanding and experience of history. It can only be likened to the original act of creation. It is not merely a miracle, it is an *Urwunder* (a "primal miracle").[53]

The resurrection reality includes, secondly, the new existence of Jesus. This new existence of Jesus "can only be described with ontological statements".[54] Jesus lives in a new "spiritual bodily reality" ("pneumatisch-leibhafte Wirklichkeit"). He is neither merely a historical person, nor is he a supernatural angelic being. He has a new existence, "in which his historical humanity has been transposed into a metahistorical reality of being."[55]

These massive ontological assertions are modified somewhat by Künneth's observation that the resurrection reality cannot be adequately described in static and objectifying ontological categories. Divine reality is dynamic and personal, and the resurrection reality must therefore be depicted in personal, dynamic, and relational terms.[56] The God who created the world and who raised Jesus from the dead wants to enter into a relationship of trust with his creatures.

---

46. Künneth, *Entscheidung heute* (1966), pp. 66–71.
47. Künneth, *The Theology of the Resurrection* (1965 [1933]), p. 96.
48. Künneth, *Entscheidung heute* (1966), pp. 40, 89.
49. Künneth, *Entscheidung heute* (1966), pp. 75, 81.
50. Künneth, *Entscheidung heute* (1966), p. 158, compare pp. 154–161.
51. Künneth, *Entscheidung heute* (1966), pp. 78–82.
52. Künneth, *Entscheidung heute* (1966), p. 79, compare pp. 79–82.
53. Künneth, *Entscheidung heute* (1966), p. 81; *The Theology of the Resurrection* (1965 [1933]), p. 73.
54. Künneth, *Entscheidung heute* (1966), p. 82.
55. Künneth, *Entscheidung heute* (1966), p. 84, compare the whole section pp. 82–89.
56. Künneth, *Entscheidung heute* (1966), pp. 36, 85–89.

Thus relational categories need to be added to ontological categories in order
to formulate an appropriate understanding of the resurrection of Jesus Christ.

EDWARD SCHILLEBEECKX: A TRANSHISTORICAL EVENT

It may be controversial whether Edward Schillebeeckx (1914-) should be located within this model. He is certainly more restrained in his assertions than
both Barth and Künneth,[57] and he may be viewed as providing a mediating position between the "liberal" and the "evangelical" approach. Like many contemporary theologians, Schillebeeckx is concerned to communicate the
Christian faith to the modern person: "I have tried to bridge the gap between
academic theology and the concrete needs of the ordinary Christian."[58] Since
the believer is at the same time a modern human person, faith and critical rationality need to protect each other "from becoming totalitarian and detrimen-
tal to freedom."[59] He recognizes that the certainty of faith cannot be given by
reason, "but from the moment I speak of my faith (and I do so as soon as I have
it) I have already left this storm-free zone and become vulnerable to the exi-
gencies of critical rationality. . . ."[60]

With his emphasis that Christian faith must be accessible to historical reason, that faith is centered in the historical Jesus, and yet, that faith does not need
any historical crutches, one may tend to include Schillebeeckx in the "liberal"
model.[61] But in fact Schillebeeckx explicitly disassociates himself from views
that do not take seriously what happened to Jesus himself after his death, and
he considers this to be a necessary presupposition for Christian faith.[62] He affirms the personal resurrection of Jesus which "'precedes' any faith-motivated
experience."[63] Jesus is "exalted to be with the Father" and he "is with us, in an
altogether new way."[64] An "empiricist objectivism"[65] cannot grasp this. Yet it is

---

57. We are referring here mainly to: Edward Schillebeeckx, *Jesus. An Experiment in
Christology* (New York: Crossroad, 1987 [1979; orig. Dutch 1974]), pp. 320–397,
439–550, 644–649 (= *Jesus*); *Interim Report on the Books Jesus & Christ* (New York:
Crossroad, 1981 [orig. Dutch 1978]), pp. 64–93, 134–139 (= *Interim Report*).
58. *Jesus* (1987), p. 5.
59. Schillebeeckx, *Jesus* (1987), p. 32.
60. Schillebeeckx, *Jesus* (1987), p. 32.
61. Schillebeeckx shifts the emphasis from the "empty tomb" and the "appearances"
to a religious "conversion", because the latter is more accessible to the modern person.
He also maintains that the disciples never totally lost their faith in Christ, so that the
continuity between the pre-Easter Jesus and the risen Christ could be found in the faith
of the disciples, rather than in a new eschatological act of grace that created something
new out of the disciples' crisis and loss of faith.
62. *Jesus* (1987), pp. 645, 647; *Interim Report* (1981), p. 78.
63. *Jesus* (1987), p. 645.
64. *Jesus* (1987), p. 646.
65. *Jesus* (1987), p. 644, compare p. 647.

also more than a subjective experience of the disciples. The God who raised Jesus from the dead led the disciples to a conversion in which they experienced forgiveness, renewal, and a new relationship to the Lord whom they had denied. The resurrection of Jesus is a transhistorical[66] or a metahistorical event[67] which is as such only open to the eyes of faith. Schillebeeckx wants to find a way between objectivism and fideism,[68] and therefore he asserts that the resurrection of Jesus Christ says something about Jesus, about God, about the disciples, and about us.

The Easter message is related to a religious conversion in which the disciples experienced the forgiveness of the risen Christ after the tragic failures surrounding the events of Jesus' arrest and death.[69] The "Easter experience" is therefore not "a Christian interpretation of the earthly, that is, pre-Easter Jesus," but it is a new experience after Jesus' death.[70]

First Peter[71] and then, on his initiative,[72] the disciples experienced a "conversion"[73] in which the gracious God ("a pure act of grace on God's part"[74]) forgave them for their failure and renewed their life.[75] This conversion is not to be identified with the appearance narratives in the New Testament, and it does not necessarily include visual elements.[76] It was also not merely an individualistic and private religious experience. It had a public character and was a communal reality in that the same disciples who had forsaken Jesus at the cross, now, in consequence of their conversion, gathered and formed a new community.

Schillebeeckx speaks of a process of conversion.[77] Analogous to the Damascus Road experience of Paul,[78] the disciples recognized that they had made a mistake in abandoning Jesus, and they were converted to a new faith in him. The elements contributing to this process of conversion were: "the recognition of their paucity of faith";[79] their recollection of their relationship with Jesus, and recalling his ministry and his message of the kingdom of God; remembering his warning that they might display a lack of faith; remembering their experience of the God of grace whom they had come to know in the

---

66. *Interim Report* (1981), p. 75.
67. *Interim Report* (1981), p. 77.
68. *Jesus* (1987), p. 647; *Interim Report* (1981), p. 80.
69. *Jesus* (1987), p. 394; *Interim Report* (1981), p. 81: "This renewed gathering of the disciples who were scattered after Jesus' death is the fruit of the new presence of the now glorified Christ."
70. *Jesus* (1987), pp. 393f.
71. *Jesus* (1987), pp. 385–390.
72. *Jesus* (1987), p. 389.
73. *Jesus* (1987), pp. 321, 329–334, 379–397.
74. *Jesus* (1987), p. 383.
75. *Jesus* (1987), p. 545.
76. *Jesus* (1987), p. 369.
77. *Jesus* (1987), p. 381; *Interim Report* (1981), p. 75.
78. *Jesus* (1987), pp. 381, 347–352, 360–379.
79. *Jesus* (1987), p. 381.

presence of Jesus;[80] and recalling how he helped people in distress, how he ate and drank with sinners and promised salvation to them.

> And then finally there was their recollection of the quite special temper prevailing at the farewell meal. . . . These remembered aspects of their life shared in fellowship with Jesus and of Jesus' whole line of conduct are essential elements in the process of conversion undergone by these men who did indeed fail, but had not in the end lost their faith in Jesus. They had been thrown off balance rather than been deliberately disloyal.[81]

This conversion then led to the conviction that God had raised Jesus from the dead. So, between the death of Jesus and the failure of the disciples on the one hand, and the formation of the new community and their courageous preaching on the other, there stands the experience of conversion caused by the risen, exalted, and glorified Christ.

It is interesting that Schillebeeckx seeks to maintain this emphasis on the conversion-event without basing either the resurrection of Christ or the experience of the disciples on the empty tomb and/or the appearance narratives. For him the Easter reality "was already present even before the traditions about the tomb and appearances had arisen. The Easter faith emerged independently of these two traditions."[82]

Like Bultmann and Knox he is obviously concerned to safeguard the resurrection as a reality to which only faith has access,[83] and faith caused by the risen Christ does not need the historical verification of the visual appearances or the empty tomb. Having thus dismissed the theological necessity of the visual appearances and the empty tomb, Schillebeeckx, in harmony with the stated intention for writing his book, can say: "There is not such a big difference between the way we are able, after Jesus' death, to come to faith in the crucified-and-risen One and the way in which the disciples of Jesus arrived at the same faith."[84]

Schillebeeckx achieves this emphasis by making a shift from a christology in which the understanding of the resurrection is built on the appearances and the empty tomb to a *parousia christology*.[85] Not 1 Corinthians 15:3–8 or the appearance narratives and the empty tomb stories in the gospels, but the pre-Pauline traditions in 1 Thessalonians 1:9f. (". . . how you turned to God . . . and to wait for his son from heaven, whom he raised from the dead . . .") and 4:14–17 (". . . since we believe that Jesus died and rose again, even so, through Jesus

80. *Jesus* (1987), p. 545.

81. *Jesus* (1987), p. 382, compare p. 387.

82. *Jesus* (1987), p. 334, compare p. 397.

83. *Interim Report* (1981), p. 79: "Without the Christian experience of faith we have no organ which can give us a view of Jesus' resurrection."

84. *Jesus* (1987), p. 346.

85. *Jesus* (1987), pp. 346f., 405–423, 438; *Interim Report* (1981), p. 71: ". . . parousia christology is the mother of all Christianity: Jesus is 'the one who is to come'."

God will bring with him those who have fallen asleep. . . . For the Lord himself will descend from heaven. . . .") provide the basis for this emphasis. Christ's revelation "from heaven" caused the conversion experiences, and these are therefore theologically independent of the visual appearances and the empty tomb.

How then did the empty tomb and the appearance traditions evolve? The empty tomb tradition emerged as an "aetiological cult-legend" which was "intended to shed light on the (at least) annual visit of the Jerusalem church to the tomb in order to honour the risen One there,"[86] and the appearance stories developed in analogy to religio-historical parallels. Jesus was identified with the spirit-filled, religious eschatological prophet who was to appear at the end of time;[87] and there are Jewish conversion stories in which a Gentile through a vision is converted to the law.[88] "What happens in the Christian resurrection vision (the Easter appearances) is a conversion to Jesus as the Christ, who now comes as the light of the world."[89] To experience the forgiveness of sins ("an act of sheer grace on God's part")[90] after forsaking Jesus, and to acknowledge Jesus as Lord in the total context of their lives, including the failure of forsaking Jesus when he was captured and killed, that "is what I call the 'Easter experience'."[91]

In conclusion we may say that for Schillebeeckx Jesus was raised by God from the dead. The disciples did not see the resurrection nor did they experience the appearances which are reported in 1 Corinthians 15:3–8 and in the gospel narratives. What they did experience was a conversion as an act of grace by the same God who raised Jesus from the dead. At first they interpreted this conversion within the context of a parousia christology, and then, later, with the help of religio-historical parallels, a resurrection theology emerged as we find it in the "appearance" narratives and the "empty tomb" traditions.

SUMMARY

The "evangelical" approach maintains the intention of the "traditional" approach insofar as it seeks to present a faithful picture of the biblical historical emphasis on the resurrection of Jesus. At the same time the "evangelical" theologians could not escape the reality that has led to the "liberal" approach. No theologian and no interpreter of the biblical message can bypass the challenge as to how God and history, faith and historical methodology, can be related. While the "liberal" approach tended to formulate theological statements that

---

86. *Jesus* (1987), p. 336.
87. *Jesus* (1987), pp. 441–515; *Interim Report* (1981), pp. 64–74.
88. *Jesus* (1987), pp. 382–384.
89. *Jesus* (1987), p. 384.
90. *Jesus* (1987), p. 390, compare pp. 390–392.
91. *Jesus* (1987), pp. 387.

would not contradict that which was accessible to modern historical investigation, the "evangelical" approach insists on making theological statements that are not accessible to historical reason. In contrast to the "traditional" approach they realize that a divine event cannot be measured and validated by generally acceptable scientific, historical, and rational methods. The assertions that the tomb was empty, that Jesus was bodily raised from the dead by a sovereign act of God, that he appeared to the disciples, and that he as Lord will determine the future of the world are therefore confessions of faith rather than statements of reason. They insist that since the resurrection is an act of God and of God alone, its depth and reality is only accessible to faith. Yet with the same emphasis they also maintain that the resurrection event contains historical manifestations, like the empty tomb, the appearances to the disciples, or a religious conversion that are open to historical investigation.

QUESTIONS AND ISSUES

The "evangelical" approach also gives rise to a number of comments and questions. Since it appears to be a very promising model, we must pay special attention to its promises and problems.

Appreciation

It is important to appreciate the theological intentions of the theologians that can be associated with this approach. They are interested to avoid a number of theological dangers.

Firstly, they want to resist any attempt to dissolve the resurrection of Jesus Christ into statements of human existence; or to limit the resurrection reality to assertions about human experience. They want to speak of the resurrection of Jesus Christ and consequently they want to give discernible biblical content to it.

Secondly, they believe that the resurrection should not be interpreted on exactly the same level as other historical events, such as Jesus' baptism or even his death. It can, of course, not be questioned that such other events also have dimensions that are not open to historical reason, but this is even more so with the resurrection, since God alone is the subject of raising Jesus from the dead.

Thirdly, the "evangelical" approach maintains that Jesus' resurrection is not simply *a* miracle. If anything, it is *the* miracle; a unique, a divine, and an eschatological event that can only be likened to the *creatio ex nihilo* and to the salvation of the sinner *sola gratia* and *sola fide* (compare Rom 4:5.17).

Fourthly, they fear that if the historical nature of the resurrection were to be surrendered, then it would lose its concrete relevance for our human historical existence. They emphasize the soteriological effect of the resurrection and the present experience of the risen Christ, and they want to guard the truth and reality of that experience by safeguarding the truth and historical nature of the resurrection. Summarily it may be said that the "divine" dimension of the resurrection needs to be asserted in order to protect its soteriological thrust (Jesus as savior, not just as a moral example), while the "historical" dimension needs to be maintained, so that the salvation which was accomplished by Christ really makes a difference in the world, in our lives and on the stage of history.

As a fifth point we may note the dissatisfaction of these theologians with affirming merely "that" Jesus lived and died and was raised. Rather, they assign new importance to the questions as to who the risen Christ is, and how he can be known.

Having these positive intentions in mind, we shall now try to locate those problem areas that we need to be aware of in developing our own understanding of the resurrection.

The Interpretation of "Space and Time"

We must ask whether it is wise to say that an event has occurred "in space and time", if at the same time one wants to maintain that such an event cannot be perceived and verified within the scientifically acceptable laws of space and time. These theologians insist that the resurrection is not a historical fact like other historical facts, and therefore it cannot be examined by accepted historical methodology. It is said that the resurrection is a different sort of historical event, one that cannot be recognized by historical reason. But few, if any, criteria are offered to describe this "different sort" of historical event.

We shall therefore need to investigate further the "space and time" dimension of the resurrection. In doing so we should reject the false dichotomy of whether something happened to Jesus or to the disciples. We need to find a way to perceive the resurrection as an event which includes Jesus, the disciples, the church, our own life, the world and its future.

The Apologetic and Kerygmatic Nature of Many New Testament Texts

This brings us to a further problem. Many of the New Testament texts that are used to give content to the resurrection as an event "in time and space" are taken from the Lukan and Johannine resurrection narratives where the risen Christ is portrayed as eating and drinking with his disciples, as being among them for forty days, as being able to be seen, heard, and touched. In addition, empty tomb narratives are found in all four gospels.

These are often the same narratives which, with the possible exception of the empty tomb tradition, can be better understood in terms of theological apologetics and kerygmatic embellishments rather than as historical reports. These are stories which the earliest Christian preachers used to communicate the resurrection, and to safeguard its reality against those who doubted it or who wanted to explain it away as an inner-personal or merely spiritual experience.

We must learn to appreciate that such apologetic and kerygmatic interests were important to protect the reality of the resurrection, and these interests could only be carried out with the scientific and literary means and methods that were available in first-century Palestine and its surrounding regions. With the means available to them, the early Christians wanted to underline the reality of the event, yet at the same time resist its objectification. Christ therefore walks through closed doors, and at first he is not recognized by his former followers.

A number of theologians have too quickly assumed what first needs to be established, namely, that the resurrection narratives are all historical reports. In order to discern the intention of a text—and that is the declared intention of these theologians!—one must ask in each case what the nature of a text is, what it wanted to convey, and how we can best appropriate its message in our situation. The empty tomb narratives, for instance, could in fact witness to the historical discovery of an empty tomb, but this would not prove the theological claim that God raised Jesus from the dead; and is it not significant that in the gospel account it is an angelic being, a divine messenger, who conveys that message (Mark 16:5f., par. Matt 28:5, Luke 24:4f.)?

Let us also not forget that there is another very strong New Testament tradition which stands in tension with the above approach if the apologetic and kerygmatic intentions are not taken into consideration. When the apostle Paul, for instance, speaks of the resurrection body, he speaks of a "spiritual" body, a "celestial" body, a body that "God has given," a body whose "glory" is quite different from perishable things. It is a body which is concomitant with the kingdom of God, while "flesh and blood cannot inherit the kingdom of God" (1 Cor 15:35–50). Here Paul seems to represent quite a different view of the resurrection body than that indicated by some synoptic texts. And no one should accuse Paul of underestimating the reality and importance of the resurrection! Rather, one must face the hermeneutical challenge and try to discern the reality of the resurrection that was formative in creating these texts.

If the texts are understood in their original context, and if the interpreter asks for the intentions of the texts, then the apparent differences between Paul and the gospels need not be contradictions! The different emphases arose when the early Christian preachers looked for effective forms to communicate this new reality, and when the early Christian theologians sought to safeguard the reality of the resurrection against spiritualizing tendencies. The first testimonies to the resurrection were formulated in confessional or catechetical formulas like "God raised Jesus from the dead." But the resurrection called for communication in preaching and teaching; consequently resurrection narratives emerged. These narratives included different historical information about the Easter events, but at the same time they had to fulfill the theological function of preaching the resurrection as gospel and not as law, to preach it into a certain situation, and to counteract trends that tended to dissolve the reality of the resurrection of Jesus into an other worldly "spiritual" phenomenon. Many of the resurrection narratives in the gospels are therefore intended to safeguard the same reality of the resurrection which is explicated in Paul's teaching.

The Situational Nature of Theological Statements

The above is related to a further theological challenge. All theologians want to understand the New Testament message and want to preserve the intention of the New Testament texts. But the New Testament is not as unified as we may assume. There is, for instance, an obvious difference in emphasis between some of the gospel texts and the Pauline view, a difference which was necessitated, as we have said, by hermeneutical and theological considerations. Such differences are therefore situational and functional rather than essential. Depending on the situation, such differences are necessary in order to communicate the message and to safeguard it against distortions.

This has often been overlooked by theologians. They tend to be selective in their choice and interpretation of texts. They have not been sufficiently self-critical to realize that the criteria for their selection may have been their own theological situation! We should not overlook, for instance, that a number of theologians who can be placed in this model have formulated their theology in explicit opposition to Rudolf Bultmann and his followers. Therefore it appears that similar to some of the synoptic texts, a number of their emphases seem to have an eristic or even apologetic character.

In developing our own view, we therefore need to ask what place the situation in which we find ourselves should play in developing a responsible understanding of the resurrection of Jesus Christ, and how we can best understand and explicate the historical nature of the resurrection.

The Biblical View of History

Some theologians who could be placed within this model insist that accepting the authority of the Bible must also include accepting the biblical understanding of history and reality. They would urge that we must not criticize the worldview of the text, but that we must surrender our understanding of history and reality to that of the text.

But questions remain: to which text? to what level of the respective texts? and how are these texts to be interpreted? On the surface it may appear, for example, that Luke 24:36–43 with its emphasis on the material and tangible aspects of the body of the risen Christ implies a different view of history than 1 Corinthians 15 where, with all the emphasis on the theological and soteriological necessity for the resurrection as an event that reaches into history, Paul never loses sight of the divine origin and the eschatological nature of the resurrection. Or one may think of John 20:26–29 where Thomas is invited to touch the body of the risen Lord. Yet the same Christ who issued that invitation had just entered through closed doors (20:19.26), and he commends a faith that has not seen (20:29)!

The biblical interpreter needs to ask therefore for the nature and intention of the biblical text. Only when that has been discerned, can we draw theological conclusions. This does not mean that we submit the texts to our scientific methodology and let them say only what we want to hear. But it does mean that we pay attention to the nature of the texts and ask, for instance, whether a text is a historical report, an apologetic story, or a kerygmatic narrative. Determining the literary form of a text and discerning the theological intention of a text is necessary for understanding its message. Acceptance of the authority of the Bible necessitates a considerable caution not to force the text into the framework of our philosophical and theological presuppositions. It should therefore be part of our exegetical discipline to understand the form and intention of a text; without that it will be difficult to comprehend its message.

A serious question remains. Can we or should we surrender our modern understanding of reality and our modern scientific methodology to those of a biblical text? The spirit of our time challenges us to be critical. We should not simply make arbitrary authoritative statements. We must give an account for what we think and say: "Always be prepared to make a defense to *any one* who calls you to account for the hope that is in you, yet do it with gentleness and reverence" (1 Pet 3:15, emphasis mine). This accountability should therefore not only be directed to the "inner circle" of those who agree with us already; it must be directed to the forum of the public to whom we want to communicate a faithful rendering of the gospel.

We are therefore confronted with a moral and a theological problem. The moral problem is whether it is still responsible scholarship to reason from the perhaps logical possibility that the resurrection could have happened in space and time to the conclusion that in fact it did so.[92] We might also question if one can really square the assertion that the resurrection happened in space and time with the insistence that with historical methodology, i.e., the methodology of space and time, we cannot perceive it! The theological problem is whether with that insistence the theologian is not erecting a stumbling-block that is foreign to the gospel. Whatever view of the resurrection we may develop, it must be clear that it is the cross of Christ and our unwillingness to believe, not any historical or intellectual difficulties, that is the true stumbling-block of Christian faith. The New Testament challenges us to maintain the emphasis on the historical reality of the resurrection, but we must ask how we can best perceive, appropriate, and manifest this historical reality.

The Nature of Faith

Related to the above is the insistence of some representatives of this approach that Christian faith includes intellectual assent to the tangible objectivity of the synoptic resurrection stories. Any discussion or questioning are often strangled by the uncritical postulate that "the Bible says so." Some

---

92. The moral problem involved in historical investigations is addressed by Van Austin Harvey, *The Historian and the Believer* (1966), compare e.g. pp. 153–159.

"evangelical" theologians relativize or even ignore the results of critical New Testament scholarship. This may leave the critical inquirer in a moral and spiritual dilemma. It includes the inherent danger of making faith as personal trust in a God who is love dependent on rational and intellectual assertions that some believers find difficult to make. If the impression is conveyed that such intellectual assent is necessary for faith, then the stumbling block of the gospel and its foolishness is misunderstood. Theological reflection is and must be rational. But it is always the second act, following the event of faith, ~/3 and trying to understand it.

At the same time, we must not forget the important reminder that faith has content and that this content must be received from the Christ-event. It remains our task to explicate the nature of faith in such a way that it becomes clear that it is faith *in Jesus Christ*.

This will also help us to avoid reducing faith to an individualistic and private religious experience. Here the emphasis on the bodily resurrection of Jesus and on the communal nature of resurrection faith serves as a constant reminder that faith must take on flesh in the world, and that faith has a revolutionary impulse to oppose any ideological attempt to define reality to suit our own interests.

CONCLUSION

We have seen that the "evangelical" approach tries to avoid the theological dangers of the "traditional" and the "liberal" approaches, and develop an acceptable alternative. Together with the "liberal" approach the "evangelical" / theologians emphasize that faith is the proper mode to know and to respond to the risen Christ. But they refuse to develop their view of the resurrection within the parameters of modern science.[93] Consequently, within the circle of faith, they tend to affirm the biblical historical details about the life of the risen Christh.

Our main difficulty with this position is a theological one. Is this approach 3 conducive to proclaim and represent the Christian gospel in our modern world? God wants to come to people. He wants to share in their lives. He wants to give them the certainty that they are loved by him. Theology must be an instrument to facilitate God's coming to his creation. Theology must not erect false fences to hinder people from opening their lives to God. The only true stumbling block is, according to the New Testament, the cross of Christ, because of human pride or unwillingness to accept God on his terms. But this unwillingness must not be seen primarily as an intellectual reluctance to accept that Jesus as risen Lord

---

93. The exception may be Edward Schillebeeckx whose emphasis on "conversion", rather than on the "visual appearances" and the "empty tomb", may be understood as an attempt to explicate the resurrection faith in terms that are more acceptable to modern human experience and modern historical reason.

could be touched or that he ate fish—that would be a false stumbling block! The real stumbling block is whether people are willing to admit that on their own they are estranged from the source of real life and that their soul is restless until it finds rest in God. This model would therefore have to carefully guard against the same danger that we have mentioned in our criticism of the "traditional" model.

It *is* important, however, that we maintain the emphasis on history. Not in order to speculate what happened long ago, but to responsibly manifest the reality of the resurrection of Jesus Christ today.

Chapter 4

The "Liberation" Approach

Promise and Praxis

INTRODUCTION

We saw that the "traditional" approach is primarily concerned with protecting the identity of faith against the critique of atheism, agnosticism, and secularity. It wanted to present the Christian faith as a real and rationally accessible option for the modern "post-Enlightenment" person. The "liberal" approach set out to show that the identity and content of faith in Christ does not negate the parameters set by modern science. As such it argues that faith and reason are not in conflict with each other if the function and limits of both are recognized. The "evangelical" theologians resisted allowing modern science to dictate the agenda for theology to explicate its own specific vision of reality. They maintained that the resurrection of Christ is an objective fact, but that this particular objective fact is not wholly accessible by secular historical reason. With the rise of the *Theology of Hope* (Jürgen Moltmann), *Political Theology* (Johann Baptist Metz), and various liberation theologies (Gustavo Gutiérrez, Jon Sobrino, Rosemary Radford Ruether, James Cone) a new theological emphasis has entered the scene. It may be gathered into the maxim: the promise of revelation and the praxis of discipleship.

This new emphasis was born out of the existential shock that the Christian gospel, rooted in the poverty of Jesus, must have something to say to people whose life and dignity is broken, spoiled, and destroyed; it must have something to say about structures of injustice that reward the rich and powerful, and punish the voiceless, the poor, and the powerless. This existential shock was intensified with the awareness that the Christian churches have often been found on the side of the oppressor, rather than the oppressed; supporting the slave owner, rather than the slave; being an advocate for the rich, rather than providing support to the poor; furnishing balm for the conscience of those who hunger for power, rather than encouraging and sustaining those who are passionately involved in the struggle for justice and peace; using its

85

human and material resources to protect their own interests and assure their own survival, rather than employing them to raise the consciousness of those who experience life as fated, and helping them to stand up and begin to seek ways by which they can participate in shaping their own future. Out of the experience of oppression and out of solidarity with the oppressed, theologians began to recall and retrieve that God is not a slave owner, but that he liberated his people from slavery in Egypt; that the prophets were not paid religious functionaries who provided divine validation for political and economic interests and ambitions, but that they spoke the "Word of the Lord" to those who trampled the poor under their feet; that Jesus was not the sweet and apolitical Son of God who saved people's souls, but that he was concerned with the salvation of people's lives, and that therefore he forgave sins, preached good news to the poor, and promised liberation to the oppressed, so much so, that he was opposed, arrested, and killed in a very short time for manifesting the kingdom of God in such a concrete way; that the earliest churches sought the presence of Christ not only in the preaching of the word and the administration of the sacraments, but that Christ was also present in the poor and the others who were pressed to the margin of life (Matt 25:31–46); that the history of the church is not only replete with political and ecclesiastical leaders that celebrate and maintain the *corpus christianum*, the great merger between politics and Christianity that has lasted from the 4th century to the present day, but that there are also persons like Bartholomé de las Casas, Oscar Romero, Mother Theresa, Martin Luther King, and Nelson Mandela whose faith was intimately related to the passion for justice and liberation. With this new awareness many theologians began to relate the riches of the Christian faith to the situations of injustice, oppression, the ecological crisis, and to the question of theodicy. History, ecology, the world and its future were put on the theological agenda. It was discovered that in traditional philosophy and theology the concentration on God and the individual self was so determinative that concern for the world and its future receded into the background,[1] while it "is the task of theology to expound the knowledge of God in a correlation between understanding of the world and self-understanding."[2]

Although this approach takes up elements from the other approaches, there is a definite change in emphasis. Some of Karl Barth's insights are now shaped into a theological program. Barth not only insisted that all of Christian theology must be eschatological,[3] but in his later work he also explicated the revolutionary and social-ethical content of God's revelation. For Barth Jesus existed

1. Jürgen Moltmann, *Theology of Hope. On the Ground and the Implications of a Christian Eschatology* (London: SCM, 1967 [1964]), pp. 62f.

2. Moltmann, *Theology of Hope* (1967), p. 65.

3. *The Epistle to the Romans* (London: Oxford University Press, 1933 [6th ed. 1928]), p. 314.

"analogously to the mode of existence of God."[4] By sharing his life with the despised and forgotten, Jesus revealed that God is a God who "ignored all those who are high and mighty and wealthy in the world in favour of the weak and meek and lowly."[5] Barth even speaks of the "partiality" of God[6] for the poor and oppressed. God is therefore to be found in the below, and he looks at life from the below, thereby transfiguring all values.[7] God is understood more as a disturber questioning the status quo and desiring to change it, rather than the transcendent deity who is often used to validate the status quo.[8] Salvation is no longer quantitative and heaven oriented, but it is qualitative, relating to the situation in which God has placed humanity here and now. Sin is not only understood in personal and individual terms, but also in its structural and dehumanizing manifestations. Mission must therefore not only tell the story of Jesus with the purpose of saving people's souls, but it must also be directed to changing political and economic structures that deny equality and equal opportunities to two-thirds of humankind. Faith must therefore not be primarily related to propositional truths and historical facts, but it must concretely be practiced to further justice and liberation.

CONTEXT[9]

"Paradigm shift" may be too big a claim. Nevertheless, it has meant a major reorientation for theological thinking when the crisis of justice and human rights, the crisis of economic exploitation, the crisis of racism and sexism, and the ecology crisis were not merely perceived as moral problems and social

---

4. Karl Barth, *CD* IV/2 (1958), p. 166.

5. Barth, *CD* IV/2 (1958), p. 168. In the original German text Barth mentions specifically the "poor" which the English translation omits (*KD* IV/2 [1955], p. 188). He adds: "There should be no softening of the starkness with which wealth and poverty are there contrasted and estimated . . . even in the economic sense." (p. 169).

6. The English translation "prejudice" (CD IV/2 [1958], p. 168) is inadequate for the German *parteiisch* (*KD* IV/2 [1955], p. 188). Barth, without denying or relativizing Jesus as Savior and Son of God who is God's radical YES to humanity, insists that this Jesus cannot be really known "if we do not know Him as this poor man, as this (if we may risk the dangerous word) partisan of the poor, and finally as this revolutionary." (*CD* IV/2 [1958], p. 180).

7. Karl Barth, *CD* IV/2 (1958), p. 169.

8. Karl Barth says in the above context: "The conformity of the man Jesus with the mode of existence and attitude of God consists actively in what we can only call the pronouncedly revolutionary character of His relationship to the orders of life and value current in the world around Him." (*CD* IV/2 [1958], p. 171).

9. Compare: Robert McAfee Brown, *Theology in a New Key. Responding to Liberation Themes* (Philadelphia: Westminster, 1978); David Batstone, *From Conquest to Struggle. Jesus of Nazareth in Latin America* (Albany, N.Y.: State University of New York Press, 1991); Jon Sobrino, *The True Church and the Poor* (London: SCM, 1985); Jürgen Moltmann, "The Course of Theology in the Twentieth Century," and "Mediating

ethical challenges; but when it was realized that they challenge the very content of our faith and the way that we have traditionally done theology. How can
we think of God in light of these crises? Out of the experience of oppression
and exploitation, and out of the solidarity with that experience, there have
emerged liberation theologies that interrelate God and salvation with the challenge of justice and liberation. As "North Atlantic" theologians, the least we
can do is to show our respect, to indicate our willingness to learn, and not ". . .
to dismiss liberation theology as no more than the latest fad."[10] This new way
of doing theology has also provided the context for a distinct way of understanding the resurrection of Christ. The resurrection is understood as inspiring
a passion for justice, as containing the promise that justice will ultimately triumph, and that it is therefore worthwhile to show constructive solidarity with
the oppressed here and now. Let us recall the context before we discuss its effect on understanding the resurrection.

There is first of all the startling awareness that the experience of oppression
and the solidarity with the oppressed is an eminently theological experience in
which one's own experience can be interrelated with the passion of God as it
is manifested in the stories of the exodus, and of the death and resurrection of
Christ.[11] While traditionally the church's attention has been focused on the non-
believer, liberation theologies want to give due attention to those whose human
dignity is denied.[12] While traditionally theology was mainly concerned with the
salvation of individuals and their future in the presence of God, an increasing
number of theologians retrieve the theological insight that God is not only redeemer but also creator, and that therefore he is concerned about the quality of
human life in the context of nature and society here and now.[13] What God has
created here and now deserves to be recognized as such here and now! This

---

Theology Today," both in: *Theology Today. Two contributions towards making theology
present* (London: SCM, 1988). The consequences for mission and evangelism are well
stated in Orlando E. Costas, *Christ Outside the Gate. Mission beyond Christendom*
(Maryknoll, N.Y.: Orbis, 1982). The consequences for theological methodology are ably
discussed by Juan Luis Segundo, *Liberation of Theology* (Maryknoll N.Y.: Orbis, 1976).

10. McAfee Brown, *Theology in a New Key* (1978), p. 11.

11. Gustavo Gutiérrez speaks of the "irruption" and the "new presence" of the poor:
"Liberation theology is closely bound up with this new presence of those who in the
past were always absent from our history." (*A Theology of Liberation. History, Politics,
and Salvation*. Revised Edition with a New Introduction [Maryknoll, N.Y.: Orbis, 1988
[1971], pp. xxf.).

12. "The traditional doctrine of the rescue of the soul into a heaven beyond must be-
come the doctrine of the future of the kingdom of God which renews heaven and earth."
(Jürgen Moltmann, "The Course of Theology in the Twentieth Century," in: *Theology
Today* [1988, pp. 1–51], p. 23).

13. Moltmann insists, for instance that "salvation . . . must also be understood as shalom
in the Old Testament sense. This does not mean merely salvation of the soul, individual rescue from the evil world, comfort for the troubled conscience, but also the realization of the eschatological hope of justice, the humanizing of man, the socializing of
humanity, peace for all creation. This 'other side' of reconciliation with God has always

concern is given cosmic relevance with Moltmann's emphasis that Christ is not merely the omega point of the evolutionary process, but rather the redeemer of the victims of that process.[14] On that promise and on that promise alone it is worthwhile to show solidarity with the victims here and now.

This is related to a second emphasis. If the "wretched of the earth" are given the theological status that they deserve, then all of reality must be viewed from below.[15] Not the wisdom of philosophical speculation, not the power politics of a social Darwinism, not the security syndrome of "Western" democracies, but the cross of the risen Christ becomes the hermeneutical key for interpreting reality. Christ is seen not only in the proclamation of the word and the proper administration of the sacraments, but he is also to be sought in the face and in the fate of the poor and oppressed (Matt 25:31–46). Reality is perceived not from the perspective of the priest and the Levite who come from their worship service and who (with good theological reasons!) walk past the man who lies half-dead on the side of the road, but from the perspective of the one who has been robbed and is now lying there on the side of the road of life (Luke 10:29–37).

This implies thirdly that we can no longer interpret the statement "God is love" in romantic and individualistic terms. Rather, it means that God takes sides and those who believe in him cannot escape into the safe harbor of a so-called neutrality. Neutrality is an illusion. Claiming to be neutral means in fact supporting the status quo. Religion in general and Christian churches in particular must question their traditional role of being used to provide the divine validation for the structures and values of those who enjoy the privilege of economic wealth, political power, and social status in a given society. Faith in Christ must learn to be suspicious of such interests.[16] It must retrieve the dangerous memory of Jesus and participate in the impatient struggle for *shalom*.

However, the God who takes sides is the God who creates ex nihilo, who raised Jesus from the dead, and who justifies the sinner. This means, fourthly, that human life is not fated.[17] Deprived people can begin to understand that their

---

been given too little consideration in the history of Christianity, because Christians no longer understood themselves eschatologically and left earthly eschatological anticipations to the fanatics and the sects." (*Theology of Hope* [1967], p. 329).

14. *The Way of Jesus Christ: Christology in Messianic Dimensions* (London: SCM, 1990), pp. 301–305.

15. Jürgen Moltmann, *The Way of Jesus Christ* (1990), pp. 38f.

16. Compare David Batstone, *From Conquest to Struggle. Jesus of Nazareth in Latin America* (1991), pp. 25f.

17. To explicate this and to raise the consciousnness of people to this fact is, according to Jürgen Moltmann, an important task of theology: "It is in a particular way a task of Christian theology, since this theology is the reflection of a historical, not a mystical faith. Because it speaks of God for Christ's sake, like Jewish theology it is directed towards historical recollection and the testimony which hands that collection on. It must 'make present' the fundamental historical recollection of Christ, in order to interpret the present in the light of that and to open up the future which is being headed for in that

situation is a result of historical constellations. They can be informed that these
constellations can be changed, and they can be helped to stand up and begin,
however slowly, to walk towards a more promising future. This walk will not
be easy. It will mean struggle and it will call for sacrifice. The Pharaohs of this
world will need to be opposed, and the principalities and powers will need to
be exposed. Often people will long to go back to the fleshpots of Egypt. But
the gospel will speak into their life that the struggle for liberation is worthwhile.
In this struggle more help will come from the social, political, and economic
sciences than from philosophy which has been the traditional dialogue partner
of theology. The main problem in this new theological emphasis is not atheism
and secularity, but exploitation and injustice.[18] Consequently the needed response is not apologetics, but the praxis of liberation based on and fueled by
God's promises made known in the resurrection of Jesus from the dead. Theory
and practice will be inter-related so that a new, a holistic way of knowing can
evolve. Theology will have the privilege of communicating hope, of raising the
consciousness of people, and of entering the struggle to "preach good news to
the poor" and "proclaim release to the captives" (Luke 4:18f.). And such proclamation is not aimed at saving a person's soul for the life beyond, but at re-
specting, safeguarding and healing God's creatures and God's creation here and
now.

We finally note that with this theological emphasis history is not perceived
in static, but in dynamic terms: "The resurrection of Christ is impossible unless it in turn launches history."[19] God is not the "totally other" as he has been
traditionally perceived, but He is the One who changes things.[20] Theology must
help the church to tune into God's dynamic passion for justice and thereby create analogies to God's being in the world.[21]

---

historical past." (*Theology Today* [1988], p. viii, compare "The Course of Theology in
the Twentieth Century," in: ibid., pp. 2–8).

18. Jon Sobrino comments: "Broad segments of humanity today live with a deep
yearning for liberation." While in the European enlightenment the major emphasis was
in "the liberation of reason from dogmatic faith," in the Latin American continent liberation must take on the challenge of "the liberation of the whole person from a religious outlook that supported or at least permitted social, economic and political
alienation." (*Christology at the Crossroads. A Latin American Approach* [Maryknoll
N.Y.: Orbis, 1978], p. 348; compare: *The True Church and the Poor* [1985], chapt. 1).

19. Jon Sobrino, *The True Church and the Poor* (1985), p. 87; compare: Jürgen
Moltmann, *Theology of Hope. On the Ground and the Implications of a Christian
Eschatology* (London: SCM, 1967), pp. 180f., 212.

20. Compare: Jürgen Moltmann, *Way of Jesus Christ* (1990), p. 232; "God and
Resurrection. Resurrection Faith in the Forum of the Question of Theodicy," (1968), in:
Jürgen Moltmann, *Hope and Planning* (New York: Harper & Row, 1971, pp. 31–55),
pp. 36, 51.

21. Here we recall Moltmann's often quoted modification of Karl Marx's 11th thesis
against Ludwig Feuerbach: "The theologian is not concerned merely to supply a different interpretation of the world, of history and of human nature, but to transform them
in expectation of a divine transformation." (*Theology of Hope* [1967], p. 84).

JÜRGEN MOLTMANN: REVELATION, PROMISE, AND DISCIPLESHIP[22]

Jürgen Moltmann has interpreted the resurrection of Jesus Christ in different literary and theological contexts. Nevertheless, from his earliest and ground-breaking book on eschatology (*Theology of Hope*, 1967 [1964]) to his more recent work on christology (*The Way of Jesus Christ*, 1990 [1989]) the resurrection of the crucified Christ has remained a or even *the* central and determining symbol for his theology. God is understood as the One who raised the crucified Jesus from the dead,[23] and the resurrection of the crucified One is the foundation ("der Grund") for christology and for the Christian church.[24]

The resurrection is an integral part of the "Way of Jesus Christ." This way is grounded in the history of Israel, it includes Jesus' messianic mission as the prophet of the poor, his apocalyptic suffering, his eschatological resurrection, and its fulfillment with the parousia of Christ. This christological process is related to Moltmann's insistence that revelation grounded in the resurrection of the crucified Christ has "constitutively and basically the character of *promise*. . . ."[25] Revelation is not the epiphany of the eternal in time, nor can it be tied to the historical verification of past events. It does not simply uncover what has always been, always is, and always will be, but it opens up new possibilities for the future, a future that is understood as the future of Christ: "The revelation of the risen Christ is not a form of this epiphany of the eternal present, but necessitates a view of revelation as apocalypse of the promised future of the truth."[26] This truth is not identical with what nature and history already contain, but it includes the *novum* that is indicated by theological symbols such as the "creation of the world", the "resurrection of Christ", and the "justification of the sinner".

---

22. For Moltmann's view on the resurrection consult: *Theology of Hope* (1967), especially pp. 15–36, 84–94, 95–120, 139–229, 272–303; *The Crucified God. The Cross of Christ as the Foundation and Criticism of Christian Theology* (1974), chapt. 5; *The Way of Jesus Christ: Christology in Messianic Dimensions* (1990), chapts. V–VII; "The Hope of Resurrection and the Practice of Liberation," (1972), in: Jürgen Moltmann, *The Future of Creation* (London: SCM; 1979), pp. 97–114; "God and Resurrection. Resurrection Faith in the Forum of the Question of Theodicy," (1968), in: Jürgen Moltmann, *Hope and Planning* (New York: Harper & Row, 1971), pp. 31–55.

23. *The Crucified God* (1974), pp. 187–196.

24. *The Way of Jesus Christ* (1990), pp. 76, 139, 213. Moltmann's distinction between the death of Christ as *Seinsgrund* ("ontological foundation") and his resurrection as *Erkenntnisgrund* ("epistemological foundation") in his discussion of cosmic christology (*The Way of Jesus Christ* [1990], pp. 281–283) is problematic in light of Moltmann's own criticism of Barth and Bultmann for whom the resurrection adds nothing new to the meaning of the death of Jesus.

25. *Theology of Hope* (1967), p. 85 (emphasis mine); compare ibid., chapt. I, § 8: "The Eschatology of Revelation", chapt. II: "Promise and History"; *The Way of Jesus Christ* (1990), pp. 223, 237–240.

26. *Theology of Hope* (1967), p. 84, compare pp. 84–94, 224f., 228f.

Moltmann strongly affirms the reality of the resurrection as the presupposition for faith, but he questions whether this particular reality can be understood
in terms of modern historical reason. How can historical reason that by its very
nature is delimited by death capture an eschatological event that has relativized
the limitations of death? "The symbol of 'resurrection from the dead' means a
qualitatively new life which no longer knows death and therefore cannot be a
continuation of this mortal life."[27] Given the modern "anthropocentric" understanding of history, which does not allow for actions of God, "it is plain that
on this presupposition the assertion of the raising of Jesus by God is a 'historically' impossible and therefore a 'historically' meaningless statement."[28]
Affirming the resurrection of Christ as a real event therefore implies a challenge for the most adequate understanding of reality as such: "In so far as . . .
the cross of Jesus is a scandal and foolishness in the world, his resurrection cannot be demonstrated to this world, except through the *freedom of a faith which
runs contrary to this world* and is therefore constantly on trial. *It lies with reality in the dispute over the future of true being*."[29]

Consequently, the resurrection can only be comprehended if it is understood
on its own terms: "The path leads here from the historic and unique to the universal, because it leads from the concrete event to the general. . . ."[30] Theology
must recognize this if it wants to remain true to its own Christian identity. For
theology, therefore, the resurrection is the hermeneutical key for its own particular understanding of history and reality. "To talk about Christ's resurrection
is meaningful only in the framework of the history which the resurrection itself opens up—the history of the redemption of human beings and nature from
the power of death. In the framework of a history determined in any other way
it has no meaning."[31]

Moltmann further clarifies this by distinguishing between a historical fact
and an eschatological event.[32] While the death of Jesus is a historical fact, and
while there were historical phenomena associated with the resurrection—the
visionary experiences of the disciples in Galilee, of the women in Jerusalem,
and of Paul on the road to Damascus; the disciples' courageous return to
Jerusalem; the discovery of the empty tomb[33]—the resurrection is an event of
a different order. It "means the annihilation of death,"[34] it refers to a "qualitatively new life which no longer knows death and is not a continuation of this
mortal life,"[35] indeed "it breaks the power of history and is itself the end of

27. *The Crucified God* (1974), pp. 169f.
28. *Theology of Hope* (1967), p. 174.
29. *The Crucified God* (1974), p. 173 (emphases mine).
30. *Theology of Hope* (1967), p. 142.
31. *The Way of Jesus Christ* (1990), pp. 236f.
32. *The Way of Jesus Christ* (1990), pp. 213–215.
33. *The Way of Jesus Christ* (1990), pp. 215–227.
34. *The Way of Jesus Christ* (1990), pp. 214, 222.
35. *The Way of Jesus Christ* (1990), p. 222.

history."[36] While the death of Christ symbolizes the apocalyptic end of world history, his resurrection stands "at the beginning of the new creation of the world."[37]

"Historical", therefore, is open to misunderstanding and almost certainly suggests a reduced understanding of the resurrection. Moltmann prefers to speak of the resurrection as a *history creating event*.[38] This has a double meaning in that the resurrection of Christ challenges and questions the adequacy of our modern understanding of history, and at the same time it is a reality that infuses new life into the historical process. "The 'resurrection of the dead' has no significance of its own, but is thought of as a *conditio sine qua non* for the universal achievement of righteousness in the judgement upon righteous and unrighteous."[39] The resurrection of Christ is therefore intimately interwoven with the divine promise that God's justice will triumph over the estranging and exploiting forces of death. It alone issues the promise that ultimately the oppressors will not "triumph over their innocent victims".[40] This is the important thrust of Moltmann's understanding of the resurrection. Against "liberal" theologians he insists that in the resurrection something happened to Jesus himself, in dialogue with "evangelical" theologians he argues that the resurrection of Jesus is part of God's passion for justice, and against the "traditional" rationalistic theologians he maintains that the risen Christ can only be known by people who are willing to follow him.

The human correlative to the resurrection as a history creating event which carries within itself the promise of the triumph of justice is therefore the understanding of faith as hope and as the praxis of discipleship.[41] Faith unfolds itself into hope, and hope becomes the determining reality of the believer's thoughts and deeds.[42] This hope becomes concrete in the praxis of discipleship:

---

36. *The Way of Jesus Christ* (1990), p. 214.
37. *The Way of Jesus Christ* (1990), p. 214.
38. *Theology of Hope* (1967), pp. 180f., 212.
39. *The Crucified God* (1974), p. 177.
40. *The Crucified God* (1974), p. 175, compare pp. 174–178. In the *Theology of Hope* (1967) Moltmann had located the question of the reality of the resurrection in direct confrontation with the modern experience of the "death of God" (pp. 163–172). That was the problem of the 1960s. However, already in his response to the criticism of his *Theology of Hope* Moltmann has interpreted this theological "location" in terms of justice. Theology must show solidarity with the poor; it must concretely address the problems of the situation and it must be concerned with changing things in the direction of justice: "Antwort auf die Kritik der Theologie der Hoffnung," in: Wolf-Dieter Marsch, ed., *Diskussion über die "Theologie der Hoffnung" von Jürgen Moltmann* (München: Kaiser, 1967, pp. 201–238), pp. 202, 230, 232f.
41. *The Way of Jesus Christ* (1990), chapt. V, §6; "The Hope of Resurrection and the Practice of Liberation," (1972), in: *The Future of Creation* (1979), pp. 97–114; "God and Resurrection. Resurrection Faith in the Forum of the Question of Theodicy," (1968), in: *Hope and Planning* (1971), pp. 46–50.
42. "As long as hope does not embrace and transform the thought and action of men, it remains topsy-turvy and ineffective." (Moltmann, *Theology of Hope* [1967], p. 33).

"Anyone who enters upon Christ's way will discover who Jesus really is; and anyone who really believes in Jesus as the Christ of God will follow him along the way he himself took. Christology and christopraxis find one another in the full and completed knowledge of Christ."[43] The first witnesses to the resurrection were therefore called to mission.[44] They were drawn into God's future, being allowed to experience a foretaste of the future of the crucified Christ.[45] This experience makes the believer restless and dissatisfied with the present.

> That is why faith, wherever it develops into hope, causes not rest but unrest, not patience but impatience. It does not calm the unquiet heart, but is itself this unquiet heart in man. Those who hope in Christ can no longer put up with reality as it is, but begin to suffer under it, to contradict it. Peace with God means conflict with the world, for the goad of the promised future stabs inexorably into the flesh of every unfulfilled present.[46]

The only adequate response to the resurrection is therefore not ". . . assent to a dogma and the registering of a historical fact," but rather "participating in this creative act of God. A faith of this kind is the beginning of freedom."[47]

Faith, therefore, does not provide the social cohesive for the stability of a given society, or the divine validation for the status quo. But, grounded in Christ's resurrection and anticipating his future, faith has "mobilizing, revolutionizing and critical effects upon history."[48] "The expected 'resurrection of the body' is already present in 'the Spirit of the resurrection' and is effective here and now. Life in the Spirit of God is consequently a life in the power of the resurrection."[49] Concretely this means that in the power of the reconciling life of Christ the believer and the community of faith resists the estranging forces of death. The exploitation and oppression of humanity and of nature is resisted by a struggle for economic justice, human rights, and the rights of nature.[50] Against the separation of body and soul the equal dignity of the body in its togetherness with the soul is affirmed. Against the tendency to devalue less

---

Moltmann therefore reformulates the traditional methodological principles of theology—*fides quaerens intellectum* and *credo, ut intelligam*—into *spes quaerens intellectum* and *spero, ut intelligam* (ibid.).

43. *The Way of Jesus Christ* (1990), p. xiv, compare pp. 41–43, 116–119, 240f., chapt. IV, §6.

44. *Theology of Hope* (1967), pp. 84–94, 188, 283–303; *The Crucified God* (1974), pp. 166–168; *The Way of Jesus Christ* (1990), p. 219.

45. For the believer, awareness "of history is awareness of mission, and the knowledge of history is a transformatory knowledge." (*Theology of Hope* [1967], p. 89).

46. *Theology of Hope* (1967), p. 21, compare pp. 102, 196, 224f., 226.

47. *The Way of Jesus Christ* (1990), pp. 240f., compare p. 237.

48. *Theology of Hope* (1967), p. 15, compare pp. 100, 334.

49. *The Way of Jesus Christ* (1990), p. 263.

50. *The Way of Jesus Christ* (1990), pp. 265–273; chapt. VI, §5.

productive stages of life (e.g., old age) the equal dignity of all stages of human life, including the life before birth, is affirmed. Against the individualistic tendencies in modern "Western" societies the importance of life in the context of community is underlined. The self-centeredness of the present generation is relativized by accepting responsibility for future generations. And faith in Christ makes believers aware of the essential interrelationship of human culture with nature and instills in them a new reverence for the dignity of life and a responsibility for nature.

Faith as hope and discipleship lives from the trust that God can and God will be true to his promises. God's "essence is not his absoluteness as such, but the faithfulness with which he reveals and identifies himself in the history of his promise as 'the same'."[51] In the Christ-event God reveals the truth and his faithfulness to his promise. "Between this once-for-all validation of the promise and its fulfilment in the glory of God there stands only the dependability of God himself."[52] Again: this has consequences for the way human beings can know God. Knowing the God of promise is

> . . . a peculiarly hopeful knowledge . . . an interested knowledge, a practical knowledge, a knowledge that is upheld by confidence in the promised faithfulness of God. . . . Knowledge of God is . . . an anticipatory knowledge of the future of God, a knowledge of the faithfulness of God which is upheld by the hopes that are called to life by his promises. Knowledge of God is . . . a knowledge that draws us onwards—not upwards—into situations that are not yet finalized but still outstanding.[53]

But can the believer be certain that God's promises are true, and that God will keep his promises? Moltmann replies with reference to the resurrection of Christ: ". . . because he [God] has raised Christ from the dead, therefore the fulfilment of his promise is certain."[54] This implies, of course, that the resurrection is a *real* event. It is not simply an existential or psychological phenomenon. It is real. It is not a human possibility. It happened outside the human person. The earliest witnesses

> . . . did speak of a fact and an event whose reality lay for them outside their own consciousness and their own faith, whose reality was indeed the origin of their consciousness in remembrance and hope. . . . Their statements contain not only existential certainty in the sense of saying, 'I am certain,' but also and together with this objective certainty in the sense of saying, 'It is certain.'[55]

good

---

51. *Theology of Hope* (1967), p. 143.
52. *Theology of Hope* (1967), p. 147, compare pp. 116, 143–148.
53. *Theology of Hope* (1967), p. 118.
54. *Theology of Hope* (1967), p. 145.
55. *Theology of Hope* (1967), pp. 172f.

We finally want to recognize that Moltmann breaks new theological ground when he discusses the resurrection of Christ not only in the context of the traditional paradigm of history, but relates it also to the emerging paradigm of nature and its cosmological dimensions.[56] The human being is not only related to history, but it is ontologically woven into nature and cosmos. Nature and cosmos provide the context in which history is being shaped. Apart from a functioning environment and a "friendly" cosmos, the human race cannot survive.

How then is the resurrection of Christ related to nature and cosmos? Two emphases are important. There is, first of all, the biblical conviction that the death and resurrection of Christ have soteriological significance for the whole universe including nature and the cosmos:

> In the ancient world, cosmic Christology confronted Christ the redeemer with a world of powers, spirits and gods. The proclamation of 'universal reconciliation' liberated believers from their fear of the world and their terror of demons. Today a cosmic christology has to confront Christ the redeemer with a nature which human beings have plunged into chaos, infected with poisonous waste and condemned to universal death; for it is only this Christ who can save men and women from their despair and preserve nature from annihilation.[57]

Secondly, Moltmann attributes new and important significance to the bodily resurrection of Christ. It is not only Jesus' "Spirit" or "die Sache Jesu" ("the cause of Jesus") that is raised from the dead, but his whole person. With his bodily resurrection "Christ leads human nature into the kingdom of God."[58] And since human persons with their bodies are bound into nature and the cosmos, the resurrection of Christ contains the promise of salvation for all creation, indeed for the whole cosmos: "the coming of Christ in glory is accompanied by a transformation of the whole of nature into its eternal discernible identity as God's creation."[59]

When it is asked how one can imagine such a bodily resurrection and what the resurrection body would be like, Moltmann refers to analogies of resurrection in nature: spring following winter, a new day following the night. But these can only serve as analogies for the "new creation"—when death and its estranging power will be no more and when love will reign in the kingdom of God. There is continuity and there is discontinuity between the old and the new: "The vulnerability . . ., its mortality, its sins, its suffering and its grief will be overcome," but at the same time, the personal identity, "the whole person, body and soul," as it is shaped in relationship to God will remain because God remembers it, and what God remembers death cannot destroy.[60]

---

56. *The Way of Jesus Christ* (1990), chapt. V/§§ 4–6 and chapt. VI.
57. *The Way of Jesus Christ* (1990), pp. 274f., compare pp. 280–286.
58. *The Way of Jesus Christ* (1990), p. 257.
59. *The Way of Jesus Christ* (1990), p. 280, compare pp. 257–263.
60. *The Way of Jesus Christ* (1990), p. 262.

With what body has Christ been raised and what shall the resurrection body of believers be like? It is the "body of love",[61] where the estrangement between body and soul, nature and history, life and death has been reconciled and at the same time transfigured[62] into the festive liberation of eternal life: "The first exodus led out of a historical tyranny into a historical freedom. Christ's exodus leads out of the tyranny of history into the freedom of the new creation."[63]

For the future this means that the future is not merely the unveiling of that which has already been accomplished in Christ, but it is the final fulfillment "of the promised righteousness of God in all things, the fulfilment of the resurrection of the dead that is promised in his resurrection, the fulfilment of the lordship of the crucified one over all things that is promised in his exaltation."[64] This means, for instance, that Christ is not the inner driving force or the inner *telos* of the process of history and evolution, but that he is "the Redeemer of Evolution": "The raising of the dead, the gathering of the victims and the seeking of the lost bring a redemption of the world which no evolution can ever achieve."[65]

JON SOBRINO: RESURRECTION AND JUSTICE[66]

Jon Sobrino acknowledges his debt to Moltmann's theological insights[67] as he develops his christology in the context of the Latin American struggle for justice and liberation. Since liberation theology in general and Sobrino in particular are often (unjustly![68]) accused of reducing christology to the "historical", the "pre-Easter" Jesus, and thereby truncate a holistic christology, it needs to be emphasized that Sobrino affirms the divinity of Christ and that he acknowledges the foundational character of the resurrection: "The starting point for the christology of liberation is the resurrection."[69]

---

61. *The Way of Jesus Christ* (1990), pp. 260–263.

62. Moltmann uses the biblical picture of the seed that is sown into the ground, "dies", and then blooms into life again. "Here we are shown a transition, not a total breach and a new beginning. That is why Christ is called 'the first fruits' of the dead (I Cor. 15.20)." (*The Way of Jesus Christ* [1990], p. 249, compare especially p. 257).

63. *The Way of Jesus Christ* (1990), pp. 257f.

64. *Theology of Hope* (1967), p. 229, compare pp. 210f.; *The Way of Jesus Christ* (1990), p. 223.

65. *The Way of Jesus Christ* (1990), p. 303, compare p. 239.

66. Jon Sobrino, S.J., *Christology at the Crossroads. A Latin American Approach* (Maryknoll, N.Y: Orbis, 1978 [1976]), especially chapts. 7, 8, and 11 (= *Christology*); *Jesus in Latin America* (Maryknoll, N.Y.: Orbis, 1987 [1982]), especially chapts. 1, 2, and 7; *The True Church and the Poor* (London: SCM, 1985 [1981]), chapt. 4.

67. *Christology* (1978), pp. 257f.[10]; this influence is also evident in *The True Church and the Poor* (1985).

68. Hans Kessler, *Reduzierte Erlösung? Zum Erlösungsverständnis der Befreiungstheologie* (Freiburg: Herder, 1987).

69. *Jesus in Latin America* (1987), p. 14, compare the whole of chapt. 1 where he addresses some of the criticisms that were voiced against his *Christology* (1978).

He agrees with Moltmann's insistence that the resurrection of Christ cannot be reduced to doctrinal, existential, and historical issues. The resurrection cannot be discussed in isolation from the cross, from the crosses in this world, and from the church's mission of justice and liberation.[70] The resurrection of Jesus is an eschatological event which entails a new vision of life and of reality. Only by making this new vision of life one's own and by participating in the new understanding of reality can the risen Christ be known: ". . . the meaning of Jesus' resurrection cannot be grasped unless one engages in active service for the transformation of an unredeemed world."[71]

Like Moltmann, Sobrino seeks to develop a relational Christology. The resurrection of the crucified Jesus from the dead and "the vindication of God's justice" are interrelated:[72] ". . . the hermeneutical locale for understanding the resurrection of Jesus . . . is to be found in the questioning search for justice in the history of suffering."[73] Important for understanding the resurrection is not whether the tomb was empty or with what body Jesus was raised. Important is the theological conviction that with the resurrection of Jesus "the triumph of justice" is at stake: "Who will be victorious, the oppressor or the oppressed?"[74] The resurrection of Jesus is the foundation for the promise of justice and liberation: "God has raised a crucified one, and from this moment forward there is hope for the crucified of history."[75]

To believe in the risen Christ is not the affirmation of a dogma or the agreement to the facticity of an event. Rather it means "grasping the future as a promise."[76] The believer and the believing community are drawn into God's mission of justice and liberation, which is grounded in the resurrection of Christ and longs for its ultimate fulfillment in the future when God will be all in all. "This means that it is possible to verify the truth of what happened in the resurrection only through a transforming praxis based on the ideals of the resurrection."[77] Therefore in all of his writings we meet the insistence that Jesus can only be known as the Christ in the praxis of discipleship.

---

70. ". . . the first question addressed to the church, precisely when it seeks to proclaim Jesus' resurrection, is whether the church is indeed united to the cross and to the numberless other crosses of current history." (*Jesus in Latin America* [1987], p. 157).

71. *Christology* (1978), p. 380.

72. *Christology* (1978), p. 243.

73. *Christology* (1978), p. 244.

74. *Christology* (1978), p. 244; compare *Jesus in Latin America* (1987), p. 149. In an interview Sobrino said: "The Resurrection of Jesus is primarily a symbol of hope for the victims of this world. At least in one case, a crucified victim triumphed over his executioners." ("The greatest Love," *Sojourners* [April 1990, pp. 16–21], p. 19).

75. *Jesus in Latin America* (1987), p. 151.

76. *Christology* (1978), p. 252.

77. *Christology* (1978), p. 255.

SUMMARY

With the "liberation" approach a shift of emphasis has entered the theological scene. It has challenged the traditional way of doing theology and of perceiving the very task and function of theology. As it was the case with the
"traditional" approach, the "liberation" approach is concerned with history.
However, here history is not seen as the stage on which God reveals himself in
historical events which can then be investigated and verified as such with historical reason. Rather, history is experienced as the process of remembrance and
anticipation. The believer and the believing community remember the resurrection of the crucified Christ and at the same time they anticipate the ultimate triumph of justice, of that *shalom* for which Jesus lived and died. This becomes
concrete by engaging themselves with word and deed for justice and liberation
here and now. Faith and hope are therefore perceived not in rationalistic terms,
but in terms of the praxis of discipleship.[78] History is not there to provide facts
for God's existence or God's revelation, but history invites responsible involvement. Accepting responsibility for the "wretched of the earth", for future generations, and for the ecosystem calls for change into the direction of justice.

With the "evangelical" and in contrast to the "liberal" approach, the "liberation" approach is very suspicious of the generally accepted status quo. It is critical of any attempt to give theological status to scientific, social, cultural,
political, and economic givens. Even more so than the "evangelical" approach
it wants to change things. It wants to find ways to let the kingdom of God im-
pinge upon the present and draw it into its future. Freedom is therefore not perceived primarily in "Western" terms, justifying its individualistic, consumer,
and success-oriented cultures which have to be defended by sophisticated military machineries and which have to seek ever new markets in order to survive.
Rather, freedom is understood in terms of liberation. The antislavery movement,
the labor union movement, and human rights traditions are remembered, the
passion of Jesus' engagement for the poor and oppressed was retrieved, and in
the power of the Spirit the liberation and justice of the poor and oppressed is
sought in the here and now. Freedom is defined not in terms of protecting the
interests of those who have power and wealth, but freedom is sought at the point
of pain where those who are disadvantaged and fated need to be enabled to lift
up their heads, get up, and walk. Understanding freedom in terms of liberation
is done in conscious and intentional critique of religion in general and the
Christian churches in particular, because they have allowed themselves too often
to be used as a social cohesive providing divine validation for the status quo.[79]

---

78. Jürgen Moltmann, *The Crucified God* (1974), p. 173: "The resurrection of Jesus
from the dead by God does not speak the 'language of facts', but only the language of
faith and hope, that is, the 'language of promise'."

79. Jürgen Moltmann: ". . . one cannot help noting that the basic anti-revolutionary,
conservative option has determined the historical form of Christian religion, the way in
which it is given form in the church and presented in theology, down to the present day."

In contrast to the other three approaches, the primary focus of the "liberation" approach is not on the individual's existential problems and questions and
longing for personal salvation, instead the individual is seen in her or his social, historical, and ecological context. The tragedy of those who feel fated in
situations of oppression is given theological status. The concern for the dignity
of women and children whose dignity is being denied and spoiled is understood
not only as a moral but also as a theological problem. The realization began to
dawn that in light of the ecology crisis we need not only deny a natural theology but at the same time and urgently call for a theology of nature. The witness to the gospel must therefore not only be directed to peoples' minds and
consciences, but in our time it must be addressed especially to the structures of
injustice that reward the rich and powerful and punish those who have no friends
and no voice and no power. Sin is therefore not only seen in its individual and
personal dimensions, but also in its structural manifestations. Salvation is not
only the forgiveness of individual sins and the assurance that the "saved" individual will go to heaven; it is the grateful acceptance of God's gift here and
now, and therefore it tunes in to God's passion for the dignity of human life and
for the preservation of his creation here and now.[80]

QUESTIONS AND ISSUES

Being a "North Atlantic" theologian it is difficult to be fair to this approach.
One is very conscious of the fact that this theological emphasis stands in potential judgment of one's own theology, one's own church, and one's own culture. And since none of us is able to or wish to distance ourselves from our
own theology, church, and culture, it is understandable that we tend to become
defensive at this challenge to our own position, and even feel guilty for not
being on the side of the answer but rather being part of the problem.
Defensiveness and guilt, however, are bad counselors for developing a responsible theology. They tend to result in aggression. They do not allow us to
become vulnerable to the insights and passion of this approach. We then tend
to caricature this approach by absolutizing some of its emphases, and then
criticize them in light of our own traditional theology, rather than asking
whether some of these emphases may not be required by the content of our
faith in Christ, may not be more biblical, and may not be more relevant to the

---

("The Course of Theology in the Twentieth Century," in: *Theology Today* [1988, pp.
1–51], pp. 5f., compare pp. 3f.).
    80. Gustavo Gutiérrez speaks of three levels of a holistic understanding of liberation:
firstly the aspiration of the oppressed to be freed from political, economic, and social
structures that dehumanize them. Secondly, the conscious awareness that people are not
fated but that they can assume responsibility and begin to shape their own destiny. Thirdly
the liberation from sin "which is the ultimate root of all disruption of friendship and of
all injustice and oppression." (*A Theology of Liberation. History, Politics and Salvation*
[Maryknoll, N.Y.: Orbis, rev. ed. 1988], pp. 24f. compare chapt. 9).

challenges of our time. Here is not the place to provide a detailed evaluation of Moltmann's or Sobrino's theology or of the various theologies of liberation. We can only try to become aware of questions and issues that are related to our attempt to understand the resurrection of Christ on its own terms.

Appreciation

The emphasis on revelation as promise, and discipleship as the corresponding way of knowing, is well taken and is a necessary corrective of an understanding of revelation that can more easily functionalize God into validating the status quo. In light of our contemporary situation it must also be appreciated that this model seeks to give more theological prominence to the problems of injustice, the denial of human rights, and the ecology crisis. It is indeed an important challenge to contemporary theology to give a more adequate theological status to the "wretched of the earth", and to develop a theology of nature including a cosmic christology that does not deny or relativize its theological continuity with the life, death, and resurrection of Christ. This implies the emphasis of retrieving the "dangerous memory of Jesus", and this in turn helps us to give a more adequate status to the critical and prophetic function of theology. This model forcefully reminds us that theology does not only have a priestly and eristic but also a prophetic task. Theology must measure the church's faith and practice by its confession to the crucified and risen Christ and thereby be suspicious of the many subtle ways in which we functionalize our theology to validate the status quo and thereby serve the interest of those who are in power.

The Novum of Christ and His Resurrection

The intention of Moltmann and Sobrino is clear. They want to ground their theology in the Christ-event, and at the same time recognize that the God of Jesus is none other than the God of Abraham, Isaac, and Jacob, the God of the Exodus, and the God of the prophets. In light of present religious pluralism and in light of the contemporary challenge for a theology of religions the question must be asked: is Jesus and his resurrection really the foundation of the Christian faith, as both Moltmann and Sobrino emphasize, or is Jesus Christ the confirmation, the fulfillment, the clarification, the interpretation and in that sense the incarnation of the God of the Old Testament? In what does the "novum" of Christ consist? Is it a quantitative or a qualitative *novum*?

While the category of "promise" is extremely helpful to capture the dynamic and the future and justice oriented dimensions of faith, it must not be seen as an alternative but rather as an expression of the saving work of Christ.[81] In that sense the Christ-event as an event of salvation and as an event of promise are

---

81. This is presented as an alternative in Moltmann, *Theology of Hope* (1967), p. 158; however, in his response to criticisms of the *Theology of Hope* Moltmann admits that the Christ-event is both an event of redemption and an event of promise. God mediates

not alternatives, but they complement and interpret each other, with the proviso, however, that procedural priority must be given to understanding the Christ-event as an event of salvation. In Christ, God has become flesh (John 1:14), and in him he has reconciled the world to himself (2 Cor 5:18–21). Christ therefore is the fulfillment of God's promises and the unconditional Yes of God for us and for his creation (2 Cor 1:18–22). Faith is therefore grounded in the work of Christ and lives from the promise that this work of Christ will be fulfilled because God is faithful to his promises.

Salvation and Liberation

Properly understand, both concepts, "salvation" and "liberation", mean the same. Salvation describes total well-being here and now, with the promise of a future life in the presence of God. Liberation refers to the freeing from law, sin, and death, and bringing us into contact with the source of all life, God. The problem is that traditionally "salvation" has been understood in more personal and individualist terms ("eyeball to eyeball" evangelism; preaching only to personal needs) and operating with a deficient anthropology (the mortal body as the prison of the immortal soul), while "liberation" was understood in terms of social and political revolution often with Marxist overtones. An adequate understanding of the resurrection must remain aware of this problem.[82] The risen Christ ministered to personal needs by forgiving sins, and at the same time the resurrection of the crucified Christ is God's great protest against injustice, and it contains the promise that ultimately the oppressors will not triumph over their victims.

Personal and Structural Evil

Again, traditionally evil and sin have mainly been understood in personal terms. The implication being that by changing and converting individuals, structures of injustice will also be changed. This has proven to be an illusion. Evil and sin are not only found in our hearts. They are also manifest in political, economic, military, and social structures that dehumanize people and hinder them from lifting up their heads, standing up, beginning to walk, and thus starting to shape their own future. Many people feel and in fact are fated. Structures need to be changed in order to create room for people to move and become creative. This approach has pointed out the peril of structural evil. We shall need to remember, however, that both personal and structural evil need to be dealt with.

---

his future in the representative suffering and in the atoning death of Christ and thereby overcomes the power of sin and death: "Antwort auf die Kritik der Theologie der Hoffnung," in: Wolf-Dieter Marsch, ed., *Diskussion über die "Theologie der Hoffnung" von Jürgen Moltmann* (München: Kaiser, 1967, pp. 201–238), pp. 227f.

82. Compare: Jan Milic Lochmann, *Reconciliation and Liberation* (Philadelphia: Fortress, 1980).

The Partiality of God and the "Preferential Option for the Poor"

These assertions are experienced as a constant threat to traditional theology. Does God not love poor and rich, oppressor and oppressed alike? Do not the rich and the oppressor also have to be liberated from their materialism and their stress, as much as the poor and the oppressed have to be liberated from the bondage of poverty and oppression? These questions contain, of course, an element of truth. God does want to share his life with all people, rich and poor, slave owner and slave. God loves the world and through Christ he has reconciled the world with himself. Nevertheless, God raised the crucified Jesus from the dead; this particular Jesus, who fleshed out a certain vision of reality and a certain understanding of God. Jesus would not have been crucified if he had uncritically accepted the political and religious establishment. He showed partiality for the poor and lame and sick, and for this partiality he was prepared to pay with his life. By raising this Jesus from the dead, God affirmed and effectively enacted the partiality of Jesus. This in no way means that God does not love all people, but he expects the rich to share their riches and he expects the oppressors to repent and stop their oppression. In that sense the partiality of God and the preferential option for the poor are the concrete expressions of love. And that is what the confession to the resurrection of the crucified Christ is all about. An awareness of the partiality of God forces us therefore to interpret our life. Neutrality is an illusion. By trying to be neutral or apolitical we simply support the status quo. Faith in the risen Christ entails the imperative to decide where the believer will take her or his stand.

The Moralizing of Faith

Protestant theologians, with their commitment to the Reformation rediscovery of the Pauline *sola fide*, are rightly suspicious of any moral distortion of faith.[83] Since much of liberation theology is Roman Catholic, and since Moltmann stands in the Barthian tradition which some Lutheran theologians tend to suspect of moralizing faith and thereby distort the Reformation emphasis on *sola gratia* and *sola fide*,[84] it must be asked whether this approach does not make the unconditional Yes of God dependent on human performance.

---

83. Compare Paul Tillich's discussion of the "voluntaristic" distortion of faith in *Dynamics of Faith* (1957), in: Carl Heinz Ratschow, ed., *Paul Tillich, Main Works/Hauptwerke*, vol. 5 (Berlin/New York: De Gruyter, 1988, pp. 231–290), pp. 247–249.

84. So Gerhard Ebeling's criticism of Karl Barth's theology: "Karl Barths Ringen mit Luther," in: *Lutherstudien*, Band III: Begriffsuntersuchungen—Textinterpretationen—Wirkungsgeschichtliches (Tübingen: Mohr, 1985), pp. 428–573, explicitly pp. 550f., 557f.; compare also Gerhard Ebeling, "Über die Reformation hinaus? Zur Luther-Kritik Karl Barths," *ZThK*. B 6 (1986, pp. 33–75), pp. 57, 66–75. In the same volume see Eberhard Jüngel's response, and defense of Barth position: "Zum Verhältnis von Kirche und Staat nach Karl Barth," ibid., pp. 76–135.

For many this fear becomes even more compelling when they become aware of the positive reception that some Marxist insights have received in the thinking of Moltmann and of liberation theologians. Although such fears are mostly unfounded, we need to be aware of this danger. The resurrection of Christ helps us to understand that faith is the undeserved gift of God. He is the subject in raising Jesus from the dead and in creating faith. But it was Jesus who was raised from the dead, and faith does therefore have a content which must become manifest in the life of the believer and in the community of faith.

A Selective Use of the Bible

It has often been said that the theologians of this approach are very selective in their use of the scriptures. They appear to be mainly interested in the Exodus motif and the social critical prophets from the Old Testament, and in the New Testament they tend to refer mainly to texts like Luke 4:18–30 and Matthew 25:31–46 that highlight the social and political relevance of Jesus. The fact as such is unavoidable. All theologians and all Christians read the Bible from what they perceive to be its theological center. This entails a certain danger of subjectivism and distortion. Moltmann and Sobrino have both been aware of this danger, and especially Moltmann has based his theology on a wide exegetical basis. However, we shall remain aware of this problem and try to avoid it by providing a careful biblical basis for our discussion of the resurrection.

Who Is Subject in the Historical Process?

Liberation theologies have also been accused of removing God from the stage of history and putting the human being in his place. Nevertheless, we saw that both Moltmann and Sobrino emphasize that God is active in the historical process, that he has raised Jesus from the dead, and that in the eschaton God will make *all things* new. This raises certain questions: what is the relationship between God's activity and human activity in the process of history? What theological significance, if any, does human activity have? Does human work ultimately make any difference if God in the end makes all things new? Is obedience to Christ and the praxis of discipleship worthwhile, and on what theological basis is it worthwhile? We need to keep these questions in mind as we try to discern the nature and content of resurrection faith.

Spirituality and Worship

The emphasis on justice, the necessity to protest against and to resist the structures of injustice, and the call to understand faith in terms of the praxis of discipleship, *can* lead to an activism which then may overlook the importance of a spirituality of liberation and the need for worship and praise in order to keep faith alive and focused in God. Liberation without spirituality easily turns into legalism and moralism. Any concern for justice needs to be kept alive and focused by the story of Jesus, lest the struggle for liberation turns sterile. Moltmann, Sobrino and other theologians who may be associated with this approach have realized this and therefore emphasize the importance of worship, praise, prayer, and joy in the struggle for justice on the way to *shalom*.[85] In our deliberations we shall therefore not forget that through Christ "we have been born anew to a living hope through the resurrection of Jesus Christ from the dead" (1 Pet 1:3). This "new birth" does not only include the response of service but at the same time and together with it the response of worship.

CONCLUSION

This approach has emphasized that the resurrection of the Crucified Christ is related to history as a history creating event. By raising Jesus from the dead, God has infused history with a promise. This promise is grounded in God's history with Israel and in the saving event of Christ's life, death, and resurrection. The believer and the community of faith are being drawn into that promise by being called to a mission of justice, liberation, and salvation. Faith as response to that call is experienced as hope, longing for the fulfillment of God's promises. Believing that God will be faithful to his promises, believers stake their lives on that promise. They become dissatisfied with the self-interest and injustice around them, and in anticipation of God's final *shalom* they become instruments of life, justice, and liberation. The emphasis on the bodily resurrection underlines the conviction of faith that God's activity becomes concrete in the world, and at the same time it contains the assertion that life must not be separated into holy and profane, into body and soul, but that the promise of God's salvation covers the totality of human life and of nature and the cosmos, apart from which human life would not be possible.

The "liberation" approach takes up motifs from the other approaches and then relates them to the creation of hope and justice in the world. It insists that liberation is the anticipation of salvation in the here and now. Theology, therefore, has a priestly and a prophetic function. With the "traditional" approach "liberation" theologians share the emphasis on history, but they ask the question as to how the historical event of the resurrection modifies our history in the direction of justice here and now. With the "liberal" approach of Bultmann and Knox these theologians share the emphasis on faith as the mode of recognizing God's revelation. But they understand faith not primarily in terms of a

---

85. See for instance: Gustavo Gutiérrez, *We Drink from Our Own Wells: The Spiritual Journey of a People* (Maryknoll,: Orbis, 1984); Jon Sobrino, *Spirituality of Liberation: Toward Political Holiness* (Maryknoll,: Orbis, 1988); Robert McAfee Brown, *Spirituality and Liberation. Overcoming the Great Fallacy* (Philadelphia: Westminster, 1988); Jürgen Moltmann, *Experiences of God* (London: SCM, 1980); Jürgen Moltmann, *Theology and Joy* (London: SCM, 1973); Jürgen Moltmann, *The Spirit of Life. A Universal Affirmation* (London: SCM, 1992).

private and personal religious experience, but rather in terms of the praxis of discipleship. This is the praxis of faith that must be involved in changing the world and participate in shaping its future. With the "evangelical" approach "liberation" theologians share a certain suspicion about letting the world determine the theological agenda. But this suspicion is not so much directed to scientific methodology. Rather, "liberation" theologians want to unmask social, political, economic, and ecclesiastical structures that create and sustain injustice, and they want to relate the gospel, grounded in the resurrection of the Crucified Christ, as a liberating and saving reality to these structures of injustice. By doing that they believe that theology is fulfilling its priestly and its prophetic task.

Conclusion and Transition

Where do we stand? We have surveyed some contemporary theological approaches to the resurrection of Christ. We have seen different emphases, and we have, at least in part, explained and appreciated these differences by taking into consideration the context in which the theologians are writing and to which they respond. A further differentiating factor was the philosophical or sociological orientation of the respective theologian. The cultural tradition and the perception as to where the real challenge to the Christian faith is located today also led to different responses. Of course, there is also the very human need to define a particular position in as clear-cut a manner as possible in order to see it as an alternative to other proposals. Nevertheless, with most or with all the theologians that we have surveyed, we have recognized the genuine interest to be faithful to the intention of the biblical message and the real concern to relate that message to the modern situation. Sometimes the situation was understood more in personal terms, which led to an eristic or existential thrust; at other times the situation was perceived more in sociopolitical terms, calling forth a passion for justice. Since all approaches meet the basic theological criterion of attempting to be faithful to the Christian message and to relate that message in a meaningful way to the present situation, they have all resulted in important insights that we should not forget as we attempt to develop our own understanding of the resurrection.

Both, the "traditional" and the "evangelical" approaches, have forcefully reminded us of the *extra nos* of faith. Jesus was really crucified (killed), and that Jesus has really been raised from the dead! The resurrection of Jesus is the presupposition for faith; it is not the product of faith. Any attempt to dissolve the resurrection into the faith of the believer or into the memory of the church must be resisted. Something happened to Jesus, and as such the resurrection is not only a "divine" but also a "historical" event.

While theologians of the "traditional" approach are confident that reason, if it is objective and neutral, can acknowledge the resurrection, "evangelical" theologians think that the divine riches of the resurrection cannot be grasped by the poverty of human reason. I tend to agree with the "evangelical" approach at this point. Reason is important and reason can do much. But it is not able to recognize an "act of God". The place of reason in theological reflection must therefore be carefully assigned. In the realm of theology reason is important to explore the reality and content of faith, but it cannot take the place of faith, nor should it claim priority over faith. In any case, neither reason nor faith can pos-

tulate the resurrection. The resurrection is an "act of God" which faith "receives" and reason then, as a second act, acknowledges and reflects about.

The "liberal" approach has made us painfully aware of the difficulty of understanding and communicating an "act of God" in our post-Enlightenment,
modern, and secular world. How can an event that has no analogies in our day
to day experiences of life be made accessible to a modern person? With a genuine concern to present the Christian faith as a viable option to the modern person, "liberal" theologians have explained the meaning of the resurrection in
such a way that the conflict with a "modern" world view is minimized. They
have shifted the attention from the resurrection of the dead Jesus to what this
resurrection may mean or signify with respect to phenomena that are historically more accessible. Consequently, the resurrection has either become a symbol for the eschatological significance of the pre-Easter Jesus, or it symbolizes
the soteriological and ecclesiological significance of faith in Christ. Again, some
of the emphases need to be kept in mind. It is certainly an important biblical
insight that the risen Christ comes to people in the event of faith, and that this
faith creates a community in which Christ remains present. It is also important
that the risen Christ must be seen in togetherness and continuity with the historical Jesus. But our hesitancy with this approach has been that the resurrection as such has been relativized and that therefore the ground of faith has been
reduced to the historical Jesus and his cross. Thereby faith either constitutes itself, or it tends to be reduced to an intellectual and moral commitment to a person who lived 2000 years ago and excites our moral imagination. To avoid the
extremes of fideism and moralism we must therefore insist that the resurrection of Jesus is not only of symbolic or noetic significance but that it is the ontological ground for faith, and indeed, that it also belongs, together with the life
and death of Jesus, to the content of faith.

The "evangelical" approach remains attractive with its clear commitment to
biblical authority, while at the same time avoiding the danger of biblicism.
Important is also the "evangelical" intent to protect the divine reality of the resurrection against the interest of secular reason. We must indeed be careful not to
reduce the reality of the resurrection to our possibilities of understanding. Even
if our reason is not able to grasp the nature of the resurrection, that in itself is insufficient to deny its being.[1] Do we not confess and affirm God's being, without
claiming that we can rationally prove God's existence? Just as we confess that
God has revealed himself in certain events and persons, so also the reality of the
resurrection has become known in certain manifestations. Must we not pay more
attention to the fact that the New Testament does not actually narrate the resurrection of Jesus, but speaks of the appearances of the risen Christ and of the gift
of the Holy Spirit. Although we have found the "evangelical" approach very

---

1. The German word for "reason", *Vernunft*, comes from *vernehmen*, which means
"receive" or "hear". This suggests the primary function of reason, not to postulate reality, but to analyze and reflect about the reality which it "receives".

attractive, our hesitation has been that it still remains too much in the realm of theological reflection and does not really gather the dynamic reality, the life-changing and history-creating quality of the resurrection of the crucified Christ.

This is better developed in and with the "liberation" approach. Responding to the experience of oppression, and out of a heartfelt solidarity with the oppressed, a much neglected aspect of the biblical understanding of God has been redis-covered and has been retrieved as a liberating dimension of faith in Christ. Some theologians have become newly aware of the "dangerous memory of Jesus"; they have retrieved the theological significance of reading in the Bible that God "hears" the cries of the oppressed and "knows" their suffering, that in the crucified Christ God made his own being vulnerable to the agony of estrangement and separa-tion, and that by raising the crucified Jesus from the dead, God has spoken a con-crete and liberating word of promise and hope into the historical process. We have been reminded that the "novum" of the resurrection does not only apply to Jesus, but it also entails the promise that the God who raised Jesus from the dead will make all things new and will ultimately fulfill what he has begun with the story of Jesus. These theologians have made us aware that sin is not only an in-dividual and personal reality, but that it also creates structures of injustice. In re-sponse to such a radicality of sin, salvation must also be understood in holistic terms. It cannot be limited to the salvation of a postulated soul in an afterlife, but it must include the liberation from structures of injustice here and now. God is neither a slave owner nor an oppressor. Consequently, with the resurrection of Jesus from the dead, God has spoken the promise into the world that ultimately the slave owner and the oppressor will not triumph over their victims. This promise shapes faith into an active anticipation of that ultimate promise. Faith therefore understands itself in terms of discipleship which entails the inherent knowledge that it is worthwhile to engage oneself for justice here and now. Such passion for justice is not only the moral consequence to faith, but it is the praxis of faith it-self. This model tries successfully to interlock the identity and the relevance of the Christian faith. The temptations that may be inherent to this model is that faith may result into a moral activism. This danger can only be resisted if the *extra nos* of faith is maintained and a spirituality of liberation is developed.

We could have, and perhaps we should have, examined further approaches. It would have been of special interest and promise to explore how Eastern Orthodox theologians have understood the resurrection. Their emphasis on the trinity, and, within the trinity, on the Holy Spirit as a "person" with its own identity and activity, on a cosmic christology and the implied all-encompass-ing salvation, and on the importance of the resurrection for the liturgy and the worship experience of the church, would have provided further valuable re-sources.[2] They have intentionally resisted "Western" rationalism. They affirm

---

2. Although Eastern Orthodox christology is, like traditional Anglican theology, pri-marily an incarnational christology, it is generally held, that through the resurrection the triumph of Christ over death ushers in the new humanity, which through faith, baptism,

the reality of the resurrection without wanting to remove its mystery. The resultant language appears speculative, but in fact it is a language of praise that seeks to correspond to the resurrection as a new and as a divine event. Nevertheless, both space and competence have prevented us from exploring this further.

---

and the eucharist is conferred on the church and on Christians and as such begins to shape their life. The general resurrection is the ultimate fulfillment of the resurrection of Christ and as such the consummation of his victory over death. For a first orientation of Eastern Orthodox christology see: Sergei Bulgakov, "Meditations on the Joy of the Resurrection," (1938), in: Alexander Schmemann, ed., *Ultimate Questions. An Anthology of Modern Russian Religious Thought* (Crestwood, N.Y.: St. Vladimir's Seminary Press, 1977), pp. 299–309; N. O. Lossky, "The Resurrection of the Body," *AThR* 31 (1949), pp. 71–82; Georges Florovsky, "The Resurrection of Life," *HDSB* I (1952), pp. 5–26; Timothy Ware, *The Orthodox Church* (Hammondsworth: Penguin Books, 1963), chapts. 2 and 11; Frank C. Senn, "Berdyaev, Orthodoxy, and the Theology of Hope," *JESt* 7 (1970), pp. 455–475; John Meyendorff, *Byzantine Theology. Historical Trends and Doctrinal Themes* (London & Oxford: Mowbrays, 1974), chapt. 12; Georges Florovsky, *Creation and Redemption*, vol. III in the Collected Works (Belmont, Mass.: Nordland Publishing Company, 1976), pp. 111–149, 213–240; Paul N. Tarazi, "Witnessing the Dynamics of Salvation," *SVSQ* 22 (1978), pp. 179–191; Bishop Kallistos Ware, *The Orthodox Way* (London & Oxford: Mowbray, 1979), pp. 110–117; Vladimir Lossky, *Orthodox Theology: An Introduction*. (Crestwood, N.Y.: St. Vladimir's Seminary Press, 1978), pp. 110–118; Georges Klinger, "La doctrine de la Croix et de la Résurrection de Rudolf Bultmann en confrontation avec la théologie de l'Eglise d'Orient," *Ist.* 25 (1980), pp. 176–211; Georges I. Mantzaridis, *The Deification of Man. St Gregory Palamas and the Orthodox Tradition*. With a foreword by Bishop Kallistos of Diokleia (Crestwood, N.Y.: St. Vladimir's Seminary Press, 1984), chapt. V; Boris Bobrinskoy, "The power of the resurrection," in: *Jesus Christ—the Life of the World. An Orthodox Contribution to the Vancouver Theme*. Ion Bria, ed. (Geneva: WCC, 1982), pp. 102–105; Protopresbyter Michael Pomazansky, *Orthodox Dogmatic Theology. A Concise Exposition* (Platina, Ca.: Saint Herman of Alaska Brotherhood, 1984), pp. 215–221; Nicilaos P. Vassiliades, "The Mystery of Death," *GOTR* 29 (Spring 1984/1), pp. 269–282; Damaskinos Papandreou, "Christologie und Soteriologie im Verständnis der Kirchenväter," in: *Orthodoxie und Ökumene. Gesammelte Aufsätze von Damaskinos Papandreou*. Ed. by Wilhelm Schneemelcher (Stuttgart: Kohlhammer, 1986), pp. 58–70; Georgies D. Metallinos, "Betrachtung des Menschen im Lichte der Auferstehung," in: *Begegnung mit der Orthodoxie. Vorträge von "Seminar für Orthodoxe Liturgie und Spiritualität", Frankfurt 1985* (München: Kloster des HI. Hiob vonPocaev, 1986), pp. 67–83; John Meyendorff, *Christ in Eastern Christian Thought* (Crestwood, N.Y.: St. Vladimir's Seminary Press, 1987); John Meyendorff, "New Life in Christ: Salvation in Orthodox Theology," *TS* 50 (1989), pp. 481–499; Dumitru Staniloae, *Orthodoxe Dogmatik*. Transl. by Hermann Pitters. Foreword by Jürgen Moltmann. II. Band (Zürich: Benziger Verlag/Gütersloh: Gerd Mohn, 1990), pp. 123–149; Christoph Künkel, *Totus Christus. Die Theologie Georges V. Florovskys* (Göttingen: Vandenhoeck & Ruprecht, 1991), chapt. 4; Stanley Samuel Harakas, "Resurrection and Ethics in Chrysostom," *Ex Auditu* 9 (1993), pp. 77–95.

Having surveyed how the theological community has understood the resurrection, we must now enter that discussion ourselves. In our appreciation and evaluation of the different approaches, a number of our theological conclusions have already been anticipated. Nevertheless, since there is no consensus as to how the resurrection should be understood, we must enter the debate ourselves. Wherever possible we shall rely on biblical scholarship, but at the present stage of research, every theologian must analyze the sources anew and draw his or her own conclusions.

Part II

FOUNDATIONS

The Resurrection of the Crucified Christ as a Foundational Event

Introduction to Part II

So far we have shown our appreciation for the theological community. We have seen how responsible and respected theologians have wrestled to understand the reality of the resurrection, and in our discussion with the various approaches we have become aware of some major issues related to the understanding of the resurrection.

It is now time for us to enter the process of understanding and begin to outline our own view of the resurrection of the crucified Christ. Like other theologians we shall seek to remain faithful to the primary sources, the New Testament traditions; we shall remain in dialogue with the various theological attempts to understand the resurrection; and we shall be sensitive to the biblical postulate: "Always be prepared to make a defense to any one who calls you to account for the hope that is in you, yet do it with gentleness and reverence." (1 Pet 3:15).

The first Christians proclaimed the resurrection of Christ as a necessary and integral part of the foundational reality for the Christian faith and the Christian church. The apostle Paul verbalizes this early Christian consensus: "if Christ has not been raised, then our preaching is in vain and your faith is in vain." (1 Cor 15:14). Christians have affirmed this consensus throughout the ages to the present day.

It is, of course, important to remember that the resurrection must be seen in the context of Jesus' life and his death on the cross. Nevertheless, it is equally significant to insist that the resurrection is more central to the New Testament witnesses than other theological assertions. For example, early Christian theologians may vary in the way they narrate the divinity of Christ. The apostle Paul and the Gospel of John, for instance, do it with the concept of "pre-existence", while the Gospel of Matthew and the Gospel of Luke point to the same reality with their concept of the "virgin birth". But all New Testament witnesses agree on the centrality and the necessity of the resurrection as the ground and basis for faith.

In our theological reflections we must therefore distinguish between foundational doctrines and supportive doctrines. The resurrection of Jesus Christ is a foundational reality. No Christians and theologians who are bound in their conscience to the authority of the biblical message can therefore ignore that the resurrection of Jesus Christ is an integral and constitutive part of the Christian faith. It calls for understanding and interpretation, not for relativization or even elimination!

Chapter 5

The Resurrection as an "Act of God"

The New Testament writings portray the resurrection of Jesus Christ as an "act of God".[1] One of the earliest Christian confessions—still transparent in texts like Romans 4:24, 8:11, 10:9; 1 Corinthians 6:14, 15:15; 2 Corinthians 4:14; 1 Thessalonians 1:9f; Galatians 1:1; Colossians 2:12; Ephesians 1:20; 1 Peter 1:21; and Acts 3:15, 4:10, 5:30, 10:40, 13:30.37—had the content: "*God raised Jesus from the dead!*"[2]

THE *NOVUM* CHARACTER

The "divine event" character of the resurrection of Jesus Christ is underlined by the fact that it breaks all categories of expectation, of historical methodology, and of language. It was a new and unexpected act of God.

This *novum* character has been controversial amongst theologians and church historians. There have been historical, religio-historical, and psychological explanations that tend to relativize the novum character of the resurrection. Such explanations seek to portray the continuity from the historical Jesus to faith in him in immanent historical categories that do not necessitate a new act of God. We therefore need to face the question, whether there are religio-historical parallels to the resurrection of Jesus Christ that would have made it possible or

---

1. Placing "act of God" in quotes in no way questions the effective and history-changing reality of the event. It simply intends to indicate that an "act of God" cannot be viewed on the same plane and cannot be understood by the same methodology as a human historical act.

2. Texts that speak of Jesus Christ himself being the subject of his own resurrection— "Jesus rose from the dead" (for instance: I Thess 4:14; Rom 14:9; Mark 8:31, 9:9.31, 10:34, 16:9; Luke 18:33, 24:7.34; Acts 10:41, 17:3; John 2:19.21, 10:17f.)—show a trinitarian development in thought. This development, however, in no way contradicts or questions the divine initiative in the event of resurrection.

probable for Jesus and his disciples to expect his resurrection from the dead. If that were the case, then indeed there would have been no need for the disciples to flee when Jesus was arrested and sentenced to death. If, on the other hand, the resurrection was an unexpected, new and unique event, then we need to face the further question as to whether and how language is able to grasp and contain something that is new and unique.

The Religio-Historical Question

The religious scene surrounding the earliest Christians was very diverse.[3] Although there were groups like the Sadducees that denied the doctrine of the resurrection, one may say that generally within Judaism, Hellenism, and Hellenistic Judaism it was not an unusual thought that people could rise or could be raised from the dead.

The Jewish God can raise people from the dead (e.g., 1 Sam 2:6),[4] and he will do so at the end of time in order to reward those who have kept the law, and punish those who have disregarded it (e.g., Dan 12:2; Isa 26:19).[5] In the most important prayer of Judaism which the Israelite must recite three or even five times a day, God is blessed as the One "who makest the dead alive."[6] Recent discussions have shown, however, that there is little evidence that in pre-Christian

---

3. George W. E. Nickelsburg comments: ". . . in the intertestamental period there was no single Jewish orthodoxy on the time, mode, and place of resurrection, immortality, and eternal life." (*Resurrection, Immortality, and Eternal Life in Intertestamental Judaism.* HThSt XXVI [Cambridge: Harvard University Press, 1972], p. 180).

4. Other texts that imply the conviction that God is master over life and death are: Gen 5:24; 2 Kgs 2:11; Ezek 37:1–14; Ps 73:24; Job 19:25–27; Wis 2:23, 3:1; 4 Macc 18:23f.

5. Compare also: Jub 23:30; Test. Judah 25:4; Test. Ben 10:6–10; 2 Macc 7:9.14; 1 Enoch 51, 91:10, 92:3f.; 2 Apoc Bar 30:1–5, 49–51; Pss Sol 3:12.

6. So the second of the "Eighteen Benedictions" (the Shemoneh 'Esreh): Text and discussion in Emil Schürer, *The History of the Jewish People in the Age of Jesus Christ* (175 B.C.-A.D. 135). A New English Version, revised and edited by Geza Vermes, Fergus Millar, Matthew Black (Edinburgh: Clark, 1979 [1885]), vol. II, pp. 455–463. Compare Gerhard Friedrich, "Die Auferweckung Jesu, eine Tat Gottes oder ein Interpretament der Jünger?" *KuD* 17 (1971, pp. 153–187), pp. 167–169, who argues that the reference to the resurrection may be a later addition arising from the polemic of the Pharisees against those who denied the resurrection. The Jewish concept of the resurrection immediately preceding and during the rise of the earliest Christian Churches is presented and discussed by: Kurt Schubert, "Die Entwicklung der Auferstehungslehre von der nachexilischen bis zur frührabbinischen Zeit," *BZ NF* 6 (1962), pp. 177–214; Paul Hoffmann, *Die Toten in Christus. Eine Religionsgeschichtliche und exegetische Untersuchung zur paulinischen Eschatologie* (Münster: Aschendorff, 1966), pp. 58–174; George W. E. Nickelsburg, *Resurrection, Immortality, and Eternal Life in Intertestamental Judaism.* HThSt XXVI (Cambridge: Harvard University Press, 1972); Günter Stemberger, *Der Leib der Auferstehung. Studien zur Anthropologie und Eschatologie des palästinischen Judentums im neutestamentiichen Zeitalter* (ca. 170 v. Chr.-100 n. Chr.). AnBib 56 (Rome: Biblical Institute Press, 1972).

times the resurrection and the appearance of an individual messianic figure was expected.[7]

While within Judaism there developed an expectation of the corporate nature of the resurrection at the end of time, Hellenism and Hellenistic Judaism also know of individuals who after their death have risen again and have appeared to people.[8] But these stories are not really resurrection stories. They are stories about people who after their death have been exalted into another world

---

7. Joachim Jeremias, *New Testament Theology. The Proclamation of Jesus* (New York: Charles Scribner's Sons, 1971), pp. 308f.; Gerhard Friedrich, "Die Auferweckung Jesu, eine Tat Gottes oder ein Interpretament der Jünger?" *KuD* 17 (1971, pp. 153–187), pp. 166–170; Ulrich Wilckens, *Auferstehung*. Themen der Theologie 4 (Stuttgart: Kreuz Verlag, 1970), pp. 114–144; C. F. D. Moule, in: C. F. D. Moule and Don Cupitt, "The Resurrection: A Disagreement," *Theology* 75 (1972, pp. 507–519), p. 508; Anton Vögtle, "Wie kam es zum Osterglauben?" in: Anton Vögtle/Rudolf Pesch, *Wie kam es zum Osterglauben?* (Düsseldorf: Patmos Verlag, 1975), pp. 107–117. This is also the scholarly opinion resulting from the discussion of Klaus Berger's thesis about the pre-Christian expectation of an eschatological prophet (*Die Auferstehung des Propheten und die Erhöhung des Menschensohnes. Traditionsgeschichtliche Untersuchungen zur Deutung des Geschickes Jesu in frühchristlichen Texten* [Göttingen: Vandenhoeck & Ruprecht, 1976]); compare: Eduard Schweizer's book review in: *ThLZ* 103 (1978), pp. 874–878; Martin Hengel, "Ist der Osterglaube noch zu retten?" *ThQ* 153 (1973, pp. 252–269), pp. 257–260; Johannes M. Nützel, "Zum Schicksal der eschatologischen Propheten," *BZ* 20 (1976), pp. 59–94.

8. Herodotus (approx. B.C. 490-425/20) reports a story that he had heard about a certain poet Aristeas who had died in a fuller's shop at Proconnesus. When the fuller went to tell the family of Aristeas that the poet had died, the report was disputed by a man from Cyzicus who said that he had met Aristeas and spoken with him. And indeed, when the family came to get his body, the body was not found. (*Herodotus*. With an English Translation by A. D. Godley. In four Volumes. Vol. 2, Books 3 and 4. The Loeb Classical Library [Cambridge, Massachusetts: Harvard University Press, 1963], Book 4, §§ 13–15 [pp. 212–217]).

Lucian of Samosata (approx. A.D. 120–180) tells a similar story about a trustworthy gray-haired man who had seen a person named Proteus in a white robe after he had died. ("The Passing of Peregrinus," in: *Lucian*, with an English translation by A. M. Harmon. Vol. 5. The Loeb Classical Library [Cambridge, Mass.: Harvard University Press, 1962, pp. 1–51], §40 [pp. 44–47]).

Philostratus (approx. A.D. 170–250) narrates the life of Apollonius of Tyana who prophecies to his disciple Damis where he will appear to him after his death: "'. . . turn aside to the sea-shore where the island of Calypso lies; for there you shall see me appear to you.' 'Alive,' asked Damis, 'or how?' Apollonius with a smile replied: 'As I myself believe, alive, but as you will believe, risen from the dead.'" ("The Life of Apollonius of Tyana," Book VII, §41, in: Philostratus, *The Life of Apollonius of Tyana*. With an English Translation by F. C. Conybeare. Vol. 2. The Loeb Classical Library [Cambridge, Mass.: Harvard University Press, 1950], pp. 262f.). When towards the end of his life Apollonius has to defend his life before the emperor, he disappears from the court room and appears to his disciples far away (ibid., Book VIII, §10, pp. 356–359). Forty days he speaks with them (ibid., Book VIII, §19, pp. 379–383), and during that time he convinces them that he is not merely a ghost, but that he is with them in body (ibid., Book VIII, §12, pp. 360–365). Then he enters the temple and is taken up to heaven, accompanied by a chorus of maidens singing: "Hasten thou from earth, hasten thou to Heaven, hasten." (ibid., Book VIII, §30, pp. 398–401). After his death he appears to a

and from there they appear to some people on earth. The resurrection of Jesus is narrated quite differently. Here the crucified Christ is transfigured by God into a new mode of existence. This new mode of existence, however, does not negate or relativize the life and death of Jesus, but rather reveals and manifests their eschatological and soteriological significance. The resurrection of the crucified Jesus is an act of God that qualifies and changes history. There are worlds of difference between the exaltation of a "divine man" to another world, and the resurrection of the crucified Christ.[9] Indeed, the Greek word-group usually associated with Hellenistic appearance stories—ἐπιφάνεια (epiphaneia), ἐπιφαίνεσθαι (epiphainesthai)—is not used in the New Testament at all. This indicates that either the New Testament writers did not know these stories, or they consciously avoided them, because they found them inappropriate as analogies to the resurrection of Jesus Christ. It is therefore unlikely that the Hellenistic and Hellenistic-Jewish literature influenced the thinking of the earliest Christians at this point.

The most that one can say is that in first-century Palestine it would have been possible to think of the resurrection of dead people as an act of God. But to conclude from this observation that the resurrection of a messianic figure in general, and of the crucified Jesus of Nazareth as the Messiah in particular, was expected, is inadmissible.[10] It is not the general religio-historical possibility of a resurrection, but only the specific event of the resurrection of the crucified Jesus which can account for the confession of the first Christians that God raised Jesus from the dead.

We must therefore conclude that neither the Semitic nor the Hellenistic or Hellenistic-Jewish religio-historical background can offer adequate analogies to the event of the resurrection of the crucified Christ.

The Historical Question: The Flight of the Disciples

It has been suggested that the faith of the disciples, or at least the faith of Peter, never came into a theological and existential crisis, and that therefore the "flight of the disciples" is a legend created by some New Testament scholars.[11] The

---

youth in his dream to convince him about the immortality of the soul (ibid., Book VIII, §31, pp. 402–405).

9. Compare Gerhard Friedrich, "Die Auferweckung Jesu, eine Tat Gottes oder ein Interpretament der Jünger?" *KuD* 17 (1971, pp. 153–187), pp. 170–179.

10. It is more likely that the Hellenistic-Jewish literature has influenced the New Testament narratives about the resurrections of Lazarus (John 11:1–44), Jairus' daughter (Mark 5:22–24.35–43 par.), and the widow's son at Nain (Luke 7:11–17). There is, however, an essential difference between the resurrection of these people and the resurrection of Jesus. They will have to die again, while Jesus has conquered death and will therefore "never die again" (Rom 6:9).

11. For instance: Hans von Campenhausen, "The Events of Easter and the Empty Tomb," in: *Tradition and Life in the Church. Essays and Lectures in Church History*

theological implication of such a proposal is, of course, that the continuity between the historical Jesus and the risen Christ could be sought in the continuing
faith of the disciples. In other words, the disciples through the religious worldview of their day, through their association with Jesus and through his teachings, could have—and perhaps even would have—expected that Jesus would be
raised after his death, or that at least the "Sache Jesu" (the cause of Jesus) would
continue after his death. If they had such expectations, then one may indeed
wonder whether and why they should have fled from Jerusalem to Galilee.

The New Testament evidence, however, so strongly favors the fact that the
disciples fled after Jesus' arrest, that one may suspect that behind the denial of
the flight there is a theological interest to play down the *novum* character of the
resurrection. The historical question therefore has theological significance. We
shall briefly summarize the arguments that make the flight of the disciples the
most probable explanation of the available evidence.[12]

The texts in Mark 14:27a, Mark 14:50, and John 16:32b imply that the disciples despaired sometime between the arrest and the crucifixion of Jesus, and
that consequently they fled from Jerusalem. John 16:32b mentions specifically
that they went "home", which for them was Galilee. It would have been unlikely for the early church to have created such texts, because the fact that the
disciples fled in the crisis hour was obviously an embarrassment to the early
church.[13] Indeed, Mark 14:27 explains that the flight was predicted by Jesus

---

(Philadelphia: Fortress, 1968 [1960], pp. 42–89), pp. 78–84. He argues "that the disciples
first remained in Jerusalem, and were still there when the tomb was discovered empty."
(p. 78). The disciples must have expected the death of Jesus (p. 80), and Peter remained
loyal to the end (p. 82). ". . . Peter had never, even after the crucifixion of Jesus, gone
astray in his regard. In spite of all, he had preserved his 'faith', and so finally won over
the others." (p. 81). Hans Conzelmann, "Auferstehung Christi. I. Im NT," in: *RGG* 3rd.
ed. Vol. 1 (1957, pp. 698–700), p. 699, states that the flight of the disciples has no basis
in the texts, and is indeed excluded by them. Eugen Ruckstuhl—in Eugen Ruckstuhl und
Josef Pfammatter, *Die Auferstehung Jesu Christi. Heilsgeschichtliche Tatsache und
Brennpunkt des Glaubens* (München: Rex Verlag, 1968), pp. 39–43—suggests that when
Jesus was detained, the disciples, with the exception of Peter, Judas, and John, fled to
Galilee. Peter remained in Jerusalem, although in hiding, and only later after the death,
burial, and discovery of the empty tomb did he go to Galilee to inform the other disciples.
Willi Marxsen postulates: "The legend about the flight of the disciples to Galilee should
now be laid to rest!" (*Der Evangelist Markus. Studien zur Redaktionsgeschichte des
Evangeliums* [Göttingen: Vandenhoeck & Ruprecht, ²1959], p. 52, fn. 1, my translation).
   12. Compare: Thorwald Lorenzen, "Ist der Auferstandene in Galiläa erschienen?
Bemerkungen zu einem Aufsatz von B. Steinseifer," *ZNW* 64 (1973, pp. 209–221), pp.
209–211; Wolfgang Schrage, "Das Verständnis des Todes Jesu im Neuen Testament,"
in: Fritz Vierig, Hg., *Das Kreuz Jesu Christi als Grund des Heils* (Gütersloh: Mohn,
1967, pp. 49–89), pp. 57–59; Gerhard Lohfink, "Der Ablauf der Osterereignisse und die
Anfänge der Urgemeinde," *ThQ* 160 (1980, pp. 162–176), pp. 162–164; Anton Vögtle,
Die Dynamik des Anfangs. Leben und Fragen der jungen Kirche (Freiburg: Herder,
1988), pp. 11–13.
   13. Compare: Erich Fascher, "Johannes 16:32. Eine Studie zur Geschichte der
Schriftauslegung und zur Traditionsgeschichte des Urchristentums," *ZNW* 39 (1940, pp.
171–230), pp. 172–176.

and the Old Testament (Zech 13:7). This obviously plays down the failure of the disciples and tends to excuse them. Not their failure, but God's providence was the reason for their flight! Also in Mark 16:7 the flight is interpreted positively as the presupposition for the appearances of Jesus in Galilee.

Luke may have felt the embarrassment that the disciples fled when Jesus was arrested, although Luke also had good theological reasons for locating the resurrection appearances in and around Jerusalem. He omits the "flight" texts Mark 14:27 and 14:50. In Luke 24:6 he reformulates the reference indicating that the risen Christ would appear in Galilee (Mark 16:7), and he adds to Mark 15:40 that not only women, but also "all his acquaintances" stood at the cross (23:49).[14] In John it is the male authority figure of the Johannine community, the "beloved disciple", who is present at the cross (19:26), and both he and Peter discover the empty tomb (John 20:3–8).

Obviously the need was felt in the early Christian communities to "explain" the somewhat embarrassing episode that the disciples had fled from Jerusalem. At the same time there was the tendency to associate male disciples with the scene that is of fundamental importance for the Christian faith, the crucifixion.

Historically speaking, the earliest records know of no male disciples at the cross, at the burial, or at the empty tomb (Mark 15:40–16:8). Not a disciple, but a friend (Joseph of Arimathea) had to arrange the burial, and only women were associated with the scene of the crucifixion and with the discovery of the empty tomb. In the ancient world women were considered to be inferior witnesses. It is therefore very unlikely that these stories would have evolved in the early church. Indeed, the fact that the dominant role of the women was reported at all shows the high regard that the earliest Christians had for historical traditions. But in that cultural context the later tendency to associate male disciples with the decisive event of Jesus' death and resurrection is quite understandable. John[15] and Luke[16] associate Peter, the beloved disciple, and other disciples with the cross and the empty tomb. Behind this tendency there stood the apologetic interest to associate the male authorities in the early churches with the foundational events of the Christian faith.[17] Historically we would have to conclude, therefore, that Peter and the disciples did not remain in Jerusalem.

---

14. A reference to the continuing faith of Peter could be found in the pre-Lukan text Luke 22:31f.: "Simon, Simon . . . I have prayed for you that your faith may not fail; and when you have turned again, strengthen your brethren." For Luke this may indeed have meant a reference to the exceptional faith of Peter in contrast to the other disciples. But the parallel text in John 21:15–17 (and Matt 16:18f.) suggests that the original reference was to the Easter situation when Peter experienced the forgiveness of the risen Christ and as such was enabled to strengthen the brethren.

15. John 19:26f, 35: the beloved disciple; 20:2–10: Peter and the beloved disciple.

16. Luke 23:49: Jesus' "acquaintances"; 24:12: Peter; 24:24: some disciples.

17. Compare: Thorwald Lorenzen, *Der Lieblingsjünger im Johannesevangelium. Eine redaktionsgeschichtliche Studie.* SBS 55 (Stuttgart: Katholisches Bibelwerk, 1971), pp. 87–109; note also that the pre-Pauline tradition in 1 Corinthians 15:5–7 includes only males.

The disciples' flight from Jerusalem to Galilee is also confirmed by the fact that the first Easter appearances to male disciples most probably occurred in Galilee (John 21:1ff.; Mark 16:7; Matt 28:16). Luke has theological reasons for locating the appearances in and around Jerusalem. Jerusalem and its temple is the center of the Jewish religion, there Jesus died, there he must therefore appear, and from there the church must spread the gospel "to the end of the earth" (Luke 24:49–53; Acts 1:1–11). Luke therefore places the appearance tradition that is linked with Galilee (John 21:1–14) back into in the life of Jesus (Luke 5:4b–6.8). The location of the appearance stories in Matthew 28:9f. and John 20 is given by their literary context.

We would therefore have to conclude that both the explicit references to the flight of the disciples and to the first appearances to male disciples in Galilee suggest that the flight of the disciples is not a legend created by some New Testament scholars, but that it remains as the best explanation of the available evidence. For our investigation this means that the psychological makeup of the disciples—flight, theological crisis, disappointment, fear, sadness—was such that an affirmation of the resurrection of the crucified Christ could not have been the product of their hearts and minds. For them the cross of Jesus was the crisis of their faith. They fled. The resurrection was for them an unexpected *novum*.

It must not be overlooked at this point that Jesus' female disciples stayed in Jerusalem. They observed the crucifixion, they discovered the empty tomb, and to them the risen Lord appeared. If the continuity from the historical Jesus to the Christ of faith is explained merely in immanent historical categories then it must have been the women who remained in Jerusalem that provided that continuity. This is in itself an important discovery in a male-dominated church. However, we shall see that affirming the resurrection of Jesus Christ in no way diminishes this discovery. If the risen Christ should have first appeared to the women in Jerusalem, then this would even intensify the theological challenge to draw consequences from such a historical discovery.

The Psychological Question

Another way to explain the resurrection of Jesus Christ within immanent historical categories and thereby relativize its *novum* character is the psychological explanation. We have already referred to it when we presented and criticized the subjective-vision theory of David Friedrich Strauss.[18]

The resurrection of Jesus Christ would then not be the cause for and the basis of the faith of the disciples, but it would be a theological symbol resulting from the faith of the disciples. Thus it would be seen primarily not as a new act of God but as a conflation of historical events, of theological factors,

---

18. Compare: pp. 50f., 61f. above. A good discussion of this problem can be found in Hans Grass, *Ostergeschehen und Osterberichte* (Göttingen: Vandenhoeck & Ruprecht, ⁴1970 [1956]), pp. 233–249.

and of subjective psychological conditions producing visionary experiences which led to the conviction that Jesus was alive and as such, given their world-view, that he had been raised from the dead.

It is argued that the memory of Jesus recaptured their hearts and minds when the disillusionment associated with his arrest and his death faded: his impressive personality, his authoritative teaching and preaching, his own predictions of his arrest, death, and resurrection (Mark 8:31, 9:31, 10:33f.), and the intense fellowship they had with him at the passover meal. This reassessment was augmented by new insights into the scriptures where they found prophecies for the resurrection of the Messiah (compare for instance the Old Testament references cited to predict the resurrection in Acts 2:24–36, 13:30–37). They may have heard of the dying and rising deities in the Hellenistic world, and they certainly knew about the exaltation of the righteous sufferer in pre-Christian Judaism. These ideas they could have transferred to Jesus. In addition, consciously or unconsciously, they had to deal with their own psychological needs: their fear of an uncertain future; their guilt for having forsaken their Lord in his hour of crisis; and their need to find new reason and hope for continuing their life. Given their psychological and cultural disposition toward ecstasies and visions—such experiences are reported of Paul (2 Cor 12:1–4), Peter (Acts 10:9–16), and Cornelius (Acts 10:1–8)—this could all have resulted in an experience of intensely personal and emotional reality which they could only interpret as "having seen the Lord."

The continuity between Jesus of Nazareth and faith in him after he had been crucified would then not be provided by a new act of God, but it could be explained with reference to the psychological disposition and experiences of the disciples.

Such an explanation should not be dismissed too easily. There are a number of observations that would speak in its favor. Visions belong to the common experience of humanity from ancient to modern times. People have had and are still having visions of Christ, or Mary, or the Buddha. Why should God not reveal himself through visions, as Paul, Peter, and Cornelius believed and experienced (2 Cor 12:1–4, Acts 10:1–8.9–16)? The vision theory would also be supported by the observation that the appearances of Christ were no public phenomena; only those who believed or came to faith "saw" the risen Christ. Such a theory as this to explain the basis and content of the Easter faith would certainly be more conducive and credible to the modern scientific mind.

Yet, however logical or convenient such a theory may appear to us, we could only adopt it if the sources would permit it. That, however, does not seem to be the case. There is a widespread agreement that the New Testament sources speak of a real encounter of the risen Christ with the disciples, that this encounter was initiated by God himself, that it was not produced by the psychological makeup of the disciples, but that it happened from the outside to the disciples, and that something happened, not only to the disciples, but also to Jesus himself.

The exegetical argument is supported by the historical argument that a dramatic change took place in the lives of the disciples. A change from fear to courage, from fleeing to Galilee to returning to Jerusalem, from returning to their former lives to becoming courageous proclaimers of the gospel, and from the guilt of failure and denial to the restoration of fellowship and the call to the pastoral office (Peter). These changes can only be adequately explained if something decisive and unexpected happened to the disciples. Of course, remembering Jesus, interpreting the scriptures, and compensating their psychological needs most likely played a role in interpreting their encounter with Christ. These factors helped them to understand and shape their new experience of faith. But by themselves they would not have been strong enough to provide the cause and the sustaining basis for their new faith, life, love, mission, and hope.

The exegetical and historical arguments are supplemented by the theological observation that the experience of faith confesses Jesus Christ as "the same yesterday and today and forever" (Heb 13:8). The reality of Easter faith does not merely witness to an event in the past, which ongoing generations must then remember and confess, but it lives from the present reality of the risen and exalted Christ.

We must therefore conclude that the psychological explanation is an attempt to explain the resurrection of Christ with categories that are drawn from an immanent worldview. These categories are inadequate to fathom the reality of the resurrection of Christ as it is portrayed in the New Testament traditions. This does not mean, of course, that the Easter experiences did not include visionary elements. The disciples must have "seen" something. But this "seeing" was not the result of their own remembering or their psychological disposition. It resulted from a reality created as a new act by God. To understand this reality of the resurrection of Jesus Christ the category "vision" is misleading and therefore inadequate.

THE PROBLEM OF LANGUAGE

The *novum* character of the resurrection implies that we can never completely understand it, and our attempts to speak about it can never capture the full meaning of the event.

When the New Testament speaks of the "resurrection" of Jesus Christ it uses two word groups that are very similar in meaning: the verbs ἀνίστημι (anhistēmi) and ἐγείρω (egeirō) (or ἐξεγείρω [exegeirō]) and the corresponding nouns ἀνάστασις (anastasis) and ἔγερσις (egersis).[19] These words were not created to describe the resurrection of Jesus Christ. They were already in use. They had meanings like: "to raise up" someone who is crouching down; "to rise" in order to speak; "to wake up" someone from his sleep; "to install" a person into an office; "to set up" or "to erect" pillars or walls or buildings; "to raise up" persons who were dead, or "to rise up" from the dead. Similarly,

---

19. Where other words are used—e.g. Rom. 14:9: "to live"—they are normally an adaptation to the context.

the corresponding nouns to these transitive and intransitive verbs could mean: "erection" of buildings, "arising" from sleep, the "resurrection" of dead persons, and the "waking up" from sleep.[20]

The earliest Christians, having been compelled by an experiential encounter with the risen Christ, began to speak about the resurrection of Jesus Christ in their own words; in language drawn from their cultural traditions and environment. These words only approximated what they wanted to say. They were the best "pointers" or "signposts" available to them to express the newly discovered reality. But these words did not exhaust the whole reality and meaning of the event. The event itself gave new meaning to these words.

We must therefore be careful that we do not limit the event itself to the traditional meaning of given words. Rather, we must allow the event to determine the content of the words used. Admittedly, interpreters find themselves in a hermeneutical circle. The event of the resurrection is only accessible through the experiences and the words that witness to it, and yet, neither the experiences nor the words can really capture the event. We must be aware of this dilemma, and yet attempt to give procedural priority to the event, so that the event determines the language rather than vice versa.

Applied to the question at hand, the earliest Christians certainly did not want to say that Jesus was "raised" or "delivered" from pain or agony. Neither did they want to say that Jesus was "raised" or "restored" from unconsciousness. For them Jesus was dead and yet through his appearances revealed himself as the Living One. For them the resurrection of Jesus was also different from "resurrections" of which they had heard in the Old Testament or from Hellenistic-Jewish culture. Jesus' resurrection for them was not like the "resurrection" of Lazarus (John 11:38–44), or the "resurrection" of Jairus' daughter (Mark 5:21–24a.35–43), or that of the widow's son at Nain (Luke 7:11–15). These were understood to be supernatural miracles: uncommon but not unheard of. It was clearly understood that these persons were raised back to earthly life and that, consequently, they would have to die again. They were not delivered from the power and realm of death. We may say that theirs was a resuscitation from death to earthly life—which as such is a life unto death; it was not a resurrection from death into the eternal presence of God.

CONCLUSION

Whatever else will have to be said about the resurrection of the crucified Christ, it is first and foremost an act of God. More precisely: it is a new act of God which cannot be explained within religious, historical, and psychological

---

20. For details see: Albrecht Oepke, "ἀνίστημι κτλ.," (anhistēmi ktl.) in: *TDNT* I (1964 [1933]), pp. 368–372; Albrecht Oepke, "ἐγείρω κτλ.," (egeirō ktl.) in: *TDNT* II (1964 [1935]), pp. 333–339.

categories of expectation. It was an unexpected surprise of joy, hope, and promise. When one searches for categories that may provide analogies to this new, unique, and unexpected event, the events of creation and salvation come to mind. In Romans 4 the apostle Paul can therefore speak of God as the One "who gives life to the dead", who "calls into existence the things that do not exist", and "who justifies the ungodly" (Rom 4:17.5). It is important to note that this act of God is not an arbitrary demonstration of power, but that it manifests God's nature as being radically for his creation.

Chapter 6

The Appearances of the Risen Christ

We saw that the most likely explanation for the disciples' faith subsequent to Jesus' arrest and death is the New Testament insistence that after the crisis of the cross Jesus was raised from the dead and appeared to the disciples. To this we must add the fact that the early Christians experienced Christ through the ministry of the Holy Spirit. Whatever else the resurrection may be and may mean, at the point of the encounter between the risen Lord and the disciples, and in the experience of the Holy Spirit, it reached into history and modified the lives of the disciples. Indeed, it radically changed the existence of the early disciples, it led to the formation of the Christian church, and it caused a change in our understanding of history and of the world.

Whether the empty tomb should be mentioned in this connection is debatable. On one hand it can be said with a fair degree of historical reliability that Mary of Magdala discovered an empty tomb, and that she was convinced that it was the tomb into which the corpse of Jesus had been laid. On the other hand there is a strong resistance in the New Testament to use the empty tomb as a historical proof for faith in the resurrection of Jesus Christ; and the apostle Paul does not use it in his theological explication of the resurrection of Jesus Christ. Only John 20:8—which portrays the beloved disciple entering the tomb "… and he saw and believed"—may convey a different impression. But even there the fourth evangelist immediately guarded against false theological conclusions by insisting: "Blessed are those who have not seen and yet believe" (20:29).

Whatever position we may want to adopt, there can be no doubt that any attempt to replace faith by sight, or to ground faith in the risen Christ on the historical veracity of the empty tomb narratives, would run counter to the confessional character of the New Testament and to the New Testament understanding of faith.

In order to understand the genesis and the content of the Easter faith we shall therefore discuss in that order: the "appearance" narratives, the experience of the Holy Spirit as an experience of the risen Christ, and the "empty tomb" stories.

A critical reading of the earliest New Testament traditions leads to the conclusion that soon after his death Jesus appeared as the risen Lord to Peter and possibly to other followers in Galilee. Most likely he also appeared to Mary Magdalene and possibly also to James and to the five hundred brethren in Jerusalem. Finally, two years later, on the road to Damascus, he also appeared to Paul.[1] These appearances were given a special dignity by being limited to a certain period of time, and to a select group of people.[2] Paul speaks of his Christophany as the last one (1 Cor 15:8); and in the Lukan writings the ascension stories (Luke 24:50–53 and Acts 1:9–11) serve the purpose of indicating that the appearances of Christ have come to an end. The heavenly messengers therefore proclaim that Jesus will not be seen again until the end of history (Acts 1:11).

These appearances are not identical with the resurrection of Jesus Christ. They are the consequence of and the witness to the resurrection. But since the New Testament sources never describe the resurrection of Jesus Christ itself, the appearances are as close as we can actually get to the event of the resurrection. For that reason alone it is essential to investigate the texts about the resurrection appearances and ask what actually happened and what that means for our understanding of the resurrection.

"CHRIST APPEARED TO ..."

The sources use different terminology to describe that some people, after Jesus' arrest, death, and burial, "saw" the risen Lord: ὁράω (horaō) = to see (1 Cor 15:5–8), ἀποκαλύπτω (apokalyptō) = to reveal (Gal 1:16), ὀπτάνομαι (optanomai) = to appear (Acts 1:3), ὑπαντάω (hypantaō) =

---

1. The literature dealing with the appearance traditions in the New Testament is vast; compare, for instance: Peter Carnley, *The Structure of Resurrection Belief* (1987), pp. 223–249, also: pp. 62-72, 204–211, 259–265; Hans Grass, *Ostergeschehen und Osterberichte* (Göttingen: Vandenhoeck & Ruprecht, ⁴1970 [1956]); Karl Lehmann, "Die Erscheinungen des Herrn. Thesen zur hermeneutisch—theologischen Struktur der Ostererzählungen," in: H. Feld und J. Nolle, Hrsg., *Wort Gottes in der Zeit*. Festschrift K.H. Schelkle zum 65. Geburtstag (Düsseldorf: Patmos, 1973), pp. 361–377; Karl Lehmann, *Auferweckt am dritten Tag nach der Schrift. Früheste Christologie, Bekenntnisbildung und Schriftauslegung im Lichte von 1 Kor. 15,3–5*. Quaestiones Disputatae 38 (Freiburg: Herder, 1968); Anton Vögtle, "Wie kam es zum Osterglauben?" in: Anton Vögtle/Rudolf Pesch, *Wie kam es zum Osterglauben?* (Düsseldorf: Patmos Verlag, 1975), pp. 9–131.

2. This point has recently been emphasized again by Daniel Kendall, S. J. and Gerald O'Collins, S. J. ("The Uniqueness of the Easter Appearances," *CBQ* 54 [1992], pp. 287–307). However, their ecclesiastical intention is fairly obvious. They seek to undergird the normative role of the male apostles, and consequently they neglect the appearance to Mary Magdalene, a woman! A few years earlier the same authors wrote an article in which they argue for Mary being a major witness to the resurrection: Gerald O'Collins, S. J. and Daniel Kendall, S. J., "Mary Magdalene as major witness to Jesus' resurrection," *TS* 48 (1987), pp. 631–646.

to meet (Matt 28:9), θεωρέω (theōreō) = to look at, to perceive (John 20:14), and φανερόω (phaneroō) = to reveal, to show (John 21:1.14). Of these, ὤφθη ([ōphthē] aorist passive of ὁράω [horaō] = to see) followed by the dative case—e.g. "Χριστός ... ὤφθη Κηφᾷ" (Christos ... ōphthē kēpha)—seems to have acquired special significance to describe the appearances of the risen Christ (1 Cor 15:5–8; Luke 24:34, Acts 9:17, 13:31, 26:16; 1 Tim 3:16).

Focusing our attention on ὤφθη (ōphthē) has the added advantage that we can draw on the further evidence of a primary witness: the apostle Paul. In 1 Corinthians 15:5–8 he uses ὤφθη (ōphthē) to list his own Christophany alongside others:

> Christ ... appeared to Cephas, then to the twelve.
> Then he appeared to more than five hundred brethren at one time, most of whom are still alive, though some have fallen asleep.
> Then he appeared to James, then to all the apostles.
> Last of all, as to one untimely born, he appeared also to me.

At other places Paul uses different terminology to describe the same event. In Galatians 1:16 he says that God "was pleased to reveal (ἀποκαλύψαι [apokalypsai]) his Son to me." In 1 Corinthians 9:1 Paul asks: "Have I not seen (ἑώρακα [heōraka]) Jesus our Lord?" Also 2 Corinthians 4:6 ("For it is the God who said, 'Let light shine out of darkness,' who has shone in our hearts to give the light of the knowledge of the glory of God in the face of Christ") and Philippians 3:4–16 ("... I have suffered (pass. !) the loss of all things,... because Christ Jesus has made me his own") are representative texts pointing to the radical impact that the resurrection appearance of Christ has made on the apostle. In addition we shall ask what Luke's account of Paul's encounter with the risen Christ on the Damascus Road (Acts 9:1–19a, 22:3–16, 26:9–18) could add to our understanding of the appearance event.

VARIOUS INTERPRETATIONS OF "CHRIST APPEARED TO ..."

The phrase "Χριστός ... ὤφθη Κηφᾷ" ([Christos ... ōphthē Kēpha] 1 Cor 15:3–5, compare Luke 24:34) can be translated and interpreted in several ways. It remains controversial as to who the determinative subject of the action is. Has God made Christ visible to Peter, so that the decisive activity lies with God? Or has Christ appeared or shown himself to Peter, so that Christ is the acting subject? Or was Christ seen by Peter, so that the receptive activity of Peter is emphasized? It is also uncertain how ὤφθη (ōphthē) was used and understood at the time when the earliest Christians formulated their faith. It is clear, however, that it was a well-known word, that it was often used in the Septuagint, and that therefore it had become a fixed concept to describe divine appearances.

The most popular interpretation is that Jesus Christ, shortly after his death, made himself known (from heaven) in such a way that Peter, Mary, Paul, and possibly the others could see him, recognize him, and even hear him speak. The initiative for this appearance laid therefore with Jesus Christ himself. And the emphasis is that Peter, Mary, Paul, and possibly the others really saw him.

Another interpretation is offered by Wilhelm Michaelis,[3] who understands the early Christian usage of ὤφθη (ōphthē) against the background of its use in the Septuagint. There in the major prophets, Michaelis maintains, "hearing" is emphasized over "seeing". He argues that the accent is not on the "perception with the eye",[4] but on "the presence of revelation as such with no necessary reference to its sensual perceptibility."[5] For the Septuagint "ὀφθῆναι (ophthēnai) means that man comes face to face with God in a religious and spiritual encounter."[6] This interpretation of ὤφθη (ōphthē) in Septuagint usage becomes determinative when Michaelis turns to the New Testament appearance narratives: "The visual aspect is never stressed."[7] "It seems that when ὤφθη (ōphthē) is used as a tt. [= terminus technicus] to denote the resurrection appearances there is no primary emphasis on seeing, as sensual or mental perception."[8] Consequently "ὤφθη Κηφᾳ (ōphthē Kēpha) etc. does not mean in the first instance that they saw Him, with an emphasis on seeing …,"[9] but it describes the appearances "as manifestations in the sense of revelation rather than making visible."[10] It seems, however, that for Michaelis the reception of that revelation was not merely an abstract intellectual knowing, because he insists that Jesus Christ "encountered them as the risen, living Lord; they experienced His presence."[11]

A third interpretation is offered by Karl Heinrich Rengstorf.[12] In contrast to Michaelis he maintains that ὤφθη (ōphthē) refers to a perception with the eyes,[13] and then he emphasizes, with reference to Acts 10:40, that it is God who is the acting subject in the resurrection appearances of Jesus Christ.[14]

We have already met a fourth interpretation.[15] A number of scholars understand "Christ appeared to Peter … to the twelve … to James … to the

3. Wilhelm Michaelis, "ὁράω κτλ.," (horaō ktl.) in: *TDNT* V (1967) pp. 315–381, especially pp. 324–334 and pp. 355–361.

4. Wilhelm Michaelis, "ὁράω κτλ.," pp. 324f.

5. Wilhelm Michaelis, "ὁράω κτλ.," p. 327, compare p. 358.

6. Wilhelm Michaelis, "ὁράω κτλ.," p. 325.

7. Wilhelm Michaelis, "ὁράω κτλ.," p. 356.

8. Wilhelm Michaelis, "ὁράω κτλ.," p. 358.

9. Wilhelm Michaelis, "ὁράω κτλ.," p. 359.

10. Wilhelm Michaelis, "ὁράω κτλ.," p. 359.

11. Wilhelm Michaelis, "ὁράω κτλ.," p. 358.

12. *Die Auferstehung Jesu.* Form, Art und Sinn der urchristlichen Osterbotschaft (Witten/Ruhr: Luther Verlag, 1967).

13. Ibid., p. 119, compare pp. 56f.

14. Ibid., p. 57.

15. Pp. 52–54 above.

apostles ... to Paul ..." as *Legitimationsformeln*.[16] These would have had the function "of authenticating particular leaders of the congregation."[17] The appearance formulas, then, do not primarily point to a christological event, nor do they in the first instance make a statement about Jesus Christ, but they have the ecclesiastical function of authorizing the leadership roles of Peter, James, Paul and the apostles in the early church. For Wilckens it is possible that behind the "formulas of divine validation" there stands a historical event of Peter's encounter with the risen Lord,[18] while in the essay of Pesch such an event is considered to be very unlikely.[19]

DIVINE "APPEARANCES" IN THE SEPTUAGINT

So far we have seen that ὤφθη (ōphthē) is a dominant concept in the New Testament appearance tradition, that this term was probably intentionally chosen to express the reality and importance of the resurrection appearances, and that it is part of a well established literary formula which Paul took over from his tradition.

In order to understand what ὤφθη (ōphthē) means in the christological context we need to recognize its usage in the Septuagint. There it is used as a technical term to speak of the appearance of YHWH or his messengers. Since the early Christians were probably well aware of this when they used ὤφθη (ōphthē) to relate the resurrection appearances of Christ, we need to ask whether the use of ὤφθη (ōphthē) in the Septuagint can be helpful to our inquiry.

In the Septuagint ὤφθη (ōphthē) is a translation of the Niphal perfect (נִרְאָה [nir'â]) and Niphal imperfect (יֵרָאֶה [yērā'eh]) of ראה (r'h) "to see". The Niphal expresses a reflexive and resultative dimension of the verb, which would suggest a literal rendering such as: "the Lord made himself 'seeable' to Abram" or to "Isaac" or to "Jacob" or to "Moses" (Gen 12:7, 26:24, 35:1.9; Exod 3:2, 6:2f.). God is clearly initiating and completing his self-communication, and it is understood that this self-communication becomes real and perceivable to the people who were part of the encounter. Since in the appearance formulas "Christ" is clearly delineated as the subject of the action, we may then, in analogy to the LXX usage, conclude that in the appearance formulas 1 Cor 15:5–8 and Luke

16. Ulrich Wilckens, "The Tradition-history of the Resurrection of Jesus," in: C.F.D. Moule, ed., *The Significance of the Message of the Resurrection for Faith in Jesus Christ.* Studies in Biblical Theology, 2nd Series, 8 (London: SCM, 1968, pp. 51–76), p. 73; Rudolph Pesch, "Zur Entstehung des Glaubens an die Auferstehung Jesu. Ein Vorschlag zur Diskussion," *ThQ* 153 (1973, pp. 201–228), pp. 212–218.

17. Ulrich Wilckens, "The Tradition-history of the Resurrection of Jesus," (1968), p. 73.

18. Ulrich Wilckens, "The Tradition-history of the Resurrection of Jesus," (1968), pp. 73f.

19. Rudolph Pesch, "Zur Entstehung des Glaubens an die Auferstehung Jesu. Ein Vorschlag zur Diskussion," *ThQ* 153 (1973), pp. 212–218.

24:34 Jesus Christ himself is understood to be the initiator and subject of his own appearance: "Christ appeared [made himself seeable] to Cephas...." But this still does not answer the question as to what actually happened in the appearance encounters, or whether the appearance formulas were merely literary devices to emphasize and validate the authority of important religious leaders.

At this point the use of ὤφθη (ōphthē) in the Septuagint becomes more elusive. In recent years Old Testament scholarship has dealt carefully and thoroughly with the language, literary forms, and content of the appearances of YHWH in the Semitic traditions and the surrounding cultures.[20] Also the use of ὤφθη (ōphthē) in the Septuagint has been carefully examined.[21] Different kinds of "appearances", their *Sitz im Leben*, and the corresponding literary forms have been isolated. There seems to be an increasing consensus that stories of appearances of God or his messengers were told to validate cultic centers or sacred sites,[22] to announce special promises to people, to appoint persons to perform a certain mission,[23] and to authenticate the author-

---

20. Compare the brief summary by Rudolf Pesch, "Materialien und Bemerkungen zu Entstehung und Sinn des Osterglaubens," in: Anton Vögtle/Rudolf Pesch, *Wie kam es zum Osterglauben?* (Düsseldorf: Patmos Verlag, 1975, pp. 133–184), pp. 136–156. Further: J. Kenneth Kuntz, *The Self-revelation of God* (Philadelphia: Westminster, 1967); Samuel Terrien, *The Elusive Presence.* Toward a New Biblical Theology. Religious Perspectives, 26 (New York; Harper & Row, 1978); Jörg Jeremias, "Theophany in the OT," in: *IDB* Supplementary Volume (1976), pp. 896–898; Jörg Jeremias, *Theophanie.* Die Geschichte einer alttestamentlichen Gattung. WMANT 10 (Neukirchen-Vluyn: Neukirchener Verlag, 1965).

21. Wilhelm Michaelis, "ὁράω κτλ. (horaō ktl.)," in *TDNT* V (1967, pp. 315–381), pp. 324–327; Claus Bussmann, *Themen der paulinischen Missionspredigt auf dem Hintergrund der spätjüdisch-hellenistischen Missionsliteratur.* Europäische Hochschulschriften XXIII/3 (Bern: Herbert Lang, 1971), pp. 97–101; Karl Heinrich Rengstorf, *Die Auferstehung Jesu.* Form, Art und Sinn der urchristlichen Osterbotschaft (1967), pp. 119–121; Hans Werner Bartsch, "Inhalt und Funktion des urchristlichen Osterglaubens," in: Hildegard Temporini und Wolfgang Haase, Hg., *Aufstieg und Niedergang der Römischen Welt. Geschichte und Kultur Roms im Spiegel der Neueren Forschung,* II.25.1: *Religion (Vorkonstantinisches Christentum: Leben und Umwelt Jesu; Neues Testament [Kanonische Schriften und Apokryphen]).* Hg. Wolfgang Haase. (Berlin, New York: Walter de Gruyter, 1982, pp. 794–890), pp. 820–836.

22. Appearances to prominent persons are often linked with the foundation of a cultic place: "Then the Lord *appeared* to Abram, and said, 'To your descendants I will give this land.' So he built there an *altar* to the Lord, who had appeared to him." (Gen 12:7f.; similar: Gen 26:24f., 28:12–19, 35:1–15).

23. Of special import are the *theophanies to Moses:* "And the angel of the Lord *appeared* to him (Moses) in a flame of fire out of a bush ..." (Exod 3:2, compare 3:16, 4:1.5). These are interrelated with other appearances: "And God said to Moses, 'I am the Lord. I *appeared* to Abraham, to Isaac, and to Jacob ...'" (Exod 6:2f.); "... the Lord *appeared* to Abram, and said to him, 'I am God Almighty; walk before me, and be blameless. And I will make my covenant between me and you, and will multiply you exceedingly.' ..." (Gen 17:1-8; similar in emphasis are the appearances to Solomon [1 Kgs 3:5, 9:2] and Isaiah [Isa 6:1-9]). In Genesis 18:1-15 "the Lord appeared" to Abraham in the form of "three men" and promised that his wife Sarah would have a son. The "angel of the Lord"

ity of leaders.[24] It is also widely felt that ὤφθη (ophthē) can neither be reduced to the word of revelation and the subsequent hearing of faith, nor can it be limited to the experience of seeing. It has the wider connotation of a holistic revelatory experience in which seeing, hearing, vision, ecstasy, and dreaming cannot be clearly distinguished from each other.[25]

The main question for us is this: does the language about the "appearance" of God refer to an actual experience in which God is encountered, or is it a literary device to emphasize the importance of a cultic place or to validate the authority of spiritual leaders?[26]

The fact that in certain Septuagint texts ὤφθη (ōphthē) was frozen into a literary formula does not necessarily imply that it does not preserve the memory of real, divine, and foundational events in the history of the people of Israel. The Old Testament, for instance, gives a special place to God's encounters with Moses,[27] and especially to the Sinai-theophany (Exod 19–24). Jörg Jeremias has investigated the Sinai tradition, and he comments that with it Israel witnesses to the experience of a foundational and unique event in which YHWH became their God and they became his people.[28]

We conclude therefore that the meaning of ὤφθη (ōphthē) should not be reduced to its functional and literary use. The Old Testament "appearance" narratives remain helpful at the following points. They must be seen, firstly, within

---

appeared to Gideon with the promise that the Lord was with him (Judg 6:12), and to a barren woman "the angel of the Lord *appeared*" with the promise that she would "conceive and bear a son." (Judg. 13:3). It should be noted, however, that the prophets do not usually use the "appearance" formula to validate their call. The closest are Isaiah: "In the year that King Uzziah died I saw (LXX: εἶδον [eidon]) the Lord ..." (Isa 6:1), and Ezekiel: "when I saw (LXX: εἶδον [eidon]) it (i.e. the appearance of the likeness of the glory of the Lord), I fell on my face ..." (Ezek 1:28).

24. For a summary statement see: Jörg Jeremias, "Theophany in the OT," in: *IDB* Supplementary Volume (1976), pp. 896–898.

25. Rudolph Pesch, "Materialien und Bemerkungen zu Entstehung und Sinn des Osterglaubens," in: Anton Vögtle/Rudolf Pesch, *Wie kam es zum Osterglauben?* (1975), 136f., 140, referring to the research of Friedrich Ellermeier (*Prophetie in Mari und Israel.* Theologische und orientalische Arbeiten 1 [Herzberg 1968]) and Johannes Lindblom (*Gesichte und Offenbarungen. Vorstellungen von göttlichen Weisungen und übernatürlichen Erscheinungen im ältesten Christentum.* Acta Reg. Societatis Humaniorum Litterarum Lundensis LXV [Lund 1968]); Heinrich Schlier, *Über die Auferstehung Jesu Christi.* Kriterien 10 (Einsiedeln: Johannes Verlag, 1968), pp. 31–39.

26. Compare Rudolph Pesch, "Materialien und Bemerkungen zu Entstehung und Sinn des Osterglaubens," in: Anton Vögtle/Rudolf Pesch, *Wie kam es zum Osterglauben?* (1975, pp. 133–184), p. 138.

27. In Numbers 12:6–8 God's encounter with Moses is given special status by distinguishing it from prophetic visions and dreams. With Moses, God speaks "mouth to mouth" (Num 12:8), or "face to face" (Exod 33:11, Deut 34:10), and Moses alone "beholds the form of the Lord" (Num 12:8).

28. Jörg Jeremias, *Theophanie.* Die Geschichte einer alttestamentlichen Gattung. WMANT 10 (Neukirchen-Vluyn: Neukirchener Verlag, 1965), p. 154.

the context of the Old Testament emphasis on the Godhood of God. Moses is told: "you cannot see my face; for man shall not see me and live" (Exod 33:20). Only when God makes special provision for it, is Moses allowed to see his "back; but my face shall not be seen" (Exod 33:23). God, therefore, cannot be objectified (Exod 20:4–6, 32:1–14). He cannot be defined on the basis of our possibilities of perception and understanding. God's holiness is mysterious and unfathomable. Therefore, people who participate in a divine encounter generally respond with fear and reverence. When the "angel of the Lord" appeared to Moses and "God called him out of the bush", then "Moses hid his face, for he was afraid to look at God" (Exod 3:1–6).[29]

Nevertheless, secondly, it must be asserted with equal emphasis that throughout the Old Testament this same sovereign God steps out of his elusive mystery and reveals himself in a real and perceptible way to people.[30] God or his messengers "appear" and "speak", and the people "see" and "hear". When the early Christians spoke of the appearance of Christ they thereby conflated their experiences of the risen Christ with the tradition of the appearances of God, who in the history of Israel appeared for the salvation of his people.

Thirdly, the consequence of the appearance of God is often the radical call to a divine task. Abraham, Isaac, and Jacob are given promises and are called to build altars (Gen 12:7f., Gen 26:24f., 28:12–19, 35:1–15), Moses is called to bring the children of Israel out of Egypt (Exod 3), and Elijah is called to appoint his successor and to anoint the kings of Syria and Israel (1 Kgs 19:9–18). Neither the "appearances", nor the promises and calls, can be objectified. They create obedience in the life of the hearer.[31]

At one point, however, all analogies and similarities break down: the Christian faith and the Christian church is grounded in the resurrection appearance of One who died the ignominious death of a criminal. This is the center of Paul's theology and it will be helpful to recall his experience of the risen Christ.

---

29. Compare also Moses' reluctance to respond to God's call: Exodus 3:11, 4:1.10.13, 6:10-13. Similar responses are known from the prophetic call narratives: "... when I saw it (i.e. the appearance of the likeness of the glory of the Lord), I fell on my face ..." (Ezek 1:28); "Woe is me! For I am lost; for I am a man of unclean lips, ...; for my eyes have seen the King, the Lord of hosts!" (Isa 6:5).

30. J. Kenneth Kuntz, *The Self-revelation of God* (Philadelphia: Westminster, 1967) has listed the various elements that make up a typical appearance narrative in the Old Testament (pp. 30–46). They include, for instance, that "the theophany is appallingly real" (p. 31), that it "is initiated by, and only by the deity himself" (p. 32), that it "is manifested as a temporal event" (p. 33), and that the "intensity" of the encounter is such that "the effects ... upon the life of one who attends the apparition of the deity may seem to be permanent indeed" (p. 34).

31. This close relationship between hearing and obeying is still preserved in some languages, for instance German: *hören—gehorchen*; Latin: *audire—oboedire*; Greek: ἀκούειν (akouein)—ὑπακούειν (hypakouein).

PAUL'S ENCOUNTER WITH THE RISEN CHRIST

We are in the fortunate position of having a first-hand account of one who claims to have "seen" the risen Christ. Although the resurrection/exaltation of Christ was known before Paul's own encounter with Christ on the road to Damascus, this would not be sufficient reason to question the veracity of Paul's own testimony. And since in 1 Corinthians 15 he uses the same terminology to list his own experience alongside that of the others, we may assume that he considered his experience to be similar in form and content to theirs. Paul's testimony may therefore further help us to discover what the earliest disciples actually "saw".

We may begin with the general observation that Paul makes a distinction between "visions and revelations of the Lord" (2 Cor 12:1) of which he probably had many, and the one decisive encounter with the risen Christ which caused a radical reorientation of his life and included the divine call to become an apostle to the Gentiles. The "visions and revelations" are not important to Paul. He feels forced to speak about them and as such he speaks "as a fool" (2 Cor 11:21, 12:11), while the encounter with the risen Christ forms the very foundation of his life and apostleship.

In 1 Corinthians 15:1–11 Paul describes the appearance which occurred to him as the "last" one (v. 8) in a series of resurrection appearances. For him, then, the appearances are limited to a certain period of time, and consequently they should not to be expected by Christians of all ages. This is a strange but important assertion. It was made in a culture and in an environment where visions, dreams, miracles, and ecstatic experiences were not unusual. When Paul describes his experience of an encounter with the risen Lord as the "last" one, he is safeguarding the reality of the Christian faith against a possible misunderstanding. For Paul, Peter, and the others it was clear that the encounters with the risen Lord neither replaced faith, nor made faith easy. They were life-changing encounters that created and sustained faith. As time went on, however, the appearances could easily have been misunderstood and misinterpreted as objective and public manifestations through which God revealed himself in an objectifiable and empirically verifiable manner in advance to a person's faith in him.[32] To counter such misunderstanding Paul postulates his encounter with the risen Christ as the "last" one.

---

32. In this context we should also be reminded of Paul's generally critical attitude towards a "miracle" faith. Especially in 2 Corinthians, Paul makes it quite clear that faith is centered in the crucified Christ, and to believe in him means "being crucified with him", which implies a life of hardship, sacrifice, and radical commitment. Against his Christian opponents in Corinth Paul boasts not in miraculous manifestations of strength, but in his trials, sleepless nights, beatings, and imprisonments, in order that it might become evident that the Christ who is revealed in and through his existence is the Crucified One! (See: Erhardt Güttgemanns, *Der leidende Apostel und sein Herr.* Studien zur paulinischen Christologie [Göttingen: Vandenhoeck & Ruprecht, 1966]).

For Paul, the encounter with the risen Lord radically changed his life. He used to be a persecutor of the church of God (v. 9). Now he became the most significant builder and motivator of new churches. This radical reorientation of life, which resulted from a radically new understanding of God, could not have evolved in Paul's psyche. It originated in an event which happened to him, not merely in him.

Through this event Paul feels himself to be given equal status with the other apostles (vv. 5–8), and he stresses that his apostolic message is in continuity with that of the other apostles: "whether then it was I or they, so we preach and so you believed" (v. 11).

However, in 1 Corinthians 15:1–11 Paul's main interest is neither to describe what he actually saw, nor to validate his own apostolic authority. He quotes a pre-Pauline tradition (vv. 3b-5.7) to support his theological argument that Jesus Christ has really been raised from the dead, and that this resurrection is the basis and content of faith. In the traditional formula the "appearances" support the reality that "he has been raised", just as the reference to the burial supports that he had really died. Paul then adds the reference to the five hundred brethren "most of whom are still alive", implying of course, that they can be asked about the veracity of their experience. With the long list of witnesses Paul follows the same theological intention as the tradition in Luke which affirms that "the Lord has risen indeed [ὄντως(ontōs)], and has appeared to Simon!" (Luke 24:34).

In Galatians 1:11–17 Paul's main interest is not to verify the reality of the resurrection, but to authenticate the gospel that he preaches, and the apostolic mission to which he had been called. He uses the concept "revelation" to speak of his encounter with the risen Lord: Paul did not receive his gospel from or through human authorities, "but it came through a revelation of Jesus Christ" (v. 12). God "was pleased to reveal his Son in me, in order that I might preach him among the Gentiles" (v. 16). Paul's main concern was to ground his apostolic mission in God himself. The content of the gospel and the authority of his ministry is not based on teaching or tradition, his commissioning does not come from the church in Jerusalem, but God himself had singled out Paul for a specific mission. Paul is speaking here of "a personal experience, divine in its origin ..., personal to himself and effectual."[33]

That this experience is qualified as a "revelation" gives to it a unique status and content. God has revealed his Son as the center of history and of all reality. In this encounter the eschaton has been made known proleptically.[34] Here

---

33. Ernest De Witt Burton, *A Critical and Exegetical Commentary on the Epistle to the Galatians.* ICC (Edinburgh: T. & T. Clark, 1921), p. 41; similar: Heinrich Schlier, *Der Brief and die Galater.* KEK (Göttingen: Vandenhoeck & Ruprecht, 1951), pp. 26f.; Heinrich Schlier, *Über die Auferstehung Jesu Christi.* Kriterien 10 (Einsiedeln: Johannes Verlag, 1968), pp. 33f.

34. Compare: Dieter Lührmann, *Der Brief an die Galater.* Zürcher Bibelkommentare NT 7 (Zürich: Theologischer Verlag, 1978), pp. 23f.; Dieter Lührmann, *Das Offenba-*

for a moment in time the secret meaning of history has been revealed. Here Paul has experienced what rational reflection, scientific research, and philosophical speculation cannot offer. The "new creation" which God has ushered in with the Christ event has become a personal and effective reality for Paul. This encounter changed his life—"I persecuted the church of God violently and tried to destroy it" (v. 13)—and conveyed to him the commission which determined his existence for the rest of his life (v. 16).

It is interesting that Paul interprets this call experience by using language which is adapted from the call narrative of Israel's great prophets, Deutero-Isaiah (Isa 49:1.5f.) and Jeremiah (Jer 1:5). In continuity with their ministry, he understands himself as called by God, sent to the nations, and he knows that it will be a ministry of hardship.

In 1 Corinthians 9:1 Paul refers to his encounter with the risen Lord—"Have I not seen the Lord?"—to validate his apostolic ministry ("Am I not an apostle?"), and to show that his "workmanship in the Lord" is a valid expression and result of the ministry which Christ himself had begun in and through him. It is again possible that Paul interprets his own calling consciously in analogy to the call of Israel's great prophets; both Isaiah and Ezekiel witness to having seen the Lord or his glory (Isa 6:1.5; Ezek 1:28). The use of the perfect tense (ἑώρακα [heōraka]) indicates that for Paul the "seeing" is not an observation that took place in the past, but that it was a life-changing event that continues to shape his present existence.[35]

In 2 Corinthians 4:6 Paul may not refer directly to his Damascus Road experience, but this text certainly explicates the fact that is central for the understanding of Paul's theology, that in his encounter with the risen Lord he was overcome with the conviction that the glory of God—God's nature, God's presence, God's character—is not to be seen or sought in the Torah but in Jesus Christ. And the context (vv. 7–18) makes quite clear that Jesus Christ is the crucified and risen Lord who continues to reveal himself in and through the apostolic existence. Indeed, the life of the crucified and risen Christ flows over into the apostolic existence so that the cross and the resurrection find analogies in the existence of the apostle:

We are afflicted in every way, but not crushed;
perplexed, but not driven to despair;
persecuted, but not forsaken;
struck down, but not destroyed;

rungsverständnis bei Paulus und in Paulinischen Gemeinden. WMANT 16 (Neukirchen-Vluyn: Neukirchener Verlag, 1965), pp. 73–81, 156–164.

35. F. Blass, and A. Debrunner, *A Greek Grammar of the New Testament and Other Early Christian Literature.* Trans. and ed. Robert W. Funk (Chicago: Chicago University Press, 1961), § 342.

always carrying in the body the death of Jesus,
so that the life of Jesus may also be manifested in our bodies.

(2 Cor 4:8–10)

Also Philippians 3:4–16 makes abundantly clear that Paul's conversion to
Christ cannot be grounded in his own religious needs or psychological makeup. Indeed, he confesses that his religious dedication, moral uprightness, and
cultural nobility was a hindrance in coming to know God personally. "I have
suffered the loss of all things,… because Christ Jesus has made me his own"
(vv. 8, 12). The source of his conversion is Christ himself who "grasped" him
and radically reoriented his existence. This encounter with the risen Lord was
so overwhelming in its reality and quality that everything else in life took on
secondary significance: "… whatever gain I had, I counted as loss for the sake
of Christ. Indeed I count everything as loss because of the surpassing worth of
knowing Christ Jesus my Lord" (vv. 7f.).

Romans 3:21f. may be cited as a representative text to remind us that the
coming of Christ is not to be reduced to the conversion or call of an individual.
Rather, it is a cosmic event with universal implications. "But now [νῦν (nyn)]
the righteousness of God has been manifested apart from law,… the righteousness of God through faith in Jesus Christ for all who believe." The "now"
has a twofold dimension. In its universal dimension it wants to say that with
Jesus Christ a new aeon has broken in. But, and this is the second dimension
of the "now," this new aeon aims at becoming a personal reality for each individual. In the horizon of Paul's theology we may say that Jesus Christ has been
exalted through the resurrection to be the Lord of the universe, and as such he
has drawn the apostle into the realm of his Lordship in order to use him in making his universal Lordship concrete and real on earth.

Before we summarize our findings we need to make a brief reference to
the Lukan accounts of Paul's Damascus Road experience: Acts 9:1–19a,
22:3–16, 26:9–18. These are not eyewitness accounts and therefore they cannot serve as primary sources. They are secondary witnesses in which Luke's
view of things and his historical information merge together, so that it is difficult to arrive at historically reliable information. All three reports mention,
however, how Paul, who was on the way to Damascus where he was to capture Christians in order to bring them back to Jerusalem (9:2, 22:5, 26:12),
saw "a light from heaven" (9:3, 22:6, 26:13). He fell to the ground (9:4, 22:7,
26:14), and he heard a voice: "Saul, Saul, why do you persecute me?" (9:4,
22:7, 26:14). Paul answers: "Who are you, Lord?" (9:5, 22:8, 26:15), to which
he hears the reply: "I am Jesus, whom you are persecuting" (9:5, 22:8, 26:
16–18).

For our inquiry it is important that the narrator is uncertain about the objec-
tifiability of the event of Paul's encounter with the risen Lord. In 9:7 we read:
"The men who were travelling with him stood speechless, hearing the voice but
seeing no one." Thus, while Paul saw a light from heaven (v. 3), his companions saw nothing. In 22:9 it seems to be the other way around: "Now those who

were with me saw the light but did not hear the voice of the one who was speaking to me."

What we need to notice is that there is a distinction between Paul and his companions. The text, on one hand, wants to underline the reality and objectivity of the event; on the other hand, this objectivity does not mean that the event is objectifiable—it is an event of revelation which by its very nature is only perceivable with the eyes of faith.

In conclusion we recall briefly what we have learned from Paul's encounter with the risen Christ.[36] Both Paul himself and also the Lukan accounts speak of an unexpected, unique, and objective event that happened at a certain period of time to this persecutor of the church.

This event was real, but it was not public. It created faith in Jesus Christ as Lord, which for Paul meant a total reorientation of life, a new understanding of God, a new view of reality, and a call to a new mission. The experience of faith included the whole person (Phil 3:12). He therefore "saw" and "heard" Christ, and Christ was revealed in him (Gal 1:16). Our modern alternatives of faith or sense experience, revelation or vision/audition are obviously inadequate to contain what Paul is speaking about.

In this encounter with Christ, God "revealed" himself as creator of heaven and earth. The God who was in Christ "reconciling the world to himself" (2 Cor 5:19), through raising his Son from the dead, had begun to make this reconciliation concrete in the world, and he called Paul to participate in this mission of salvation (Gal 1:15f.). Paul, therefore, does not consider his encounter with the risen Christ to be an individualistic, private religious experience. He considers himself being drawn into a cosmic event, a new era, a time, in which God—starting with the resurrection of Jesus Christ—has commenced to make all things new. In this mission of God to win back his world Paul has become a "fellow worker with God" (1 Cor 3:9).

Paul uses the language of revelation to show that although the event was objective, it was not objectifiable. It was not a supernatural miracle that can be seen, heard, and understood by a neutral bystander, and which then as such could be verified with empirical historical methodology. It is understood to be an "act of God", and as such it can only be appropriated with the obedience of faith (2 Cor 5:7).

Paul interprets his encounter with the risen Christ with the help of Old Testament texts. He sees himself being placed in the tradition of Israel's great prophets (Gal 1:15f.; 1 Cor 9:1),[37] and of the apostles (1 Cor 15:5–8; 9:1) of the earliest church, with whose message he identifies his own (1 Cor 15:11). Whenever his apostolic authority and mission are questioned then he refers back to his life-changing encounter with the risen Christ (Gal 1:11–17; 1 Cor 9:1).

---

36. For details see: Josef Blank, *Paulus und Jesus. Eine theologische Grundlegung* (München: Kösel, 1968), pp. 184–248.

37. Formative prophetic texts for Paul were Jer 1:4–10; Isa 6:1–3; Isa 49:1–6.

DID THE FIRST APPEARANCE OCCUR TO MARY—A WOMAN?

It is usually argued or presumed that the first appearance of the risen Christ happened to Peter in Galilee. The earliest formulas (1 Cor 15:5; Luke 24:34), the fact that the disciples fled to Galilee when Jesus was arrested and crucified, and the accumulation of Petrine resurrection narratives (John 21:1–14 [Luke 5:1–6.8], 21:15–17.18–22; [compare Luke 22:31f.; Matt 16:17–19]) certainly point in that direction. Nevertheless, a healthy suspicion must also remind us that there was a tendency in the earliest churches to down play the role of women, and to highlight the witness of male apostles.

It deserves therefore our special attention that the resurrection narratives in the gospels also speak about an appearance of the risen Christ to Mary Magdalene—a woman:[38] Matthew 28:9f. and John 20:14–18. Indeed, in the later ending of Mark, this appearance to Mary of Magdala is described or interpreted as being the "first" one, preceding the other appearances (Mark 16:9).[39] The appearance to Mary is located in or outside Jerusalem at the empty tomb. In the Matthean version the command of the angel to the women that they should go and tell the disciples that their Lord had risen from the dead and that he will appear to them in Galilee (28:7) is repeated before the encounter with the risen Christ is narrated. This is certainly a Matthean attempt to provide a link to the Galilean appearance stories. In contrast to the Matthean text, the Johannine version emphasizes that Mary should not "touch" or "hold" the risen Christ. John guards here against a possible misunderstanding that Jesus could have returned to an earthly existence. The pre-Johannine source was probably similar to the Matthean version where Mary "took hold of his feet and worshiped him" (Matt 28:9). But with his warning to Mary—"Do not hold me ..."—the fourth evangelist resists any objectification of the resurrection. This emphasis is not contradicted by the Thomas episode (John 20:26–29), because there the invitation to Thomas (v.27) to touch the risen Christ served to underline the reality of the resurrection, while immediately following the objectification of the risen Christ is rejected: "Blessed are those who have not seen and yet believe" (20:29).

While the differences between the Matthean and the Johannine version can be explained, it is unlikely that the early church would have invented a tradition in which Jesus appeared to Mary. It is of course possible that such an appearance tradition was formed to underline that the tomb was indeed empty; and since Mary had discovered the empty tomb while the disciples had fled to Galilee, it would follow the inherent logic of the tradition that Jesus must have appeared to Mary. But knowing the juridical stipulations that the testimony of women was, like that of children and imbeciles, not valid, and recognizing the

---

38. In Matthew there are two Marys. But that is clearly an adaptation to Matthew's version of the "empty tomb" narrative (28:1–8, see v. 1).

39. Luke may have discarded this appearance to Mary because for him the first appearance of Christ occurred to Peter (Luke 24:34).

hesitancy of early Christian authors to have women serve as the main witnesses to important events, it is more than likely that the first appearance of the risen Christ was indeed to a woman—to Mary in, or outside of, Jerusalem.[40] This is confirmed by the discernible tendency to add male witnesses to events like the cross and the empty tomb, where in the tradition only women were present (compare Luke 23:49 and John 19:26 with Mark 15:40; John 20:2–10 and Luke 24:12 with Mark 16:1–7). Therefore Mark 16:9, although a later addition to the first gospel, may in this case have preserved the accurate historical information. The fact that the pre-Pauline tradition in 1 Corinthians 15:5–7 does not include this testimony is probably due to the juridical situation, coupled with a male-dominated church that began very early to suppress the important place that Jesus gave to women.

If these observations are correct, it would belong to the great and tragic ironies of the history of the Christian church that right from its beginning the church has failed to understand the revolutionary character of God's revelation through the resurrection of the crucified Christ. If the resurrection appearances are foundational events for the Christian church, and if Jesus first appeared to a woman, then this would be a tremendous indictment on a church that for 2000 years has suppressed the equal dignity of women and men, and has since its beginning refused to grant the proper recognition to the ministry of women in the structures of the church. That in many churches this resistance is still being continued must be considered a direct and wilful denial of the very foundational event of the Christian church, the resurrection of the crucified Christ.

SUMMARY, CONCLUSION, INTERPRETATION

Having surveyed the information that is available about the resurrection appearances of Christ, we are now in the position to summarize our findings and to ask what they mean for our understanding of the resurrection of the crucified Christ.

First of all, we can say with reasonable certainty that Mary Magdalene, Peter, Paul, and possibly other early Christians (for instance James, the "twelve", and the "more than five hundred brethren" whom Paul mentions in 1 Cor 15:5–7) had surprizing and unexpected encounters with Jesus Christ after his death.

---

40. Elisabeth Schüssler Fiorenza therefore calls Mary Magdalene "the primary apostolic witness to the resurrection." (*In Memory of Her. A Feminist Theological Reconstruction of Christian Origins* [London: SCM, 1983], pp. 332 and 333). Compare also the careful analysis of Martin Hengel, "Maria Magdalena und die Frauen als Zeugen," in: Otto Betz, Martin Hengel, Peter Schmidt, eds., *Abraham unser Vater. Juden und Christen im Gespräch über die Bibel*. Festschrift für Otto Michel zum 60. Geburtstag (Leiden/Köln: Brill, 1963), pp. 243–256, who argues that the prestige that Mary Magdalene had in the early church can only be explained if the first appearance of the risen Christ occurred indeed to her (pp. 251, 256).

These encounters led to the conviction that Jesus was alive, the obvious conclusion being that God had raised him from the dead.

Historically, it is possible that the encounters with the risen Christ can be reduced to three: to Mary in Jerusalem, to Peter in Galilee, and to Paul on the road to Damascus. From among these, the resurrection appearances to Mary and to Peter obviously had some kind of a foundational character. With reference to Mary this foundational character was not adequately recognized, and soon, in a patriarchal society where the testimony of women was neglected, and in an emerging male-dominated church, the appearance to Mary became more and more marginalized while the appearance to Peter gained special significance in a number of the early churches. Paul's encounter with the risen Lord is clearly attested by himself and by Luke. It was probably the last appearance of the risen Christ. The other appearances that are reported in 1 Corinthians 15:5–8 and in the gospel narratives would then indicate that the earliest Christians and their leaders accepted the foundational appearance encounter of Peter, Paul, and possibly the others mentioned, and that on that basis they were prepared to follow the risen Christ. The appearance to Mary, while it was marginalized in the New Testament writings is mentioned in the later ending of Mark as being the "first" one (Mark 16:9) and in some circles of early Christianity it received theological attention and ecclesiastical recognition.

Secondly, the encounters with the risen Christ were real. They cannot be reduced to subjective visions, dreams, or ecstasies that have their origin within the psychological disposition or the theological reasoning of the disciples; they cannot be adequately explained as intellectual affirmation of religious truths, or in terms of inner religious conversions; they were also not told merely to authenticate the leadership roles of Peter, Paul, James, and the apostles. These encounters were initiated by God. They can only be understood as "acts of God" happening to them and only as such also in them.[41] The texts therefore emphasize that they "saw" the risen Christ; and there are other texts that emphasize that they "heard" him speak.[42] Also the fact that ὤφθη (ōphthē) is found in the New Testament both in its religious and theological use as well as in its ordi-

---

41. Compare the interesting debate between C.F.D. Moule and Don Cupitt, "The Resurrection: A Disagreement," *Theol* 75 (1972), pp. 507-519.

42. The Gospels report that Jesus was not only seen, but that he was also heard. He greeted his disciples when he appeared to them (Matt 28:9; John 20:19.21.26; Luke 24:36); he held conversations with them (Luke 24:13–32; John 20:15–17.26–29, 21:4–13.15–23); he interpreted the scriptures to them (Luke 24:25–27, 44–49); he made important theological statements (Luke 24:38f.; John 20:21.29; Matt 28:18); he authorized the disciples to forgive sins (John 20:23); he installed Peter to a leadership role in the church (John 21:15–17); he sent the disciples to teach and preach the Christian message in all the world and to baptize the new converts (Matt. 28:19f.; John 20:21); and to all who follow him he promised his comforting presence (Matt 28:20). Even though these narratives are interpretations of the event of the resurrection appearances, they emphasize the realistic nature of that event.

nary secular use[43] supports the conclusion that on the basis of the available texts we would have to say that the disciples after the crisis of the cross had "sense-communications from God ... a very specific sort of 'revelation', and an exceptional sort ... not comparable with private 'visions'."[44]

This "seeing" and "hearing" were not public events. It included the call to faith and mission, and only those who responded to the call "saw" and "heard". In the encounters Christ grasped whole persons including their senses. The encounter did not just convey some kind of information to the disciples; it did not simply release this or that thought or memory in them. In the encounter the whole existence of the disciples was grasped. They experienced the restoration of their fellowship with Jesus and felt a call to radical discipleship, which in the case of Peter and James meant becoming leaders in the early church, and in the case of Paul meant becoming the missionary apostle to the Gentiles. At this point one can only surmise that Mary of Magdala had a similar call to ministry which the churches of that time could or would not recognize. The information that a number of the earliest (house) churches were led by women preserves the contribution that women have made to the growth and formation of the church right from the beginning.[45]

These personal "Easter" experiences led the earliest Christians to the confession that Jesus had "really" (Luke 24:34) risen from the dead. In our terminology this means that for them the resurrection of Jesus was a historical event. What makes our perception so difficult at this point is that their understanding

---

43. The religious and theological use of ὤφθη (ōphthē) is dominant in the New Testament. Examples are: Moses and Elijah "appeared" to Peter, James, and John on the Mount of Transfiguration (Mark 9:4 [Matt 17:3]); the angel of the Lord "appeared" to Zechariah (Luke 1:11); an angel from heaven "appeared" to Jesus (Luke 22:43); at Pentecost tongues of fire "appeared" from heaven (Acts 2:3); Stephen said that the glory of the Lord "appeared" to Abraham (Acts 7:2); an angel "appeared" to Moses in the wilderness (Acts 7:30, compare 7:35); the Lord Jesus "appeared" to Saul (Acts 9:17, 16:9, 26:16); the Lord Jesus "appeared" to the disciples (Acts 13:31); the exalted Christ "was seen" by angels (1 Tim 3:16); Christ "will appear a second time" (Heb 9:28); great signs "appeared in heaven" (Rev 12:1.3). Examples for the ordinary secular use of seeing something that appeared or someone who appeared are: Moses "appeared" to the Israelites (Acts 7:26); the ark of the covenant "was seen within the temple" (Rev 11:19).

44. C. F. D. Moule, in: C.F.D. Moule and Don Cupitt, "The Resurrection: A Disagreement," *Theol* 75 (1972, pp. 507–519), p. 516; similar Heinrich Schlier, *Über die Auferstehung Jesu Christi* (1968), pp. 31–39; Gerhard Lohfink laments the scholarly hesitancy to give serious attention to the phenomena of visions *and* auditions. He argues that the Easter experiences can be seen psychologically as visions and at the same time theologically as acts of God: "Der Ablauf der Osterereignisse und die Anfänge der Urgemeinde," *ThQ* 160 (1980, pp. 162–176), pp. 165–168.

45. We know of the house-church leaders Phoebe (Rom 16:1), Nympha (Col 4:15), Lydia (Acts 16:14f.40), Mary, the mother of John Mark ((Acts 12:12), probably also Priscilla, who is often mentioned before Aquila (Rom 16:3.5a; Acts 18:18.26; 2 Tim 4:19). We must also recall that at least in Romans 16:7 reference is made to a female apostle, Junia (often overlooked by male interpreters and translators). Together with Andronicus she is referred to as being "of note among the apostles"!

of history was different from ours. We tend to examine history under the principle of analogy, believing that we live in a "closed" universe, and that consequently all events are related or relatable to each other. In the framework of such an understanding, there would be no room for the resurrection as a new event and as an act of God. But even if we modify this view of history to include the accidental, unexpected, contingent, and particular, we would still not be able to capture the resurrection of Jesus Christ as a new act of God in which the end has been anticipated and has been revealed in the present. At this point the believer and the theologian must enter the struggle for the most adequate understanding of what is meant by "history". We need to engage in a dialogue with a philosophical understanding of history that allows no room for the resurrection of Jesus Christ, while claiming at the same time to have an adequate understanding of historical reality. Here we must insist that there are realities which cannot be grasped with our historical understanding and our historical methodology. The resurrection of Jesus Christ is such a reality. It is real and it reaches into history in and through the lives of those who participate in it. In the next part we shall discuss what manner of perception is most appropriate to the event of the resurrection. So far, we want to maintain that the resurrection of Jesus Christ has manifested itself, through the appearances of the risen Christ and the call to faith and mission of those to whom he has appeared, as a history-creating event.

Thirdly, the privilege of the encounter with the risen Christ gave special status to some of those who experienced it. The encounters, therefore, also validated and authorized certain functions of leadership and spiritual authority in the early church: we know this to be true for Peter, James, Paul, the "twelve", and the "apostles". The appearance formulas can therefore also be interpreted as *Legitimationsformeln*. It is deplorable, however, that the early church failed to recognize the foundational appearance to Mary as an event that should have decisively determined the developing structures of the early churches. The cultural influences and the self-interest of the male leadership were probably too strong for according adequate recognition to this revolutionary aspect of revelation. Today we can only wonder what difference it would have made to the history of Christianity if the equality of male and female in the Christian churches had been recognized from the beginning.

We need to emphasize that the christological event has procedural priority over its soteriological and ecclesiological significance, although it cannot be separated from these consequences. For that reason, we do not agree with those who deny or relativize the encounter event as a necessary basis for validating the faith of the early Christians and the commissions for some of them.

We recognize, fourthly, that not all who participated in the encounters were Christian believers before Christ appeared to them: for instance Paul and James. Faith in Jesus Christ was therefore not a necessary presupposition for the appearances. Not all—for instance Paul—knew the historical Jesus personally. Although, as it was in Paul's case, they all may have had contact with people who had known Jesus and who were familiar with his claims and the earliest interpretations of those claims. The fact that Paul persecuted the earliest Christians, and that the Greek-speaking Jewish Christians under the leadership of Stephen were persecuted and expelled from Jerusalem (compare Acts 6–8) shows that the Christian message was heard and known very early after Jesus' death and resurrection and had caused offense to religious Judaism.

However, all who participated in the appearances emerged from these as believers. Thus faith must be considered to be a necessary ingredient for the proper understanding and appropriation of the resurrection of Jesus Christ. Therefore, there were no neutral, unaffected, and in that sense objective witnesses of the resurrection appearances. The resurrection of Jesus Christ aims at faith. In these encounters it becomes clear that objective and subjective elements together constitute the resurrection of Jesus Christ.

It would therefore be false to think that Mary, Peter, and Paul were converted by sight, while we receive Christ by faith. We must resist explanations that on one hand try to understand the resurrection apart from faith, and on the other tend to dissolve the resurrection into faith. The resurrection of Jesus is an objective event, but it is not objectifiable. It is a relational event in which Christ, the believer, the church and the world are part—with an ontological and procedural priority for the risen Christ. It cannot be grasped with historical reason, but it is a history-creating event.

This leads us to consider, as a fifth point, the verification of the resurrection of Jesus Christ. Historically we can say that the disciples claim to have experienced—"seen" and "heard"—a personal reality which they recognized as Jesus Christ. But such a claim—even if it were accepted as historical proof—is not yet a verification of the resurrection of Jesus. The resurrection of Jesus aims at the creation of faith and at the liberation and salvation of the world. For us human beings this means that the faith and obedience of believers must become part of the verification of the resurrection. And since faith becomes visible in love (Gal 5:6), this in fact means that our deeds, our whole existence becomes part of the verification of the resurrection of Jesus Christ. Just as we have to say with Paul: "If Christ has not been raised, then ... your faith is in vain" (1 Cor 15:14), so we must also say with Paul that as a consequence of the resurrection of Christ "you must...consider yourselves dead to sin and alive to God in Christ Jesus. Let not sin therefore reign in your mortal bodies ..." (Rom 6:8–14). If the believer has not been raised by faith to newness of life, then, as far as we humans are concerned, the resurrection of Jesus Christ has not reached its intended aim.

This holistic verification, however, must have an authentic quality and a definite content. We recall therefore as a sixth point that this content is given and determined by the One who died on the cross and was raised from the dead. To appreciate that content we need to ask, moreover, what understanding and what interpretation the encounters with the risen Lord released in the lives of the disciples. In the appearance encounters the disciples recognized the One who appeared as Jesus Christ. This led to the conviction and confession that God had raised Jesus from the dead. The language in which the resurrection was then explicated was gathered from a Jewish apocalyptic worldview according to which the resurrection of all the dead was expected at the end of time. But the interest of the Jewish apocalyptic texts is not in the resurrection itself, but in the resurrection as the presupposition for the final establishment of justice, and as an expression of their conviction that God is stronger than death, the great enemy of life.

We have seen that especially for Paul a further ingredient was important; to confess that the God who called him to the Gentile mission is the same who called the great prophets to speak to the nations, and in consequence of that call to accept a life of hardship (Jer 1:4–10; Isa 49:1–6; compare also Isa 6:1–3). If we add to this linguistic and religio-cultural observation that it was Jesus Christ Crucified who was raised from the dead (compare John 20:20.27; Luke 24:39), then the meaning of the resurrection appearances begins to emerge.

In the life, death, and resurrection of Jesus Christ, God has begun to concretely realize what was expected to take place at the end of time: to establish justice and to struggle against the powers of death. In Jesus Christ God has implanted his righteousness into history. The same Jesus who spent his life with and for the despised and neglected and maimed and poor, God raised from the dead and thereby revealed himself as the Father of all who are tossed to the margin of life. God wants to have justice granted to all whom the "world" treats unjustly. God wants to have the forces of death opposed wherever they appear, and God wants all people to have the free opportunity to come to faith in him and live in free and harmonious relationship to their fellow humans and with their environment.

This means that those who believe in Jesus Christ as risen and whose existence is determined by Jesus Christ, will become instruments of life, opposing the forces of death and thus actualizing the righteousness which God is establishing on earth.

All of this has very personal implications for our own understanding of faith. There are certain things in life which we can only know by participating in them. Love is one such reality. God is another. With acts of God it is the same. We can only "know" that Jesus Christ is risen from the dead, when in our life the gospel has created new life. We can only know the power of the resurrection if we have accepted the call and cost of discipleship and have become engaged in the passion of God to make human life whole.

Chapter 7

The Experience of the Holy Spirit

This brings us to a second dimension that must be mentioned when we speak about the effect of Christ's resurrection on history. It has been implied all along, but it must now be made explicit: it is the experience of the presence of the risen and exalted Christ in the lives and ministries of the believers and the believing communities.[1] The early Christians interpreted these experiences in terms of the ministry of the Holy Spirit. The Spirit of God makes the reality of the resurrection of the crucified Christ effective and real in history. This work of the Spirit of God is the logical and necessary consequence of the theological confession that the God who raised Jesus from the dead is love, that he is God "for us". As the Spirit, God effectively communicates and applies what he has wrought in and through the life, death, and resurrection of Christ.

---

1. This interrelation between the resurrection of Christ and the work of the Spirit is generally acknowledged. Karl Barth says: the Holy Spirit is "no other than the presence and action of Jesus Christ himself: His stretched out arm; He Himself in the power of His resurrection, i.e., in the power of His revelation as it begins in and with the power of His resurrection and continues its work from this point." (*Church Dogmatics* IV/2 [1958], pp. 322f.); Ernst Käsemann: ". . . The Spirit is the earthly presence of the exalted Christ. . . . More exactly, the risen One manifests himself in his resurrection power. This resurrection power is more than ecstatic or miracle power. It is the power by which the risen Christ claims the world and ushers in the new creation." ("Geist und Geistesgaben im NT," in: *RGG* II [³1958, cols. 1272–1279], col. 1274 [my translation]); Eduard Schweizer: the power of the Spirit "is not anonymous or unknown. It is identical with the exalted Lord once this Lord is considered, not in Himself, *but in His work towards the community.*" ("Πνεῦμα κτλ.," [Pneuma ktl.] in: TDNT VI [1968, pp. 396–455], p. 433 [emphasis mine]); Peter Carnley: "It seems clear enough that the Spirit is the reality of the raised Christ *in so far as the raised Christ is experienced." (The Structure of Resurrection Belief* [1987], p. 256, compare pp. 248–265); Hendrikus Berkhof: ". . . the Spirit is the name for the exalted Christ acting in the world." (*The Doctrine of the Holy Spirit* [Atlanta: John Knox Press, 1977], p. 115, compare pp. 23–29); compare further: James D. G. Dunn, *Jesus and the Spirit. A Study of the Religious and Charismatic Experience of Jesus and the First Christians as Reflected in the New Testament* (Philadelphia: Westminster, 1975), pp. 95–156, 188, 193f.; José Comblin, *The Holy Spirit and Liberation.* (Maryknoll, N.Y.: Orbis Books, 1989), pp. 1–42.

The evangelist Luke in Peter's sermon at Pentecost (Acts 2:14–42) explains the interlocking between God's promises, the story of Jesus, and the experience of the early Christians this way: the foundational charismatic experiences of the early Christians did not result from religious or worldly enthusiasm ("these men are not drunk" [v. 15]); they were grounded in the history of God's promises for his people (vv. 16–21), and they were inherently related to the story of "Jesus of Nazareth, a man attested to you by God with mighty works and wonders and signs which God did through him in your midst,. . . this Jesus . . . you crucified and killed. . . . This Jesus God raised up, and of that we are all witnesses. Being therefore exalted at the right hand of God, and having received from the Father the promise of the Holy Spirit, he has poured out this which you see and hear" (vv. 22–33).

Also in the Johannine church the activity of the Spirit was interlocked with the story of Jesus. In the farewell discourses (John 14–16) it is not only the Father who will send the Παράκλητος (Paraklētos), the Spirit of Truth (14:16f.), and the Παράκλητος (Paraklētos) will not only be sent in Jesus' name and remind them of what Jesus had taught (14:26), but Jesus himself will send the Holy Spirit (15:26, 16:7), and in that manner he (Jesus) will be and remain present with them (14:18). For the Johannine church Easter and Pentecost (as well as Christmas, the Ascension, and the Second Coming) are essentially interrelated; it was the risen Christ who "breathed on them, and said to them, 'Receive the Holy Spirit' " (20:22).

EASTER AND PENTECOST

What then about the Christian calendar that includes the two great Christian festivals of Easter, celebrating the resurrection of Christ, and, 50 days later, Pentecost, celebrating the coming of the Holy Spirit? This chronological sequence has been adopted from the evangelist Luke who wants to distinguish clearly between the resurrection (40 days [Acts 1:3]), the Ascension (Luke 24:50f.; Acts 1:9), and the coming of the Spirit at Pentecost (Luke 24:49; Acts 1:4f.8, 2:1–4). This scheme conveys the impression that after the first Easter there was a period of 50 days when there were no manifestations of the Spirit. But historically that is quite improbable. It is more likely that Luke used that scheme to highlight his theological emphasis that the reality of the resurrection was to become public and universal in and through the power of the Spirit. It is the Spirit who would empower the church and send it on its mission to the ends of the earth: ". . . you shall receive *power* when the *Holy Spirit* has come upon you; and you shall be *my* witnesses [i.e., the witnesses of the crucified and risen Christ!] in Jerusalem and in all Judea and Samaria and to the end of the earth" (Acts 1:8, emphasis mine).

Theologically, we should appreciate the Lukan emphasis. The distinction between Easter and Pentecost helps us not to freeze the resurrection into the past, and not to dissolve the resurrection into its consequences. Christ promises to send the Spirit so that the reality of the resurrection becomes effective in the world. Yet the resurrection remains the necessary ground and content for the work of the Spirit. At the same time, the Spirit is not merely a function of Christ; the Spirit has its own identity, although this identity is interrelated with Jesus Christ.

This legitimate theological emphasis can easily be lost if the Lukan chronological scheme is absolutized. Other New Testament authors and traditions have therefore chosen different literary means to make the same theological point. The fourth evangelist has the risen Christ breathing upon the disciples and saying to them: "Receive the Holy Spirit" (John 20:22). This means that Easter and Pentecost are in fact not two events, but two dimensions of one and the same event.[2] More precisely: whenever Jesus appears as the Christ, he appears in the power of the Spirit, and whenever the Holy Spirit is active, it manifests the reality of Christ. The theological challenge is to develop a pneumatic Christology and a christological Pneumatology.[3] The uniqueness of Christ and of the Spirit must be spelled out without neglecting their relationship to each other.

THE QUALITATIVE INTENSIFICATION OF THE EXPERIENCE OF THE SPIRIT THROUGH THE RESURRECTION OF CHRIST

The Spirit of God was, of course, a well-known reality in Israel's tradition. It was known as the giver and sustainer of life (Ps 104:29f.). No one could therefore flee from the Spirit of God (Ps 139:7–9). Through his Spirit God had enabled men and women to perform exceptional tasks of leadership (Gen 41:25.28;6 Deut 34:9; Num 11:25; Judg 3:10, 6:34, 11:29, 13:25, 14:6, 15:14; 1 Sam 11:6, 16:13), prophecy (1 Sam 10:5f., 19:20–24; 2 Kgs 2:9–15; Ezek 2:1f.; Isa 61:1; Mic 3:8), or artistry (Exod 28:3). Kings were anointed by the Spirit (1 Sam 16:13f., 18:12). The Spirit would lead people to a proper knowledge of God (2 Sam 23:2; Job 32:8); the Spirit would kindle the passion for justice, and light the candle of hope in the believer; indeed the future Messiah would be endowed with the Spirit of God (Isa 11:2, 42:1, 61:1). One day God would pour out his Spirit upon all people (Joel 2:28f.). He would replace his people's heart of stone with a heart of flesh that is able to receive the new Spirit that he will place within them (Ezek 36:26f., compare Jer 31:31–34).[4]

---

2. Compare: Joachim Jeremias, *New Testament Theology* (New York: Scribner's, 1971), pp. 307f.

3. This is called for by Hans-Joachim Kraus, *Heiliger Geist. Gottes befreiende Gegenwart* (München: Kösel, 1986), pp. 32–51; it is developed by Jürgen Moltmann, *The Way of Jesus Christ* (London: SCM, 1990), part III: "The Messianic Mission of Christ" (pp. 73–150); Jürgen Moltmann, *The Spirit of Life* (1992), III/§§ 1 and 3 (pp. 60–65 and 71–73).

4. Summary statements describing the Old Testament understanding of the Spirit may be found in: Hans Heinrich Schmid, "Ekstatische und charismatische Geistwirkungen im Alten Testament," in: Claus Heitmann/Heribert Mühlen, eds., *Erfahrung und*

It is also a common conviction that although Jesus did not speak much about the Holy Spirit, the Spirit of God was active in and through Him.[5] When he lifted his heart in intimate communion to God and called God "Abba", when he asserted an authority that transcends that of Moses (Matt 5:21–48), when he healed the sick and exorcized demons, when he forgave people's sin and broke the sabbath laws, then he did all this in the power of the Spirit. The presence of the Spirit in his life constituted the theological ground for Jesus' authority, confidence, and freedom.

Nevertheless, with the reality of Easter there came a new and unexpected renewal of the Spirit. Pentecost stands for a qualitative intensification of the experience of the presence of Christ in the power of the Spirit,[6] which the early Christians could only interpret in eschatological categories (Joel 2:28–32, quoted in Acts 2:16–21). We saw in our discussion of the biblical witness to the resurrection that its reality can only be explained as a *novum*. It is a reality that transcends historical, psychological, and religious categories. This is what theologians mean when they call the resurrection an "eschatological" rather than a "historical" event. It is this newness of the reality of the resurrection that flows over through the ministry of the Holy Spirit into the world, into history, and into human experience. The Holy Spirit makes real and effective the rich reality of the resurrection of the crucified Christ.

Theological reflection must therefore acknowledge and explain the fact that the reality of the resurrection arrives in the life of the believer and in the community of faith, that it is known by them, and that it shapes their individual and communal life. The resurrection life of Christ flows over into the life of the believer so that the New Testament can speak of the resurrection of Christ and the resurrection of believers in parallel fashion: "If the Spirit of him who raised Jesus from the dead dwells in you, he who raised Christ Jesus from the dead

---

Theologie des Heiligen Geistes (Hamburg: Agentur des Rauhen Hauses, München: Kösel, 1974), pp. 83–100; Claus Westermann, "Geist im Alten Testament," *EvTh* 41 (1981), pp. 223–230; Alasdair I. C. Heron, *The Holy Spirit* (Philadelphia: Westminster, 1983), pp. 2–38; Eduard Schweizer, *The Holy Spirit* (Philadelphia: Fortress, 1980), chapters 2 and 3, pp. 10–45; R. Albertz/C. Westermann, "*ruah*, Geist," in: *THAT* II (1976), cols. 726–753; Friedrich Baumgärtel, Werner Bieder, Erik Sjöberg, "πνεῦμα κτλ. [pneuma ktl.] Spirit in the OT," in: *TDNT* VI (1968 [1959]), pp. 359–389; Werner H. Schmidt, Peter Schäfer, "Geist/Heiliger Geist/Geistesgaben I und II," in: *TRE* XII (1984), pp. 170–178.

5. Compare: Ferdinand Hahn, "Das biblische Verständnis des Heiligen Geistes. Soteriologische Funktion und 'Personalität' des Heiligen Geistes," in: Claus Heitmann/Heribert Mühlen, eds., *Erfahrung und Theologie des Heiligen Geistes* (Hamburg: Agentur des Rauhen Hauses, München: Kösel, 1974, pp. 131–147), pp. 135–137; Eduard Schweizer, *The Holy Spirit* (Philadelphia: Fortress, 1980), pp. 46–50. Compare also the careful investigation by James D. G. Dunn, *Jesus and the Spirit* (Philadelphia: Westminster, 1975), pp. 15–92, although Dunn seems to emphasize too much Jesus' consciousness of the Spirit.

6. Compare Wolfhart Pannenberg, *Systematische Theologie*. Bd. III (Göttingen: Vandenhoeck & Ruprecht, 1993), pp. 13–33.

will give life to your mortal bodies also through his Spirit which dwells in you" (Rom 8:11; compare 1 Cor 15; Phil 3:21; Rom 6:8, 8:29). It is therefore important to ask in which sense the Holy Spirit is necessary to bring out the significance of the resurrection of the crucified Christ.

THE AMBIGUITY OF RELIGIOUS EXPERIENCE

Soon it became evident in the early church that in Christian experience the riches of God's Spirit became mixed up with the selfishness of the human spirit. The apostle Paul, for instance, was frustrated with the church in Corinth, not because they practiced the charismatic gifts, but because they had divorced the practice of these gifts from their concern for the latecomers (1 Cor 11:7–22.33f.) and from their orientation to the outsider (1 Cor 14:1–5.23–25). If it is the resurrection of the Crucified One that determines the Christian community, then the presence of the Spirit must be a manifestation of love and justice which concretely shows itself in the missionary orientation of the church, and in the partiality of the church for the marginalized people.

It was and is therefore imperative to deal with the known fact that religious, spiritual, and enthusiastic experiences are not necessarily Christian, and to ask the question as to what makes a spiritual experience "Christian". In all religious traditions people can experience conversion and illumination. An unknown and undefined power (good or evil) can take hold of people and heal or destroy them. Such spiritual experiences can manifest themselves in healings, glossolalia, singing, dancing, jumping, and ecstatic movement.[7] The apostle Paul shows awareness of this when he reminds the Christians in Corinth that already before their conversion to Christ they "were led astray to dumb idols, however you may have been moved" (1 Cor 12:2).

The need was therefore felt in the early churches to understand, interpret, and measure Christian experience. They wanted to bring their spiritual experiences and their ministry into correlation with the One whom they experienced in the Spirit and in whose name they ministered. Those who spoke in tongues had to be interpreted in order to make their message transparent for the "outsider" (1 Cor 14:5.13.27). A charisma for "the ability to distinguish between spirits" was discovered (1 Cor 12:10). "Do not quench the Spirit,. . . but test everything; hold fast what is good" (1 Thess 5:19–21). "Beloved, do not believe every spirit, but test the spirits to see whether they are of God" (1 John 4:1). The churches therefore realized very early that spiritual experiences needed to be evaluated, and they developed ways to do so.

---

7. Compare: Carl A. Keller, "Enthusiastisches Transzendenzerleben in den nichtchristlichen Religionen," in: Claus Heitmann/Heribert Mühlen, eds., *Erfahrung und Theologie des Heiligen Geistes* (Hamburg: Agentur des Rauhen Hauses, München: Kösel, 1974), pp. 49–63; James D. G. Dunn, *Jesus and the Spirit* (1975), pp. 302–307.

In theological reflection the ambiguity of Christian experience has led to the question whether the ministry of the Holy Spirit is necessarily related to human experience. Could the Christian understanding and identity of the Holy Spirit not be better preserved if one were not to link it to its conscious and empirical manifestation in human experience? One could then argue that the Spirit's saving and sustaining work transcends the conscious experience of humanity. Religious experiences could then be described as natural and psychological possibilities that are common to all human beings.

There is, of course, some truth to this theological reasoning. The Holy Spirit is "transcendent" in the sense that it cannot be identified with or be reduced to its human and historical manifestations. It is equally true, however, and it has been the common conviction of Christians through the centuries and around the world, that the Holy Spirit aims at concrete manifestations, and that these manifestations include human experience. It is not possible to speak of God as God unless he makes himself known in our experience. It is therefore inadequate to deal with the ambiguity of Christian experience by placing the sphere of the work of the Holy Spirit above and beyond human experience.

Other ways in which the church has tried to deal with the ambiguity of Christian experience is to link the work of the Spirit to the institutional church and its offices, liturgies, sacraments, and doctrines. However, this has led to an ecclesiological captivity of the Spirit, so that the Spirit was limited to what the church experienced, understood, and defined as the work of the Spirit. Not the Spirit itself, but the limited appropriation of the church set the parameters for the Spirit's ministry.

Within the Protestant tradition the church has tried to deal with the ambiguity of Christian experience by linking the work of the Spirit to the text of the Bible or to the preaching of the Gospel. Consequently, the Word (preached or written) became the determinative element, and it was the Spirit's function to create, interpret, and empower the Word.

Naturally, it is true that experience, the church, the Bible, and the preaching of the Word are all related to the work of the Spirit. Potentially they are the manifestations of the Spirit; indeed they need the work of the Spirit to become what they are. But they are not identical with the Spirit. Their Christian identity and integrity consist in their being the work of the Spirit, but the Spirit is not limited to, or dissolved into its manifestations.

We may say, therefore, in conclusion, that while the experience of Christ in and through the Spirit raises the questions of the relationship between Christ and the Spirit, and what the Spirit "adds" to the Christ-event, the ambiguity of spiritual experiences calls for reflections about the Spirit's nature and content. Is there a way to measure whether spiritual experiences or spiritual manifestations are resulting from the Holy Spirit, from the Spirit of God? Not that one could empirically prove where God is, and where he is not. But given the reality of the presence of God through the ministry of the Spirit, is there a way to measure or to evaluate this ministry of the Spirit? These questions have often been addressed by discussing the relation between the experience of the Spirit, and the life, death, and resurrection of Jesus Christ.

THE CHRISTOLOGICAL CONTENT AND NORM

The New Testament has addressed the problem of the ambiguity of spiritual experiences and manifestations by recognizing and explaining that the work and ministry of the Spirit is interrelated with the story of Jesus. Jesus was raised and exalted through the power of the Spirit (Rom 1:3f., 8:11; 1 Cor 6:14; 2 Cor 3:4; 1 Pet 3:18; Heb 9:14), and from the perspective of Easter and Pentecost the whole life of Jesus was then interpreted in relation to the work of the Spirit: his birth (Luke 1:35; Matt 1:18), his baptism (Mark 1:10 par.), his temptations in the desert (Mark 1:12 par.), and his liberating words and deeds (Luke 4:18f.; Matt 11:4f).[8] Through the resurrection of the crucified Christ the "Spirit *of God*" bound itself to the story of Jesus and in that sense it can also be called the "Spirit *of Christ*".

Through the ministry of the Spirit the reality of the resurrection of the crucified Christ flows over into the existence of believers so that the early Christians could not only speak of the "Spirit of God" (1 Cor 2:11f.14, 3:16, 6:11, 7:40, 12:3; 2 Cor 3:3; Phil 3:3; Rom 8:9.11.14), or the "Holy Spirit" (Luke 11:13; 1 Thess 4:8; Eph 1:13, 4:30), but also of the "Spirit of Christ" (Rom 8:9; Phil 1:19; Gal 4:6; 1 Pet 1:11). On that basis they could make parallel statements about their life "in Christ" and their life "in the Spirit" (Rom 8:1.9–11).

> . . . you are not in the flesh, you are in the Spirit, if the Spirit of God really dwells in you. Anyone who does not have the Spirit of Christ does not belong to him. But if Christ is in you, although your bodies are dead because of sin, your spirits are alive because of righteousness. If the Spirit of him who raised Jesus from the dead dwells in you, he who raised Christ Jesus from the dead will give life to your mortal bodies also through his Spirit which dwells in you (Rom 8:9–11).

This interlocking of the Spirit with the story of Jesus can be illustrated with a brief reference to a number of New Testament traditions.

In the letters to the seven churches in Asia Minor in the Book of Revelation (Rev 2:1–3:22) we are told that the *human author*, "John", "was *in the Spirit* on the Lord's day" when he received the heavenly command to write to the seven churches in Asia Minor (1:10f. emphasis mine). The one who gave the command, and who dictated the letters, was no other than the crucified and risen Christ (1:12–20). Each letter is therefore introduced with a christological

---

8. Compare: Jürgen Moltmann, *The Way of Jesus Christ* (1990), Part III: "The Messianic Mission of Christ" (pp. 73–150).

formula: "The words of him who holds the seven stars in his right hand . . ."
(2:1); "The words of the first and the last, who died and came to life" (2:8);
"The words of the Son of God . . ." (2:18); "The words of the Amen, the faithful and true witness, the beginning of God's creation" (3:14). Following the
christological introduction, the text of each letter is presented in the "I"-form,
identifying Christ as the real author of these letters. But then, at the end of each
letter, there is a clear reference to the Spirit: "He who has an ear, let him hear
what the Spirit says to the churches" (2:7.11.17.29, 3:6.13.22). Even though
the actual human author of these letters is John of Patmos, the real author is
Christ who manifests himself to the churches in and through the Holy Spirit.
The Spirit applies and makes real to all who want to hear what Christ wills for
his church. Particularly interesting here is the universalizing tendency of the
ministry of the Spirit. While each letter has a specific church in mind—the
church in Ephesus, Smyrna, etc.—it is the Spirit who universalizes the message to all the churches.

In 1 Corinthians 11–14 Paul reminds the Christians in Corinth that spiritual
experiences as such are not specifically Christian: "You know that when you
were heathen, you were led astray to dumb idols, however you may have been
moved" (1 Cor 12:2). The genuine Christian confession, arising from the ministry of the *Holy* Spirit, is that "*Jesus* is Lord" (1 Cor 12:3). The consequence
of such a "christological" confession is that the church in its worship should
not neglect the latecomers (1 Cor 11:17–34), that they should be concerned
with the edification and the building up of the community (1 Cor
14:4f.12.26.31), and that they should be an open church, ready to share the gifts
of grace with the world (1 Cor 14:16.24f.). In these ways it would become manifest that the ministry of the Spirit is interlocked with the story of Jesus, and
that therefore the work of the Holy Spirit can only be a concrete expression of
love (1 Cor 13).[9]

The same is clearly spelled out in 1 Corinthians 1:18–2:16. The "secret and
hidden wisdom of God, which God decreed before the age for our glorification
. . . God has revealed to us through the Spirit" (2:7–10). This wisdom of God
is none other than the crucified Christ (1:18–26, 2:2). On that theological basis
Paul can sarcastically refer to the Corinthian theology of glory (1 Cor 4:8), and
then, in a moving contrast, illustrate what it means when the crucified Christ
becomes real in the power of the Spirit:

. . . I think that God has exhibited us apostles as last of all, like men sentenced to death; because we have become a spectacle to the world, to angels and to men.
We are fools for Christ's sake, but you are wise in Christ.

9. For further details see: Thorwald Lorenzen, "The Crucified Christ as Lord of the
Church. Theological Reflections on 1 Corinthians 11–14," to be published by Peter Lang,
Bern in a *Festschrift* for Athol Gill.

We are weak, but you are strong.
You are held in honour, but we in disrepute.
To the present hour we hunger and thirst,
we are ill-clad and buffeted and homeless,
and we labor, working with our own hands.
When reviled, we bless;
when persecuted, we endure;
when slandered, we try to conciliate;
we have become, and are now, as the refuse of the world, the off-scour-
ing of all things (1 Cor 4:9–13).

If it is the crucified Christ that becomes real in the Spirit, and since the resurrection does not relativize the cross, but gives it divine dignity, Paul can interpret human weakness theologically: in human weakness the believer
experiences the power of God (2 Cor 12:9, 13:4). Paul can be utterly frustrated
with the church in Corinth (1 Cor 11:17–22), and he can be aghast at the church
in Galatia (Gal 4:12–20), because they seem to forget that their spiritual experience remains tied to the story of the crucified Christ, and in consequence they
seem to lose their concern for the marginalized people and their appreciation
of human weakness.

Also Luke ensures that the ministry of the Holy Spirit will not be separated
from God's revelation in Jesus Christ. Jesus had promised to the apostles the gift
of the Holy Spirit and that such a gift would empower them to be witnesses for
Christ (Acts 1:1–8). When Judas had to be replaced to complete the apostolic
group, it was stipulated that the new man "must have accompanied us *during all
the time that the Lord Jesus went in and out among us*, beginning from the baptism of John until the day when he was taken up from us . . ." (Acts 1:21f., emphasis mine). Thus, in contrast to Paul (Gal 1:16; 1 Cor 9:1, 15:8), Luke ties the
apostolic office not only to the resurrection of Jesus, but to his whole life. This
is Luke's way of saying that the ongoing ministry of the Holy Spirit in the history of the church and of the world will create analogies to the "life of Jesus".

In the Johannine church the same theological emphasis is given with different arguments. We have already seen how in the farewell discourse of the fourth
Gospel (John 14–16) the Spirit and Christ are interrelated. In the ongoing history of the Johannine church this must have become a problem, because in 1
John 4 it is insisted that true manifestations of the Spirit must make their continuity with the story of Jesus evident:

Beloved, do not believe every spirit, but *test the spirits to see whether
they are of God*; for many false prophets have gone out into the world.
By this you know the Spirit of God: every spirit which confesses that
Jesus Christ *has come in the flesh* is of God, and every spirit which does
not confess *Jesus* is not of God. This is the spirit of antichrist, of which
you heard that it was coming, and now it is in the world already (1 John
4:1–3, emphasis mine; compare 1:1–3, 2:22, 5:6–12, 2 John 7).

Keeping these references to a number of New Testament traditions in mind we can conclude that the early Christians were aware of the ambiguity of religious experience, and they dealt with it by verbalizing the fact that in their experience the Holy Spirit was interrelated with the story of the crucified and risen Christ. This resulted in the following emphases:[10]

Firstly, for the early Christians the content and norm of the Spirit was Jesus Christ. Not that they thought that the Spirit whom they experienced was a different Spirit than the Spirit of God in their religious tradition. But given their experience of the resurrection of the crucified Christ, and given their awareness of the ambiguity of religious experience, they now confessed that for them, as Christians, the Spirit of God had bound itself to the story of Jesus. Again, not that the Spirit is simply identical with Christ, but that Jesus the Christ had provided the content, norm, and measure of the Spirit.

Secondly, in analogy to the risen Christ, the Spirit is also understood in terms of an experience that is open for the future, waiting and longing for fulfillment, but at the same time, not fleeing from the world, but accepting responsibility for life in the "here and now". The risen Christ was understood to be "the first fruits [ἀπαρχή (aparchē)] of those who have fallen asleep" (1 Cor 15:20; compare Col 1:18). By analogy, the Spirit is the present "downpayment" (ἀρραβών [arrabōn]; 2 Cor 1:22, 5:5; Eph 1:14) of the future reality of salvation. The Spirit draws the believer into the reality of the resurrection of the crucified Christ so that "we ourselves, who have the first fruits (ἀπαρχή) [aparchē]) of the Spirit, groan inwardly as we wait for adoption as sons, the redemption of our bodies" (Rom 8:23). The believer is drawn into the process of the reality of the resurrection. The *telos* of that process is anticipated in the resurrection of the crucified Christ and in the experience of the Holy Spirit. At the same time "Easter" and "Pentecost" are the theological anchors by which that process is fuelled and guided. The Christian exists in the tension between the "already" and the "not-yet". This tension makes the followers of Christ restless with the status quo, and they want to shape their own lives and the world in analogy to the future of the One who has come.

Thirdly, the Spirit does not only make the riches of the resurrection of Christ real to the believer, but at the same time it opens the believer up towards God, so that with Jesus, and in the power of the Spirit, the believer can pray to God as "Abba" (Gal 4:4–6; Rom 8:15).

It is important, fourthly, that it is the crucified Christ who was raised from the dead and who becomes a present reality through the ministry of the Spirit. On that theological basis Paul can interpret his own suffering not as weakness, or lack of faith, or a "messenger of Satan" (2 Cor 12:7) as his opponents probably tried to do, but as the manifestation of the power of God, whose "power is made perfect in weakness" (2 Cor 12:9, compare 11:30). While his oppo-

---

10. For details see: James D. G. Dunn, *Jesus and the Spirit* (1975), pp. 293–300, 308–342; Eduard Schweizer, *The Holy Spirit* (Philadelphia: Fortress, 1980), pp. 85–108, 126–134.

nents ("superlative apostles": 2 Cor 11:5.13, 12:11) try to manifest their authenticity with demonstrations of worldly power, visions, ecstasies, miracles, glossolalia, and with eloquent rhetoric, Paul boasts in his "weaknesses": "we are weak in him" (2 Cor 13:4)! The marks of the "true apostle" (2 Cor 12:12) must make evident that it was the crucified Christ whom God raised from the dead. He interprets his existence christologically! And the "weaknesses" of which he speaks are not primarily human disabilities or illnesses (as in Gal 4:12–20). Rather, they are the consequences of a concrete obedience to the call of Christ in a hostile world: "insults, hardships, persecutions, and calamities" (2 Cor 12:10).[11] Paul can say that he and his co-workers share "abundantly in Christ's suffering" (2 Cor 1:5). That was important, because it made them "rely not on ourselves, but on God who raises the dead" (2 Cor 1:9). And just as God displayed his power by raising Jesus from the dead, so he now displays his power by creating new life out of the suffering existence of the apostle:

> For as we share abundantly in Christ's suffering, so through Christ we share abundantly in comfort too. If we are afflicted, it is for your comfort and salvation; and if we are comforted, it is for your comfort, which you experience when you patiently endure the same suffering that we suffer (2 Cor 1:5f.).

The controversy which Paul had with the church in Galatia (see especially Gal 4:12–20) can only be understood if one realizes that under the influence of a different theology ("they make much of you . . ."), the church in Galatia had forgotten that it was the Crucified One who had been raised from the dead, and who in the power of the Spirit shapes Christian existence. At first, at the founding of the church, they received Paul with his human weakness "as an angel of God, as Christ Jesus"; indeed, they would have shared their most precious possessions with him: "For I bear you witness that, if possible, you would have plucked out your eyes and given them to me." But now their attitude had changed. Paul laments: "What has become of the satisfaction you felt?" Their attitude to weakness and suffering had changed because they no longer saw the power of God manifest in the crucified Christ, and consequently, they could not relate in their thinking the power of the Spirit with human weakness and suffering.

When Paul, therefore, speaks of Christ flowing over into the life of the believer through the power of the Spirit, he does not speak in triumphant terms, nor does he negate the world. He confesses that it is "the death of Jesus" that he carries in his body, "so that the life of Jesus may also be manifest in our bodies" (2 Cor 4:10). And this dialectic of the death and resurrection of Christ finds its analogy in the apostle's concrete existence:

---

11. Further texts which illustrate this are: 1 Cor 4:8–13; 2 Cor 1:3–11, 4:7–12, 6:3–10, 7:4–6, 11:16–32, 12:1–13, 13:1–4; Gal 6:17; compare: Mark 13:9.11; Matt 10:19f.; Luke 12:11f. (compare Klaus Berger, "Geist, Heiliger Geist, Geistesgaben III. Neues Testament," in: TRE XII [1984, pp. 178–196], p. 182).

We are afflicted in every way, but not crushed;
perplexed, but not driven to despair;
persecuted, but not forsaken;
struck down, but not destroyed;
always carrying in the body the death of Jesus,
so that the life of Jesus may also be manifested in our bodies.

(2 Cor 4:8–10)

A further criterion for measuring the authenticity of Christian experience is, therefore, that it must become evident that charismatic experiences form analogies to the life and death of Jesus. Concretely this means the readiness to accept suffering and hardship as a necessary ingredient of Christian discipleship.[12]

This brings us to a fifth important criterion. Already in the Old Testament it was clear that one must distinguish between true and false manifestations of the Spirit (Jer 5:12f., 14:14, 23:16–32). The distinguishing mark was the passion for truth and justice. This has become even clearer in the interrelation of the work of the Spirit with the story of Jesus. We saw that the Spirit universalizes the work of the Son. This universalizing tendency has the intention to seek and save that which is lost, to liberate those who are oppressed, and to feed those who are hungry. The universalizing tendency of the Spirit includes the manifestation of a partiality of God for the marginalized people. It is for that reason that in the beatitudes eschatological salvation is pronounced upon the poor and hungry and persecuted (Luke 6:20–23); and when in the Gospel of Luke Jesus introduces his vision of reality to the world he places himself in the prophetic tradition that links the work of the Spirit with the passion for justice (Luke 4:17–21 quoting from Isa 61:1f. [compare Isa 58:6]).[13]

This implies, as the sixth criterion, the insistence that what determines people at the center of their existence is revealed in the "fruits" that they produce (Matt 7:16, compare Gal 5:22f.; 1 Cor 13:4–7; Eph 5:9; Matt 5:13–16.20, 7:21f.)! Most of the writings in the New Testament insist that the imperative of the

---

12. In 1 Corinthians 12–14, for instance, Paul makes clear that he recognizes glossolalia as a gift of the Spirit, that he has that gift himself, and that he acknowledges its usefulness for personal edification. Yet, at the same time, he clearly criticizes the importance that this gift had acquired in the church in Corinth. When Paul lists the charismata, he places glossolalia towards the end (12:4–11.28), he argues that love must be the criterion (12:31–14:1), and that therefore "prophecy" (what we would today call "preaching") is more important because it communicates the riches of faith to the unbeliever and the outsider (14:1–33). Eduard Schweizer emphasizes that for Paul the manifestation of the Spirit is not characterized by being "extraordinary" but by being tied to the crucified Christ: "πνεῦμα κτλ.," (pneuma ktl.), in: *TDNT* VI (1968, pp. 396–455), pp. 424–428.

13. The importance of this is seen within the context of the many liberation theologies (compare: Richard Tholin, "The Holy Spirit and Liberation Movements: The Response of the Church," in: Dow Kirkpatrik, ed., *The Holy Spirit* [Nashville: Tidings, 1974], pp. 40–75).

Christian life must be grounded in the indicative of salvation, and that the nature of the indicative is revealed in the "fruits" that it produces. The liberation which the resurrection of Christ brings must be made manifest in a struggle for justice and liberation in order that it becomes evident that it was the crucified Christ who was raised from the dead. The Spirit makes Christ real in the church by building up and edifying the church (1 Cor 14), and by making the church partial for the poor and oppressed (1 Cor 11:17–34). Thus it is in the concrete manifestations of love (1 Cor 13) where it becomes visible that the crucified Christ is Lord of the church. This is visibly celebrated in the Christian community by the acknowledgement that it is the crucified Christ (". . . the Lord Jesus on the night when he was betrayed took bread . . ." [1 Cor 11:23]) who is host at the Lord's Supper, and head of the church. The church is the "body of Christ" in the sense that it creates room for the Crucified One to manifest himself through the power of the Spirit in liberating and saving the world.[14]

So far then we have seen how for the early church the liberating experience of the Spirit was clarified by their awareness that the ministry of the Holy Spirit is interwoven with the story of Jesus. We shall now try to clarify a little further why the interrelation between the story of the Spirit and the story of the Son is necessary, and what they contribute to each other.

THE SPIRIT, THE FATHER, AND THE SON

The question has arisen as to how the interlocking of the Holy Spirit with the crucified and risen Christ can best be explained without removing the specific identity of either the Spirit or of Christ.

This has been the major issue in the so-called *filioque*-controversy, which to the present day has remained the symbol for the separation between Eastern and Western Christianity, and which, at the same time, has been the major focus for debating the trinitarian nature of God in general, and the relationship between Christ and the Spirit in particular.[15]

The original version of the Niceno-Constantinopolitan Creed of 381 C.E. reads in its section about the Holy Spirit that "we believe in the Holy Spirit", that this Holy Spirit "proceeds from the Father", and that "with the Father and the Son he is worshipped and glorified." The Holy Spirit is therefore recognized as the object of faith and worship, and it is grounded in the God who is described as "Father". The identity and the equal dignity of the Spirit along-

---

14. This concrete manifestation of the Spirit as love in openness to God and neighbour is emphasized by Eduard Schweizer, "πνεῦμα κτλ.," (pneuma ktl.), in: *TDNT* VI (1968, pp. 396–455), pp. 430–432.

15. For details compare the ecumenical statement and the essays in: Lukas Vischer, ed., *Spirit of God, Spirit of Christ*. Ecumenical Reflections on the *Filioque* Controversy. Faith and Order Paper No. 103 (Geneva: WCC, London: SPCK, 1981).

side the Father and the Son is affirmed. One may only speak of a logical priority of the Father in the sense that the Spirit proceeds from him.

In the Western church there soon developed the practice of saying that the Holy Spirit proceeded not only from the Father, but from both from the Father *and the Son (filioque)*, while the East insisted that "the Spirit proceeds from the Father *alone*". On the insistence of Emperor Henry II the Western addition, *filioque*, was officially used in his coronation mass by Pope Benedict VIII (1012–1024) in 1014. This sealed the first great schism in the Christian church between Roman Catholicism and Eastern Orthodoxy, which then resulted in the excommunication of the Eastern church in 1054.[16]

We cannot debate this important issue here. But we can ask whether the positive intentions of East and West cannot help us to clarify the issue under discussion.[17] The Eastern church was correct in its insistence that the confession to the trinitarian nature of God implies the equality of Son and Spirit. Both have different identities and functions, but these differences cannot be expressed in hierarchical terms of superiority and inferiority. We must therefore resist attempts to subordinate the Spirit to the Son, or to functionalize the Spirit to serve merely as the effective application of the work of the Son. The original version of the creed confirms the biblical testimony that the Spirit has its own "personal" identity in distinction from the Father and the Son. The Father is uncreated, the Son is "eternally *begotten* of the Father", the Spirit "*proceeds* from the Father". Spirit and Son can be worshipped and glorified together with the Father. Any description of "Spirit" and "Son" must therefore be careful to preserve their distinctiveness and, at the same time, their interrelationship. The *filioque* addition becomes problematic when it is interpreted to mean that the Spirit has two sources, and that therefore it is subordinate to the Father and the Son. Together with the biblical texts we must affirm that the Spirit "proceeds from the Father" (John 15:26; compare 14:26: ". . . whom the Father will send in my name", 14:16–17: ". . . the Father . . . will give you another Counsellor,. . . the Spirit of truth . . ."). The Spirit is the effective communicative life-giving, liberating, and saving power of the Father. The Spirit was active in creation, it empowered the judges, it ordained the kings, it inspired the prophets. It was present in the birth of the Son, it empowered the Son in his baptism, it sustained the Son in his temptations, and through the power of the Spirit the Son was raised from the dead.

But the Spirit "takes" from the Son (John 16:14), it will be sent in Christ's name (John 14:26), and it will bear witness to Christ (John 15:26) and glorify

---

16. The history of the *filioque*-controversy is sketched by Dietrich Ritschl, "Historical Development and Implications of the Filioque Controversy," in: Lukas Vischer, ed., *Spirit of God, Spirit of Christ* (1981), pp. 46–65.

17. Compare: Jürgen Moltmann, "Theological Proposals toward the Resolution of the Filioque Controversy," in: Lukas Vischer, ed., *Spirit of God, Spirit of Christ* (1981), pp. 164–173; Jürgen Moltmann, *The Trinity and the Kingdom of God. The Doctrine of God* (London: SCM, 1981), pp. 178–190.

him (John 16:14). When the New Testament speaks of the "Spirit of Christ" alongside of the "Spirit of God", and when the risen Christ is portrayed as giving or sending or being himself the Spirit (John 15:26, 20:22; Acts 2:33; 1 Cor 15:45; 1 John 2:1), then this does not question that the Spirit, like the Son, is grounded in and related to the Father "alone". The emphasis is, rather, that God is a relational reality of Father, Son, and Holy Spirit, and as such a relational reality one cannot speak of any of the three persons of the Trinity without implying the other two. This then brings us to the intention of the West.

When the Western church added *filioque* it did not question that the Father is the source of the Spirit, but it wanted to insist that the Father as "Father", and therefore the Spirit who proceeds from the Father, have a certain distinctive and discernible nature. God is not only creator, but also redeemer, liberator, comforter, burden-carrier, and sustainer—he is "Father". God is not an anonymous or faceless deity. He is the Father *of the Son*, and *as such* he has sent the Spirit. The Spirit, therefore, proceeds from the Father of the Son. And since it is the Son who reveals the nature of the Father (John 1:18), the content of the Spirit's work must be the riches of the resurrection of the crucified Christ. The intention of the *filioque* is not to deny that the Father is the source of the Spirit, but to specify that within the trinitarian nature of God the Spirit brings to effective reality the nature of the Father as it is revealed in the Son.[18] This is important, because if it is not clear that the norm and content of the Spirit is the crucified Christ, then any and every religious manifestation could be validated with reference to the Spirit.[19] It is therefore not sufficient to designate God's Spirit as "spirit of life", but more concretely, it is also the Spirit who gave birth to Jesus,

---

18. The interrelationship of Father, Son and Holy Spirit is expressed well in a Pentecostal prayer of the Syrian Orthodox Church of South India: "When we say 'Father', the Son and the Holy Spirit come from him. When we say 'Son', the Father and the Holy Spirit are recognized through him. When we say *Ruho* (Spirit), the Father and the Son are perfect in him. The Father is the Creator, unbegotten; the Son is begotten and does not beget; the Holy Spirit [Ruho] proceeds from the Father and receives from the Son the person and the being of the Father." (Quoted by Jürgen Moltmann, "Theological Proposals toward the Resolution of the Filioque Controversy," in: Lukas Vischer, ed., *Spirit of God, Spirit of Christ* [1981, pp. 164–173], p. 171).

19. This theological concern to preserve the Christian integrity and identity of Christian faith was the reason why Karl Barth has defended the theological necessity of the *filioque: CD* I/1 (1975 [1932]), pp. 466–489. It has become customary to neglect or criticize Barth at this point. However, if one remembers that Barth's intention was not to question the identity of the Spirit, but to clarify the Spirit's identity with reference to the Son, and to maintain the *sola gratia* in the event of salvation, then the christological orientation of Barth's pneumatology, and his insistence that the Spirit is "God's appropriation by man" (p. 474, "Aneignung" [*KD* I/1, p. 497]), or "recognition" (p. 480, "Erkenntnis" [*KD* I/1, p. 504]), or the subjective side of revelation (p. 466) becomes understandable. The question remains, however, whether in actual fact Barth has not reduced the work of the Spirit to become a function of the work of the Son. Yet, later on, Barth himself resisted any reduction of the Spirit to the subjective dimension of revelation when he designates the Spirit as also being operative in creation and providence

who empowered him in his mission and ministry, and who raised the crucified Jesus from the dead. It is therefore the Spirit who resists the forces of death and encourages the forces of life. Where the hungry are fed, where the lost are saved, and where the oppressed are liberated, there the Spirit of God can be presumed to be at work.

The filioque-controversy therefore confirms our previous observations. The Spirit did not enter the stage with Jesus; it can therefore not be seen merely as a gift of Christ. Indeed the Spirit was operative in the birth of Christ (Luke 1:35), Jesus' earthly life and death was related to the activity of the Spirit (Heb 9:14), he was raised and exalted in the power of the Spirit (Rom 1:4). When the New Testament then adds that the risen and exalted Christ also sent the Spirit (Acts 2:33; John 20:22), or even was identical with the Spirit (1 Cor 15:45), then it wants to say that with the resurrection of the crucified Christ there came a new intensity and a new quality of the ministry of the Spirit. The Spirit reveals the riches of Christ's salvation to us and at the same time enables us to receive these riches and let them shape our life.

THE SPIRIT AND CHRIST COMPLEMENTING EACH OTHER

Our reflections have led to the conclusion that the Holy Spirit and the risen and exalted Christ are interrelated, but that they are not to be identical. Their interrelationship is essential for the identity of both, the Son and the Spirit. The Spirit receives from the Son its content, without losing its own identity, its mysterious strangeness, and its life-giving and life-sustaining reality. The christological orientation of the Spirit does not eliminate the distinctiveness and identity of the Spirit, nor is the Spirit functionalized to express the significance of Jesus. The christological content of the Spirit protects the deity and integrity of the Spirit against our human and religious self-interest. The Son, on the other hand, acquires through the Spirit universal validity and public significance. The Johannine Christ says that the Spirit "will take what is mine and declare it to you" (John 16:14).

When we ask what the Spirit "receives" or "takes" from the Son, we would say, firstly, that the activity of the Spirit is clarified through its interwovenness with the story of Jesus. The christological orientation and content provides a measure to test the Spirit, whether it is of God. The measuring stick is Jesus as the Christ. Concretely, we may say that the Spirit of God can be presumed to be at work wherever salvation, justice, liberation, and peace become an event.

(*CD* III/2 [1960], pp. 356–360). Compare the discussion of the dual role of the Spirit in creation and redemption in: George S. Hendry, *The Holy Spirit in Christian Theology*. Revised and enlarged edition (Philadelphia: Westminster, 1965), pp. 39–52; George S. Hendry, *Theology of Nature* (Philadelphia: Westminster, 1980), pp. 163–174.

But at this point we must emphasize, secondly, that with the resurrection of Christ the ministry of the Spirit is given new content and new depth.[20] Not that the history of the Spirit is denied or declared invalid. There is continuity in the story of the Spirit: from the Spirit that empowered the judges, ordained kings and prophets, and led the people of God from slavery to freedom, to the activity of the Spirit after Easter. Yet there is also discontinuity. A new development is that with Easter and Pentecost the Spirit makes real and effective the saving and liberating passion that Christ manifested in his life, death, and resurrection. This adds a qualitative newness to the experience and understanding of sin, as well as to the experience and understanding of salvation and liberation.

This leads, thirdly, to the observation that the christological content of the Spirit opens our eyes for a new interpretation of reality. Important realities and concepts like "power" and "weakness" are being reinterpreted and transfigured. We begin to understand that it is not Pilate, Constantine, the British empire, or a racist establishment that may be the authentic representatives of true power, but Jesus, Gandhi, and Martin Luther King, Jr. We may begin to perceive that it is better to give, than to receive; that it is better to share, than to hoard. It may start to dawn upon us that true leadership consists in serving others; that true freedom is to struggle for the liberation of others. And we may begin to see that not only our future, but our identity and our authenticity is at stake in our opinion of, and our engagement for, the poor and oppressed, and our concern for the exploitation of nature.[21]

Fourthly, the christological orientation of the Spirit preserves what was obvious from the Old Testament traditions, namely, that the Spirit as the Spirit of God cannot be intellectualized or spiritualized. God's Spirit aims at incarnation. It concretely shapes and changes human and historical reality. The Spirit seeks to conscientize and empower the oppressed and those fated to a life of poverty. The Spirit seeks to give comfort to those who hurt, and become a friend to those who are lonely. But in this incarnational thrust the Spirit does not bypass human persons. It is therefore true that in saving the lost, in comforting

---

20. To emphasize this newness in the experience of the Spirit the fourth evangelist associates the coming of the Spirit with the crucifixion and resurrection of Christ (John 7:39, 16:7).

21. Claus Westermann explains the fact that the concept of Spirit hardly occurs in the Prophets with the observation that "Spirit" was too identified with the performance of massive and visible demonstrations of power, while the prophets were aware that God's power becomes real in weakness, and that therefore the prophets were called to a suffering existence. Westermann also shows how *ruah* becomes interpreted in relationship to the *servant*, rather than the king ("Geist im Alten Testament," *EvTh* 41 [1981, pp. 223–230], pp. 226–228), and that the Old Testament knows of the partiality of God for the poor and oppressed: "Das Alte Testament und die Menschenrechte," in Jörg Baur, ed., *Zum Thema Menschenrechte. Theologische Versuche und Entwürfe* (Stuttgart: Calwer Verlag, 1977), pp. 5–18.

the sad, in feeding the poor, and in liberating the oppressed, we experience the Spirit who provides the resources for this liberating passion.[22]

When we ask in which way the Spirit complements the Christ-event, we note the following points.

The Spirit helps us, firstly, to understand Jesus' special relationship to God. In him the messianic predictions of the Old Testament have found their fulfilment. His election was confirmed in his baptism, when the Spirit descended upon him. His intimate relationship with God issued into the unique prayer of calling God "abba". The Fourth Gospel summarizes: "For he whom God has sent utters the words of God, for it is *not by measure that he gives the Spirit*; the Father loves the Son, and has given *all things* into his hand" (John 3:34f., emphasis mine). In the Q-source Jesus says: "*All things* have been delivered to me by my Father . . ." (Matt 11:27/Luke 10:22, emphasis mine). The uniqueness of Christ's person and mission is therefore explicated through his relationship to the Spirit of God.

Secondly, the Spirit relates the riches of the reality of the resurrection of the crucified Christ to the shaping of history. It makes Christ public. Through the ministry of Christians the Spirit beseeches "on behalf of Christ, be reconciled to God" (2 Cor 5:20). Through the Holy Spirit the riches of Christ's salvation become a possibility for all people, calling for realization and actualization in their lives.

This implies, thirdly, that the Spirit universalizes the saving work of Christ. This universalizing tendency is known to us from the Old Testament traditions, and it is affirmed through its christological intensification. Just as the risen Christ calls the church to universal mission (Matt 28:18–20), so the Spirit is the empowerment for Christian *mission* to the ends of the earth (Acts 1:8).[23] "Pentecost" symbolizes God's passion to pour out his Spirit upon "all flesh" (Acts 2:17). The Spirit as the *Holy* Spirit is the power of God, and God is the creator of heaven and earth, and the final fulfiller of history. Through the ministry of the Spirit the creator is in the process of claiming back his creation.

The Spirit therefore, as a fourth point, tunes the believer into the resurrection reality by opening up the future as a promise rather than a threat. The Spirit is the "down-payment" ($\alpha\rho\rho\alpha\beta\dot{\omega}\nu$ [arrabōn]) for things to come. And the things to come have received their content through the resurrection of the crucified Christ.

Finally, as a fifth point, the knowledge and experience of the Spirit help us not to objectify the appearances of the risen Christ. We have seen that the resurrection appearances were not objective and in that sense public events. They

---

22. Compare Heribert Mühlen, "Soziale Geisteserfahrung als Antwort auf eine einseitige Gotteslehre," in: Claus Heitmann/Heribert Mühlen, eds., *Erfahrung und Theologie des Heiligen Geistes* (1974, pp. 253–272], p. 264).

23. This is properly emphasized by Hendrikus Berkhof, *The Doctrine of the Holy Spirit* (1977 [1964]), chapter II (pp. 30–41). Berkhof also reminds us of the mission emphasis in Karl Barth's *Church Dogmatics* IV/1–3 (ibid., p. 33).

were limited to believers, so that faith is obviously a necessary ingredient in the encounter with the risen Christ. Since the danger of objectification has been there from the beginning, it is better to speak of the experience of the risen Christ in and through the Spirit.

We may therefore say that the early Christians affirmed on one hand the experiential reality of the Holy Spirit as it manifested itself in their personal lives, in their church life, and in their ministry in the world. They experienced the risen Christ in and through the power of the Spirit. We had to ask, therefore, how the Spirit and Christ complement each other without losing their own particular identity. On the other hand Christians were aware of the ambiguity of religious experiences and manifestations, and they therefore reminded themselves that "Easter" and "Pentecost" belong together, and that through the resurrection of the crucified Christ the reality of the resurrection and the ministry of the Spirit are interrelated. The early Christians therefore confessed that in and through their spiritual experience it must become manifest that Jesus is Lord. Jesus Christ was confessed to be the norm and the content of the work of the Holy Spirit.

CONCLUSION

In considering the relationship between the resurrection of Christ and the Holy Spirit we have tried to follow a trinitarian understanding of God which calls for an equal emphasis on the Son and on the Spirit. They are not identical, but they are equal. They both have their distinctive identity and function, but one is not subordinate to the other. The Word became flesh in Jesus Christ, not in the Spirit (John 1:14–18); Christ, not the Spirit, died for our sins and rose for our justification (Rom 4:25). It is the Spirit, not Christ, who helps us in our weaknesses and complements our prayers (Rom 8:26f.). The soteriological work of Christ is the theological ground and content of the work and ministry of the Spirit. But this christological foundation finds the fulfillment of its own inner *telos* only if it arrives in the lives of people and in history; when it begins to change people and to shape history. We saw that the resurrection of Christ must be understood as an "open" event, that Christ is the "first born" from the dead, and that faith is the existence between the "already" and the "not yet". It is the Spirit that concretely manifests the work of Christ, who draws us into the passion of God for his world, who applies what has been promised with the resurrection of the crucified Christ. Not that the Spirit dissolves the "promise" character of faith into a triumphant enthusiasm of the present; but the Spirit intensifies and universalizes the promise contained in the resurrection of the crucified Christ.

The Holy Spirit complements the resurrection of the crucified Christ by making its newness real, public, and universal. As the God of the creation story breathed into man's nostrils the breath of life (Gen 2:7), so the Spirit makes real and effective that "in Christ" the believer has become part of a new creation

(2 Cor 5:17). The Spirit is therefore necessary to apply the work of Christ and to help and guide the believer to concretely live in accordance with the new being in Christ (Rom 8:9).

Yet, at the same time, it is Jesus Christ as the Crucified and Risen One who gives content, and therefore provides the norm and the measure for the work and experience of the Holy Spirit. This christological content should prevent the experience of the Holy Spirit from becoming dissolved into the human spirit. The Holy Spirit neither leads to a religious elitism, nor does it use the word "God" to validate personal and institutional interests. The Spirit wants to empower human beings to shape analogies to the Crucified Christ by concretely finding ways to make human life human. The experience of the Holy Spirit finds its real truth, freedom, and love in that it remains tied to faith in the Crucified One.

The insistence that it was the *crucified* Christ who has been raised from the dead, and that through the resurrection the crucifixion has not been left behind, but has given discernible content to the word "God", should help us to resist any attempt to divorce the reality of the resurrection and the working of the Spirit of God from the concrete shaping of our life and of history in anticipation of the one who is to come. The Spirit applies the Crucified Christ to our life. We can therefore expect the power of God in weakness, and this power becomes manifest in our world in the concrete ministry of love for which the church is motivated and enabled through the various gifts of the Spirit.

Ultimately God "is Spirit" (John 4:24) in the sense that he does not live in splendid isolation, but that his very nature is to become active. God's very being is in the constant longing to change people and to shape history as the concrete manifestation of love, because God "is love" (1 John 4:8). Wherever God, the Father of the Son, becomes real and effective, there he is present in the power of the Spirit; and wherever the Holy Spirit is, there the God who is love and who has revealed himself as such in Jesus Christ becomes real.

Chapter 8

The Empty Tomb Narratives

Besides the appearance tradition and the testimonies to the experiences of the Holy Spirit, there is another tradition that speaks about an immediate effect of the resurrection of Jesus Christ on history. It is the tradition about the discovery of the "empty tomb".

While the appearance tradition in its earliest form is located in Galilee and in Jerusalem, the tradition about the empty tomb is located only in Jerusalem. It reports that during the early morning after the death and burial of Jesus, Mary Magdalene—probably together with one or more other women—went to visit the tomb into which the body of Jesus had been laid, and she discovered the tomb to be empty. This discovery of the empty tomb, linked with a then popular Jewish anthropology that thought of resurrection in terms of a material *bodily* resurrection, suggests that God had raised the physical body of Jesus out of the tomb, so that consequently the tomb must have been empty. This is probably the way most Christians would interpret the empty tomb narratives. Indeed, for many or even for most Christians the "empty tomb" occupies such an important place in their understanding of faith, that one hesitates to raise questions related to it. Nevertheless, the perception that the tomb must have been empty is burdened with a number of difficulties.

There is, first of all, the problem of sources. Which is the earliest tradition? Is it the one found in Mark 16:1-8 about the visit of Mary (and some other women?) to the tomb, or is it the one in Luke 24:12 about Peter's visit to the tomb? Do these traditions contain reliable historical information?[1]

Then there is, secondly, the problem of the origin of and the historical basis for these sources. Numerous critical investigations of the relevant New Testament texts have led to no consensus. Contemporary New Testament

---

1. The apologetic passion that theologians exercise at this point—either affirming or denying the historical nature of the "empty tomb"—is of little help for an open inquiry into the problems and their possible solutions.

scholars can argue "that Mk created the tradition of the Empty Tomb,"[2] or that the church before Mark created the empty tomb narrative in order to explicate and/or define their faith in Jesus Christ.[3] Others think that there was a historical kernel which was then shaped and embellished in the ongoing history until Mark incorporated it, possibly as part of the pre-Markan passion story, into his gospel.[4]

There is, thirdly, the religio-historical problem whether within the religious and cultural context in which the earliest Christian communities evolved, a resurrection and even a "bodily" resurrection necessarily implied the removal and transfiguration of the earthly body.

And, finally, there is the theological problem as to what message the empty tomb narratives mean to convey, and how far their content is necessary to explain the genesis and content of faith in the risen Christ.

Since there exists no scholarly consensus on any of these questions,[5] we must briefly present and argue our own proposal.

THE SOURCES

We begin with the observation that the earliest accounts of the empty tomb narratives in the New Testament—Mark 16:1–8; Matt 28:1–8; Luke 24:1–11.12.24; John 20:1–18—can be reduced to one source: the tradition that surfaces in Mark 16:1–8, Matt 28:1–8 (if Matthew used a tradition that was

---

2. John Dominic Crossan, "Empty Tomb and Absent Lord (Mark 16:1–8)," in: Werner H. Kelber, ed., *The Passion in Mark. Studies on Mark 14–16* (Philadelphia: Fortress, 1976, pp. 135–152), p. 135.

3. Rudolf Pesch, *Das Markusevangelium, II. Teil, Kommentar zu Kap. 8,27–16:20.* HthK (Freiburg: Herder, 1977), pp. 521–527; so already Rudolf Bultmann, *The History of the Synoptic Tradition* (Oxford: Blackwell, 1963 [1931]), pp. 287–290.

4. Joachim Gnilka, *Das Evangelium nach Markus. 2. Teilband Mk 8,27–16,20* (Neukirchen: Neukirchener Verlag, Zürich: Benziger Verlag, 1979), pp. 337–340; Hans von Campenhausen, "The Events of Easter and the Empty Tomb," in: *Tradition and Life in the Church: Essays and Lectures in Church History* (Philadelphia: Fortress, 1968, pp. 42–89), pp. 54–77; Eduard Schweizer, *The Good News According to Mark* (Richmond: Knox, 1970), pp. 369f.; Peter Stuhlmacher, "The Resurrection of Jesus and the Resurrection of the Dead," *Ex Auditu* 9 (1993, pp. 45–56), pp. 46–48.

5. Since the problems are discussed in most books on the resurrection, I only mention the following sources for orientation: Hans Grass, *Ostergeschehen und Osterberichte* ([4]1970), pp. 138–168; Peter Carnley, *The Structure of Resurrection Belief* (1987), pp. 44–62, 230–233; Anton Vögtle, "Wie kam es zum Osterglauben?", in: Anton Vögtle/Rudolf Pesch, *Wie kam es zum Osterglauben?* (1975, pp. 9–131), pp. 85–98; Jacob Kremer, *Die Osterevangelien—Geschichten um Geschichte* (Stuttgart: Katholisches Bibelwerk, [2]1981), pp. 13–24, 30–54; Barnabas Lindars, "Jesus Risen: Bodily Resurrection But No Empty Tomb," *Theol* 89 (1986), pp. 90–96. For exegetical details relating to Mark 16:1–8 see the commentaries on the Gospel of Mark by Eduard Schweizer, Rudolf Pesch, and Joachim Gnilka.

independent of Mark), and in John 20:1.11–18. It spoke of the visit of Mary of Magdala to the rock tomb into which the corpse of Jesus had been laid, and that she found the tomb empty. This tradition, possibly as part of a longer passion narrative, was modified and incorporated into their gospels by Mark and John, and from Mark it was taken over into the Gospels of Matthew (who may have had a further source of the same tradition available) and Luke, and adapted to their theological context and intentions.

In Luke 24:12 (compare Luke 24:24) we encounter a further, originally isolated tradition that speaks of Peter's visit to the empty tomb: ". . . Peter rose and ran to the tomb; stooping and looking in, he saw the linen cloths by themselves; and he went home wondering at what had happened." It remains uncertain whether this text is part of the original Gospel of Luke because some important manuscripts omit this verse.[6] However, following Joachim Jeremias,[7] Kurt Aland,[8] and the most recent editions of the Greek New Testament,[9] it seems probable that this verse was part of the Gospel of Luke. It reflects a separate but late tradition of the empty tomb narrative. This tradition was also known to the fourth evangelist. He introduced the beloved disciple into the narrative and thereby shifts the emphasis from Peter to the beloved disciple. It is the latter who arrives first at the tomb and who interprets its meaning: John 20:2–10.[10]

This tradition about Peter's, and then also the beloved disciple's, visit to the tomb is certainly a late development. It served a twofold purpose. On the one hand, it enhanced the authority of Peter and the beloved disciple in their respective communities by linking them with this important tradition. On the other hand, since male witnesses were considered to be superior to female witnesses, the credibility of the empty tomb tradition was enhanced. In the

---

6. Compare the discussion of Robert Mahoney, *Two Disciples at the Tomb: The Background and Message of John 20:1–10.* Theologie und Wirklichkeit, vol.6 (Bern: Lang, 1974), chapter 2, and Anton Dauer, "Lk 24, 12—ein Produkt lukanischer Redaktion," in: F. van Segbroeck, C.M. Tuckett, G. van Belle, J. Verheyden, eds. *The Four Gospels 1992. Festschrift Frans Neirynck,* vol. II (Leuven: University Press, 1992), pp. 1697–1716.

7. Joachim Jeremias, *The Eucharistic Words of Jesus* (Oxford: Blackwell, 1955), pp. 97f.

8. Kurt Aland, "Neue Neutestamentliche Papyri II," *NTS* 12 (1965–66, pp. 193–210) pp. 205f.; Kurt Aland, "Die Bedeutung des P[75] für den Text des Neuen Testaments. Ein Beitrag zur Frage der 'Western non-interpolations'," in: *Studien zur Überlieferung des Neuen Testaments und seines Textes.* Arbeiten zur Neutestamentlichen Forschung II (Berlin: Walter de Gruyter, 1967, pp. 155–172), pp. 157, 168f.

9. Nestle-Aland, *Novum Testamentum Graece* (Stuttgart: Deutsche Bibelstiftung, 26. neu bearbeitete Auflage, 1979 and 27. revidierte Auflage, 1993); compare also Bruce Metzger, *A Textual Commentary on the Greek New Testament* (London: United Bible Societies, 1971), p. 184.

10. Compare: Thorwald Lorenzen, *Der Lieblingsjünger im Johannesevangelium. Eine redaktionsgeschichtliche Studie.* SBS 55 (Stuttgart: Katholisches Bibelwerk, 1971), §3; Robert Mahoney, *Two Disciples at the Tomb: The Background and Message of John 20:1–10* (1974), chapters 6 and 7.

Johannine community, the portrayal that the beloved disciple arrives at the tomb first and then provides the theological interpretation of the empty tomb, highlights the fact that in the Johannine church the authority of the beloved disciple was superior to that of Peter.

As the earliest source for the empty tomb tradition, we are therefore left with the tradition behind Mark 16:1–8 (Matt 28:1–8) and John 20:1.11–18.

THE HISTORICAL QUESTION

The most we can say on the basis of the tradition behind Mark 16:1–8 (Matt 28:1–8) and John 20:1.11–18 is that during the early morning after the burial of Jesus, Mary Magdalene—the other women vary in the different texts—went to visit the tomb into which the body of Jesus had been laid, and she discovered it to be empty.[11]

Such a historical verdict is supported by the following observations:[12]

1. Joseph of Arimathea probably received, on request, the body of Jesus and buried it.[13] Mark 15:47 reports, furthermore, "Mary Magdalene and Mary the mother of Joses saw where he was laid." It is therefore possible that a select circle of Jesus' friends knew the location of the rock tomb where Jesus had been buried.
2. A visit of Mary Magdalene and some of her lady friends to the tomb on the morning after the burial would not have been unusual. They may have wanted

---

11. Matt 28:1 differs from Mark 16:1f. and may refer to the time of sunset when the sabbath gives way to the first day of the week (compare J. Michael Winger, "When Did the Women Visit the Tomb? Sources For Some Temporal Clauses in the Synoptic Gospels," *NTS* 40 [1994], pp. 284–288). For our investigation this possible discrepancy is of no importance.

12. For details see: Wolfgang Nauck, "Die Bedeutung des leeren Grabes für den Glauben an den Auferstandenen," *ZNW* 47 (1956, pp. 243–267), pp. 249f., 263–265; Hans von Campenhausen, "The Events of Easter and the Empty Tomb," in: *Tradition and Life in the Church: Essays and Lectures in Church History* (Philadelphia: Fortress, 1968), pp. 42–89; Eduard Schweizer, *The Good News According to Mark* (Richmond: Knox, 1970), pp. 369f.; Leonhard Goppelt, *Theology of the New Testament.* Vol. 1. Ed. Jürgen Roloff (Grand Rapids, Michigan: Eerdmans, 1981), pp. 245f.; James D. G. Dunn, *The Evidence for Jesus. The Impact of Scholarship on Our Understanding of How Christianity Began* (London: SCM, 1985), pp. 63–69, 75f., 77f.

13. Yet even the Burial Narrative may reflect more interest in theological motifs than in historical detail: compare Johannes Schreiber, "Die Bestattung Jesu. Redaktionsgeschichtliche Beobachtungen zu Mk 15:42–47 par," *ZNW* 72 (1981), pp. 141–177. The most we can say historically, according to Schreiber, is that in the pre-Markan tradition Joseph of Arimathea had something positive to do with the burial of Jesus (p. 176). Barnabas Lindars also questions the historical reliability of the burial narrative: "Jesus Risen: Bodily Resurrection But No Empty Tomb," *Theol* 89 (1986, pp. 90–96), p. 94.

to continue their lament, and at the same time they could have fulfilled the customary ritual of anointing the body of Jesus with "spices" (Mark 16:1, Luke 24:1), which, for whatever reason, may not have been carried out or completed during the burial.

3. Given the popular Jewish anthropology of that time, it would have been difficult to proclaim the message of Easter if that message could have been invalidated by taking people to the tomb and showing them that the corpse of Jesus was still there, and that therefore he could not have risen from the dead.

4. If the early Christians had created this story in order to prove the bodilyness of Jesus' resurrection, then they would hardly have chosen a woman or women as the main witnesses. Women were considered inferior witnesses, and texts like Luke 24:12.24 and John 20:3–10 show the strong tendency to have the empty tomb validated by apostolic male witnesses.

5. The unexpected discovery of the empty tomb caused "trembling and astonishment" to the women (Mark 16:8). We do not get the impression that for them it served as a convincing proof that Jesus had really risen from the dead.

6. We have no record that Jewish opponents ever tried to discredit the fact of the empty tomb. They simply tried to explain the removal of the body, be it that the disciples had stolen it (Matt 28:13), or that a gardener had removed it (John 20:15).

7. Archaeological excavations at the Church of the Holy Sepulchre "suggest nothing on the site at the time of Christ that is incompatible with the gospel stories."[14]

8. Finally, we must apply the hermeneutic of suspicion also to ourselves and admit that within our understanding of reality it is very difficult to imagine that Jesus' material body was transformed into some kind of "spiritual body" so that the tomb which was found empty was actually the tomb into which Jesus had been laid and no human beings had removed the dead body from there.

Nevertheless, there are many scholars for whom the above arguments have not been fully convincing.[15] Most persuasive in favor of the historical

---

14. Oliver Nicholson, "Holy Sepulcher, Church of the," in: *The Anchor Bible Dictionary* 3 (1992, pp. 258–260), p. 258.

15. Compare for instance: Hans Grass, *Ostergeschehen und Osterberichte* (⁴1970), pp. 15–23, 138–168; Werner Georg Kümmel, *The Theology of the New Testament According to Its Major Witnesses, Jesus—Paul—John* (Nashville: Abingdon, 1973), pp. 99–103; Peter Carnley, *The Structure of Resurrection Belief* (1987), pp. 44–62, 230–233; Anton Vögtle, "Wie kam es zum Osterglauben?", in: Anton Vögtle/Rudolf Pesch, *Wie kam es zum Osterglauben?* (1975, pp. 9–131), pp. 85–98; Rudolf Pesch, *Das Markusevangelium, II. Teil, Kommentar zu Kap.* 8,27–16:20 (1977), pp. 536–538; Ingo Broer, "Zur historischen Frage nach der Auferstehung Jesu," *AnzKG* 80 (1971), pp. 424–434.

reliability of the empty tomb traditions is the observation that the Easter message could not have been proclaimed in Jerusalem if the opponents could have invalidated its substance by pointing to the corpse of Jesus in the tomb. Yet we do not really know as to when the Easter message was first proclaimed in Jerusalem. It is unlikely that Mary as a woman, on the basis of her experience with the risen Christ, would have proclaimed the gospel in Jerusalem. The other appearances happened in Galilee, and from there Peter and the disciples had to return to Jerusalem. That takes time, and the opposition that was directed toward Jesus would also have made his disciples cautious. We know that Peter and the disciples were back in Jerusalem by the Feast of Weeks (Pentecost) which is 50 days after the Passover Feast. Yet this chronological scheme is a Lukan construct to distinguish between the resurrection of Christ and the coming of the Holy Spirit. We simply don't know when the resurrection was first proclaimed in Jerusalem.

Furthermore, the fact that Paul speaks of the "bodily" resurrection of Christ without reference to the empty tomb makes it at least possible that when the Easter message was proclaimed in Jerusalem there may have been no necessity for a reference to the empty tomb. That could also explain why the opponents apparently showed little interest in the empty tomb. If it was possible to proclaim the Easter message without an explicit reference to the empty tomb (Paul!), then it is equally possible that the opponents did not immediately infer such a connection. The fact that Paul, who was familiar with the situation in Jerusalem, does not refer to the empty tomb, may have been due to the fact that he was writing to Corinth, not to Jerusalem. Yet in his reasoning in 1 Corinthians 15 a reference to the empty tomb would have strengthened his argument, *if* the empty tomb was deemed to be a historical fact, and *if* he knew about it. Peter Carnley is probably correct when he suggests that "the emptiness or otherwise of the tomb was not an immediate issue."[16]

At this point it must also be emphasized, however, that the then current view about the nature of the resurrection body was not as coherent as it is often thought. Besides a crude belief in a material and recognizable continuity between the earthly body and the resurrection body (see below), there are other views that speak of a new and transformed resurrection body, and even of a spiritual resurrection without a body.[17]

---

16. Peter Carnley, *The Structure of Resurrection Belief* (1987), p. 58; similar: Barnabas Lindars, "Jesus Risen: Bodily Resurrection But No Empty Tomb," *Theol* 89 (1986), pp. 90–96.

17. George W. E. Nickelsburg says that ". . . in the intertestamental period there was no single Jewish orthodoxy on the time, mode, and place of resurrection, immortality, and eternal life." (*Resurrection, Immortality, and Eternal Life in Intertestamental Judaism.* HThSt XXVI [Cambridge: Harvard University Press, 1972], p. 180). Compare further: W. D. Davies, *Paul and Rabbinic Judaism. Some Rabbinic Elements in Pauline Theology* (Philadelphia: Fortress, ⁴1980 [1948]), pp. 306–309; R. H. Charles, *A Critical History of the Doctrine of a Future Life in Israel, in Judaism, and in Christianity.* Jowett Lectures 1898–99 (London: Black, 1899), pp. 216, 239, 243f., 266; Martin Hengel,

With the present state of research being what it is, the matter must remain undecided. At the genesis of the empty tomb tradition there could have been the historical report that Mary of Magdala discovered an empty tomb. But even if that were the case, such a fact could be interpreted in many different ways. It certainly cannot serve as a convincing proof for the resurrection of Jesus and for the genesis of the Easter faith.[18] At the most it could have served as a confirmation and interpretation for the Easter appearances that happened to Mary, Peter and the others. This confirmation and interpretation would then include the conviction that God had bodily raised Jesus from the dead: "He has risen, he is not here; see the place where they laid him" (Mark 16:6). It would, furthermore, underline the uniqueness of Jesus by signifying that his resurrection is different from ours (our tombs will not be empty); and it is also different from the continuing life of martyrs whose soul would live on, while their bodies disintegrate in the grave (compare Rev 6:9–11).

Nevertheless, the fact that Paul and the pre-Pauline tradition can develop a sophisticated theology of the resurrection without explicit reference to the empty tomb, allows for the possibility that the early church created the empty tomb tradition in order to proclaim and assert that Jesus had really risen from the dead. In that case then, the empty tomb narrative was formed to protect the Christian message against docetic and spiritualizing distortions.[19] As such it served the same kerygmatic and apologetic purpose as the other resurrection narratives that underline the bodilyness of the risen Christ by inviting people to touch him (Luke 24:39; John 20:25.27), and by reporting that the Risen One ate and practiced fellowship with his disciples (Luke 24:41–43; John 21:9–11.15–17). The fact that a woman, Mary of Magdala, is reported to have discovered the empty tomb may have been due to the common knowledge that all the male disciples were absent from Jerusalem; they had fled to Galilee.

Judaism and Hellenism. Studies in their Encounter in Palestine during the Early Hellenistic Period. Vols. 1 and 2 (Philadelphia: Fortress, 1974), pp. 196–202 (vol. 1). The following surveys of the then current view of the resurrection and the resurrection body are helpful: Paul Hoffmann, *Die Toten in Christus. Eine religionsgeschichtliche und exegetische Untersuchung zur paulinischen Eschatologie* (Münster: Aschendorff, 1966), pp. 58–174; George W. E. Nickelsburg, *Resurrection, Immortality, and Eternal Life in Intertestamental Judaism* (1972); Günter Stemberger, *Der Leib der Auferstehung. Studien zur Anthropologie und Eschatologie des palästinischen Judentums im neutestamentlichen Zeitalter* (ca. 170 v. Chr.-100 n. Chr.). AnBib 56 (Rome: Biblical Institute Press, 1972); Kurt Schubert, "Die Entwicklung der Auferstehungslehre von der nachexilischen bis zur frührabbinischen Zeit," *BZ NF* 6 (1962), pp. 177–214; Anton Vögtle. "Wie kam es zum Osterglauben?", in: Anton Vögtle/Rudolf Pesch, *Wie kam es zum Osterglauben?* (Düsseldorf: Patmos Verlag, 1975, pp. 9–131), pp. 103–117. See below, fn. 28.

18. So also Eduard Schweizer, *Jesus* (London: SCM, 1971), pp. 47f.

19. Rudolf Bultmann, *History of the Synoptic Tradition* (Oxford: Blackwell, 1963 [1931]), pp. 287–290; Rudolf Pesch, *Das Markusevangelium, II. Teil, Kommentar zu Kap. 8,27—16:20* (1977), pp. 521–527.

THE THEOLOGICAL SIGNIFICANCE

We saw that at the present state of research the historical question cannot be decided. Such a seemingly negative result may open our eyes for a more appropriate perception of the reality of the resurrection.

Let us note, first of all, that in the pre-Markan narrative it is "a young man . . . dressed in a white robe" (Mark 16:5), that means a heavenly messenger, an angel, who interprets the meaning of the empty tomb: "you seek Jesus of Nazareth, who was crucified. He has risen, he is not here; see the place where they laid him" (Mark 16:6). An "angel" cannot be "seen" and "heard" with our natural capacity of historical reason. It is therefore not the intention of the empty tomb narrative to provide an empirical proof for the resurrection of Jesus. The text wants to interpret the reality of the resurrection by pointing out that "Jesus of Nazareth, who was crucified" is risen. The "interpreter" is an "angel" and as such can only be perceived by the believer.

It is of theological significance that the New Testament traditions never portray the resurrection of Jesus Christ as such. May this not be a reminder that the meaning and reality of the resurrection resists every attempt at objectification?[20] How different is the portrayal of the resurrection in the extracanonical tradition! In the Gospel of Peter (150 C.E.?), for instance, we meet the detailed historical interest that is lacking in the gospel narratives:[21]

8.28. But the scribes and Pharisees and elders, being assembled together and hearing that all the people were murmuring and beating their breasts, saying, "If at his death these exceeding great signs have come to pass, behold how *righteous* he was!", 29. were afraid and came to Pilate, entreating him and saying, 30. "Give us soldiers that we may watch his sepulchre for *three days, lest his disciples come and steal him away* and the *people* suppose that he *is risen from the dead*, and do us harm." 31. And Pilate gave them Petronius the centurion with soldiers to watch the sepulchre. And with them there came elders and scribes to the sepulchre. 32. And all who were there, together with the centurion and the

---

20. It is of interest to note that the early church was very reluctant to portray the resurrection of Christ. Until the 15th century it was mainly the crucifixion of Christ and his burial that were represented in pictures. Compare: Hans Werner Bartsch, "Inhalt und Funktion des urchristlichen Osterglaubens," in: Hildegard Temporini und Wolfgang Haase, Hg., *Aufstieg und Niedergang der Römischen Welt. Geschichte und Kultur Roms im Spiegel der Neueren Forschung, II.25.1: Religion (Vorkonstantinisches Christentum: Leben und Umwelt Jesu; Neues Testament [Kanonische Schriften und Apokryphen])*. Hg. Wolfgang Haase (Berlin, New York: Walter de Gruyter, 1982, pp. 794–890), pp. 795f.

21. Cited according to Edgar Hennecke, *New Testament Apocrypha*. Ed. Wilhelm Schneemelcher. English translation ed. R. McL. Wilson. Vol. I: Gospels and Related Writings (Philadelphia: Westminster, 1963), pp. 185f. The words and phrases printed in italics are allusions to texts in the New Testament Gospels.

soldiers, *rolled* thither a great stone and laid it against the entrance to the sepulchre 33. and *put* on it seven *seals*, pitched a tent and kept watch. **9**. 34. Early in the morning, when the Sabbath dawned, there came a crowd from Jerusalem and the country round about to see the sepulchre that had been sealed. 35. Now in the night in which the Lord's day dawned, when the soldiers, two by two in every watch, were keeping guard, there rang out a loud *voice in heaven*, 36. and they saw the *heavens opened* and two men *come down* from there in a great brightness and draw nigh to the sepulchre. 37. That *stone* which had been laid against the entrance to the sepulchre started of itself to *roll* and gave way to the side, and the sepulchre was opened, and both the young men entered in. **10**. 38. When now those soldiers saw this, they awakened the centurion and the elders—for they also were there to assist at the watch. 39. And whilst they were relating what they had seen, they saw again three men come out from the sepulchre, and two of them sustaining the other, and a cross following them, 40. and the heads of the two reaching to heaven, but that of him who was led of them by the hand overpassing the heavens. 41. And they heard a voice out of the heavens crying, "Thou hast preached to them that sleep", 42. and from the cross there was heard the answer, "Yea". **11**. 43. Those men therefore took counsel with one another to go and report this to Pilate. 44. And whilst they were still deliberating, the heavens were again seen to open, and a man descended and entered into the sepulchre. 45. When those who were of the centurion's company saw this, they hastened by night to Pilate, abandoning the sepulchre which they were guarding, and reported everything that they had seen, being full of disquietude and saying, "In *truth* he was *the Son of God*".

Here, then, we see a clear tendency toward rational explanation and objectification which as such we do not yet find in the New Testament writings.[22] The canonical texts, in fact, hesitate to assign theological importance to the empty tomb narratives. In Mark the women flee from the tomb, "for they were afraid" (16:8), in John, Mary's weeping is only dissolved when she recognized

---

22. Closest to this tendency come those gospel texts in which the tomb is guarded by soldiers (Matt 27:62–66), or where male witnesses authenticate the empty tomb tradition (Luke 24:12.25; John 20:2–10). But these texts are woven into a context. They do not acquire independent value. They are part of a story that wants to emphasise the reality of the resurrection without objectifying it. Similar to the text in the Gospel of Peter is a text from the Gospel of the Hebrews (150 c.e.?): "And when the Lord had given the linen cloth to the servant of the priest, he went to James and appeared to him. . . . And . . . the Lord said: Bring a table and bread! And immediately it is added: he took the bread, blessed it and brake it and gave it to James the Just and said to him: My brother, eat thy bread, for the Son of man is risen from among them that sleep." (§7, cited from Edgar Hennecke, *New Testament Apocrypha*, Vol. I: Gospels and Related Writings [1963], p. 165).

the risen Lord (20:16), in Luke the disciples on the road to Emmaus do not yet believe although they knew about the empty tomb (24:22–27), and Paul does not mention the empty tomb at all. Whether the empty tomb was a historical fact or whether the narrative was created by the early Christians to witness to the reality of the resurrection, we can no longer say. But it is important to note that the reality for which the empty tomb stands is made accessible only by an "interpreting angel", and that angelic message can only be perceived by faith. Faith in the risen Christ is therefore a necessary element in understanding the meaning of the empty tomb narratives.

This leads us to another, a second observation that we have already alluded to: the apostle Paul explicates and develops his theology of the bodily resurrection of Christ without explicit reference to the empty tomb; and no one would want to suggest that Paul has no interest in the bodily resurrection of Jesus Christ! It has been suggested that the empty tomb is presupposed in the statement that Christ "was buried" and then "raised" (1 Cor 15:4).[23] But this is certainly not the case as far as the inner logic of the pre-Pauline formula is concerned. There the statement that "he was buried" intensifies and validates the assertion that "he died", just as the references to the appearances strengthen the assertion that "he was raised".

Given his Jewish and Pharisaic background, one would expect that for Paul the "empty tomb" would have been an implication of his emphasis on the resurrection of Christ. It is therefore surprising that he never refers to the empty tomb tradition. Either the empty tomb tradition had not yet evolved when the tradition in 1 Corinthians 15:3–5 was created, or when during the years 53–55 Paul wrote his letters to Corinth,[24] or Paul did not know it. If the empty tomb tradition had existed in Jerusalem, it would have been unlikely that Paul had not known it, because Paul had lively contact with the Christian community in Jerusalem. Whatever may have been the case, it is clear, that Paul developed an elaborate theology of the bodily resurrection of Christ without making explicit reference to the empty tomb.

When one considers, in addition, that it would have strengthened his argument in 1 Corinthians 15 if besides listing the witnesses to the appearances, he could also have listed the "empty tomb" and the witnesses to it (even though according to the earliest tradition they were only women!), then one may suspect that in his christology Paul intentionally reinterprets a Jewish tradition that postulates a natural continuity between the old body and the new resurrection

---

23. Wolfgang Nauck, "Die Bedeutung des leeren Grabes für den Glauben an den Auferstandenen," *ZNW* 47 (1956, pp. 243–267), pp. 247f., 265; Ulrich Wilckens, "The Tradition-history of the Resurrection of Jesus," in: C. F. D. Moule, ed., *The Significance of the Message of the Resurrection of Faith in Jesus Christ*. Studies in Biblical Theology, 2nd Series, 8 (London: SCM, 1968, pp. 51–76), pp. 57f. The matter is discussed and rejected by Hans Grass, *Ostergeschehen und Osterberichte* (⁴1970), pp. 146–173.

24. So Werner Georg Kümmel, *The Theology of the New Testament According to Its Major Witnesses, Jesus—Paul—John* (1973), p. 102.

body.[25] While some rabbinic speculations insist that the resurrection bodies include, for instance, the material sinews and bones,[26] and even the scars of human illnesses (which, however, will be removed when the identity of the person is established),[27] Paul insists that "flesh and blood cannot inherit the kingdom of God" (1 Cor 15:50). In his understanding of the bodily resurrection of Jesus, Paul is obviously not so much influenced by a popular Jewish anthropology that emphasizes the material continuity between the earthly and the resurrection body, as by his encounter with the risen Christ. We should also note, however, that the then current worldview was diverse enough to allow for a "bodily" resurrection without having to think the necessity of an "empty tomb". John J. Collins, in his recent commentary on the Book of Daniel comments on the belief in the resurrection in Judaism of the first century C.E.:

> Belief in some form of resurrection was widespread in Judaism by the first century C.E. Even then, however, the form of the resurrected body was controversial. . . . The stereotypical assumption that resurrection in a Jewish context was always bodily is in need of considerable qualification.[28]

---

25. Similar is the view of Barnabas Lindars: "Thus Paul frees the concept of the resurrection of the body from the crude literalism of the popular Jewish views, shared by the Galilean fishermen, whose experience of the risen Jesus is, nevertheless, the foundation of the gospel of redemption." ("Jesus Risen: Bodily Resurrection But No Empty Tomb," *Theol* 89 [1986, pp. 90–96], p. 95).

26. Hermann L. Strack und Paul Billerbeck, *Kommentar zum Neuen Testament aus Talmud und Midrasch*. Band III: Die Briefe des Neuen Testaments und die Offenbarung Johannis erläutert aus Talmud und Midrasch (München: Beck, 1926), pp. 473f.; Band IV: Exkurse zu einzelnen Stellen des Neuen Testaments. Abhandlungen zur neutestamentlichen Theologie und Archäologie, zweiter Teil (München: Beck, 1928), pp. 815f.

27. Hermann L. Strack und Paul Billerbeck, *Kommentar zum Neuen Testament aus Talmud und Midrasch*. Band IV: Exkurse zu einzelnen Stellen des Neuen Testaments. Abhandlungen zur neutestamentlichen Theologie und Archäologie, zweiter Teil (1928), p. 1175; compare also: W. D. Davies, *Paul and Rabbinic Judaism. Some Rabbinic Elements in Pauline Theology* (Philadelphia: Fortress, ⁴1980 [1948]), pp. 300f.

28. John J. Collins, *Daniel. A Commentary on the Book of Daniel* (Minneapolis: Fortress Press, 1993), p. 398. George W. E. Nickelsburg cites Jubilees 23 and the Ethiopic Apocalypse of Enoch 102–104 as religio-historical analogies to the idea of the resurrection of people without having to postulate that the corpse of these people was removed from their tombs. *Resurrection, Immortality, and Eternal Life in Intertestamental Judaism* (1972), pp. 31–33, 123f., 174, 178f.; Günter Stemberger suggests that the anthropology of 2 Maccabees implies "a bodily resurrection, but not a resurrection of the self same body." ("Die Auferstehung ist leiblich, aber nicht eine Auferstehung eben desselben Leibes.") (*Der Leib der Auferstehung. Studien zur Anthropologie und Eschatologie des palästinischen Judentums im neutestamentlichen Zeitalter* (ca. 170 v. Chr.-100 n. Chr.) [1972], p. 24, my translation). The Syriac Apocalypse of Baruch (early second century C.E.) affirms the popular belief that there is continuity between the earthly body and the resurrection body in order that people can be recognized after the resurrection (50:1–4). But then this view seems to be transcended when the text speaks about "the glory of those who proved to be righteous . . .—their splendor will then be glorified

It seems to have been not so much Jewish anthropology but his christology, tied to his Damascus Road experience, which was the determinative hermeneutical key for Paul.

This would be further supported by the fact that, except for the pre-Pauline hymnic text in Philippians 3:20f.[29] ("the Lord Jesus Christ . . . will change our lowly body to be like his glorious body . . ."), and in contrast to the gospels (Luke 24:3; John 2:21, 20:12), and the post-Pauline tradition (Col 1:22; Heb 10:10; 1 Pet 2:24), Paul himself does not speak of a resurrection body of Christ in the sense that such a body would presuppose a material continuity with the particular human and earthly body that Jesus had at the point of his death and which was placed as a corpse into the tomb.[30]

For Paul the "body of Christ" can either be the crucified body of Jesus with the emphasis on "crucifixion" (Rom 7:4, 1 Cor 10:16, 11:27.29), or it can refer to the element of bread in the Lord's Supper (1 Cor 11:24), or it means the church (1 Cor 10:17, 12:27, Rom 12:4f.). There is an inner coherence in this varied use of the "body of Christ". In and with his crucifixion, Jesus Christ gives himself to free humanity from law, sin, and death. The church is the community of believers which knows this, which lives "in Christ", which lets its life be determined by Christ, and which celebrates this in the Lord's Supper. The church then is the sphere and the community in which the Lordship of Christ is believed and accepted, and through which this lordship is testified in word and deed to the rest of creation. Through the church as his "body" the risen Christ encounters the world with his saving and liberating grace. The body of the risen Christ is therefore not a material substance that defines the identity of the risen Christ, but it is the sphere in which his lordship is accepted, obeyed, and lived.[31]

---

by transformations, and the shape of their face will be changed into the light of their beauty so that they may acquire and receive the undying world which was promised to them." (51:1–3). They "will be like angels" (51:10), indeed "the excellence of the righteous will . . . be greater than that of the angels" (51:12). Similar is the view of the Ethiopic Apocalypse of Enoch (second century B.C.E.-first century C.E.) according to which "the righteous and elect ones shall rise from the earth. . . . They shall wear the garments of glory." (62:15). The argument that the affirmation of a bodily resurrection does not necessarily imply the resurrection of the material corpse of Jesus is positively received by a number of theologians, e.g.: Pheme Perkins, *Resurrection: New Testament Witness and Contemporary Reflection* (London: Chapman, 1984); J.I.H. McDonald, *The Resurrection. Narrative and Belief* (London: SPCK, 1989).

29. Compare the discussion by Erhardt Güttgemanns, *Der leidende Apostel und sein Herr. Studien zur paulinischen Christologie* (1966), pp. 240–247, 251f.

30. Compare: F. W. Beare, *A Commentary on the Epistle to the Philippians* (London: Black, 1959), pp. 138f.; Erhardt Güttgemanns, *Der leidende Apostel und sein Herr. Studien zur paulinischen Christologie* (1966), pp. 247–281.

31. Compare: Eduard Schweizer, *Jesus* (1971), pp. 110–115; for details see Eduard Schweizer, "σῶμα κτλ.," (sōma ktl.) in: *TDNT* VII (1971, pp. 1024–1094), pp. 1067–1074.

We must, finally, not overlook Paul's insistence that "flesh and blood cannot inherit the kingdom of God" (1 Cor 15:50). Even where Paul, citing a pre-Pauline hymnic tradition, speaks of the body of the risen Christ, it is a body "of glory" (Phil 3:21). And when Paul speaks of the resurrection body of Christians it is always a "new" body which God gives as he has chosen. Paul tries to avoid two extremes. On the one hand he cannot perceive a "naked" (2 Cor 5:3) resurrection, because what people do in and with their earthly bodies is important and has significance *coram deo* (2 Cor 5:10). On the other hand, the "bodily" resurrection does not imply a natural continuity inherent to one's earthly body.[32] It is God's act, and any continuity with the earthly body is not inherent to the human person, but it results from God's initiative and action (2 Cor 5:1; 1 Cor 15:38).

The "body" must be seen and understood in relation to its subject (1 Cor 15:39–41). Not all bodies are the same: "there are celestial bodies and there are terrestrial bodies" (1 Cor 15:40), and, continuing in the intention of the text, we must say that there are the resurrection bodies of believers and there is the resurrection body of Christ. The resurrection body of Christ differs from that of the believers, because he *is* different. He is Savior and Lord, and his body is the sphere of his lordship. Potentially this sphere includes all of creation, as the pre-Colossian hymn (Col 1:15–20) in Colossians 1:18a explicitly says, but in actual fact it is the realm where his salvation is experienced and where his lordship is confessed—the church. The author of Colossians therefore adds "the church" to the given hymnic text: "He is the head of the body, the church". What the resurrection of Christ and the future resurrection of believers have in common, however, is that in both cases the continuity between the "old" body and the "new" body is seen as an act of God's grace. The continuity does not lie in the flesh of a person but in personal identity as it is shaped in relation to oneself, to the world, to nature, and to God.[33] At this point Paul transcends popular Jewish anthropology.

This brings us, thirdly, to an observation where Paul's argument can be correlated with our own experience. We know that our tombs and the tombs of our loved ones will not be empty after we die. When we die, our bodies will disintegrate to dust. This was, of course, known to Paul. Yet with this knowledge he develops an elaborate doctrine of the bodily resurrection of believers (especially in 1 Cor 15:35–57 and 2 Cor 5:1–10) and grounds the resurrection of believers (whose tombs are not empty!) in the resurrection of Jesus Christ.

It may be argued, of course, that Paul speaks of a future resurrection of believers and that therefore at the end of time the dust of the disintegrated human

---

32. Eduard Schweizer, "πνεῦμα κτλ., (pneuma ktl.) the New Testament," in: *TDNT* VI (1968, pp. 396–455), pp. 420–422; Eduard Schweizer, "σῶμα κτλ.," (sōma ktl.) in: *TDNT* VII (1971, pp. 1024–1094), pp. 1060–1062, 1065f.

33. Compare: Eduard Schweizer, "σῶμα κτλ.," (sōma ktl.) in: *TDNT* VII (1971, pp. 1024–1094), pp. 1065f. Similar is the reasoning of Hans Grass, *Ostergeschehen und Osterberichte* ('1970), pp. 146–173, 185.

bodies will be gathered and transformed into resurrection bodies and that then, in the *eschaton*, the tombs of all human beings will be empty. This would mean that what happened to the corpse of Jesus is only an anticipation of what will happen to the corpses of all believers or of all people.[34]

Yet such a reasoning would only be compelling if it is the only view that would have been possible within the general view of Jewish anthropology, and if that anthropology is accepted as the necessary and determinative hermeneutical key for understanding Paul's thought. Neither is the case. We saw that there are different emphases in Jewish anthropology, and for Paul it is ultimately christology that is determinative in his theological reflections. It is therefore likely that in light of his christology Paul relativizes popular expectations and as such speaks of the bodily resurrection of Jesus without making reference to an empty tomb.

We remind ourselves, finally, of the unique and eschatological nature of Jesus' resurrection. In contrast to the other resurrections that we hear of in the New Testament and the surrounding religions, Jesus "will never die again; death no longer has dominion over him" (Rom 6:9).

CONCLUSION

We will therefore have to conclude that the empty tomb tradition serves a legitimate theological and apologetic function in that it seeks to protect the reality of the resurrection against certain spiritualizing distortions. In narrative form it fulfills the same intention as the ὄντως ([ontōs] "real") does in Luke 24:34, and as what Paul accomplishes by his list of witnesses, "most of whom are still alive", and could therefore be questioned! (1 Cor 15:5–8).

Its historical roots are uncertain. It may go back to a visit of Mary Magdalene's to the tomb in which Jesus had been buried and which she discovered to be empty. It may also have arisen, ten, twenty, or thirty years after the death and resurrection of Jesus to address a theological issue. The fact that Paul does not seem to know this tradition speaks for its lateness. It could easily have evolved as a rational deduction in which the confession that "God raised Jesus from the dead" is conflated with that part of Jewish anthropology that emphasizes the continuity between the earthly body and the resurrection body, and consequently would have led to the conclusion that Jesus' corpse was removed by divine action from the tomb into which it had been placed.

It is clear, however, that the New Testament sources do not intend the empty tomb narratives to provide historically verifiable proof for the resurrection of Christ and for the genesis of the Easter faith. It is also clear that Paul has developed an elaborate theology of the resurrection of Christ without reference to an empty tomb.

---

34. Such a view obviously stands behind Matt 27:52f. which was originally a "resurrection text".

The "body" of Jesus' earthly life was much more than the physical body at the point of his death. To limit the "body" of Jesus to the corpse in the tomb would be a serious reduction. His "body" was himself, his identity, his mission, his effect on the world. It included all of his life; a life shaped in relationship to God, to human beings, to nature, and to history. His "body" is the sphere of his mission, his influence, his effect on history. This "body" has been universalized in that God has raised him from the dead. Potentially his "body" includes all the world. Concretely it is the realm where his Lordship is believed, confessed, obeyed, and lived.

Summary, Conclusion, Interpretation

With the resurrection of Jesus Christ, God concretely manifests and universalizes the soteriological promises that are grounded in his promises to Israel and that have been intensified and fulfilled in the life and death of Jesus the Christ. In contrast to all expectations, even the expectations of Jesus' closest followers, God raised the crucified Jesus from the dead. The resurrection of Christ has ontologically modified the whole of reality, because it was God "the creator of heaven and earth" who raised Jesus from the dead and thereby effectively confirmed his saving passion for all of reality. As far as humanity and the ongoing historical process is concerned, the important aspect of the resurrection was and is its effect on history. God shapes, modifies, and creates history by effectively relating the riches of Christ to the poverty of human experience and to the ambiguity of the ongoing historical process. This was concretely experienced when the risen Christ through the ministry of the Holy Spirit appeared to a select group of people and created faith in them. This faith was then shaped with the help of their memory of Jesus and with certain scriptural texts in which they saw this memory crystallized. On the basis of their experience of the risen Christ they proclaimed that "God raised Jesus Christ from the dead!"

Some questions that have assumed considerable importance in historical and contemporary theology could not be conclusively answered. The question, for instance, whether the conviction that God had raised Jesus from the dead necessarily implied that the corpse of Jesus no longer remained in the tomb. Nevertheless, it can be said with reasonable certainty that for the earliest Christians the "empty tomb" was not a constitutive element for asserting and proclaiming the bodily resurrection of Christ. This conclusion has resulted from a consideration of several factors: a reading of the relevant gospel narratives, and contrasting these narratives with extracanonical testimonies; becoming aware of the diverse religio-historical background at that time, which allowed for various ways of perceiving the resurrection of people; realizing that the "empty tomb" narratives in the gospels generally do not refer to the empty tomb as a ground for faith (except perhaps in John 20:8); and especially the realization that Paul could develop his theology of the resurrection without referring to the empty tomb.

In the ongoing history of the church it became necessary to defend the reality and content of the Easter faith against various distortions and accusations. Such apologetic needs could only be fulfilled with the language and literary forms that were available and communicative at that time. Consequently, early Christian leaders modified and embellished existing narratives, and, where necessary, they also "created" stories to correct distortions, and to deal with accusations.

In Matthew 27:62–66 we read, for instance, that on their request Pilate allowed the chief priest and the Pharisees to seal the tomb securely and to command a special guard to protect the tomb. This story obviously evolved to meet the charge that the disciples had stolen the body (see also Matt 28:13). Another example is the tradition that emphasizes the fact that male rather than female disciples discovered the empty tomb (Luke 24:12.24; John 20:2–10). Such an emphasis could serve several purposes. It could heighten the credibility of the empty tomb stories because male witnesses were considered to be more trustworthy than female witnesses; it could give added authority to those disciples (Peter and the "beloved disciple") who were associated with this important discovery; and it could relativize the problem that the male disciples had forsaken their Lord in the hour of crisis, left Jerusalem, and fled to Galilee. A further example is provided by the narratives that emphasize that the risen Lord could be touched (Luke 24:39; John 20:27), and that they saw him, heard him speak, and even ate with him (Luke 24:36–49; John 20:19–28, 21:1–23). These stories were directed against the accusation that the resurrection of Jesus was an illusion, and against distortions that tended to spiritualize the resurrection. Theologically speaking, these narratives serve the same function as the ὄντως in Luke 24:34, which asserts that Jesus had "really" been raised from the dead, and the list of witnesses that Paul brings in 1 Corinthians 15 in order to verify the reality of the resurrection of Christ.

One such story was also the narrative about the "empty tomb". This story was probably not simply created. It may have unfolded around a historical report that told of Mary Magdala's visit to the tomb in which Jesus had been laid and her discovery that the tomb was empty. We know, for instance, that the tombs of holy people occupied an important place in the religious ethos of that time,[1] and therefore it would not have been unusual that a legend, with or without a historical kernel, evolved around the tomb into which Jesus had been laid.[2] It is clear, however, that Paul does not use the empty tomb narrative in developing his theology of the resurrection, and that the New Testament does not use the "empty tomb" to provide an empirically verifiable basis for the Easter faith.

---

1. Joachim Jeremias, *Heiligengräber in Jesu Umwelt (Mt. 23,29; Lk. 11,47). Eine Untersuchung zur Volksreligion der Zeit Jesu* (Göttingen: Vandenhoeck & Ruprecht, 1958); Ingo Broer, "Zur heutigen Diskussion der Grabesgeschichte," *BiLe* 10 (1969, pp. 40–52), p. 47.

2. Some scholars interpret the "empty tomb" narrative as a etiological cult legend which was used in the Jerusalem church to celebrate the annual Easter service at the tomb of Jesus. Compare: Ludger Schenke, *Auferstehungsverkündigung und leeres Grab. Eine traditionsgeschichtliche Untersuchung von Mk 16, 1–8.* SBS 33 (Stuttgart: Katholisches Bibelwerk, 1968), pp. 86–93.

In conclusion we may gather our findings into a survey of the historical events associated with the time when the resurrection of Jesus Christ began to reach and shape history. During the trial of Jesus and before his crucifixion Peter and the other disciples left Jerusalem and fled to their homes in Galilee. For them history had cast its verdict against Jesus. For them God had spoken through the events of history, "for a hanged man is accursed by God" (Deut 21:23). They considered Jesus' mission to have failed. Their faith in Jesus' understanding of God was shattered. Although they must have known about the divine possibility of raising people from the dead, they did not apply this possibility to Jesus. It obviously transcended their imagination and their expectation that God would raise this particular Jesus, marked by poverty, disrespect for law and cult, arrest, and crucifixion, from the dead. Only the women followers of Jesus, and perhaps his brother James, who at that stage was not yet a follower of Jesus, remained in Jerusalem.

Some time after the death of Jesus, the same disciples who had left their Master and had returned to Galilee, confessed that Jesus Christ was not dead, but alive; that God had raised him from the dead, and that Jesus Christ had appeared to them. They gathered together and later returned to Jerusalem even though this meant exposing themselves again to danger and death. Those who had been timid and discouraged, now displayed the courage of lions proclaiming the resurrection of Christ.

> Even the unprejudiced historian must concede that "something" must have happened in the meanwhile to make this change comprehensible—"something" which brought the disciples back to Jerusalem from Galilee, "something" which enabled them to begin their new activity, "something" which caused them to spread abroad the "Christian" proclamation and to found a community. Without this "something" the origin of the Christian Church remains historically incomprehensible.[3]

In the New Testament we find no claim that anyone saw Jesus being raised from the dead, or that they saw Jesus walking or flying or being carried out of the rock tomb into which his corpse had been placed. Paul does not refer to the empty tomb narratives in his theology of the resurrection, and in the gospels the empty tomb narratives are not used to provide empirical proof for their belief that Jesus had been raised from the dead. What had happened?

Historically, we can say with reasonable certainty that in Jerusalem Mary Magdalene and in Galilee Peter experienced an appearance in which they recognized Jesus as the Christ. It is possible that similar appearances occurred to smaller (further women, the apostles, the "twelve", and James) and larger groups (the five hundred brethren). At a later date Christ appeared to Paul on the road to Damascus.

---

3. Heinz Zahrnt, *The Historical Jesus* (New York: Harper and Row, 1963), pp. 124f.

While Peter and the other disciples were in Galilee, in Jerusalem Joseph of Arimathea had probably gotten the body of Jesus and buried it in a rock tomb. Early in the morning, after the burial, Mary Magdalene and possibly one or more other women may have gone to visit the tomb. They would have known its location from attending the burial or they could have found it out from Joseph of Arimathea. On arrival they found the tomb to be empty. This visit to the tomb and the discovery that it was empty is most likely historical. It would have been known and told from the beginning, but, most likely, it did not have the theological importance that Christians have assigned to it in post-New Testament days.

It was probably in connection with her visit to the tomb that the risen Christ appeared to Mary of Magdala and possibly to some other women. This empowering of women resonated in the fact that many of the earliest house churches were led by women. But soon the dominant and powerful patriarchal culture became determinative in the Christian churches, and consequently the appearance to Mary Magdalene was played down in the evolving history of the early church. Women were not considered to be credible witnesses, the emerging churches lived in a patriarchal society, and the male leadership of the churches had many problems to deal with. They did not sufficiently recognize that the revolutionary power of the gospel would also expect them to reshape traditional leadership patterns, and consequently manifest the equality that is given with faith in Christ and with Christian baptism in the structures of the church (Gal 3:26–28). Given the patriarchal culture of that day, given the overwhelming novum of the resurrection, and given the insignificance of the small band of believers, such lack of implementing the demands of the gospel is perhaps, if not excusable, so certainly understandable. That this lack has then been frozen into a stubborn tradition that persists in many churches to the present day,[4] is not only a tragedy for the women who have felt called to the ministry, but it has been a major factor in injuring the credibility and hindering the effective ministry of the church.

While Mary encountered the risen Christ in Jerusalem, to Peter Christ appeared in Galilee. In consequence of his encounter with the risen Christ Peter gathered other disciples around him. They may also have encountered the risen

---

4. Most recently, on May 30, 1994, the Pope has declared "that the church has no authority whatsoever to confer priestly ordination on women", and that therefore all believers definitely and finally must accept the verdict that women cannot and will not be ordained: "Priestly Ordination" ("Ordinatio sacerdotalis"). "Apostolic Letter on Ordination and Women of Pope John Paul II of May 30, 1994," *Origins* 24/4 (9 June 1994), pp. 49, 51f. For the theological reasons that have led to this verdict the Pope refers specifically to: "On the Question of the Admission of Women to the Ministerial Priesthood" ("Inter insigniores"), Declaration of Oct. 15, 1976 of the Sacred Congregation for the Doctrine of the Faith (U.S. Catholic Conference Edition with Commentary [Washington, D.C., 1977]); *Acta Apostolicae Sedis* 69 (1977), pp. 98–116. In "Inter insigniores" the first appearance to Mary is distinguished from the "official" witnesses to the resurrection, which are the male apostles (§ 2).

Christ, or they may have believed in the risen Christ on the basis of Peter's testimony. Together they affirmed the experience that Jesus was not dead but alive, and on the basis of that experience they confessed that God had raised Jesus from the dead!

The resurrection appearances revolutionized their lives. They became convinced that the end-time had begun when God would usher in the Messianic kingdom. Jesus Christ was for them the "first fruit", the down payment, the anticipation, of the general resurrection. The center of such messianic and eschatological activities would be Jerusalem and Mt. Zion.[5] There they needed to go, to Mount Zion, to Jerusalem. Some time between the Passover Feast and the Feast of Weeks (Pentecost), perhaps together with the pilgrims who went up to Jerusalem for the Feast of Weeks, they returned from where they had fled several weeks earlier, to Jerusalem.

On their return to Jerusalem they met with the other followers of Jesus. They shared their experiences, worshipped and prayed together, and in a heightened eschatological consciousness they became aware that God had done something new to them, in them, and with them. They reestablished the circle of the "twelve", representing the twelve tribes of Israel, hoping to participate in the imminent reign of the Messiah (Matt 19:28). Just as it was the case with Jesus, they also could not include any woman in the circle of the "twelve", because the "twelve" were to represent the twelve sons of Jacob, "the twelve patriarchs" (Acts 7:8), and therewith the twelve tribes of Israel. At that stage there was no intention to break with Israel. They probably lived in the conviction that God would gather all of Israel to Mt. Zion, and indeed would use them in the process of calling all of Israel to repentance and faith.

In the context of those early meetings in Jerusalem they must have had intense experiences of the presence of the Spirit. Those experiences were most likely accompanied by charismatic manifestations like the speaking in tongues (Acts 2:4). Luke highlights the importance of those gatherings in Jerusalem by separating the resurrection of Jesus (Easter) and the outpouring of the Holy Spirit (Pentecost). But that is a Lukan theological construction. In fact, it is most unlikely that there was a period between Easter and Pentecost when the Spirit of God was absent or inactive.[6] The Spirit had never been absent, but with the resurrection appearances a new and heightened awareness of its presence had begun. The evangelist John therefore correctly condenses Easter and Pentecost into one event. It was the risen Christ who "breathed on them, and said to them, 'Receive the Holy Spirit . . .' " (20:19–23).

In those charismatic community experiences the presence of God was conflated with the presence of the risen Christ. Christ was in their midst in the

---

5. Georg Fohrer, Eduard Lohse, "Ζιών, Ἰερουσαλήμ, κτλ.," (Ziōn, Ierousalēm, ktl.)," *TDNT* VII (1971, pp. 292–338), pp. 300, 309–311, 312–317, 324–327, 333f.

6. Compare: Wilhelm Thüsing, *Erhöhungsvorstellung und Parusieerwartung in der ältesten nachösterlichen Christologie*. SBS 42 (Stuttgart: Katholisches Bibelwerk, 1969).

power of the Spirit. To express this in theological reflection they employed the concepts of exaltation (Phil 2:9; Acts 2:33, 5:31) and ascension (Acts 1:1–11, 3:21). Jesus, having been exalted to the right hand of God through the resurrection from the dead, was now empowered to share his life with his followers through the ministry of the Spirit of God. At the same time these symbols of exaltation and ascension helped to distinguish the resurrection of Jesus from other resurrections, like the resurrection of Lazarus. Jesus' resurrection was not a resuscitation. "For we know that Christ being raised from the dead will never die again; death no longer has dominion over him" (Rom. 6:9; contrast John 12:9f.). The earliest Christians therefore understood the resurrection of Jesus as exaltation or ascension into the presence of God: "This Jesus God raised up, and of that we are all witnesses. Being therefore exalted at the right hand of God, and having received from the father the promise of the Holy Spirit, he has poured out this which you see and hear" (Acts 2:32f.). For that reason in the appearance stories—except perhaps in the tradition behind Matthew 28:17, certainly, however in Matthew 28:18–20—Jesus appears to the disciples coming "from heaven".

The encounter with the risen Christ meant a radically new orientation of life. Jesus was right after all! His mission had not been a failure! God himself had validated it. The crisis of faith had given way to the creation of new faith. It needs to be said clearly: the appearances of Jesus are not the products of faith, but the necessary causes of faith! And the One who appeared to them—the crucified Christ—began to shape the content of the Easter faith.

It is quite possible that the quality and immediacy of their experience of the risen Christ could have made any reflection about the corpse and the tomb irrelevant and therefore unnecessary. It would then have been later, when the reality of the resurrection was questioned, opposed, and distorted, that the question of the fate of the body of Jesus in the tomb was raised.

Part III

RESPONSE

The Nature of Faith in the Risen Christ

Chapter 9

The Dialectic of Christian Knowing

Experience, Faith, Praxis

INTRODUCTION

Can one really understand the meaning of a dance—apart from dancing it? Can one really comprehend the ethos of a festival—apart from joining in its celebration? Can one really know the fascination of a football game—apart from playing it?[1]

It is not enough to remain spectators, if we really want to know what a dance, a festival, or a football game is all about. It is also not enough merely to know the rules of the game, the rhythm of the dance, or the procedures of the festival. It is not even enough to have the game explained to us or to talk about it. The inner *telos* of a game, a dance, or a festival, can only be known by participating in them!

It is true, of course, that the dance, the festival, and the game exist apart from the participants. We know their content and their rules. And yet the dance must be danced in order to become what it is. What is a game if it is not played, and what is a festival that is not celebrated? A dance that is not danced, a game that is not played, and a festival that is not celebrated are lost in the abyss of history. The dancer, the player, and the participant are necessary to make the dance, the game, and the festival what they are! The dancer does not create the Flamenco, but she is necessary to portray and to shape it. Similarly, only with players can the game become what it is, and a festival without participants would be a contradiction in terms.

The dance and the game and the festival are given! They become what they are when the dancers decide to dance, the players decide to play, and the people begin to celebrate. Their participation takes place within given parameters.

---

1. These introductory reflections are adopted from Hans-Georg Gadamer, *Truth and Method* (London: Sheed and Ward, 1975), pp. 91–119.

191

They follow certain rules. But within these parameters and rules they freely shape the game, interpret the dance, and celebrate the festival. Indeed the *telos* of the game, the dance, and the festival is fulfilled if the participants become so much a part of the proceedings that the dance, the game, and the festival take over and determine the existence of the participant. These preliminary thoughts lead us into the purpose of this chapter.

How can we know and understand the resurrection of Jesus Christ as an act of God? Can God and his acts be known at all? How can we appreciate an act of God, and at the same time protect God's identity, and God's difference from us? At the end of his book on the resurrection of Christ, Heinrich Schlier admits that theologically we know very little about the resurrection of Jesus Christ. He then concludes that we must make a renewed attempt to develop adequate categories that can lead us to the reality of the resurrection itself.[2] That task shall now demand our attention. In the previous part we asked what the earliest sources tell us about the event of the resurrection of Christ. Now we need to ask what kind and what form of knowledge is appropriate to that event.

This approach implies a procedure that is, as far as I can see, widely recognized in the fields of modern science, philosophy, and theology, namely, that the way of knowing must correspond to the object of inquiry. We therefore do not approach the object of our inquiry with a predetermined and universally accepted scientific method. Rather, we seek to discover the way of knowing that is appropriate to the object of our study, the resurrection of the crucified Christ. Our theological thinking therefore does not create reality, but it receives and interprets a given reality. We ask before we answer; we listen before we speak. Our inquiry, as does all scientific inquiry, takes place in a circular relationship between the object of our research and ourselves who are engaged in the research. Yet within that circle, priority must be ascribed to the object of inquiry. In that sense the object of inquiry must also be its determining subject. The interpreter is not master over the text, or the event, or the object, but rather its servant.

Nevertheless, no interpreter is neutral. None of us can be neutral, objective, and disinterested thinkers. Our desire and capacity to understand is not only determined by the object of our inquiry, but also by many other things. All knowledge is determined and shaped by interests. Theologians, like all other scientists, are influenced by their context: by their church tradition, by their cultural, political, and economic interests, by those who pay their salaries, by their personal needs, and so on. Only if this is freely admitted can we be aware of it, and as such try to preserve the integrity of the event even if it collides with our interests.

The priority of the event in the process of knowing, and the awareness of our self-interest set the agenda for the next two steps. In this chapter we shall ask what kind and what form of knowledge is appropriate to the event of the resurrection; and in the final part we shall summarize the content of that knowledge. In this chapter we shall let the event and its witnesses determine our way

---

2. Heinrich Schlier, *Über die Auferstehung Jesu Christi* (1968), pp. 70f.

of knowing, while in the final part we shall problematize our self-interest by focusing on the content of that knowledge.

Both our concerns receive a clear answer from the New Testament: the knowledge appropriate to the resurrection of Jesus Christ as an act of God is the knowledge of faith; and the content of that faith is Jesus Christ. What seems to be clear on the surface, however, becomes very controversial when one tries to spell out the details. What is faith? Who is Jesus Christ?

We proceed in this chapter by showing that faith is made possible by the word that brings the story of Jesus into our present. This presupposes that the resurrection of Jesus Christ is an "open event", calling for a language of promise. In the event of remembering, the word of promise reaches believers and shapes them into being witnesses. As witnesses they are partners with God in his work of salvation and liberation. Finally, we examine how the human response to the reality of the resurrection may be understood in three dimensions: *worship, praxis,* and *knowledge.*

FAITH

The earliest Christians confessed: "*we believe* that God raised Jesus from the dead." In Romans 6:9 (emphasis mine) Paul says: "For *we know* that Christ being raised from the dead will never die again; death no longer has dominion over him." This is the knowledge of faith, and it has soteriological significance: "if you confess with your lips that Jesus is Lord and *believe in your heart that God raised him from the dead, you will be saved*" (Rom 10:9, emphasis mine). The New Testament does not speak of any unbelievers witnessing to the resurrection. Those who were unbelievers before their encounter with the risen Christ—e.g., Paul, James, and possibly some or all of the "five hundred brethren"—became believers in that encounter.

The major creeds and confessions of the church continue to portray this interlocking of the resurrection and faith: "*I believe* in God. . . . And in Jesus Christ . . ., Who . . . on the third day rose again from the dead . . ." (Apostles' Creed); "*We believe* in one God. . . . And in one Lord Jesus Christ. . . . He suffered and the third day he rose, and ascended into heaven. . ." (Creed of Nicaea); "*We believe* in one God. . . . And in one Lord Jesus Christ. . . . He was crucified for us . . ., and suffered and was buried, and rose on the third day . . ." (Constantinopolitan Creed). Faith, therefore, appears to be a constitutive element of the resurrection event.[3] How then can we think of the resurrection of Jesus Christ and faith in him as one event?

---

3. Karl Rahner formulates it well: ". . . if the resurrection of Jesus is the permanent validity of his person and his cause, and if this person and cause together do not mean the survival of just any person and his history, but mean the *victoriousness* of his claim to be the absolute saviour, then *faith* in his resurrection is an intrinsic element of this resurrection itself. Faith is not taking cognizance of a fact which by its nature could exist

Our experience teaches us that there are realities that can only be grasped in the context of a personal trust and commitment. With my reason I can say objectively: "Jill is a woman." But with that statement I have not yet grasped who she *really* is. Her real being is in her relatedness to others and to the world around her. It surfaces in statements like: "Jill is my wife" (stating more than a legal fact), or "I trust my wife, Jill." Such statements transcend the intellectual and theoretical categories of knowledge. By their very nature these latter statements demand personal commitment. It is a knowledge in which all dimensions of my being and existence are involved. Real knowledge therefore does not distance the object from the inquirer by way of definition. Real knowledge does not try to rule over the object of knowing. Real knowledge tries to understand the object of inquiry on its own terms. It grants procedural priority to the object of inquiry.

Faith grants procedural priority to Jesus Christ. It recognizes that God has raised him from the dead by responding with ultimate concern and holistic commitment.[4] In this event of faith the resurrection reaches its immediate aim, and at the same time it opens the believer for its ultimate eschatological *telos* when God will be all in all. This is what the early Christians meant when they confessed Jesus as the "Messiah" ("Christ") and "Son of God". Through the resurrection Jesus had become for them the pioneer, the basis, and the content of their ultimate trust. We shall illustrate the holistic nature of faith and its relationship to the risen Christ with a brief reference to Paul's reasoning in 1 Corinthians 15.

---

just as well without being taken cognizance of. If the resurrection of Jesus is to be the eschatological victory of God's grace in the world, it cannot be understood without faith in it as something actually and freely arrived at, and it is only in this faith that its own essential being is fully realized." (*Foundations of the Christian Faith. An Introduction to the Idea of Christianity* [London: Darton, Longman & Todd, 1978], pp. 267f.).

4. It is not possible here to elaborate on the biblical understanding of faith. Suffice it to say that in the Old Testament faith means total reliance on God for one's present and future. In a situation of crisis Abram "believed" (relied on, trusted in) the Lord's promise (Gen 15:6); the prophet Isaiah makes the promise to the house of David (2 Sam 7:9b.16a) dependent on faith when he proclaims the word of the Lord to King Ahaz: "If you will not believe, surely you shall not be established" (Isa 7:9); in Isaiah 28:14–22 the prophet ascribes to the foundational stone that assures the security of the whole building the name: "He who believes will not be terrified." (Compare further: Hans Wildberger, " 'Glauben' im Alten Testament," *ZThK* 65 [1968], pp. 129–159; "Fest, sicher," in: *THAT* I [1971], cols. 177–209). Jesus did not call for faith in himself (Matthew 18:6 is an editorial interpretation of Mark 9:42), but he interpreted people's coming to him and relying—in his presence—*on God* as "faith". (Compare: Gerhard Ebeling, "Jesus and Faith," in: *Word and Faith* [Philadelphia: Fortress, 1963], pp. 201–246). The reality of Easter finds expression in the coining of new language— "faith *in Jesus Christ*"—which is dominant in the New Testament. (Compare: Hans-Jürgen Hermisson and Eduard Lohse, *Faith* [Nashville: Abingdon, 1981]; Dieter Lührmann, *Glaube im frühen Christentum* [Gütersloh: Mohn, 1976]; Egon Brandenberger, "Pistis und Soteria. Zum Verstehenshorizont von 'Glaube' im Urchristentum," *ZThK* 85 [1988], pp. 165–198).

There Paul insists that although we cannot separate the resurrection of Jesus from the faith of the believers, we need to distinguish between the two. He reminds his readers that the faith in which they stand (vv. 1f.) affirms the resurrection of Jesus Christ as an act of God (v. 4); this resurrection was confirmed by the appearances of the risen Christ (vv. 5–8); these appearances created a life-changing faith in those to whom they occurred; this faith led to preaching (v. 11); and preaching aims at the creation of new faith (v. 11). But the story of faith continues! It continues from the resurrection of Jesus, via the faith of the believers, to the future resurrection from the dead (vv. 13.15f.18), and to the fulfillment of God's purposes for the world (vv. 20–28). All of this, the preaching, the faith, and the hope, would be invalidated if Christ had not been raised from the dead (vv. 14.18).

Paul's whole argument therefore presupposes an essential interlocking of the life of the believer, the resurrection of Christ, and the future of the world. To question one of the links would break the whole chain. Thus Paul can argue that the faith of the church and the resurrection of Christ imply the future resurrection of the dead. The Corinthians who questioned this and claimed that they have already been raised with Christ are therefore questioning, according to Paul, the whole view of history that is implied in their faith in the risen Christ. It is important that the whole argument is carried on within the circle of word and faith (vv. 1f.). Paul wants to strengthen and to correct the faith of the believers in Corinth by insisting that one must distinguish between the resurrection of Jesus and our faith. The resurrection precedes our faith, although one cannot separate the two. If the resurrection were not preached and if it were not believed then it would not be the resurrection of Jesus Christ as an act of God. This holistic and Christ-centered nature of faith can be focused further by listing a number of distortions that are current in church and theology.[5]

There is first of all the individualistic distortion of faith. It is true, of course, that faith comes to individuals, and as such it is a personal reality. But faith does not individualize people. It takes place within the context of a community, and it calls and shapes people into a community of faith. More so: faith makes the believer and the community aware that the God who has become real to them as their redeemer, is in fact also the creator of heaven and earth, and the final fulfiller of his plans for the world and for history. Believers are woven into the fabric of society and nature to be witnesses to, and instruments of, the universal and holistic salvation that God has established in Jesus Christ (compare 2 Cor 5:18–20). The communal dimension of faith and its inherent responsibility for the society, for nature, and for the future, is therefore an essential aspect of faith.

---

5. Paul Tillich's excellent little book *Dynamics of Faith* (New York: Harper & Row, 1957) is very helpful in this connection, especially chapter II; also found in: Carl Heinz Ratschow, ed., *Paul Tillich: Main Works/Hauptwerke*, vol. 5 (Berlin/New York: De Gruyter, 1988), pp. 231–290.

Related to this is, secondly, the existential distortion of faith. In our second model (Part I, chapter 2) we met theologians who argued that the resurrection of Jesus Christ is identical with the birth of faith in the disciples. The focus would then not be on the resurrection of Jesus. It would either be on the faith of the believers, or it would be on the faith which Jesus had in God, to which he remained faithful even unto death, and which conveyed to the disciples the certainty that God can be trusted even unto death. However, this position tends to absolutize the existential consequences of resurrection faith. It does not adequately recognize the ground, basis, and content of faith in the risen Christ.

Here we must also mention, thirdly, the emotional distortion of faith. As a holistic reality faith has, of course, emotional elements and it is imperative for wide areas of Christianity to rediscover the emotional elements of faith. But faith includes a certainty of divine acceptance that transcends one's experiences of it, and it has a universal and eschatological thrust that may lead to actions and to sufferings which are no longer covered by the common use of the concept of "emotion".

There is, fourthly, the ecclesiastical distortion of faith. This happens when the church understands itself as the object or even the primary reference point of faith; when the church claims to be the continuation of the incarnation and consequently assumes divine attributes; when the legitimate concern for its identity becomes an end in itself and no longer serves the church's struggle for relevance; when the church denies freedom of conscience to its own members; and when the church claims divine election for itself and has forgotten that it is called to witness to God's election of his world and his creation. Resurrection faith has a universal and an eschatological thrust. It cannot be limited to the boundaries of the church. It aims to participate in God's saving passion for the world.

Then there is, as a fifth point, the intellectual distortion of faith. We saw that in contemporary theology there are those who say that the resurrection was an objective event in space and time and as such it is potentially recognizable and understandable to anyone who wants to research the historical evidence for it.[6] So much so, it is argued, that even the opponents of Jesus conceded his resurrection:

> ... the most technically qualified representatives of the foes of Jesus conceded that the tomb was empty and that they did not have the crucified body of Jesus. The officially appointed investigator and persecutor conceded that Jesus is alive in a resurrection body and named him the promised Messiah.[7]

---

6. Compare Part I, chapter 1 above.

7. Carl F. H. Henry, *God, Revelation and Authority*, vol. III: God Who Speaks and Shows, Fifteen Theses, Part II (1979), p. 162.

In this case the resurrection would be a historical fact which confronts us with the question as to whether we regard it as true or not. We should not question that there is indeed a cognitive dimension to faith. The whole enterprise of theology stands for that fact. Faith has a source, it has content, and it has an aim. All this can be investigated by reason. But faith itself is of a different order. It is grounded in the reality of the resurrection of Christ and it cannot be reduced to any intellectual affirmation about the resurrection.

As a sixth and final point we mention the moralistic distortion of faith. Faith in Christ implies a subsequent morality. If faith is a holistic and Christ-centered reality, then it must have content and thrust. Nevertheless, faith is not identical with its moral demands. Christian theology must never tire of elaborating the unconditional nature of God's grace and the priority of the resurrection of Jesus to our faith in him.

We conclude then, that the resurrection of Jesus Christ is not an event in and for itself. It aims at the creation of faith and the shaping of history. Only when this faith has been created, has the event become what it is. On the other hand, faith is not a human possibility. It is the human person's grateful and obedient response to God's action. In our faith, God's action reaches its goal; at the same time our faith presupposes God's action. The resurrection of Jesus Christ is therefore the basis for faith, and faith is a necessary element of the reality of the resurrection. Faith, however, is a difficult and widely misunderstood concept.[8] We shall therefore try to elaborate its genesis and its nature by gathering related biblical and theological concepts that are associated with the resurrection of Christ.

WORD

How does the reality of Jesus Christ come into the present, and as such provide the basis and content for faith in him? The biblical answer and the answer of Christian experience is: through the word. The word brings the story of Jesus into our human and historical reality and thereby creates the possibility for the event of faith. The apostle Paul identifies the "coming of faith" with the "coming of Christ" (Gal 3:23–26), and in Romans 10 he explains that this happens through the word: ". . . faith comes from what is heard, and what is heard comes by the preaching of Christ" (Rom 10:17; compare 2 Cor 4:5f.13f.).

---

8. Paul Tillich's "Introductory Remarks" to *Dynamics of Faith* (1957) deserve to be repeated: "There is hardly a word in the religious language . . . which is subject to more misunderstandings, distortions and questionable definitions than the word 'faith.' It belongs to those terms which need healing before they can be used for the healing of men. Today the term 'faith' is more productive of disease than of health. It confuses, misleads, creates alternately skepticism and fanaticism, intellectual resistance and emotional surrender, rejection of genuine religion and subjection to substitutes." (p. ix; also in: Ratschow, ed., *Paul Tillich: Main Works/Hauptwerke*, vol. 5 [1988], p. 231).

The word performs what it promises. It may be helpful to recall here a distinction that the British philosopher John L. Austin makes between performative and constative utterances.[9] A constative utterance refers to an event that has already taken place; it is there apart from the utterance; the utterance informs about the event. Applied to our discussion it may, for instance, state that the tomb into which the dead body of Jesus had been laid was empty; we only need to be informed about it. Preaching would then be the imparting of the information that God has raised the dead Jesus out of the tomb. Faith would mean accepting this information as true.

A performative utterance, on the other hand, does not merely point to or inform about an event that has occurred in the past, but it "performs" an event as the spoken word modifies the situation. The event is not dissolved into the utterance, but the utterance is a constitutive part of the event of which it speaks. The event remains incomplete without the utterance. This is probably what Paul meant when in 2 Corinthians 5:18–20 he maintains that God has called forth both the event of reconciliation and the ministry of reconciliation. And because both belong together, Paul can say that God makes his appeal through us. It means that God is effectively present in the "ministry of reconciliation". Hearers of the gospel are not simply informed about what happened in the past, but the story comes to them with an existential claim upon their life.[10]

The word evokes an experience that we call the experience of faith. This experience has rich content and a variety of dimensions. It contains the historical knowledge that allows faith to measure itself and to ask whether it is in continuity with Jesus. It contains the impulse for worship and for praxis. Yet before we come to that, we shall try to understand more clearly the interrelationship between the resurrection of Jesus Christ, the faith of the believer and the believing community, and the future of the world.

PROMISE

This essential interlocking between the resurrection of Jesus and the future of the world will become a little clearer when we recognize that the resurrection is an *open event*—open to the future, seeking to create faith, and through it to shape history, and thus to determine the future.

The openness of the resurrection toward the future finds expression in the careful wording of one of the oldest confessional formulas in 1 Corinthians

9. J. L. Austin, *How to Do Things with Words*. The William James Lectures delivered at Harvard University in 1955 (Cambridge, Mass: Harvard University Press, 1962). Austin does emphasize, however, that it is often difficult to distinguish clearly between the two.

10. J. L. Austin may have had something like this in mind when he says: ". . . the performative is happy or unhappy as opposed to true or false" (ibid., p. 132).

15:3–5: "Christ died [aorist tense] . . . he was buried [aorist tense] . . . he has been raised [perfect tense] . . . he appeared [aorist tense] . . . ." The use of the perfect tense to describe the resurrection stands out. It is intentionally used to delimit the resurrection of Jesus Christ from his death, his burial, and his appearances. It is used to underline the "continuing effect"[11] of the event of resurrection. The openness of the resurrection event seeks the corresponding remembrance of faith in order to re-present the event thus making it real in the present and to determine the future.

Indeed, to confess an event as an "act of God" is to claim that it has *significance* not only for times past, but for the situation "here and now" and for the future. This *significance* must find expression in the way we respond to such an event; it must influence and shape our *way of knowing*. It is obvious, for instance, that an uninvolved, impartial, objective, and neutral description of a past event, a description that makes no difference to the one who makes it, would be an inadequate way to respond to the resurrection of Jesus Christ as an "act of God".[12] We continue to ask therefore: what categories are available to develop a way of knowing that is adequate to the resurrection of Jesus Christ as an "open event"?

Here we must recall the biblical-theological concept of "promise" which has been given the prominence it deserves by Jürgen Moltmann.[13] Jürgen Moltmann understands a promise to be a "language event" of a special kind:

---

11. F. Blass and A. Debrunner, *A Greek Grammar of the New Testament and Other Early Christian Literature*. Trans. and ed. by Robert W. Funk (Chicago: Chicago University Press, 1961), p. 176 (§ 342).

12. Karl Barth emphasizes, for instance, that the activity of God "kann ja als vollzogen gar nicht anders als in seinem *tätigen Nachvollzug* erkannt werden" (*Kirchliche Dogmatik* IV/1 [1953], p. 111, [emphasis mine]; the English translation is inadequate at this point). The same idea is contained in the subsequent sentences: "God is not idle but active. . . . therefore, man must be active too." (*Church Dogmatics* IV/1 [1956], p. 103). Compare the whole section *Church Dogmatics* IV/1, pp. 103–122, which contains helpful insights for our discussion. Barth emphasizes the openness of the established reality of reconciliation in the context of which the believer as God's partner anticipates with concrete activity the coming of the kingdom of God.

13. Compare especially: Jürgen Moltmann, *Theology of Hope. On the Ground and the Implication of a Christian Eschatology* (London: SCM, 1967). Important in this context, is the input of Old Testament studies, for instance: Walther Zimmerli, "Promise and Fulfillment" (1952), in: Claus Westermann, ed. *Essays on Old Testament Hermeneutics*. English translation ed. by James Luther Mays (London: SCM, Atlanta: John Knox Press, 1963), pp. 89–122; Walther Zimmerli, *Old Testament Theology in Outline* (Atlanta: John Knox Press, 1978), e.g. pp. 27–32; Claus Westermann, "The Way of Promise through the Old Testament" (1963), in: Bernhard W. Anderson, ed.. *The Old Testament and Christian Faith. A Theological Discussion* (New York: Harper & Row, 1963), pp. 200–224. Compare further: Christopher Morse, *The Logic of Promise in Moltmann's Theology* (Philadelphia: Fortress, 1979), who also discusses the relationship of this concept to the linguistic philosophy of J. L. Austin, Donald Evans, and John Searle (pp. 67–75).

it remembers, and as such preserves history, and at the same time it aims at the concrete historical actualization of this promise in the shaping of the future.[14] This suggestion is helpful. It can guide us in avoiding possible distortions as we try to think of the reality of the resurrection in its effect upon history. It prevents us from "freezing" the resurrection into a past event, and thereby relativizing its ongoing, dynamic effect on history. It also helps us not locate the resurrection as an event of revelation exclusively in the word of preaching or in the experience of the believer and the believing community, and thereby relativizing the importance of history. The resurrection of Jesus Christ, therefore, calls for a way of knowing that avoids the extremes of a historical positivism, of hermeneutical theology, and of historical existentialism. Historical positivism tends to absolutize the past by "freezing" an event into its so-called objective past. The emphasis is on what really happened, and the response is a theoretical affirmation or denial of that fact. Hermeneutical theology locates revelation in the "word" ("word event", "language event").[15] This is helpful because it recognizes the "performative" and "sacramental" dimension of the "word". It appreciates that the "word" is more than information about a past event. But, at the same time, it remains unclear about the truth and the reality which language brings to expression, and it fails to do justice to the historical manifestations of the resurrection. Historical existentialism tends to absolutize the present by being primarily interested in the effect of an event on the present existence of the inquirers and their life-situation.

The resurrection of Jesus Christ forces us to find a way of explanation in which the event and its effect upon us and our world are interrelated. This is because the resurrection of Jesus Christ aims at changing human existence and affecting history. This change of human existence has its theological basis in the resurrection, and it acquires its content from the One who was raised from the dead. Both belong together, with a procedural priority for the resurrection of Jesus Christ over its life-changing and history-changing effects. This "procedural priority" of Christ over his effects on history and on humanity is important, because as human beings, whose perception of reality is distorted by our self-interest, we cannot know God and his activity in the world by ourselves, and we therefore cannot adequately respond to him out of our own

---

14. Jürgen Moltmann, "Verkündigung als Problem der Exegese," (1963) in: *Perspektiven der Theologie. Gesammelte Aufsätze* (München: Kaiser, 1968, pp. 113–127), p. 126: "Eine Verheissung ist ein 'Sprachereignis', aber ein solches, das Geschichte erinnernd aufbewahrt und das auf die zukünftige Wirklichkeit geschichtlicher Erfüllung hinzielt."

15. "Word event" is the concept Gerhard Ebeling prefers, while Ernst Fuchs generally speaks of "language event": e.g., Gerhard Ebeling, "Word of God and Hermeneutics," (1959), in: *Word and Faith* (Philadelphia: Fortress, 1963, pp. 305–332), pp. 326–328; Ernst Fuchs, "What is a 'Language-event'. A Letter," (1960), and "The Essence of the 'Language-event' and Christology," (1962), both in: *Studies of the Historical Jesus* (Naperville,: Allenson, 1964), pp. 207–212 and pp. 213–228.

resources. Christians therefore speak of revelation as the basis for authentic experience and responsible talk of God. But revelation must be understood in terms of promise in order to preserve the "open" nature of an act of God. This understanding of revelation/resurrection as promise relies heavily on some Old Testament insights.

In the Exodus narrative, for instance, God, who calls Moses to participate in liberating the people of Israel from slavery, introduces himself as אֶהְיֶה אֲשֶׁר אֶהְיֶה ['ehyeh 'ăšer 'ehyeh] = imperfect of הָיָה (hāyâ) "to be", Exod 3:14]. This self-revelation of God is difficult to render into English, because, unlike the English language, Hebrew does not have past, present, and future tenses. In Hebrew the verb describes an action which is either completed in the past (perfect) or incomplete (imperfect). Applied to the above sentence, God is described as an "open" reality. Perhaps the best translation would be: "I am the One who I will show myself to be in your ongoing history."[16] The self-introduction is therefore immediately followed by the promise: ". . . I promise that I will bring you up out of the affliction of Egypt" (Exod 3:17).[17] This promise is not arbitrary. It is grounded in God's nature, and it relates God's passion to the situation: "Then the Lord said, 'I have seen the affliction of my people who are in Egypt, and have heard their cry because of their taskmasters; I know their sufferings, and I have come down to deliver them out of the hand of the Egyptians, and to bring them up out of that land to a good and broad land, . . .'" (Exod 3:7f.).

To know this God, does not call for a theoretical affirmation of his existence. Such an existence is presupposed. To know this God, would mean believing him by tuning into his promise and thus joining him in shaping history as a story of liberation for Israel.

The God who introduces himself in this way to Moses is, according to Exodus 3:6, the God of Abraham, Isaac, and Jacob. Thereby a link is established from the Exodus tradition to the patriarchal narratives in which a similar understanding of God and his relationship to history emerges.

We recall the promise of God to Abraham in Genesis 12:1–4a. The divine imperative to "go from your country" is grounded in the promise that "I will make you a great nation, and I will bless you, and make your name great, so that you will be a blessing. . . ." Abraham risks his life by tuning into the promise:

---

16. The Septuagint translates this as ἐγώ εἰμι ὁ ὤν (egō eimi ho ōn). Here a Hebrew verb (imperfect, denoting incomplete action) is made into a Greek participial noun. This has often been interpreted as a move from historical thinking to a metaphysical ontology in which God is perceived in terms of transcendence, separation from the world, and non-involvement with history. Such a change in emphasis may have been implied in the Greek world view of that time, but it should not lead to a rejection of ontology altogether. The challenge is not to reject and replace ontology, but to reshape it in a way that it takes history seriously.

17. This is, of course, a common motif in Old Testament thinking, compare: Exod 20:2f.; Deut 5:6f.; Hos 13:4.

"So Abram went, as the Lord had told him." The text makes clear that the proper response to the promise is not a theoretical acceptance that the promise is true, but the concrete dependence with one's own life and future on the reliability of that promise. The promise becomes history and begins to shape history in that people believe it, and allow their lives to be shaped by it. The promise and the blessing of God have a concrete thrust (promise of land, promise of descendants, promise of becoming a blessing to others), and the response to such a promise must also be concrete.[18]

When the apostle Paul confesses that in Jesus Christ, God has fulfilled his promises he says: "For all promises of God find their Yes in him." (2 Cor 1:20). Thereby Jesus Christ is confessed to be, not the end, but the center of history. In Christ God has spelled out his aim for his creation. This promise is being realized when people in faith and discipleship let their lives be shaped by faith in Jesus Christ.

These biblical allusions have paved the way for gathering the major elements that make the concept of promise so important for understanding the reality of the resurrection.

The Christian understanding of God affirms, first of all, that God realizes his aims for humanity and for the world in history. In the process of evolution in nature and history, God provides ever new possibilities that can be actualized to become concrete historical events by human willing and doing. The resurrection of the crucified Christ is an event that affects history, but its reality is not dissolved into a particular historical time and situation. It transcends the situation which it modifies. It affects history again and again as it

---

18. In the ongoing history of Israel the liberation from slavery and the promises to Abraham were told, remembered, and celebrated again and again. As such they provide the basis for trusting in God for one's future. In Genesis 15 Abraham is promised his own son and descendants (Gen 15:1–6), and a land in which to dwell (Gen 15:7–21). Like Abraham, every generation is asked to believe the Lord (Gen 15:6) by leaning into the promises, claiming them for shaping one's life and future. Genesis 46:1–5a tells the story of the aging Jacob who wants to go to Egypt to visit his son Joseph. He hears the promises of God: "I am God, the God of your father; do not be afraid to go down to Egypt; for I will there make you a great nation. I will go down with you to Egypt, and I will also bring you up again;. . . ." (Gen 46:3f.); and in response to these promises "Jacob set out". In Isaiah 43:1–3a the prophet reflects the same understanding of God, of his acts, and of human response. God is introduced as the creator—"he who created you, O Jacob, he who formed you, O Israel"—whereby this creating activity of God does not merely refer to a one time event in the past. It marks the continuing activity of God for the welfare of his people. Then comes the *Heilszusage* composed in the perfect tense, indicating a completed action: "Fear not, for I have redeemed you; I have called you by name, you are mine." This *Heilszusage* is followed by the promise (imperfect, indicating an incomplete action): "When you pass through the waters I will be with you; and through the rivers, they shall not overwhelm you; when you walk through fire you shall not be burned, and the flame shall not consume you." The Godhood of God—"I am the Lord your God, the Holy One of Israel, your Savior"—is experienced in history when people let their lives be shaped by those promises.

is "remembered", or better, as it is brought into the memory of people to shape their present and their future.[19]

Secondly, the fact that God as creator and redeemer wants to realize his aims concretely in history does not mean that historical acts or events on their own are the medium of God's revelation. The biblical message speaks of the correlation of an event with words and deeds that witness to it. What Walther Zimmerli says about the Exodus tradition is true for the biblical message as a whole:

> In the confession of 'Yahweh, the God of Israel since Egypt,' Israel's faith receives an intimate association with a historical event. . . . Having said this, we must still avoid the mistaken assumption that for Israel history as such became the revelatory word of Yahweh. Such an understanding of history as a phenomenon in its own right, to be taken as an independent quantity in God's revelation, is alien to the Old Testament. By the same token, an isolated fact of history is not as such simply a proclamation of Yahweh. . . . Thus we must also remember in retrospect that the 'deliverance from Egypt' was also accompanied by Yahweh's word.[20]

---

19. Jürgen Moltmann, referring to the Old Testament scholars Gerhard von Rad and Hans Walter Wolff, says : ". . . if events are thus experienced within the horizon of remembered and expected promises, then they are experienced as truly 'historic' events. They do not then have only the accidental, individual and relative character which we normally ascribed to historic events, but then they have always at the same time also an unfinished and provisional character that points forwards. Not only words of promise, but also the events themselves, in so far as they are experienced as 'historic' events within the horizon of promise and hope, bear the mask of something that is still outstanding, not yet finalized, not yet realized." (*Theology of Hope* [1967], p. 107). "Hence the events that are 'historically' remembered in this way do not yet have their ultimate truth in themselves, but receive it only from the goal that has been promised by God and is to be expected from him." (Ibid., p. 108). "It could perhaps be said that the promises enter into fulfilment in events, yet are not completely resolved in any event, but there remains an overspill that points to the future." (Ibid., p. 109). Moltmann applies this insight to the understanding of the resurrection: "The Christ-event of the resurrection is 'historical' in so far as it creates history by opening up a new future. From this event of the past, which is still in no way a past event, the present is revealed for the future as the time of hope. Theological knowledge of the truth develops from the observation of this once and for all event and can only note the significance of this event by grasping the horizon of the future which is projected and announced by this event. Theological knowledge of truth may also be designated as historical; here it anticipates at the same time a universal future." ("Theology in the World of Modern Science," [1966], in: *Hope and Planning* [New York: Harper & Row, 1971, pp. 200–223], p. 215).

20. *Old Testament Theology in Outline* (1978), pp. 24f. The same point is made by Gerhard von Rad when he insists that Israel's experience of the guidance of God in history includes the deed and the word of God: *God at Work in Israel* (Nashville: Abingdon, 1980), chs. 14 and 15, pp. 139–175; "Offene Fragen im Umkreis einer Theologie des Alten Testaments," *ThLZ* 88 (1963, pp. 401–416), pp. 406–414.

We note, thirdly, that God's concrete action in history is aimed at healing and sustaining the wholeness of human life in all its manifold relationships. As creator of heaven and earth God wants to save and liberate his creation from oppression and estrangement. What Walther Zimmerli says about Old Testament faith is also important for the Christian understanding of reality:

> The event that bears significance for the beginning of 'Israel's' faith in Yahweh has from the outset a political dimension. The beginning does not consist in the illumination of a single individual who then assembles other individuals around him, like Buddha, but in the deliverance experienced by a cohesive group. This political dimension, relating to a people defined in secular terms, will subsequently remain a hallmark of Yahwism. The individual is not forgotten and individual responsibility is increasingly stressed as time goes on, but it remains clear even in the late statements of the book of Daniel that individuals are not isolated from the people of Yahweh as a whole, nor can they take refuge in a special relationship with their God such as might remove them from the concrete events of the 'secular' world.[21]

Fourthly, since it is *God* who acts in history, our knowing and our acting should not be limited to what *we* can and do experience or what *we* consider to be possible or not. History has a goal towards which it is moving. The content of this goal is declared in Jesus Christ. He, therefore, provides the basis for our faith and hope. Faith is not the static acceptance of certain theological truths, but it is the dynamic participation in God's liberating process in his creation. The Christian's identity does not consist in affirming certain truths about God, but in being a pilgrim of the soft revolution which God has begun with the life, death, and resurrection of Jesus Christ. As Moltmann correctly observes: "The theologian is not concerned merely to supply a different interpretation of the world, of history and of human nature, but to *transform* them in expectation of a divine transformation."[22] History is therefore an open, though not an arbitrary process.

---

21. *Old Testament Theology in Outline* (1978), pp. 25f.

22. *Theology of Hope* (1967), p. 84. Again, the words by Walther Zimmerli are helpful: "Anyone who speaks of promise and fulfillment knows of veiled purposes and distressed waiting; he knows of walking, and not only of standing still; he knows of summoning, and not only of looking on. History receives a declivity (*Gefälle*) toward that which is yet to come. But this is not merely a declivity determined by empty motivating powers, but one which stands illuminated by clear words." ("Promise and Fulfillment," [1952], p. 97). And Moltmann applies this to our understanding of revelation: "The decisive question is, whether 'revelation' is the illuminating interpretation of an existing, obscure life process in history, or whether revelation itself originates, drives and directs the process of history; whether consequently, as Barth has asked, revelation is a predicate of history, or whether history has to be understood as a predicate of the eschatological revelation and to be experienced, expected and obediently willed as such." (*Theology of Hope* [1967], pp. 75f., compare pp. 103f. [§§ a and f]).

The above observations about the nature of history and God's relationship to it, must lead us, as a fifth point, to the question how we as human beings can appropriately respond to such a historical event. How does such an event arrive in our life and qualify our existence? The concept of promise reminds us that a historical event, which we qualify as an act of God, cannot be properly understood by merely making a theoretical affirmation that the event has happened in the past; nor is it sufficient to experience the subjective, existential, or psychological significance of such an event for our life. Beyond this objective-intellectual and subjective-existential knowledge we need to affirm the event with our life. We affirm such an event as true by tuning our life into the history which that event is creating and shaping. This is the knowledge of the praxis of discipleship, not of theory. To be unwilling to engage in such discipleship is to question the truth and reliability of the event. The believer is called to responsibility and to covenantal partnership. This we do in the conviction of faith that the God who has shaped the event will be faithful to his own promises. Jürgen Moltmann says correctly that knowledge of God

> . . . must be a knowledge that does not merely reflect past history . . . but it must be an interested knowledge, a practical knowledge, a knowledge that is upheld by confidence in the promised faithfulness of God. . . . Knowledge of God is then an anticipatory knowledge of the future of God, a knowledge of the faithfulness of God which is upheld by the hopes that are called to life by his promises. Knowledge of God is then a knowledge that draws us onwards—not upwards—into situations that are not yet finalized but still outstanding.[23]

This brings us to the next, the sixth, emphasis. The promise, arising from historical events which the believing community confesses to be acts of God, is not arbitrary. It is grounded in God's manifest faithfulness to his creation. The covenants in the Old Testament and the New Covenant in Jesus Christ are the Judeo-Christian symbols confessing the conviction of faith—that in spite of human faithlessness, God remains faithful; in spite of human godlessness, God remains in unconditional love committed to his creation; in spite of human

---

23. *Theology of Hope* (1967), p. 118. Compare also: "Hence the form in which Christian theology speaks of Christ cannot be the form of the Greek *logos* or of doctrinal statements based on experience, but only the form of statements of hope and of promises for the future. All predicates of Christ not only say who he was and is, but imply statements as to who he will be and what is to be expected from him. They all say: 'He is our hope' (Col. 1:27). In thus announcing his future in the world in terms of promise, they point believers in him towards the hope of his still outstanding future." (Ibid., p. 17). And again: "Theological knowledge of the coming truth of the whole becomes aware of its own temporality in the Christ event. It does not therefore have a supernatural character, but has the character of a reminiscent knowledge of hope." ("Theology in the World of Modern Science," [1966], p. 215).

estrangement, God sustains his Godhood by continually providing new possibilities which can be actualized by human beings. The God, the one who created new life out of the ambiguity of the cross, can in all times create new life out of the rubble of history.[24]

Finally, we mention the critical thrust that is implied in the concept of promise. When God is thought of in terms of metaphysical transcendence, the danger has always been that the word "God" was functionalized to validate those political, social, and economic institutions—for instance: democracy, monogamy, capitalism—that are deeply entrenched in a particular society or culture. Against such a misunderstanding of God, it needs to be emphasized that God can, and God does, create new realities, and that God wants to move human society into a new and different future. Revelation therefore does not validate the status quo but provides the content and motivation towards a more humane understanding of human life and society.[25]

The concept of promise, then, is an important reminder to understand the resurrection of Christ as an "open", purposive, and dynamic event that wants to shape and prod history in anticipation of the kingdom of God. Believers correspond to such a purposeful and dynamic event by letting this promise shape their existence.

REMEMBERING

How does the resurrection of Christ as the resurrection of the crucified One become effective in the ongoing historical process? How does the reality of the resurrection arrive in the present? What mode of knowledge corresponds to the resurrection as an "open" event? How does the risen Christ create and sustain

---

24. Jürgen Moltmann comments: "Between this once-for-all validation [*In-kraft-Setzung*] of the promise and its fulfilment in the glory of God there stands only the dependability [*Zuverlässigkeit*] of God himself." (*Theology of Hope* [1967], p. 147). Compare also: Ibid., pp. 116f.; Zimmerli, "Promise and Fulfillment," (1952), pp. 95, 121; *Old Testament Theology in Outline* (1978), pp. 174–182.

25. The dominant theme of Moltmann's *Theology of Hope* (1967) is his distinction between an understanding of revelation as an epiphany of the eternal presence which he considers to be of Greek origin, and which he rejects as being unbiblical, and a revelation of the promised future which he sees expressed in the biblical message. He prefers the latter because it contains the critical and therefore constructive elements of faith (compare for instance: pp. 28f., 40f., 42f., 95–112, 141, 143f., 154–165). Moltmann says: "Hope's statements of promise, however, must stand in contradiction to the reality which can at present be experienced. They do not result from experiences, but are the condition for the possibility of new experiences. They do not seek to illuminate the reality which exists, but the reality which is coming." (Ibid., p. 18). "If the word is a word of promise, then that means that this word has not yet found a reality congruous with it, but that on the contrary it stands in contradiction to the reality open to experience now and heretofore." (Ibid., p. 103). Compare further: Christopher Morse, *The Logic of Promise in Moltmann's Theology* (1979), pp. 31–36.

faith now? The traditional answer to this question is: the story of Jesus—the Word—through the ministry of the Holy Spirit creates faith in the life of the believer. That is certainly correct, as both the biblical traditions (e.g., Rom 10:17; John 5:24) and our experience confirm.

The early Christians clarified this further by referring to the remembering activity of faith: in the memory of the believer and of the Christian community Christ is present as Lord. In the post-Pauline tradition the act of remembering is therefore brought into correlation with the resurrection of Christ and the preaching of the gospel: "Remember Jesus Christ, risen from the dead,. . . as preached in my gospel . . ." (2 Tim 2:8). Between the remembered past and the anticipated future there stands the remembering present in which the past event is actualized and thereby effectively influences the shaping of the future.

"Remembering" is more than the psychological calling to mind of a past event and of a person who had lived in the past. "Remembering" can be the actualization (*Vergegenwärtigung*) of an event or a person in such a way that the remembered reality decisively qualifies the present situation and determines the future.

When, for instance, the church celebrates the Lord's Supper "in remembrance" of Jesus Christ (1 Cor 11:24f.; Luke 22:19), it does not merely look back to a person (Jesus) and to events in the past (his life, death, and resurrection). Rather, the church celebrates the Lord's Supper in the expectation that in the worshipping community the crucified[26] Christ himself is present as host, and that his presence will determine their future "until he comes" (1 Cor 11:26; compare Mark 14:25, par. Matt 26:29). In this celebration of its identity the church confesses that "Jesus Christ is the same yesterday and today and for ever" (Heb 13:8).[27] The church remembers the past and the future of the crucified Christ and thereby experiences the presence as consolation and challenge.

In the Johannine Farewell Discourses (John 14–16) explicit reference is made to the ministry of the Holy Spirit. Jesus says to his disciples: ". . . the παράκλητος (paraklētos), the Holy Spirit, whom the Father will send in my name, he will teach you all things, and bring to your remembrance all that I have said to you" (14:26). This means that the church in the situation after Easter continues to experience the presence of Christ through the ministry of the Spirit, who brings Christ into the remembrance of the Christians and the Christian community.

---

26. The Lord's Supper tradition in 1 Corinthians 11:23ff. obviously wants to emphasize that the celebration of the presence of Christ is grounded in the passion story of Jesus: ". . . the Lord Jesus on the night when he was betrayed took bread . . ." (v. 23).

27. The gospel narratives draw a close relationship between the celebration of the Lord's Supper and the actualization of the resurrection-reality: in Luke 24:13-35 the Lord's Supper terminology is used to show that while being "at table with them . . . their eyes were opened" (vv. 30f.); the same is true for the meal motif in the resurrection story in John 21:9–13.

We may therefore say that by remembering, an event of the past can be brought into the present so that it then interprets, qualifies, and changes the present, and opens new vistas for the future. Such an understanding has a long history in the theology of remembering in a number of Old Testament traditions (for instance the Deuteronomist, Deutero-Isaiah, Ezekiel, and the Psalms).[28] Brevard Childs speaks of "the dynamic quality of an historical event" and he continues:

> It [the historical event] enters the world of time and space at a given mo-
> ment, yet causes a continued reverberation beyond its original entry. The
> biblical events can never become static, lifeless beads which can be strung
> on a chronological chain. In direct analogy to the "history-creating" Word
> of God, the redemptive events of Israel's history do not come to rest, but
> continue to meet and are contemporary with each new generation. . . . It
> means more than that the influence of a past event continued to be felt in
> successive generations . . . Rather, there was an immediate encounter, an
> actual participation in the great acts of redemption . . . Actualization is
> the process by which a past event is contemporized for a generation re-
> moved in time and space from the original event. When later Israel re-
> sponded to the continuing imperative of her tradition through her memory,
> that moment in historical time likewise became an Exodus experience.
> Not in the sense that later Israel again crossed the Red Sea. This was an
> irreversible, once-for-all event. Rather, Israel entered the same redemp-
> tive reality of the Exodus generation.[29]

The early church tuned into this tradition by expecting God through the ministry of his Spirit to bring the resources of the risen Christ into their present experience to evaluate, interpret, and modify their situation.[30] The content of what is remembered and how this is related to the reflections and actions of the believer and the community of faith will be the focus of our discussion in the final part. Nevertheless, remembering changes us, and since as Christians we remember the resurrection of the crucified Christ, therefore it is a "dangerous

---

28. Compare especially: Brevard S. Childs, *Memory and Tradition in Israel.* Studies in Biblical Theology (London: SCM, 1962); Willy Schottroff, *"Gedenken" im Alten Orient und im Alten Testament. Die Wurzel ZAKAR im semitischen Sprachkreis.* WMANT 15 (Neukirchen-Vluyn: Neukirchener Verlag, 1964). Shorter studies can be found in: *NIDNT* 3 (1978), pp. 230–247 (K. H. Bartels and C. Brown); *ThWAT* 2 (1977), pp. 571–593 (Eising).

29. Brevard Childs, *Memory and Tradition in Israel* (1962), pp. 84f.

30. Contemporary theologians ascribing importance to this dimension include John Knox (compare our discussion, pp. 47–49 above; Karl Barth (*CD* I/2 [1956], pp. 53f., 101–121; CD III/2 [1960], pp. 442, 469f.): Richard R. Niebuhr (*Resurrection and Historical Reason. A Study of Theological Method* [1957], pp. 96–100); Johann Baptist Metz (*Faith in History and Society. Toward a Practical Fundamental Theology* [London: Burns and Oates, 1980], chapts. 6, 11–13); and Peter Carnley (*The Structure of Resurrection Belief* [1987], chapts. VII and VIII).

memory"[31] which makes us to critically interpret our life and our context in light of the story of Jesus.

WITNESS

This brings us to retrieve an important biblical-theological category that is often overlooked in theological discussions that deal with the interpretation of the resurrection of Christ. When the early Christians reflected about the manner in which an act of God is received and understood they did not only think in terms of the word, the kerygma, and of "remembering", as the "bearer" and "receiver" of the Christian message, but they spoke primarily in terms of "witness" and "testimony". This word group is found in major biblical traditions, it is used in philosophical and hermeneutical discussions, and it has also been adopted in theological reflections.[32]

Protestant theology with its emphasis on the "word" or the "word and the sacraments" as the main carriers of the gospel, and Roman Catholic theology with its emphasis on the church and the eucharist as the sacraments of God's grace, can easily lead to an individualistic or an ecclesiastical reduction of the power of the gospel. Both the credibility crisis which the churches face today and respect for the biblical traditions call for a change of emphasis. In the New Testament the word group "witness/testimony" is at least as prominent as the word group associated with "word", "proclaiming the gospel", and "kerygma".

When we reflect about our human experience in and with history, it will become immediately evident that an event needs a testimony in order to survive. Without a testimony the event sinks back into the abyss of history; it is lost as far as we are concerned. An event that is not testified to in some way cannot be remembered. It cannot affect the ongoing historical process. It will disappear.

A testimony, on the other hand, needs to derive its content from somewhere and it needs to be carried by someone. It is and remains dependent on the event to which it testifies, and it calls for witnesses who communicate it, and who with their existence are responsible for the accuracy of the testimony. If a witness distorts the testimony then the very event is distorted and it does not arrive in the present as the event that it is.

---

31. This helpful concept is adopted from Johann Baptist Metz: *Faith in History and Society. Toward a Practical Fundamental Theology* (1980), chaps. 6 (e.g. pp. 109f.), 11 (e.g. pp. 184f.), and the "Excursus: Dogma as a dangerous memory" (pp. 200–204).

32. Compare for instance: Allison A. Trites, *The New Testament Concept of Witness* (Cambridge: University Press, 1977); Paul Ricoeur, "The Hermeneutics of Testimony," (1972), in: Paul Ricoeur, *Essays on Biblical Interpretation*. Ed. with an introduction by Lewis S. Mudge (Philadelphia: Fortress, 1980), pp. 119–154; Klaus Kienzler, *Logik der Auferstehung. Eine Untersuchung zu Rudolf Bultmann, Gerhard Ebeling und Wolfhart Pannenberg* (Freiburg: Herder, 1976); Francis Schüssler Fiorenza, *Foundational Theology: Jesus and the Church* (New York: Crossroad, 1986), chaps. 1, 2 and 11.

The event, the testimony, and the witness are interrelated. They need each other. An event without a testimony and without a witness is lost. A testimony lives from the event, and it is empty apart from the event. The event therefore has priority over the testimony and the witness. A testimony needs a witness to communicate it. And the witness needs the testimony and the event to be a witness, and yet at the same time the witness is not identical with that to which he or she witnesses. Event, testimony, and witness are essentially interlocked. It is therefore not surprising that the concept of "witness" plays an important role in a number of biblical traditions.[33] Here is not the place to discuss the different theologies of "witness" in the Bible. A few illustrations must suffice to underline the importance of "witness" in the process of tradition and communication.

In Deutero Isaiah we witness a legal dispute of YHWH with other deities (the so-called "*rîb-pattern*"). YHWH calls upon Israel, whom he has chosen, to be his witness: "you are my witnesses!" (see mainly Isaiah 43:8–13, 44:6–11). At stake is the Godhood of God, the reality of his love for his people, and the effectiveness of his saving power (43:11–13, 44:6.8, 46:5.9). Is God really God? In a situation of conflict it is the function of witnesses to let their existence become an analogy to the being of God, so that in the public arena (43:9) the witnesses make transparent the fact that God can and does save and liberate. By tuning into this call of God the witnesses "know", "understand", and "believe" (43:10), and as such they show by their very existence that the idols and those who make them "are nothing" (44:9). When a person or, as in this case, a nation, accepts the role of being a witness, it must be ready to enter the dispute between God and the gods; but at the same time the witness is motivated and sustained by confidence and hope in the promises of the God who says: "I have spoken, and I will bring it to pass; I have purposed, and I will do it" (46:11).

In the New Testament it is mainly Luke (the Gospel and the Book of Acts) and John who develop a "theology of witness", and Luke relates this "theology of witness" specifically to the resurrection of Jesus Christ.[34] Although Luke can use "witness" in an everyday and juridical sense (Luke 18:20; Acts 6:13, 7:58,

---

33. For a survey of relevant texts see: H. Strathmann, "μάρτυς κτλ.," (martus ktl.) *TDNT* IV (1967 [1942]), pp. 474–514; L. Coenen, A. A. Trites, "Witness, Testimony," *NIDNT* 3 (1978), pp. 1038–1051; Allison A. Trites, *The New Testament Concept of Witness* (1977). The original setting of "testimony" and "witness" in Israelite history was the law court or the legal dispute, which was carried out at the town gate. There accuser and accused would present their witnesses. The elders would hear the evidence and after wise deliberations announce their verdict. But the theological use of "testimony" and "witness" transcends this original setting.

34. Compare: Paul Ricoeur, "The Hermeneutics of Testimony," (1972), pp. 134–136; Klaus Kienzler, *Logik der Auferstehung* (1976), pp. 202–218; Ulrich Wilckens, *Die Missionsreden der Apostelgeschichte. Form- und traditionsgeschichtliche Untersuchungen.* WMANT 5. (Neukirchen-Vluyn: Neukirchener Verlag, 3. überarbeitete und erweiterte Auflage 1974), pp. 145–150; Allison A. Trites, *The New Testament Concept of Witness* (1977), pp. 128–153, 175–198.

15:8, 22:5), most often it is used with a specific theological meaning, often interlocking the resurrection of Jesus Christ with the life of the believer and the future of the world.

In the context of the Lukan resurrection narratives the risen Christ commissions "the eleven . . . and those who were with them" (Luke 24:33): "You are witnesses of these things" (24:48). In Acts 1:8 the risen Christ further elaborates that commission: ". . . you shall receive power when the Holy Spirit has come upon you; and you shall be my witnesses in Jerusalem and in all Judea and Samaria and to the end of the earth." When a new apostle needed to be chosen, this person must be a "witness to the resurrection", and since this is the resurrection of Jesus of Nazareth who lived a definite life and was killed in response to that life (Acts 2:22–24.36, 3:13–15, 4:10, 5:30, 7:52, 10:38–40, 13:28), the witness must also be linked to the life of Jesus of Nazareth (Acts 1:21f.). Also in Peter's sermon at Pentecost and in a number of other speeches in Acts, the resurrection of Jesus Christ and the witness are interrelated: "This Jesus God raised up, and of that we all are witnesses." (Acts 2:32; compare 3:15, 5:32, 10:39.41, 13:30f.). It therefore seems natural that Luke describes Stephen, Paul, and Barnabas as "witnesses" (Acts 14:3, 18:5, 20:21, 22:15.20, 23:11, 26:16, 28:23), whose special function it was to communicate the gospel beyond the religious confines of Judaism into the world of the Gentiles.

Why is it that Luke used the concept of "witness" to speak of the resurrection of Christ? Why the concept of "witness" to relate the resurrection of Jesus Christ with the life of the believer and with the future of the world? It seems, that Luke found this concept most appropriate to describe the fact and the manner in which the Christ-event lives on after the death of Jesus. The witness and the witnessing community ensure that the fact of the story of Jesus as the Christ and the content of the Christian gospel are preserved and passed on. The witness is therefore the essential link, guaranteeing the continuity between Jesus and the ongoing church.[35] What emphases can we gather from Lukan theology with regard to the nature and function of the witness and its relation to the resurrection of Jesus Christ?

Witnesses, for Luke, have, firstly, no independent identity. Their identity is shaped by the reality to which they witness: Jesus Christ, who is present in the power of the Spirit. This does not merely mean having objective knowledge about Jesus, or about the testimonies of scripture to Jesus and his resurrection, or about the empty tomb. All of this "objective" knowledge the disciples on the road to Emmaus had, but they did not know the Lord (Luke 24:13–35)! What does it then mean for Luke to know the risen Lord?

To be witnesses means, secondly, that the past and the present dimensions of the reality of the resurrection must conflate in their existence, and thereby the event of the resurrection takes the witness into its reality and thus contributes to shaping the future. On the one hand, witnesses must therefore be anchored

---

35. Compare: Klaus Kienzler, *Logik der Auferstehung* (1976), pp. 204, 208.

with their existence in the life of the historical Jesus (Acts 1:21f.) and in the reality of the resurrection of Jesus (Luke 24:34); on the other hand, the reality of the resurrection must become a present event in the existence of the believer. Therefore it is only at Pentecost when the risen Christ comes in the power of the Spirit that the witness is fully constituted (Luke 24:49; Acts 1–2). The Spirit relates the riches of Christ to the believer and the believing community.

But it must be emphasized, thirdly, that although for Luke there is this essential interlocking between Jesus, the Spirit, and the witness, it is quite clear that within that interwovenness Luke wants to confess Jesus as the determining center. Jesus is described therefore as the Lord of the Spirit.[36] It is in the name of "Jesus" or of "Jesus Christ" that miracles are performed (Acts 4:30, 9:34, 16:18) and believers are baptized (Acts 2:38, 10:48, 19:5), yet in both actions these performances in the name of Jesus are intimately linked with the gift and the work of the Holy Spirit (Acts 8:14f., 19:5f.). It is Jesus who through the resurrection is exalted to the right hand of God, and from there he bestows the Spirit on the witnesses (Acts 2:32f.).

This means that the witnesses to the resurrection derive their identity and content neither from their own faith, nor from a theoretical affirmation of the happening of the resurrection, but from the ongoing life and reality of the One who lived, died, and was raised. Witnesses are authentic and credible when their existence matches that to which they are witnessing, namely the story of Jesus as it is present in the power of the Spirit. The "name of Jesus" alone does not do it, as some itinerant Jewish exorcists had to discover; the name must be incarnated in the existence of the witnesses (Acts 19:11–19).

For Luke, then, it is important that the resurrection of Jesus Christ has "really" happened (Luke 24:34). It is a christological event, and only as such it is also a soteriological event. Jesus Christ is the ἀρχηγός ([archēgos] Acts 3:15, 5:31), "the first to rise from the dead" (Acts 26:23), which implies, of course, that the resurrection of others will follow. Luke therefore safeguards both the *extra nos* and the content of the Christian faith.

The resurrection reality includes, fourthly, the commission to invite the addressee to become a witness and to participate in the universal mission of the Christian church (Luke 24:47f.; Acts 1:8). Here the resurrection is linked to the salvation and future of the world. It is of special interest that in his concern for the salvation and the future of the world the risen Christ does not bypass the believers but calls them to a saving and liberating activity in the world.

Since, however, it is Jesus as the Christ whom the witnesses are commissioned to represent in the world, therefore, fifthly, the witnesses must be personally involved in the event and thereby guarantee its credibility.[37] The hardship and the suffering which witnesses like Paul and Stephen had to face was part

---

36. Eduard Schweizer, *The Holy Spirit* (Philadelphia: Fortress, 1980), pp. 50–52, 58–60.

37. Klaus Kienzler describes the witnesses as "guarantors of the word, not merely its proclaimers" (*Logik der Auferstehung* [1976], p. 208, my translation).

of their identity as witnesses to the risen Christ in his essential identity with Jesus of Nazareth, who radically lived for others, and therefore suffered and was killed.[38]

We may say then, in conclusion, that for Luke "witness" is the appropriate category to speak of the resurrection of Jesus Christ, because the event character of the resurrection of Christ is preserved without freezing its reality into the past. The life of the witness is determined and shaped by Jesus Christ who is present in the Spirit. With his life and deeds and proclamation the witness re-presents the reality of the resurrection and thus contributes to the shaping of the future.

Although there are significant differences between Luke and John in their theology of witness/testimony, the Johannine understanding can further enrich our understanding.[39] As far as word statistics go, of all the New Testament writings, the word group μαρτυρέω/μαρτυρειν (martyreō/martyrein) and μαρτυρία (martyria) is most dominant in the Gospel of John: μαρτυρέω (martyreō) 33 times out of 76 times (the other main occurrences are in Luke/Acts: 12 times, Hebr: 8 times, JohEp: 12 times, Rev: 4 times); μαρτυρία (martyria) 14 times out of 37 times (the other main occurrences are JohEp: 7 times, Rev: 4 times). The fact that the noun μαρτυρία (martyria) always occurs in association with the verb μαρτυρέω (martyreō) indicates that "witnessing" is a dynamic reality. The Johannine theological emphases may be gathered into the following points:

Firstly, Jesus Christ is identified as the truth (14:6). Truth is thereby defined as a personal reality. As such it cannot be adequately understood in propositional or historical categories. The risen Christ calls for faith: "I am the resurrection and the life; he who believes in me, though he die, yet shall he live . . ." (11:25f.). Truth is the divine reality, anchored in the very being of God, revealed in Jesus Christ (1:1–18), and centered in the cross (19:34f.). Jesus Christ can therefore *be* the truth (14:6), and at the same time be the *witness to* the truth (18:37). In and with him the reality and content of truth has come to expression. He is the exegete of the being of God (1:18). This truth will seek and find ever new witnesses in the ongoing process of history. Whether it is John the

---

38. Hans Conzelmann comments: "In Luke . . . the 'necessity' of the Passion is fully brought out. . . . Not only the death, but the whole ministry of Jesus is implicit in the kerygmatic proclamation, in so far as the Resurrection casts light not only on Jesus' death, but also on his deeds and on his whole being. Luke deliberately indicates this in his account of the Resurrection." (*The Theology of St. Luke* [London: Faber and Faber, 1960], pp. 153f.). The same is true for the Gospel of Mark where first John the Baptist, then Jesus, and finally Jesus' followers are "handed over". Mark 13:9 relates this specifically to the act of witnessing.

39. Compare: Allison A. Trites, *The New Testament Concept of Witness* (1977), pp. 87–127; Klaus Kienzler, *Logik der Auferstehung* (1976), pp. 219–238; Josef Blank, *Krisis. Untersuchungen zur johanneischen Christologie und Eschatologie* (Freiburg: Lambertus Verlag, 1964), pp. 183–186, 198–230.

Baptist (1:6–8.15.19–34, 3:22–30), or the scriptures (5:39), or the disciples before and after Easter (1:35–51, 15:27), the miracles (signs) of Jesus (2:1–11.23,
4:46–54, 5:1–47, 6:1–71, 9:1–41, 11:1–57), or even the Holy Spirit (15:26,
16:12–15)—they all witness to the truth as it has come to expression in Jesus
Christ.

This means, secondly, that a witness to the truth is therefore a witness to
Jesus Christ. The truth, Jesus Christ, and the witness are closely interrelated.
The Christ event sets forth the witness, and the witness lives from the Christ-
event. Being a witness to Jesus Christ has therefore this personal dimension of
staking one's life on him because he is the truth. Discipleship is therefore the
proper response to Jesus as the Christ: "I am the light of the world; he who follows me will not walk in darkness, but will have the light of life" (8:12).

Thirdly, the Johannine resurrection stories contain a noticeable apologetic
thrust. They are witnesses to the truth of Christ (2:19–22). The risen Christ
points to the wounds of his crucifixion in order to underline the continuity between the crucified Jesus and the risen Christ (20:20.25.27). The tidy grave
clothes that the risen Christ has left behind in the tomb witness to the bodilyness of his resurrection (20:6–8).

Fourthly, there is never any doubt, however, that the aim of the witness is to
create faith (1:7, 19:35). The testimony to Jesus Christ realizes its aim in the
event of faith (4:39–42). By receiving the testimony, the life of the risen Christ
and the life of the believer conflate, and out of this event the confession arises
in word and deed "that God is true" (3:33).

In conclusion we may therefore say that Johannine theology confirms our
previous discovery that an act of God like the resurrection of Christ cannot be
objectified and then grasped in propositional or historical statements. The truth
that is grounded in the very being of God and has been revealed in Jesus Christ,
is that divine personal reality that can only be known in so far as it rules our
life. The witness is necessary to represent the Christ event in the world, and the
witness is true if it manifests an adequate interpretation of the crucified and
risen Christ.

In the Book of Revelation Jesus Christ is called the "true and faithful witness" (3:14, compare 1:5), because with his life he credibly re-presented (incarnated) the Word of God (1:2b.9b, 12:17b).[40] Christians are the followers of
this "true and faithful witness", and in following him they become themselves
witnesses (1:2a. 9a). An analogy is being shaped between Jesus Christ and those
who follow him. As the slain lamb he is the secret center of history (Rev 5),
and those who follow him must be prepared to enter a similar passion and be
counted among "the souls of those who had been slain for the word of God and
for the witness they had borne" (6:9, compare 2:13, 11:7, 12:11, 20:4). And just

---

40. Allison A. Trites shows that "testimony of Jesus" is a subjective genitive; it refers
to the testimony that Jesus incarnated, rather than to a testimony about him (*The New
Testament Concept of Witness* [1977], pp. 156–158).

as the slain lamb alone was able to open the "seven seals" of the book that contained the mysterious plan of history, so the witnesses to Jesus Christ shall be conquerors (2:7.11.17.26, 3:5.12.21), and they shall be motivated by the promise of his future (22:16). Again, we have an impressive biblical testimony of how the story of Jesus is continued in history by those who are prepared to let their lives become analogies to the crucified and risen Christ.

The apostle Paul had to defend the legitimacy of his witness to Jesus Christ against numerous opponents in a number of churches.[41] Against his opponents in Corinth, for instance, Paul defended his witness to the resurrection of Jesus Christ in the urgent self-awareness that with this defense the veracity of his preaching and of their faith was at stake (1 Cor 15:14.17), that he could be found to be misrepresenting God (1 Cor 15:15), and that their salvation could be an illusion (1 Cor 15:17f.). If the resurrection of Jesus Christ were not true then they would all be "false witnesses" (1 Cor 15:12–19). The Christians in Corinth did not deny the phenomenon of resurrection as such, but they questioned the resurrection of the dead (1 Cor 15:12–19). Paul argues that their logic has been broken at one point in history, namely in the resurrection of the dead man Jesus of Nazareth. He then undergirds his argument with a reference to Christian tradition which contains a long list of the witnesses to the resurrection of Jesus Christ (1 Cor 15:5–8).

The question remains, however, what this witness entails. If a denial of the resurrection of Jesus Christ would make them "false witnesses" (1 Cor 15:15), what then is a "true witness"? Are the witnesses in 1 Corinthians 15:5–8 simply listed to testify to the historical happening of the resurrection and the appearances of the risen Lord, or is there more to it? What is, according to Paul, the appropriate way to witness to the resurrection of Jesus Christ?

Rudolf Bultmann asserted against Karl Barth that in 1 Corinthians 15:1–11 Paul listed the witnesses in order to prove that the resurrection of Jesus Christ is an "objective historical fact".[42] Bultmann, however, criticizes Paul's argumentation and thinks that this apologetic interest is theologically fatal.

Wolfhart Pannenberg agrees with Bultmann's exegetical assessment, but in contrast to Bultmann, he fully affirms the postulated theological interest: "The intention of this enumeration (of the witnesses in 1 Cor 15:5–8) is clearly to give proof by means of witnesses for the facticity of Jesus' resurrection."[43] This would suggest that the resurrection of Christ is a historical fact which can be

---

41. Compare: Erhardt Güttgemanns, *Der leidende Apostel und sein Herr. Studien zur paulinischen Christologie* (Göttingen: Vandenhoeck & Ruprecht, 1966).

42. Rudolf Bultmann, "Karl Barth, *The Resurrection of the Dead,*" (1926), in: Rudolf Bultmann, *Faith and Understanding*, Vol. 1. Ed. Robert W. Funk (London: SCM, 1969, pp. 66–94), pp. 83f.; compare also "New Testament and Mythology," (1941), in: Hans Werner Bartsch, ed., *Kerygma and Myth: A Theological Debate.* (New York: Harper & Row, 1961, pp. 1–44), where Bultmann calls Paul's argumentation a "dangerous procedure" (p. 39).

43. Wolfhart Pannenberg, *Jesus–God and Man* (Philadelphia: Westminster, 1968), p. 89.

investigated and verified with the methods of historical science and can be recognized by human reason. The witness stands in the service of affirming the resurrection of Christ as an objective historical fact. Historical reason affirms that God has acted in history by acting in the history of Jesus of Nazareth.

However, a closer look at this text in its wider context suggests a more holistic portrayal of a responsible witness to the resurrection of Jesus Christ. Paul affirms, first of all, an essential interlocking between the resurrection of Jesus Christ and the future of the world. Jesus Christ is the "first fruits" of those who have fallen asleep (1 Cor 15:20.23). With his resurrection, the end, when God will be all in all, has begun (1 Cor 15:20–28).

This interlocking between the resurrection of Jesus Christ and the future also includes, secondly, the believers and their lives: "If Christ has not been raised, your faith is futile and you are still in your sins" (1 Cor 15:17). It was a controversial issue, however, between Paul and his opponents in Corinth, how this relationship between Jesus Christ and the believers should be understood. The opponents obviously thought that it was not the real historical Jesus who had been raised from the dead. They denied that a dead person could be raised. For them the resurrection of Jesus Christ meant that the "Christ", i.e., the spiritual, the divine, the heavenly part of Jesus Christ, had returned to unity with God, while "Jesus", i.e., the earthly, the material part of Jesus Christ, had died. They had separated "Jesus" and "Christ" in their theology and practice.[44] They had denied the essential unity between the earthly Jesus and the Christ of their faith and their experience. The Christ of their faith and experience was the Spirit Christ who had left the poverty of his life and the offense of the cross behind. They believed to have a share in Christ's triumphant and heavenly life through faith and through sacramental religious exercises. They believed that they were "already filled", that they were "already rich", that they had "already become kings", that they "already reigned with Christ and shared in his rule" (compare 1 Cor 4:8). They, in other words, had dissolved Christ into the existence and experience of faith. The charismatic riches of their faith had left behind the poverty of Jesus. This had made them insensitive to the historical Jesus and his cross, and at the same time had made them unconcerned about the fate of the disadvantaged in their midst, as the controversy about the Lord's Supper in 1 Corinthians 11:17–34 eloquently illustrates.

Against the triumphant and victorious life of his opponents who prided themselves on being "super-apostles", participating in the reign of Christ already, Paul speaks about his relationship to Christ in terms of suffering service in the world: "I die every day!" (1 Cor 15:31); and this death is not that of a martyr, nor does it refer to some kind of spiritual death, but it is the concrete consequence of a life of service as a disciple and apostle of the crucified and risen Christ that included sleepless nights, hunger, thirst, ill-clad, buffeted, reviled,

---

44. A similar docetic Christology was also prevalent in the Johannine Community (compare: 1 John 2:22, 4:2f. and the antidocetic thrust of the Fourth Gospel).

persecuted, afflicted, beaten, imprisoned, homeless, insulted, hard work . . . (1 Cor 4:8–13; 2 Cor 1:3–7, 6:1–10, 10–13; Gal 4:12–20, 6:17). It is therefore the resurrection of the crucified Christ that flows over into the existence of the believer.

Cross	*Resurrection*
We are afflicted in every way,	but not crushed;
perplexed,	but not driven to despair;
persecuted,	but not forsaken;
struck down,	but not destroyed;
always carrying in the body	so that the life of Jesus may
the death of Jesus,	also be manifested in our
	bodies (2 Cor 4:8–10).

We must recognize, thirdly, that in contrast to the Corinthian triumphant Christology and its subsequent soteriology, Paul asserts the distance and the difference between the risen Christ and the believer. Paul emphasizes the chronological distance between Christ and the believer by reminding his readers that not they, but Jesus Christ and he alone, has been raised from the dead (1 Cor 15:4.12). He is the "first fruits" of those who have died (1 Cor 15:20.23). As such he is related to but not identical with those who believe in him. Not they, but he has been raised from the dead. Their resurrection is promised, yes, it is even implied in the resurrection of Christ, but it has not yet happened. Their present existence should be an existence marked by the cross.

This chronological distance implies also the difference between Christ and those who believe in him. While his opponents in Corinth believed that the Christ whom they were experiencing in their lives had left his earthly life and the cross behind, Paul emphasized that the Christ of faith is the historical and crucified Jesus. That he, Jesus Christ, was the origin and content of their faith, but that he had not been dissolved into their experience of faith. It should not be their faith that determines who Christ is, but Jesus Christ should determine the nature and content of their faith!

This leads us to ask, fourthly, how these emphases can be brought together? How can Paul affirm the interrelationship between the resurrection of Jesus Christ and the future and the believers on the one hand, and the distance and difference between Christ and the believer and the world on the other? The answer must be seen in Paul's attempt to insist on the continuity between the risen Christ and the crucified Jesus. Although Paul affirms the essential interrelationship between the life, death, and resurrection of Jesus Christ, his theological emphasis is centered on the Crucified Christ (e.g., 1 Cor 1:18–2:13). With this theological reflection Paul resists the attempt to dissolve the resurrection of Christ into the experience of faith, and as such separate the risen Christ from the life and death of the historical Jesus.

The history of the church has shown that the symbol of the cross can easily become an empty symbol and a theoretical abstraction. To gather Paul's intention, it is therefore better to speak of the "Crucified One" as his central theological symbol. This would make sure that for Paul the cross is not the starting point for an abstract theory of atonement, but the central category for the way God shares his rich life with the poverty of the world. This is eloquently illustrated when in the context of 2 Corinthians 4:7–15 Paul interprets the presence of the risen Christ in the life of the believer as "carrying in the body the death of Jesus" (2 Cor 4:10). Here the life of the apostle and the concrete life of Jesus, i.e., that life which ended up at the cross, are given theological status. Against his opponents, who play down the significance of the earthly Jesus, Paul makes the earthly Jesus the determining content for the risen Christ.

Concretely, this means that the resurrection of Christ is confessed and affirmed in the suffering existence of the apostle. Erhardt Güttgemanns makes the important observation that while the opponents of Paul play down the historical Jesus and consider it to be a phenomenon of the past, a phenomenon that no longer has any theological importance when the redeemer has become identified with the redeemed, Paul himself upholds the theological importance of the historical Jesus who is confirmed and made present through the ministry of the Spirit.[45]

These references to some biblical traditions have underlined the important theological function that testimony and witness fulfill within the realm of faith. We have seen the essential interlocking between event, testimony, and witness. It remains to sort out these biblical insights and ask what they teach us about the way of knowing and confessing the resurrection of Jesus Christ.

We note, first of all, that the event of the resurrection calls for corresponding witnesses in order to keep the event alive in the ongoing process of history. The event needs the testimony and the witness, and testimony and witness live from the event. The testimony is given in the present, but it lives from the past. Through a testimony, a past event becomes real in and for the present. A testimony gathers up an event of the past and makes it manifest in the present. It helps us to interpret and modify the present, and thereby aids us in shaping the future.

Without such testimony an event is lost. It is left to disappear in the abyss of history. The event therefore needs a testimony in order to have a *Wirkungsgeschichte*—an effect and influence on the ongoing historical process. Through an adequate testimony people at all times and in all situations can share in the reality of a past event.

Such testimony and witness must, secondly, re-present the event. Their function is to gather up (to "remember") the event and faithfully manifest it in the present. This is done with language and with existence.

We saw earlier that the concepts of "promise" and "remembrance" can help us to understand how a past event becomes real and effective in the present.

---

45. *Der leidende Apostel und sein Herr* (1966), pp. 65f., compare pp. 94–126 and his refutation of the mystical interpretation of 2 Cor 4:10 (pp. 102–112).

Bringing an event out of the past into the present normally happens through language. Words are used, a narrative or a confession for instance, to re-present a past event and relate it to the present. Testimony therefore has normally a word or language character. This becomes immediately clear when we recall how Jesus related the power of the "kingdom of God" to the world: in parables. For the apostle Paul the saving and liberating power of the gospel was present in the word of preaching that aimed to create faith in the hearer (e.g., Rom 1:16f., 10:17). Also for the fourth evangelist it was the word that brought eternal life to the hearer (John 5:24).

Yet our references to Jesus, Paul, and John also make it quite clear that the word of testimony must be related to, and must be authenticated by, the existence of the witness. Therefore the unconditional love of God and his accepting grace became an event not only in Jesus' parables, but also in his healing ministry and in his concrete fellowship with "publicans and sinners". The same is true for the apostle Paul whose theology of the cross was essentially related to a "crucified" existence (2 Cor 4, 6, 10–13). So also in John we hear Jesus saying: "My food is to do the will of him who sent me, and to accomplish his work" (4:34).

The truth of a testimony, therefore, and the adequacy of re-presenting an event, are both at stake in the existence of the witness. Events require not only words, but also an authentic existence. If the existence of the witness does not cohere with the content of the testimony then the testimony is "broken"—it is distorted. Words of testimony, therefore, must not only be related to the event that is testified, they must also be related to the one who testifies. Persons who bear the testimony are with their existence responsible for its truth. The truth of the testimony is at stake in the existence of the witnesses, and the credibility of the witnesses is dependent on the adequacy of their representation of the event. The witnesses must be willing to suffer for their witness. Paul Ricoeur says it well: "Testimony is . . . the engagement of a pure heart and an engagement to the death. It belongs to the tragic destiny of truth."[46] Therefore the testimony and the existence of the witness, the one who testifies, belong together. Human witness belongs to the reality that makes a past event present through language and existence.

At this point we must address a controversial issue. Biblical texts suggest that there are two different elements in the concept of witness. There is, firstly, the juridical element that envisages witnesses and their testimonies in a court of law. The truth of their testimony can be discovered and verified by

---

46. Paul Ricoeur, "The Hermeneutics of Testimony," (1972), p. 130. The following words are written in the same context: "The witness is capable of suffering and dying for what he believes" (p. 129). "The witness is the man who is identified with the just cause which the crowd and the great hate and who, for this just cause, risks his life" (p. 129). In this context we must also recall that the Greek word for "witness" is μάρτυς (martus) from which the English word "martyr" derives.

investigative research. The language is juridical, and the emphasis is on a rationally convincing argument. Then there is, secondly, the existential element which emphasizes that the witnesses are willing to suffer for the truth of their testimony. The truth of the testimony depends on the credibility of the witness.

This has consequences for our investigation. The first element is emphasized by those theologians who emphasize the apologetic function of the witness. The witness then serves to provide a rational testimony for the factual character of the resurrection as a historical event.[47] I do not want to exclude that element, but I have emphasized the second aspect, because I feel that it is closer to the biblical intention and provides a more adequate and more relevant representation of the resurrection of the crucified Christ. The witnesses do not testify to an abstract fact *that* Jesus has been raised from the dead, but the witnesses and their testimony are a necessary part of the communicative event which brings the reality of the risen Christ into the present. The risen One is present in the life of the believer. Paul defines this presence as "carrying in the body [i.e., in one's existence] the death of Jesus" (2 Cor 4:10). Appropriate testimony to the resurrection is therefore not a theoretical or propositional dogmatic statement, it is also not a charismatic religious experience, but it calls for a life of discipleship in which it is existentially manifested that the risen Lord makes himself known under the shadow of the cross.[48]

It suggests a false alternative if one is asked to make a choice whether the resurrection of Christ is communicated through a pure kerygma, which as such does not need any historical support (Bultmann), and a message that is supported by historical evidence. The reality of the resurrection suggests a way of faith beyond these alternatives. The resurrection of the crucified Christ is not properly guarded by an existential decision or a rational construct, but by a credible life of following Jesus.

The resurrection of Jesus Christ is therefore, on the one hand, essentially linked to the life and death of Jesus, and, on the other hand, to the life of the witness and the witnessing community, and through the witness and the community to the life and future of the world. The unity of the Christ-event means that our perception of, and confession to, the risen Christ cannot bypass the fact that during his life Jesus ministered to, and showed solidarity with, the outcast, the poor, the oppressed, the sick. To them he communicated the colorful grace of God. It is therefore in our concrete engagement for the needs of the world

---

47. So, for instance, Allison A. Trites, *The New Testament Concept of Witness* (1977), pp. 222–230. Trites admits "that faithful witness often entails suffering and persecution" (p. 227), but her special leaning seems to be that in "a sceptical, questioning age" (p. 225) the "historical foundations of the Christian religion" (p. 224) can be given rational credibility.

48. A classical paradigm is the encounter between Jesus and Peter at Caesarea Philippi as presented in Mark 8:27–9:1. It is not merely the orthodox confession "You are the Christ" (8:29), but the concrete life of discipleship—following the suffering One—that is the appropriate response to Jesus as the Christ (8:34–38).

in our time that we show whether we believe in the Jesus who lived a certain life, was killed because of it, and was raised from the dead to show that his vision of reality is the true one which invites followers in all times and all situations. This partiality of God for those who are lost and broken must become evident in the witness to the resurrection. Otherwise the event is distorted.

Witnesses have their identity in that to which they witness; but the risen Lord is never dissolved into the life of the witness. Jesus Christ is risen, the Christians walk in newness of life (Rom 6:4). This difference between Christ and the believer on the one hand, and the visible consequences of the believer's commitment to the risen Christ on the other, must be the ingredients of a responsible witness to Christ.

This presents us, thirdly, with the question of truth. When is a testimony true, and when does it become untrue? When is a witness a true witness, and when does he or she become a false witness, a hypocrite? This is a very difficult problem, because an authentic testimony demands that we hold the language of the testimony and the existence of the witness together. The truth question therefore focuses on the testimony in its interlocking between word and existence. And for this undertaking we are ill prepared because traditionally we have only evaluated the propositional content of a testimony. We have asked, for instance, whether someone believes in the resurrection of Jesus Christ, and we have taken the "Yes" or "No" for an answer, without asking whether this "Yes" or "No" is grounded in an existence in which the life of the risen Christ is manifest or not. Believing that Jesus has been raised from the dead cannot merely be a theoretical affirmation; it must be a holistic existential manifestation.

A testimony is inadequate when it is an improper re-presentation of the event. A true testimony is in its intention an adequate representation of the event. I have said "in its intention", because a testimony can never quite represent the event. But the witnesses must not volitionally distort the event, and they must continually reexamine their own life in the light of the event to which they witness.

The measure for the truth of a testimony is therefore not inherent in the testimony or the witness. It lies outside the witness. The witnesses point away from themselves to the event to which they testify. It is only the adequate representation of the event in the word and existence of the witness which is important.

Having said that, it must be equally clear that there will remain a certain distance between the witness, the testimony, and the event. The event has priority, and the testimony and the witness will remain dependent on the event. An event without a testimony is lost; a testimony without an event is empty, and a witness that does not flesh out the testimony becomes inauthentic and therefore incredible.

We may therefore say, in conclusion, that on the descriptive level the proper understanding of a historical event demands that we think of the event, the testimony to the event, and our existence, together. Neither an objectification of the event (if that were possible) nor dissolving an event into the subjective experience of the witness does justice to reality as we experience it. Applied to our topic this means that the resurrection of Jesus includes us. It aims at the word of testimony and it wants to be credibly represented in the life of the witness.

If we keep in mind that the witness to the risen Christ is grounded in the event of the resurrection and remember the essential interrelationship between event and witness, then we will avoid the following distortions. We will not objectify the resurrection of Christ, but remember that it aims for a concrete manifestation in our life and in the world. We will not limit the resurrection reality to our experience of it, but remember that it is Jesus Christ, not ourselves, who is risen and who wants to shape our life. We will not limit verification to a theoretical proof, but we will remember that we must confess our allegiance to Christ with our whole existence. The category of witness therefore enables us to think the resurrection of Jesus Christ as determining our life and our future, without being dissolved into our experience.

PARTNERSHIP

The involvement with and the participation in God's ways with the world is further underlined by the biblical-theological concept of partnership.[49] This concept is suspect to some theologians because they associate it with the heresy of synergism (from the Greek word συνεργεῖν [synergein] = "cooperating") which maintains that the human being "cooperates" with God in the work of salvation. God's grace alone (sola gratia) would then not be sufficient for salvation. It would need the "cooperation" of the human person. At this point theological caution is in order. Nevertheless, it is equally important to ask whether our reaction against the heresy of synergism has not blinded us toward important biblical and theological insights that are implicit to God's revelation through Jesus Christ.

The biblical message portrays God as establishing a covenant with humanity and nature, and this covenant is renewed with the incarnation. In Jesus Christ God has not only revealed his love for the world (John 3:16), but in Christ God has reconciled the world with himself (2 Cor 5:18–20). Nevertheless, this divine work of reconciliation does not exclude, but it includes the call to human beings to become partners in God's ministry of reconciliation. This can be illustrated with the reference to 2 Corinthians 5:18–20. The sole authorship of the work of salvation is located in the being of God. It is he who established

---

49. Wolf Krötke has recently reminded us that this theological concept is central to the theology of Karl Barth: Wolf Krötke, "Gott und Mensch als 'Partner'. Zur Bedeutung einer zentralen Kategorie in Karl Barths Kirchlicher Dogmatik," ZThK. B 6 (1986), pp. 158–175. This is noteworthy because Barth has often been accused of dissolving the freedom and dignity of the human person into the all encompassing grace and sovereignty of God.

the event of reconciliation in Christ: ". . . all this is from God" (v. 18). But with the event of reconciliation in Jesus Christ, God also established the "ministry of reconciliation", and thereby he entrusts to the believing community the "message of reconciliation" (v. 19). The identity of Christians is in being "ambassadors for Christ". Although it is "God" who makes "his appeal", but he does it "through us" (v. 20).

It may also be necessary to give a more prominent theological status to 1 Corinthians 3:9a, where Paul interprets his work and the work of his fellow laborers as being "God's fellow workers."[50] Again the context makes clear that this in no way diminishes the sole work of God for our salvation. Referring to his and Apollos's ministry, Paul says: ". . . neither he who plants nor he who waters is anything, but only God who gives the growth" (1 Cor 3:7). It is God who as part of his saving and reconciling work (*sola gratia*) calls people into partnership with himself. Human dignity consists in being invited and being able to tune into God's passion for the world.

The same theological dignity is assigned to the work of the believer by the important text from the Sermon on the Mount, Matthew 5:13–16. The indicative is clearly spelled out: "You are the salt of the earth. . . . You are the light of the world." Not "you will be . . .", promising the dignity of the believer for the future; not "you shall or should be . . .", defining the liberating claim of God in terms of morality; but "you are . . .", interpreting the life of the believer and the believing community as an established fact, established by God (*sola gratia*). But this indicative entails the imperative: "Let your light so shine before men, that they may see your good works and give glory to your Father who is in heaven." Their "good works" have a theological dignity. They have a kerygmatic and a missionary function. In and with them the crucified and risen Christ remains present in the world. This can neither mean salvation by works, nor does it imply synergism. The good works are grounded in God's salvation and their aim is to bring glory to God, not to the doer. Thus the grace of God surrounds the life of the human person, but at the same time it calls for holistic obedience and discipleship. The grace of God becomes visible in the life of those who are called into God's passion for the world and who respond to that call.

We note further that in the Book of Revelation the church in Laodicea is severely criticized because their works do not manifest their faith in Jesus Christ: "I know your works: you are neither cold nor hot. . . . So, because you are lukewarm, and neither cold nor hot, I will spew you out of my mouth" (Rev 3:15f.).

---

50. Georg Bertram, interpreting the use of συνεργός (synergos) in 1 Corinthians 3:9, says that ". . . Paul raises a theological claim for himself and his helpers. . . . Along the lines of Is. 43:24 they thus share in God's own work with its toil and labour." ("συνεργός κτλ.," [synergos ktl.], *TDNT* VII [1971, pp. 871–876], p. 875); H.-C. Hahn says with reference to Mark 16:20 and 1 Corinthians 3:9 that the work of God with his servants "is a real co-working, in as much as the person who has been called by God to be a witness is himself no mere inactive instrument in the proclaiming event, but equally a co-operating servant of God." ("Work, Do, Accomplish," *NIDNT* 3 [1978, pp. 1147–1152 [1971]], p. 1152).

With these biblical intimations in mind it is therefore not surprising that the reality of the resurrection contains the call to mission (Matt 28:18—20; John 20:19–23, 21:15–17; Acts 1:8). The resurrection of Jesus Christ as a divine event does not exclude, but it includes human response and human activity. This is what the concept of partnership brings to expression. Within their ontological dependence upon God human beings maintain a relative independence. This relative independence is the presupposition and the ground for human responsibility. Human persons accept this responsibility for their life, and thereby they participate intentionally in shaping their life and future. In and through this responsible participation possibilities of grace become actualized in human history. The possibilities are provided by God; their actualizations include the partnership of the human person. The refusal to enter this partnership means closing oneself to the active grace of God, and as such it is sin.[51]

WORSHIP

The resurrection stories in the gospels remind us of another important aspect in the believers' and the believing communities' response to the resurrection of Christ: worship. Two narratives, one from the Johannine tradition and one from the Lukan tradition, may serve as paradigms to illustrate this aspect of knowing the risen Christ.

The Johannine narrative deals with the encounter between the risen Christ and Thomas: John 20:24–29. Not having participated in the experience of the resurrection—"Thomas . . . was not with them when Jesus came" (v. 24)—Thomas formulates the conditions under which he will accept the resurrection of Jesus as true: "Unless I see in his hands the print of the nails, and place my finger in the mark of the nails, and place my hand in his side, I will not believe" (v. 25). He demands empirical proof. He determines the way by which a potential object of knowledge can become known to him. He sets the agenda, and thereby he makes himself master over the event. The event is forced into an epistemological straitjacket which no longer allows for the event to become known on its own terms. This changes, however, when Thomas is surprised by the reality of the risen Christ: "The doors were shut, but Jesus came and stood among them, and said, 'Peace be with you' " (v. 26). The risen Christ does not withdraw from Thomas's epistemological requirements: " 'Put your finger here, and see my hands; and put out your hand, and place it in my side' " (v. 27). But then the reality of the resurrection suspends the preconceived epistemological

---

51. Karl Barth's understanding of sin as "sloth" ("Trägheit") is helpful at this point. Sin is described as the refusal, the laziness, the slowness, the sluggishness, the sleepiness, the disobedience, and the ungratefulness to join the passion which God has displayed in Jesus Christ for the world and its needs; compare: *CD* IV/2 (1958), pp. 403–483, especially 403—409; similar Jürgen Moltmann, *Theology of Hope* (1967), pp. 22–26.

straitjacket, and Thomas worships: " 'My Lord and my God!' " (v. 28). This is the most excellent christological confession in the Gospel of John, and according to some commentators, Thomas can be seen here as the spokesman of the worshipping community.[52] A sensitive theological interpretation follows: " 'Have you believed because you have seen me? Blessed are those who have not seen and yet believe' " (v. 29). Not reason, but faith is the proper mode to receive and to respond to the reality of the resurrection. And one mode of faith is the act of worship.[53]

For that reason we are not surprised to discover the motif of the eucharist or the Lord's Supper in one of the most prominent resurrection stories in the gospels. In the Lukan narrative about the two disciples on the road to Emmaus (Luke 24:13–35) it is at the meal table that the disciples recognize the stranger as the risen Christ. And the meal is portrayed in eucharist terminology: "When he was at table with them, he took the bread and blessed, and broke it, and gave it to them" (v. 30). With this story the church confesses that it was not the knowledge of the historical Jesus and his mighty words and deeds (vv. 14.19), not the historical knowledge of the crucifixion (v. 20), not the knowledge of the scriptures (v. 27), not even the historical reports about the empty tomb and the vision of the heavenly messengers (vv. 22–24), that were sufficient to remove their sadness (v. 17) and create faith in the risen Christ. It was at the table, where, although the disciples invited the stranger, the stranger immediately assumes the role as host, when "their eyes were opened and they recognized him" (v. 31). The story continues: "and he vanished out of their sight" (v. 31). What does this mean? Is this not a sensitive theological reflection about the reality of the resurrection and the continuing presence of the risen Christ? The Spirit reveals to faith what historical reason cannot perceive. And the content of what the Spirit

---

52. Raymond E. Brown, *The Gospel according to John (xiii–xxi)*. The Anchor Bible, 29A (Garden City, NY: Doubleday, 1970), pp. 1047f.

53. This is emphasized by Peter Carnley, who concludes his book *The Structure of Resurrection Belief* (1987) with the words: ". . . when we do encounter the *Christus praesens* . . . (the) more immediate response is to stand in his presence in the silent awe of worship: thanks be to God for the unspeakable gift of Christ himself, for Christ is risen: He is risen indeed" (p. 368). Carnley considers it to be "perhaps *the* glory of Anglicanism" that it has a "preference for liturgy as a way of expressing truth over the Latin proclivity for defining doctrines and dogmas" (p. 358). It is unfortunate, nevertheless, that Carnley understands the uniqueness and distinctiveness of Jesus' *agape*-love with reference to Jesus' disposition and character (chapter IX), rather than with reference to his particular and concrete life that created unrest in the world and therefore ended up on the cross. Carnley's view is in danger of reducing the reality of the resurrection to its ecclesiological consequences and thereby underestimating its significance for the world and its future. We try to avoid this danger by recognizing, on the one hand, that "worship" is only *one* dimension of resurrection faith, which needs to be complemented by an emphasis on the "praxis" of faith. On the other hand, we feel that for determining the christological content of faith, the New Testament portrayals of Jesus call for a shift of emphasis from Jesus' character and disposition to the concrete manifestations of his life in the world.

reveals, Jesus Christ, remains present after his death and resurrection in the community of faith that interprets the scriptures and celebrates its identity in the Lord's Supper.[54] The resurrection narratives, therefore, remind us of the importance of worship. It is there, in worship, where the risen Christ, again and again, visits his people to sustain, encourage, and empower them in their pilgrimage of faith.

PRAXIS

The ancient philosophical concept of praxis has experienced a renaissance in recent hermeneutical and theological reflection.[55] It is still in search of a well-defined content, but it may help us to gather some of the emphases that have emerged in our analysis of the nature of resurrection faith.

When, according to Matthew 11:2–6 (compare Luke 7:18–23), John the Baptist and his disciples ask the question of truth with regard to Jesus' messianic identity, the answer points them not to a theoretical knowledge about Jesus, but to the liberating praxis of his life, his words (in Matthew: the Sermon on the Mount, especially the Beatitudes; in Luke: Luke 4:18f., 6:20–23) and his deeds (in Matthew: chapters 8 and 9; in Luke: the miracles as the signs of the presence of the kingdom of God):

Go and tell John what you hear and see: the blind receive their sight and the lame walk, lepers are cleansed and the deaf hear, and the dead are raised up, and the poor have good news preached to them. And blessed is he who takes no offense at me.

---

54. It is therefore not surprising that the meal motif, even portrayed with eucharistic terminology, is also found in other resurrection stories: John 21:9–14; Luke 24:41–43; Acts 1:4, 10:41b (compare Mark 16:14a). It is of course a widespread conviction that the Lukan narrative is an excellent example as to how early Christians reflected about the origin, nature, and content of their faith; compare: Hans Dieter Betz, "The Origin and Nature of Christian Faith According to the Emmaus Legend (Luke 24:13–32)," *Interp* 23 (1969), pp. 32–46; Joachim Wanke, " '. . . wie sie ihn beim Brotbrechen erkannten.' Zur Auslegung der Emmauserzählung Lk 24,13–35," *BZ* 18 (1974), pp. 180–192.

55. For a scientific introduction to the subject see: Clodovis Boff, *Theology and Praxis. Epistemological Foundations* (Maryknoll, N.Y.: Orbis Books, 1987). For briefer descriptions see: Gustavo Gutiérrez, *A Theology of Liberation. History, Politics and Salvation* (Maryknoll, N.Y.: Orbis Books, rev. ed. with a new introduction 1988); Enrique Dussel, *Ethics and Community* (Maryknoll, N.Y.: Orbis Books, 1988), chaps. 1, 2, 8, and 20; Robert McAfee Brown, *Theology in a New Key. Responding to Liberation Themes* (Philadelphia: Westminster, 1978), chaps. 2 and 3; David Tracy, *The Analogical Imagination. Christian Theology and the Culture of Pluralism* (London: SCM, 1981), pp. 69–79; Frederick Herzog, *God-Walk. Liberation Shaping Dogmatics* (Maryknoll, N.Y.: Orbis, 1988); Max L. Stackhouse, *Apologia. Contextualization, Globalization, and Mission in Theological Education* (Grand Rapids: Eerdmans, 1988), especially chapters 6 and 11.

The praxis of his life reveals who Jesus is. This suggests an intimate inter-locking between faith in Christ ("blessed is he who takes no offense at me") and the activity of salvation and liberation. It is this interrelationship that we seek to gather up into the concept of "praxis".[56]

"Praxis" from a theological perspective seeks to know whether God is ac-tive in the world, and what he is doing there. These questions are inherent to the experience of faith. The Christian and the Christian community want to be part of God's saving and liberating activity in the world. That God is active as savior and liberator is the theological conviction which the community of faith has learned from its own experience and from the biblical message. Within the community of faith it is the task of theological reflection to examine whether the believer and the believing community are in fact part of that liberating ac-tivity, or whether they have (mis)used the resources of faith to compensate or validate needs and interests that are no longer in continuity with the ground and content of faith.

With the following major emphases we seek to discern the concept of "praxis" as it applies to our discussion. "Praxis" calls, first of all, for a shift of empha-sis in the theological task. While it is not false to say that "faith seeks under-standing", it is certainly one-sided and therefore misleading. The important question is whether faith itself calls primarily for understanding. Or is this fas-cination with one aspect of faith perhaps due to cultural circumstances, and to soteriological uncertainties within a dominantly intellectual context? The fact is that traditional theology was fascinated with theory rather than with prac-tice. Its reference point was philosophy and its attempt to grasp and explain re-ality intellectually. The intellectualizing of faith led to a tendency to freeze the living and dynamic revelation of God into historical facts or propositional doc-trines, which were then expected to be accepted as true. This tendency to pet-rifying God's revelation into doctrine, or freeze it into the past, underestimates the fact that the content of faith does not primarily seek understanding, but the transformation of reality.

Theological reflection must serve this transforming thrust of faith. It ana-lyzes the content of faith and then measures the theory and practice of the church by that content. Theology reminds the believer and the community of the trans-forming nature of faith. Theology is not identical with faith. It serves faith and

---

56. We must recall here the biblical emphasis on the essential interrelationship be-tween the *indicative* of salvation and the *imperative* of a praxis of life that is appropri-ate to it. Both in the Decalogue (Exod 20:1–17; Deut 5:6–21) and in the Sermon on the Mount (Matt 5–7), for instance, the indicative of salvation (Exod 20:2; Deut 5:6; Matt 5:1–11) is followed by the imperatives that are contained in that salvation. There are many biblical texts that warn against a faith that remains theoretical or ritualistic and does not issue into a concrete concern for justice, e.g.: 1 Sam 15:22; Amos 5:21–25; Hos 6:6; Isa 1:10–17, 58:1–12; Mic 6:6–8; Mark 12:28–34 [Matt 22:34–40; Luke 10:25–28]; Matt 5:23f., 7:15–27, 21:10–17, 23:23, 25:31–46; 1 Cor 10–14; Gal 5; 1 John 4; James 2:14–26; Rev 2–3.

its transforming power. Faith does not only seek understanding, but also obedience, commitment, and a corresponding activity in the world. Theological reflection must therefore constantly ask whether the praxis of faith corresponds to the content of faith. Given the fact that all knowledge is interested knowledge,[57] it is the task of theology to inquire what interest is inherent in faith, and then distinguish the interest of faith from the many other human interests.

The ground and content of faith, Jesus Christ, was not killed because he engaged in an intellectual debate about the most adequate understanding of reality, but because he struggled for a proper understanding of reality by moving it in the direction of justice. His primary reference point was not the theological speculations of the rabbis and the Sadducees, but the concrete life situation of the sick and the poor, whose need it was to experience hope, healing, and salvation. This does not exclude the necessity for theology to engage in the apologetic and eristic task, and to explain faith against the onslaught of reason. But we must be reminded that this cannot be the only task and, in our contemporary world situation, certainly not the major task of theology. When the humane survival of the human race is at stake, then theology cannot merely speak with the philosopher and explain itself to the forum of reason; it must also try to understand and interpret concrete reality (society, economics, politics). This it must do by appropriating sociological, political, and economic research, and then help the church to relate the resources of faith to the struggle for a more humane society and a more just world order. The praxis of faith seeks to help transform the world in the knowledge and anticipation of the kingdom of God. Theology therefore needs to seek closer relationship with the social sciences in order to understand our world and ask how it can change in the direction of justice.[58]

This is related, secondly, to another task of theology: to remind the believer and the believing community of the incarnational thrust of faith. Christian faith seeks to create analogies to Jesus Christ, and therefore it leads to concrete action in and for the world. The resurrection of Jesus Christ is not yet understood when we affirm with our intellect that the tomb was empty or that the earliest disciples "saw" the risen Christ. The reality of the resurrection calls for a commitment to stake one's life on its promise.

The praxis of faith does not reduce faith to activism, nor does it make God's justifying "Yes" in any way dependent on human response. It simply recognizes that faith wants to become active and visible in love (Gal 5:6; James 2:14–26; Matt 5:13–16). Since the praxis of faith is grounded in the resurrection of Jesus Christ, it must become evident that believers are attempting to create analogies to the Christian vision of reality. Jesus Christ is the criterion by which Christian praxis must be measured.

---

57. Compare: Jürgen Habermas, *Knowledge and Human Interest* (Boston: Beacon Press, 1971).

58. Clodovis Boff, *Theology and Praxis. Epistemological Foundations* (1987), pp. 1–62.

The incarnational thrust of faith implies an inherent bias toward the marginal people.[59] Just as Jesus shared his life with the leper, the sick, the poor, and the oppressed, so Christian praxis is especially aimed at liberating those who are pressed to the margin of life.

Faith in the risen Christ is therefore not world denying, but world affirming. It recognizes that as redeemer, God does not negate but save what he has created. The risen Christ is the "first born from the dead"; he is the promise for the liberation and salvation of all creation. Theological reflection must therefore point faith into the one history that God wants to write with his creation. Faith does not remove the believer and the believing from that history but makes them creative participants in it.

We must consider, thirdly, that human beings are relational beings, woven into an intricate network of relationships with other human beings, with God, with nature, and with history. Through responsible participation in this network of relationships we become who we are. If we "are raised with Christ" then this resurrection reality takes shape in our relationship with God, with each other, with nature, and with history. Christian praxis must reflect these relationships. The praxis of faith, therefore, includes an existential involvement with God (conversion, worship, prayer), an intentional commitment to the neighbor (mission, evangelism, justice, liberation), a concern for nature (ecological lifestyle), and responsibility for the future (politics, economic justice). Praxis is the activity of grace and, because it is the grace of the crucified and risen Christ, it can neither be dissolved into private religious experiences, nor merely result in moralistic activity. It is the expression of the festival of life, that seeks to include and invite all, and especially those who have no friends and no power and no voice.

Since "praxis" wants to give expression to love in a concrete situation, it aims, fourthly, at a festival of life in the Christian community and in the world.[60] When life is being honored and restored, then praxis reaches its aim. Praxis is more than "doing". Its soil is "*being* in Christ". It includes the "sabbath" of worship, reflection, and promise; the healthy interruptions in life, when it is asked what we are doing and why we are doing it.[61]

As a fifth point we must recognize the eschatological dimension of praxis. It includes and lives from the certain hope that the solidarity with the poor and oppressed now and the engagement for justice now, stands under the promise of eschatological verification: "Blessed are you that hunger now, for you shall

---

59. We recall here Jürgen Moltmann's important reminder that the Christian view of reality focuses on the underside of history and manifests a special promise for the victims of evolution (*The Way of Jesus Christ* [1990], pp. 38f., 63–69, 301–312).

60. Enrique Dussel, *Ethics and Community* (1988), p. 12.

61. Compare: Jürgen Moltmann, *God in Creation. An Ecological Doctrine of Creation: the Gifford Lectures 1984–1985* (London: SCM, 1985), chapter 11.

be satisfied. Blessed are you that weep now, for you shall laugh" (Luke 6:21). These words are not meant to encourage passivity, or to point people to the future for their lives' fulfillment. Rather, they interpret God as the One who takes his stand with the poor and oppressed, and who longs for their liberation. Early Christians were sensitive to this when they recognized that faith in Christ must become concrete now in a liberating service for the poor and oppressed (Matt 25:31–46).

This implies, as point six, that Christian praxis has a critical thrust. By reflecting on human activity in light of the word of God, theology must serve as a constant reminder that our engagement in the world is often marked by convenience and self-interest; that at times we even use our theology to validate the status quo. When the church claims to be neutral and impartial, then theology must raise its voice to say that such a stance is not possible. A silent or an apolitical church always supports the status quo and even provides, willingly or unwillingly, religious sanction for it. Praxis demands that the believer and the believing community leave their secure position of a comfortable status quo and take sides.[62] In light of the incarnation Christian "praxis" adopts an attitude "from below". Thereby it recognizes in a concrete situation that the resurrection is the resurrection of the Crucified One. "Praxis" calls the community of faith back to its very identity in Christ.

We conclude by saying that "praxis" reminds us that the resurrection of Christ has changed the world, and its reality aims at continually changing the world in anticipation of the kingdom of God. It is not interpretation but action,[63] not historical fact in the past, but historical act in the present, that forms the primary emphasis of the resurrection of Christ. The risen Lord calls us to service in the world, and theology then asks whether this service, its ends, and its means, are proper reflections of the crucified Christ.

---

62. Clodovis Boff, *Theology and Praxis* (1987), pp. 159–174.

63. This is an important emphasis in the contemporary understanding of reality. Jürgen Moltmann says: "It is no longer asked whether a theological doctrine is true or false; instead, the doctrine is tested practically to see whether its effects are oppressive or liberating, alienating or humanizing. With this method, praxis becomes the criterion of truth. This criterion is true not only for Marx; it also is operative from Kant to Sartre; it is the characteristic feature of the modern spirit." ("Political Theology and Political Hermeneutic of the Gospel," in: *On Human Dignity. Political Theology and Ethics* [London: SCM, 1984, pp. 97–112], p. 98). The same in: "Gott in der Revolution," (1968), in: Ernst Feil und Rudolf Weth, Hg., *Diskussion zur "Theologie der Revolution"* (München: Kaiser, Mainz: Matthias Grünewald, ²1970, pp. 65–81), pp. 73–75; compare further: *Theology of Hope* (1967): "The theologian is not concerned merely to supply a different *interpretation* of the world, of history and of human nature, but to *transform* them in expectation of a divine transformation." (p. 84); Clodovis Boff defines "praxis" as "the *complexus of practices* orientated to the transformation of society, the making of history." (*Theology and Praxis* [1987], p. 6; compare chapter 12 [pp. 195–205]: "Praxis as Criterion of Truth").

KNOWLEDGE

We have said that the word brings the reality of the resurrection into the present and thereby creates a situation in which a life-changing faith becomes possible. This faith issues into worship and praxis. Since faith is faith in God or in Christ, it also has a cognitive element. It contains the seed of and therefore the desire for knowledge. The "word" is the story of Jesus. It speaks of a person; a person who lived a particular life, who in consequence of that life was killed, and who was raised from the dead by God. The word therefore also contains information, and this information protects the identity of faith against subjective political and ecclesiastical distortions. Faith must constantly be reminded of its ground and content, otherwise it can easily be functionalized to serve other interests. Faith in Christ therefore contains the seed of knowledge which keeps it focused in the story of Jesus.

This may be illustrated by referring to the history of the resurrection tradition. At the outset the event was referred to with brief kerygmatic confessions that "God raised Jesus from the dead",[64] and that "Christ appeared to Cephas" (1 Cor 15:5; Luke 24:34) and to others (1 Cor 15:5–8). However, with increasing chronological distance from the resurrection event, and with the challenge to relate that event into different situations, it became necessary to expand the resurrection and appearance formulas into more or less extensive narratives as we find them in the gospel traditions. Confessional formulas are brief, abstract, and matter-of-fact. They presuppose that the preacher who uses such formulas, or the listener who hears them, can, from their own knowledge of the event, "fill in" and "add color" to the concise information. The formulas summarize more extant information, and at the same time they can tease such information into actuality. We may therefore say that the seed of narrative is contained in such formulas. They can be expanded into narratives, and modified to relate the event to the needs of the situation; be it to make the resurrection faith known in its many facets and its mysterious depth, or be it to defend this faith against skeptics and critics within and without the church.

CONCLUSION: DISCIPLESHIP

We have tried in this part to understand the nature of faith in the resurrection of the crucified Christ. Having recognized that the New Testament, the traditions of the church, and Christian experience designate faith as the proper mode of responding to the reality of the resurrection, we have tried to determine how

---

64. This confession can be reconstructed from a number of New Testament texts in which it recurs in a variety of forms: Rom 4:24, 8:11, 10:9; 1 Cor 6:14; 15:15; 2 Cor 4:14; 1 Thess 1:9f; Gal 1:1; Col 2:12; Eph 1:20; 1 Pet 1:21; Acts 3:15; 4:10; 5:30; 10:40; 13:30.37.

that faith comes about, what elements and dimensions it contains, and what consequences it calls for.

The resurrection of Jesus Christ and our faith in him must be distinguished from each other, but they cannot be separated. The resurrection must be understood as an "open" event in that it aims for the creation of faith; and faith lives from the reality of the risen Christ. This reality shapes the believers so that they understand their existence as having been raised with Christ to newness of life. This "new life", however, does not remove the believer from the world. It does not call for a privatized religious faith or for a community that defines its existence apart or in isolation from the world. Quite the opposite. The reality of resurrection faith draws believers and the believing community into God's saving and liberating passion for the world. Believers become "witnesses" who in and with their own existence manifest Jesus as the risen Christ. They become "partners" with God in the work of salvation and liberation that he has begun with raising Jesus from the dead. In the event of faith believers are beginning to recognize that in Jesus Christ, God is sharing his own life with them. The response to that can only be the worship of praise and prayer, and the praxis of Christian discipleship. But in order to preserve the Christian identity of that worship, and the Christian relevance of that praxis, the believer must constantly engage in the theological task of measuring the reality of faith against the basis and content of that faith, Jesus Christ. Thus knowledge is an important aspect of faith. The content of that knowledge shall demand our attention in the next part.

Contemporary theology has gathered this holistic way of responding to God's revelation in the resurrection of the crucified Christ into the biblical concept of discipleship.[65] It was Dietrich Bonhoeffer who in our century has reminded the church of the danger of understanding "grace" as "cheap grace":

> Cheap Grace is the deadly enemy of our Church. We are fighting today for costly grace. Cheap grace means. . . . Grace without price; grace without cost! . . . Cheap grace means grace as a doctrine, a principle, a system. It means forgiveness of sins proclaimed as a general truth, the love of God taught as the Christian "conception" of God. An intellectual assent to that

---

65. The concept of discipleship has received much attention in recent theology: e.g., Eduard Schweizer, *Lordship and Discipleship*. SBT 28 (London: SCM, 1960); Eduard Schweizer, "Discipleship and Church," in: *The Beginnings of the Church in the New Testament* (Edinburgh: Saint Andrew Press, 1970), pp. 85–104; Athol Gill, *Life on the Road. The Gospel Basis for a Messianic Lifestyle* (Scottdale, Pa.: Herald Press, 1992); Athol Gill, *The Fringes of Freedom. Following Jesus, Living Together, Working for Justice* (Homebush West: Lancer, 1990); Ferdinand Hahn, "Pre-Easter Discipleship," in: *The Beginnings of the Church in the New Testament* (Edinburgh: Saint Andrew Press, 1970), pp. 9–39; Martin Hengel, *The Charismatic Leader and His Followers* (Edinburgh: Clark, 1981); August Strobel, "Discipleship in the Light of the Easter-event," in: *The Beginnings of the Church in the New Testament* (Edinburgh: Saint Andrew Press, 1970), pp. 40–84; Segundo Galilea, *Following Jesus* (Maryknoll, N Y: Orbis, 1981); Reiner Strunk, *Nachfolge Christi. Erinnerungen an eine evangelische Provokation* (München: Kaiser, 1981).

idea is held to be of itself sufficient to secure remission of sins. . . . Cheap grace therefore amounts to a denial of the living Word of God, in fact, a denial of the Incarnation of the Word of God. . . . Cheap grace is the grace we bestow on ourselves. Cheap grace is the preaching of forgiveness without requiring repentance, baptism without church discipline, Communion without confession, absolution without personal confession. Cheap grace is grace without discipleship, grace without the cross, grace without Jesus Christ, living and incarnate. . . . The word of cheap grace has been the ruin of more Christians than any commandment of works.[66]

Only when Christians and the Christian church can rediscover grace as "costly grace" can they retrieve their identity and relevance:

Costly grace is the treasure hidden in the field; for the sake of it a man will gladly go and sell all that he has. . . . it is the call of Jesus Christ at which the disciple leaves his nets and follows him. . . . Such grace is *costly* because it calls us to follow, and it is *grace* because it calls us to follow *Jesus Christ*. It is costly because it costs a man his life, and it is grace because it gives a man the only true life.[67]

Already the "Anabaptists"[68] of the 16th century had suspected a distortion of faith and a reduction of the gospel when the magisterial reformers made a distinction between justification and sanctification, and when they located the presence of Christ in the word and in the (proper) administration of the sacraments. They agreed with the magisterial reformers in their insistence on *sola gratia, sola fide,* and *sola scriptura,* but they insisted that faith means more than the individual and personal appropriation of salvation. It means "following Jesus" in the context of an intentional Christian community. They criticized the reformers' understanding of faith as being superficial and shallow[69] In their understanding the reformers preached "a sinful sweet Christ",[70] who does not lead to a "betterment of life".[71]

---

66. Dietrich Bonhoeffer, *The Cost of Discipleship* (New York: MacMillan, 1963 [1937]), pp. 45–47 and 59.

67. Ibid., p. 47.

68. This name, meaning "rebaptizers", was given to the "Anabaptists" by their opponents. They themselves did not consider their "believers' baptism" a "rebaptism". For them it was the only baptism called for by the New Testament. In German the distinction is made between *Täufer* ("baptizers") and Wiedertäufer ("rebaptizers"). "Anabaptists" understood themselves as *Täufer,* not as *Wiedertäufer*!

69. Conrad Grebel, "Letters to Thomas Müntzer," in: George Hunston Williams and Angel M. Mergal, eds., *Spiritual and Anabaptist Writers.* The Library of Christian Classics XXV (Philadelphia: Westminster, 1957, pp. 73–85), p. 74.

70. Conrad Grebel, "Letters to Thomas Müntzer," in: *Spiritual and Anabaptist Writers* (1957), pp. 78f.

71. Balthasar Hubmaier writes: "Faith alone makes us holy [*frumm* = *Fromm*] before God . . . Such faith can not remain passive but must break out [*aussbrechen*] to God

Dietrich Bonhoeffer retrieves that passion and laments—backing up his words with a life of credible witness—that "the outcome of the Reformation was the victory, not of Luther's perception of grace in all its purity and costliness, but of the vigilant religious instinct of man for the place where grace is to be obtained at the cheapest price."[72] When Christ calls persons, so Bonhoeffer insists in ever new variations, he frees them "from all man-made dogmas, from every burden and oppression, from every anxiety and torture which afflicts the conscience."[73] But this is only possible when the person hears the call and obeys it by following him in radical discipleship.

---

in thanksgiving and to mankind in all kinds of works of brotherly love." ("Eighteen Theses," (1524), in: W. R. Estep, ed., *Anabaptist Beginnings* [1523–1533]. A Source Book [Nieuwkoop: B. De Graaf, 1976, pp. 23–26], p. 24); Conrad Grebel writes to Thomas Müntzer: " ... today ... every man wants to be saved by superficial faith, without fruits of faith, without baptism of trial and probation, without love and hope, without right Christian practices, and wants to persist in all the old manner of personal vices...." (C. Grebel, "Letters to Thomas Müntzer," in: *Spiritual and Anabaptist Writers* [1957], p. 74); Jakob Kautz challenged the Protestant clergy of the city of Worms on June 13, 1527 by insisting: "Jesus Christ of Nazareth did not suffer for us and has not satisfied (for our sins) in any other way but this: that we have to stand in his footsteps and have to walk the way which he has blazed for us first, and that we obey the commandments of the Father and the Son, everyone according to his measure. He who speaks differently of Christ makes an idol of Christ." (Cited from R. Friedmann, *The Theology of Anabaptism. An Interpretation* [Scottdale, Pa.: Herald Press, 1973], p.85); perhaps Hans (John) Denck has most clearly expressed this concern: "... none may truly know (Christ) unless he follow after him with his life. And no one can follow after him except in so far as one previously knows (*erkennet*) him." ("Whether God is the Cause of Evil," [1526], in: *Spiritual and Anabaptist Writers* [1957], pp. 88–111], p.108). Further literature discussing the Anabaptist view of discipleship: Harold S. Bender, "'Walking in the Resurrection'—the Anabaptist Doctrine of Regeneration and Discipleship," *MennQR* 35 (1961), pp. 96–110; J. Lawrence Burkholder, "The Anabaptist Vision of Discipleship," in: Guy F. Hershberger, ed., *The Recovery of the Anabaptist Vision* (Scottdale, Pa.: Herald Press, 1957), pp. 135–151; John Driver, *Community and Commitment* (Scottdale, Pa.: Herald Press, 1976); Walter Klaassen, ed., *Anabaptism in Outline. Selected Primary Sources* (Kitchener, Ont.: Herald Press, 1981), pp. 85–100; Philip LeMasters, *Discipleship for All Believers. Christian Ethics and the Kingdom of God* (Scottdale, Pa.: Herald Press, 1992); Franklin H. Littell, "The Discipline of Discipleship in the Free Church Tradition," *MennQR* 35 (1961), pp. 111–119; John C. Wenger, "Grace and Discipleship in Anabaptism," *MennQR* 35 (1961), pp. 50–69.

72. Dietrich Bonhoeffer, *The Cost of Discipleship* (1963 [1937]), pp. 52f., see further, for instance, the "Introduction" and chapter 1 on "Costly Grace". In a sermon on the Magnificat in Luke 1:46–55 Bonhoeffer says that we can only adequately know the Christian story of Advent if we cease to be spectators and become active participants in God's dealings with humanity. (*Predigten, Auslegungen, Meditationen I*, 1925–1935 [München: Kaiser, 1984], p. 412, cited from Bertold Klappert, "Die Rechts-, Freiheits- und Befreiungsgeschichte Gottes mit dem Menschen. Erwägungen zum Verständnis der Auferstehung in Karl Barths Versöhnungslehre (*KD* IV/1–3)," *EvTh* 49 [1989, pp. 460–478], pp. 472f.).

73. *The Cost of Discipleship* (1963 [1937]), p. 40.

Karl Barth has acknowledged the importance of Bonhoeffer's contribution and has wholeheartedly agreed with his emphasis.[74] In all of his writings Barth seeks to maintain that God's freely given grace implies and therefore includes the call to radical discipleship. God's very being, the fact that in the humanity of Christ he is for us, liberates the believer to active obedience.[75] The content of this discipleship is given by the humanity of Christ through whom God has revealed and thereby confirmed his partiality for the poor and oppressed.[76]

Discipleship has also become the dominant commitment within the various manifestations of liberation theologies. Jon Sobrino speaks for many when he says: "Confronted with Jesus' eschatological proclamation, we cannot continue to live on the inertial routine of our past life. . . . Jesus calls for radical trust in God and discipleship in the service of the kingdom."[77] Related to the resurrection this means "that the meaning of Jesus' resurrection cannot be grasped unless one engages in active service for the transformation of an unredeemed world."[78]

The resurrection of the crucified Christ calls for Christian discipleship so that the identity of Christian faith is preserved; Christian discipleship needs the reality of the resurrection so that its liberating manifestation of the gospel is not reduced to the moralism of a merely human activity.

---

74. *CD* IV/2 (1958), pp. 533–553.

75. Karl Barth emphasizes, for instance, that the activity of God "kann ja als vollzogen gar nicht anders als in seinem *tätigen Nachvollzug* erkannt werden" *(Kirchliche Dogmatik* IV/1 [1953], p. 111, [emphasis mine]; the English translation is inadequate at this point). The same idea is contained in the subsequent sentences: "God is not idle but active. . . . therefore, man must be active too." (*CD* IV/1 [1956], p. 103). Compare further the important essays "Gospel and Law" (1935) and "Church and State" (1938), both in: Karl Barth, *Community, State, and Church. Three Essays* (Gloucester, Mass.: Peter Smith, 1968), pp. 71–100, 101–148. "Barmen 2" may serve as a summary statement: "As Jesus Christ is God's comforting verdict [*Zuspruch*] of the forgiveness of all our sins, so, and with equal seriousness, he is also God's vigorous announcement of his claim [*Anspruch*] upon our whole life. Through him there comes to us joyful liberation from the godless ties of this world for free, grateful service to his creatures." ("The Barmen Theological Declaration," [1934], § 2, emphasis mine, in: J.H. Leith, ed., *Creeds of the Churches* (Richmond: Knox, rev. ed. 1973) pp. 517–522; a newer translation in *JTSA* 47 (June 1984), pp. 78–81.

76. *CD* IV/2 (1958), §64,3 (pp. 154–264), explicitly for instance on p. 166: Jesus "exists analogously to the mode of existence of God." Therefore the "royal man shares . . . the strange destiny which falls on God . . . —to be the One who is ignored and forgotten and despised and discounted by men" (p. 167). Jesus manifested the partiality of God in that "He ignored all those who are high and mighty and wealthy in the world in favour of the weak and meek and lowly" (p. 168).

77. *Christology at the Crossroads* (1978), p.360.

78. Ibid., p. 380.

Part IV

CONTENT

*Consequences of Faith in the
Resurrection of the Crucified Christ*

Introduction to Part IV

In this final part it must become clear that faith and the church need not and therefore should not produce their own content. Their content is *given*, and as such it must be *received*. The apostle Paul therefore emphasizes that with the "coming" of faith, Christ "comes" to the believer (Gal 3:23–25); and the gospels tell the fascinating story of Jesus in order to constantly remind faith of its content. This content is the reality that shapes the existence of the believer and of the church.

Having discussed the resurrection of Jesus Christ as the foundational event for the Christian faith and for the Christian church, and having analyzed the nature of faith in the risen Christ, we must now point out, however briefly, what consequences this has for the content of faith.

It belongs to the abiding task of theology to remind the church and to remind the believer that the content of their faith is *extra nos*, and that this content must constantly be safeguarded against the believers' and the church's self-interest. The question that shall guide our discussion is this: what does it mean that God raised Jesus from the dead, and that this risen Christ must be seen in essential continuity with the crucified Jesus?

In principle we would need to discuss all theological doctrines. There is no Christian doctrine that is not affected by the fact, that for Christians, God is the One who raised Jesus from the dead. Nevertheless, we had to limit ourselves; and we limited ourselves to those theological themes that are immediately present in the biblical resurrection texts. I had planned a separate chapter on eschatology—the future of the crucified and risen Christ—but that would have gone beyond the limitations of the present essay.

Chapter 10

Holistic Christology

The resurrection manifests Jesus Christ as the ground and content of faith. Jesus, his life and his death, is not relativized, or "left behind", but with his resurrection the theological significance of his life and death is revealed, enhanced, and enacted. Faith in the risen Christ forces us therefore to develop a holistic christology in which the unity of Jesus' life, death, and resurrection is affirmed. An absolutization, or a relativization of any one aspect of "Jesus Christ"—his life, or his death, or his resurrection—must be resisted. If, for instance, Jesus' life would be absolutized and his resurrection would be relativized, then Jesus may be admired as a courageous hero or an ethical teacher or a moral example, but his saving and liberating reality is forfeited. If, on the other hand, his death is absolutized and his life is relativized, then Jesus may be regarded as an abstract God-Man who is necessary for a theory of atonement to bridge the gulf between God and humanity, but the particularity of his life, his poverty, and his prophetic critique is being lost. If, to use a further example, his resurrection is absolutized and his life is relativized, then Jesus may be understood as a "superman" or a miracle worker, but the offense that his life provoked and the subsequent way to Gethsemane and Calvary become theologically irrelevant. The theological challenge is therefore, to develop a holistic christology in which the life, death, and resurrection of Jesus are essentially interrelated, and complement each other.

THE LIFE OF JESUS

We may recall that the early Christians used the motifs of "ascension" and "exaltation" to interpret the significance of the resurrection: "he ascended into heaven and is seated at the right hand of the Father."[1] In response to Jesus' obe-

---

1. The quotation is from the "Ecumenical Creed" of 381 C.E. Since Judaism also knows of the ascension or exaltation of people to heaven who have not passed through death, we must emphasize that when we speak of "ascension" and "exaltation" as christological

240

dience unto death—"even death on a cross"—". . . God has highly exalted him and bestowed on him the name which is above every name, that at the name of Jesus every knee should bow, in heaven and on earth and under the earth, and every tongue confess that Jesus Christ is Lord, to the glory of God the Father" (Phil 2:9–11).[2] The "ascension/exaltation" motif was well known in Judaism. The righteous believer who, as a result of his radical obedience to God, suffers, and thereby atones for the sins of the people of Israel, is at his death received into God's glory.[3] Eduard Schweizer comments:

> Judaism frequently speaks of the righteous one who humbles himself or who voluntarily accepts humiliation by suffering and death in obedience to God. Suffering in particular is very valuable as atonement for one's own sins or vicarious atonement for other people's. As a reward the righteous one is exalted by God, secretly already on earth, but especially in the world to come, where he finds his seat reserved for him in heaven, the throne of glory, and there acts as a judge and executioner. This exaltation can also be pictured physically as an assumption from the earth, as an ascension to heaven.[4]

Jewish ascension/exaltation language was therefore conducive to describe and confess the divine significance of Jesus. It means that this particular Jesus, who lived his specific life and was crucified for it, is God's Son and humanity's savior. He is the mediator between God and humanity, he is the messianic ruler.[5]

---

motifs, we mean, of course, the ascension and exaltation of the dead Jesus into the presence of God. Only as such can ascension/exaltation language serve as an interpretation of the resurrection of the crucified Christ. Gerhard Lohfink shows how in the early church the message of the resurrection was explicated with the exaltation motif suggested by a number of Old Testament texts: Gerhard Lohfink, *Die Himmelfahrt Jesu. Untersuchungen zu den Himmelfahrts- und Erhöhungstexten bei Lukas* (München: Kösel, 1971), pp. 94–98; compare also the discussion by Gerhard Friedrich, "Die Auferweckung Jesu, eine Tat Gottes oder ein Interpretament der Jünger?" *KuD* 17 (1971, pp. 153–187), pp. 170–184.

2. Explicit references to the interpretation of the resurrection as exaltation are found in Acts 2:32–35, 5:30–32, Rom 1:3f., 8:34, and Eph 1:19–22. Other New Testament texts reflecting this interpretation are: 1 Thess 1:10; Rom 14:9; Col 3:1; Eph 2:6, 4:8–10; 1 Pet 1:20f., 3:18–22; Heb 1:3, 4:14, 5:5, 7:26, 8:1, 10:12, 12:2; 1 Tim 3:16; Mark 16:19; Matt 28:18b-20; Luke 9:51f., 24:26; Acts 1:1f. 21f., 3:19–21, 13:32f.; John 3:14, 12:32.34.

3. Compare Pss 18:48, 73:23–28, 75:7.10; Isa 26:7–19, 52:13–15.

4. Eduard Schweizer, *Lordship and Discipleship*. SBT 28 (London: SCM, 1960), p. 30, see especially pp. 22–31.

5. "Ascension" and "exaltation" are therefore theological symbols that intend to express the theological meaning of the resurrection, and the divine aim and significance of the risen One. The evangelist Luke was the first theologian who shaped these motifs into a story of Christ's ascension (Luke 24:50–53; Acts 1:9–11) and thereby suggests that the ascension may have been a historical and visible event; for details see: Gerhard Lohfink, *Die Himmelfahrt Jesu* (1971), pp. 242–283.

By raising Jesus Christ from the dead, God revealed, confirmed, verified, and enacted the mission of the life and death of Jesus. The resurrection is God's concrete and unconditional "Yes" to Jesus' life and death. At the same time, the ministry of Jesus also gives content to the resurrection. Christological reflection must therefore affirm a theological continuity between the risen Christ and the life of Jesus.

The Jesus who was raised from the dead was a particular person; he had lived a specific life, to which his death was intimately related. The "life of Jesus" must therefore not remain an empty symbol, into which everyone can read a content that serves best their own personal and institutional interests. In order to understand the resurrection as the resurrection *of Jesus Christ*, we need to ask whether it is possible to give discernible content to the "life of Jesus".

Space does not permit us to debate the so-called "quest for the historical Jesus", and, related to it, the problem of the "historical-critical method".[6] Suffice it to say that the biblical sources neither allow nor encourage us to compose a biography of Jesus. Nevertheless, faith must remain in continuity with Jesus if it is not to receive its content from the believers' or the church's self-interest.

I think that it is possible to give content to the "life of Jesus" if we find a way to gather up his life intention without having to focus our attention on every single word or every single deed that was attributed to Jesus. What was the catalyzing effect in his life, that led some people to follow him in radical discipleship, while others opposed him with equal zeal? Jesus, the carpenter from Nazareth, who had no other passion than to concretely live out in a humane and nonviolent manner what he had heard in the first commandment— why was he captured, condemned, and crucified? The answers to these questions promise to reveal the main passion and intention of Jesus' life. Not how he psychologically perceived it, but as it became historically manifest. Our historical interest concentrates therefore on those aspects of his life that on the one hand led people to follow him in radical discipleship, and on the other hand incited the opposition of the religious establishment, and then finally led to his crucifixion.[7]

---

6. A good review and discussion of the problems and challenges related to the quest for the historical Jesus is: Ferdinand Hahn, "Methodologische Überlegungen zur Rückfrage nach Jesus," in: Karl Kertelge, ed., *Rückfrage nach Jesus. Zur Methodik und Bedeutung der Frage nach dem historischen Jesus* (Freiburg: Herder, 1974), pp. 11–77.

7. We are not asking for Jesus' "messianic consciousness" or "personality", nor are we primarily interested in his personal "disposition" or his "character". It is difficult to answer these questions from the New Testament texts, and, what is much more important, those enquiries often lead to an existential or ecclesiastical reduction of "Jesus Christ". This would be my main criticism against the otherwise excellent book by Peter Carnley, *The Structure of Resurrection Belief* (Oxford: Clarendon Press, 1987). By trying to discern the reasons that caused the conflict between Jesus and his opponents, we are on safer historical grounds, and we are more in line with the theological tendency of the New Testament message. It is not Jesus' personality, but his effect on history, that is the content of the incarnation.

With this attempt to approach the life of Jesus from the perspective of his crucifixion, we take up the intention of the various New Testament traditions that seek to protect the identity of Christian faith not simply by pointing to "Jesus Christ", but by interpreting "Jesus Christ" with reference to his crucifixion. The apostle Paul, for instance, in his struggle for Christian identity and relevance with the church in Corinth, states his central theological interest in this way: ". . . I decided to know nothing among you except Jesus Christ *and him crucified*" (1 Cor 2:2). The Letter to the Hebrews tells us that "Jesus also suffered outside the gate in order to sanctify the people through his own blood" (13:12). In the Book of Revelation it is "the lamb who was slain" who rules, and who alone is worthy to reveal God's plan for the world (Rev 5). In the Gospel of Mark the first adequate christological confession arises in view of the *crucified* Christ: "This man was truly a Son of God" (15:39), whereby the "was" ties the Crucified One to the particular life that he lived. And in the Gospel of John the glorification of Jesus takes place on the cross (12:23; 17:1). These texts make clear that the early Christians viewed the life of Jesus from the perspective of the cross. Jesus can only be properly understood in relationship to the cross. It is in the cross where the intention of Jesus' life becomes centered.

Viewing Jesus' life from the perspective of the cross would mean to recognize that the death of Jesus was neither the result of an accident, nor of a judicial error. Given the religious, economic, and political situation of Jesus' day, his death was the "natural" and as such predictable consequence of his way of life. The opposition against him, and his execution was a response to his understanding of God and the resultant unconditional love for human beings.

Conflict with the authorities accompanied Jesus all of his active messianic life. The religious leaders charged him with being a friend of publicans and sinners. To them it was presumptuous that Jesus (rather than God) would grant faith and forgiveness to people; that in the name of God he would restore people and convey to them hope and dignity; that he would claim those who were socially suspect and religiously unqualified to be the object of God's saving and liberating passion. His opponents rightly understood his lifestyle as questioning and even attacking the final and absolute authority of the foundational pillars of the contemporary Jewish religious establishment: the Torah, the temple, and the cult. What offended the religious establishment was not so much that Jesus understood and interpreted the regulations of the law and the rules of the cult differently, but that he in fact acted upon his understanding. That under certain circumstances, when human need was evident and calling, he assumed the authority to break the Sabbath and suspend the cultic rules of ritual purity and fasting. For his religious opponents he was a blasphemer and seducer of the people (Deut 13 and 17), and as such he deserved the death penalty (Lev 24:16).

By blessing the poor and oppressed, by showing solidarity with the wretched of the earth, and by proclaiming their liberation, he also challenged the economic interests of those in power. Anyone who suggests that the fate of the poor may not be their own fault, or may not be the will of God, but may indeed be the byproduct of societal structures that favor the interests of the rich and powerful, was perceived as dangerous by the establishment.

This would also explain why his activity was brought to the attention of the political authorities of his day, whose interest it was to maintain social stability, and who readily cooperated in removing one person in order to maintain law and order for the rest of society.

Jesus threatened the religious, political, and economic structures of his day by his radical obedience to God and the resultant radical commitment to make human life human wherever he saw it breaking or broken. This understanding of God and the resultant vision of reality clashed with the views and interests of the religious and political establishment. They could not contain and incorporate the newness of Jesus' vision of the βασιλεία τοῦ θεοῦ (basileia tou theou). In their understanding of reality, condemning Jesus to death was an act of self-preservation, and at the same time it was perceived to be a necessary act of obedience to their perception of the will of God.

When this particular Jesus, who with his life fleshed out a particular understanding of God and of the dignity of human life, was raised from the dead, this life was revealed as having divine and eternal dignity.

By raising the crucified Christ from the dead, God himself revealed that this particular person, Jesus of Nazareth and the life he lived, must serve to define the content of "divinity" and therewith the content of resurrection faith. Concretely this means that the deity of Christ is revealed in his radical obedience to God and his radical commitment to broken humanity. Deity, therefore, does not withdraw from the world, but it is the healing and reconciling reality in the world. It does not in the first place mean commitment to religious institutions and religious rules and dogmas, but the concrete engagement for the alleviation of human need: "The Sabbath was made for man, not man for the Sabbath; so the Son of man is lord even of the Sabbath" (Mark 2:27f.).

All this has consequences for our understanding of the person of Jesus Christ. His sovereign liberty over against law and cult, his radical call of people to follow him, his claim that in and through his ministry the βασιλεία τοῦ θεοῦ (basileia tou theou) had become a present reality, entailed a tremendous claim. The implied claim was that he was the true representative of the βασιλεία τοῦ θεοῦ (basileia tou theou). That in him the reality "God" was manifest. This claim was verified and confirmed by raising the crucified Jesus from the dead. The resurrection therefore revealed and reveals who Jesus was, and who God is.

THE DEATH OF JESUS

The resurrection does not only help us to appreciate the theological importance of the life of Jesus, but it also illuminates the theological meaning of his death. It reveals that the death of Jesus has more significance than being the end of his earthly life. At the same time, the death of the risen Christ reminds us that Christian existence is an existence "under the cross". Believers carry in their existence the "death of Jesus" and only as such "the life of Jesus" is also manifested in their existence (2 Cor 4:10).

On the basis of God's raising the crucified Jesus from the dead, and on the basis of their experience of Christ as savior, the early Christians confessed that "Christ died for our sins" (1 Cor 15:3), and that he liberated them from the estranging powers in the cosmos. This soteriological significance of the death of Christ was then expressed in a great variety of symbols, such as: expiation (Rom 3:25), sin offering (Rom 8:3; Heb 9:11–14.28), ransom (Mark 10:45; Rev 5:9), reconciliation (Rom 5:10f.; Col 1:22), representation (Rom 4:25, 5:6–8), redemption (Rom 3:24; Eph 1:7; Heb 9:15), justification (Rom 3:24), blood sacrifice (Rom 3:25, 5:9; Eph 2:13; Heb 10:19; 1 Pet 1:2; 1 John 1:7; Rev 1:5; Acts 20:28), covenant sacrifice (Mark 14:24, 1 Cor 11:25; Heb 9:17–21, 13:20), passover lamb (John 1:29.36, 19:36; 1 Pet 1:19; Rev 5:6, 7:14, 12:11), cosmic reconciler (Col 1:20), destruction of the devil (Heb 2:14), forgiveness (Heb 9:22).

With these and other symbols the early Christians expressed their conviction that in the death of Jesus Christ, God has dealt with the estranging powers of sin, evil, and death. In the death of Jesus, God himself opened his being to the forces of sin and estrangement, and through the resurrection it has been revealed that ultimately the estranging power of sin and death has been broken. In consequence of that victory, believers can therefore know that "in Christ" their relationship with God is established, they are reconciled with God, their sins have been forgiven, and they have been liberated to become servants of life and reconciliation, creatively participating in God's saving and liberating passion for the world.

The resurrection therefore does not interpret the death of Jesus as a transition to his real existence in the presence of God. Rather, it reveals that in and with the death of Jesus, God has continued in a decisive way what Jesus began during his life—to struggle against the forces of sin, evil, and death—and from this struggle God has emerged as the victor. That is the triumph of the resurrection of the crucified Christ. Christian faith must understand, however, that for our existence in the world this ultimate victory still stands under the provisional "not yet", and must therefore be lived here and now by displaying the solidarity of love in the certain hope that the God who raised Jesus from the dead provides the necessary resources in the struggle for truth and justice now, and that he will also ultimately stand by those who have lived in obedience to Christ.

THE RISEN LIFE OF CHRIST

The resurrection is not only the verification and revelation of the theological significance of Jesus' life and death. The biblical motifs of "ascension" and "exaltation" also remind us that we must speak of the "existence" of the risen

Christ.[8] The problem is, of course, how this "existence" can be gathered into thoughts and words. How can we best describe this dimension of christological "newness" in the resurrection? In our discussion of the historical dimension of the resurrection we have already said that through the resurrection Jesus' whole life has arrived in the presence of God. The New Testament speaks therefore of a "bodily" resurrection. "Bodily" here does not refer to that particular body which Jesus had at the point of his death. It does not even necessarily presuppose an empty tomb. It means that the whole person of Jesus with all his accomplishments and relationships, i.e., that person which was formed in and through his relationships and ministries, has arrived in the presence of God. Not only his "soul", but his whole being was taken into God and was thus given a "new" existence. From within God the risen and exalted Christ appeared to Mary, Peter, and Paul, not in his earthly body, but, as the later ending of Mark correctly says, "in another form" (Mark 16:12), a form that can no longer be grasped by empirical or historical reason, but that becomes real to the life of faith. This same risen Christ continues to minister to us and to the world through the Holy Spirit.[9]

CONCLUSION

With respect to a holistic christology, the "exaltation/ascension" motif reminds us, firstly, that through the resurrection Jesus Christ has been installed as *Kyrios*. Thereby the life and ministry of Jesus Christ has been universalized. With the resurrection the vision of Jesus' life, the all-determining passion of his ministry, the theological content of his death, all of this has been given universal relevance.

This enthroning of the Crucified Christ to be the *Kyrios* of the world serves, secondly, as the basis for the Christian hope in life after death. We cannot know the details of such a life, but we can have the certainty of faith that the God who

---

8. This would be the starting point for a cosmic Christology which we cannot develop here (but see pp. 284–294 below). Compare: Allan D. Galloway, *The Cosmic Christ* (London: Nisbet, 1951); George A. Maloney, S. J., *The Cosmic Christ. From Paul to Teilhard* (New York: Sheed and Ward, 1968); Jürgen Moltmann, *The Way of Jesus Christ. Christology in Messianic Dimensions* (London: SCM, 1990), pp. 274–312. Interesting is also Karl Barth's brief reference to Christ's "third form of existence" as "the *Pantocrator* who already reigns. . . ." (*CD* IV/3, Second Half [1962], §72:1, p. 756).

9. That this is not *mythological* but *theological* language is well argued by Wilhelm Thüsing, *Die Neutestamentlichen Theologien und Jesus Christus. I: Kriterien aufgrund der Rückfrage nach Jesus und des Glaubens an seine Auferweckung* (Düsseldorf: Patmos Verlag, 1981), pp. 118–139; see also: Wilhelm Thüsing, "Neutestamentliche Zugangswege zu einer transzendental-dialogischen Christologie," in: Karl Rahner— Wilhelm Thüsing, *Christologie—Systematisch und Exegetisch. Arbeitsgrundlagen für eine interdisziplinäre Vorlesung* (Freiburg: Herder, 1972, pp. 79–303), pp. 167–177.

received Jesus into himself will also receive us. With Jesus "the first fruits" of humanity (1 Cor 15:20) have arrived at their ultimate destiny.

Thirdly, the "ascension/exaltation" motif explains that the resurrection of Christ does not set an end to Jesus' life and ministry. Rather, through the resurrection, Jesus Christ is exalted to a place of power (the "right hand of God") from where he can continue his ministry, now not hindered by the limitations of time and space. On this basis we can affirm the priestly work of Christ. The risen Christ grants forgiveness and reconciliation to the believer (1 John 1:7.9), and makes intercession on our behalf to God (Heb 7:25; Rom 8:34). Because God has taken Jesus into himself, therefore the same grace which became real to people through the earthly life of Jesus becomes real now to the believer who obediently responds to God's word.

Fourthly, the "existence" of the risen Christ is the basis for our experience of the presence of Christ in our lives. Not only the "cause of Jesus" (die "Sache Jesu") lives on after his death, but a very personal reality confronts us in our lives through the ministry of the Holy Spirit. The theological intention of the "exaltation/ascension" motif is therefore not that Jesus through the resurrection is spatially removed from the world. Quite the opposite. It is the symbolic presentation that the Crucified Christ is no longer limited in his ministry by time and space. He has been exalted to a position of power (to the "right hand of God"), from where, through the ministry of the Spirit, he continues his healing, saving, and liberating presence on the earth.

This, finally, guards us against the danger of understanding Jesus (the historical Jesus and/or his death) in terms of a "moral law" or as part of an abstract theory of atonement. The life-vision of the historical Jesus and the soteriological depth of his death must ever anew, under the guidance of the Holy Spirit, be applied to new situations. The indicative of the reality of the resurrection must not be dissolved into the imperative of the "newness of life" (Rom 6:4). Rather, the former serves as the necessary presupposition for the latter.

Chapter 11

The God Who Raised the Crucified Jesus from the Dead

We saw that the "exaltation/ascension" motif continues to remind us that through the resurrection Jesus Christ did not return to an earthly life, a life marked by the parameters of history and death; rather, he was "exalted" to a new existence in the presence of God. Death no longer has any power over the risen Christ, "he will never die again" (Rom 6:9).

In the New Testament the life of the risen Christ is described as a life unto God: "the life he lives he lives to God" (Rom 6:10).[1] This is not merely mythological language; it means in fact that the life of God itself has been changed through the resurrection of the crucified Christ. It is therefore not surprising that the early Christians shaped their understanding of God in light of the resurrection of Christ. The God of Abraham, Isaac, and Jacob was described as the one "who gives life to the dead and calls into existence the things that do not exist" (Rom 4:17).[2] We shall therefore need to ask what consequences the resurrection of Christ has for our understanding of the nature and being of God.

---

1. Other texts that explicitly emphasize the God orientation of the risen Christ are: 1 Cor 3:23 ("Christ is God's"); 1 Cor 15:28 (in the eschaton "the Son" will be subjected to the Father, so "that God may be everything to every one"); Gal 4:6 ("God has sent the Spirit of his Son into our hearts, crying, 'Abba! Father!' "); Rom 8:34 (". . . Christ Jesus . . ., who was raised from the dead, who is at the right hand of God . . ."); Col 3:1 (Christ is "seated at the right hand of God"); Heb 9:24 (". . . Christ has entered . . . into heaven itself, now to appear in the presence of God on our behalf"); Heb 12:2 (". . . Jesus the pioneer and perfecter of our faith, . . . is seated at the right hand of the throne of God"); Matt 28:16–20 (the risen Christ appears from heaven, i.e., from the presence of God); John 17:1–5 (The Son glorifies the Father "in thy own presence with the glory which I had with thee before the world was made"); John 17:21 ("even as thou, Father, art in me, and I in thee. . . .").

2. Similar emphases are found in Rom 8:11; 1 Cor 6:14, 15:12–20; 2 Cor 1:9, 4:14; Gal 1:1; Col 2:12; 1 Pet 1:21.

248

JESUS AND THE "SHAPE" OF GOD

By raising Jesus from the dead, God affirmed Jesus' understanding of God. Jesus lived and died in a religious world. His life and death must, amongst other things, be seen as a struggle for the right understanding of God. With his words and deeds he came into conflict primarily with the religious forces of his time.[3] Although the Romans executed him for what in their understanding was a political crime, the driving force behind the opposition that led to his arrest and ultimately to his death was the religious establishment. For the religious leaders and for the people that followed them Jesus was a blasphemer and one who led the people astray. His understanding of God and the imperative included in that understanding clashed with their religious convictions and political interests. "God" stood against "God". They understood their opposition to be a religious duty and a religious service. They wanted to protect the integrity of their faith and they wanted to assure the future of their religion and culture. One of the questions, therefore, which confronts us from the life and death of Jesus is: whose understanding of God is right, that of Jesus or that of his contemporaries and his opponents?[4]

---

3. It is true, of course, that one cannot clearly distinguish between the religious and the political realm in the Jewish society during Jesus' time (E. P. Sanders, *Jesus and Judaism* [London: SCM, 1985], p. 296); but at the same time it is probably a tendentious interpretation of the sources to make the Roman authorities and political expediency the major motivations behind the opposition to Jesus. With the same rigor that Sanders criticizes other views, it must therefore be said that the following summary statement is an inadequate representation of the historical facts that he himself elaborates: "He was executed by the Romans, and *if* Jews had *anything* to do with it—that is, *if* he were not executed simply because he caused public disturbance—the instigators of his death *would have been* those with access to Pilate. Chief among these were the leaders of the priesthood." (*Jesus and Judaism* [1985], p. 293, emphasis mine).

4. It is obvious that at this point historical research is intimately interwoven with theological conclusions. There is no consensus among New Testament scholars as to what party constituted the major opposition to Jesus (the Sadducees? the Priests? the Pharisees? the Romans?), and for what reasons he was opposed, arrested, and killed (for his messianic self-claim? his opposition to and conflict with the Torah? his criticism of the temple? his political disturbance?). Since we cannot go into details here, I would suggest the following for further information: Günter Bornkamm, *Jesus of Nazareth* (London: Hodder & Stoughton, 1960), chs. II, V, VII; Herbert Braun, *Spätjüdisch-häretischer und frühchristlicher Radikalism. Jesus von Nazareth und die essenische Qumransekte.* BHTh 24/I & II. 2 vols. (Tübingen: Mohr, 1957); Herbert Braun, *Qumran und das Neue Testament.* Band II (Tübingen: Mohr, 1966), §§ 3 and 5; Ernst Käsemann, "The Problem of the Historical Jesus," in: *Essays on New Testament Themes.* SBT 4 (Naperville, Ill.: Allenson, 1964), pp. 15–47; Eduard Schweizer, *Jesus* (London: SCM, 1971), ch. II; C. H. Dodd, *The Founder of Christianity* (New York: Macmillan, 1970), chs. VII and VIII; Joachim Jeremias, *New Testament Theology. The Proclamation of Jesus* (1971), §§ 7, 11, 12, 13, 14, 17, 18, 19, 22; Martin Hengel, *The Charismatic Leader and His Followers* (Edinburgh: Clark, 1981); Leonhard Goppelt, *Theology of the New Testament.* Volume One (Grand Rapids, Mich.: Eerdmans, 1981), §§ 9, 12, 21; Ben Meyer, *The Aims of Jesus* (London: SCM, 1979); James D. G. Dunn, *Jesus, Paul and*

While some of the negative characterizations of Jesus' opponents (especially of the Pharisees) reflect the early church's sentiment—e.g., the negative portrayal of the Pharisees in the gospels of Matthew and John—there can be no doubt that Jesus' critical attitude to the Sabbath and the temple with its manifold activities, his liberal attitude towards cultic practices like washing of hands and fasting, his solidarity with "sinners", his openness to the "people of the land", to women and children, to the publicans, and even the Gentiles, must have been perceived to be a radical critique of the traditional and then current understanding of God. This historical conflict therefore raises the theological question concerning the most adequate understanding of God.

When we try to understand the situation in which the conflict between Jesus and certain religious groups and movements of his time arose, we may say that their central focus on Torah and cult was motivated by their hope for the restoration of the true Israel. Although this was also Jesus' concern, he was critical of tendencies that led to a national and religious elitism and exclusivism.

The passion for the restoration of Israel manifested itself by strictly adhering to the Torah. God's will and God's revelation could only be discovered by studying the Torah. The Torah was seen as the mediator between God and humanity. Although Israel knew of a gracious God, in fact the dominance of the Torah in their theology and practice tended to shape a legalistic, formal, and fixed understanding of God.

Another important element shaping the common picture of God was the cult. The temple cult in Jerusalem suggested that God could be pleased by meticulous cultic performances. Cultic practices like ceremonial washings, Sabbath observance, fasting, and tithing, were based on the conviction that these religious

---

the Law. Studies in Mark and Galatians (London: SPCK, 1990), pp. 10–88; Otto Betz, "Probleme des Prozesses Jesu," in: Hildegard Temporini und Wolfgang Haase, Hg., Aufstieg und Niedergang der Römischen Welt. Geschichte und Kultur Roms im Spiegel der Neueren Forschung, II.25.1 (Berlin, New York: Walter de Gruyter, 1982), pp. 565–647; Jürgen Roloff, Die Kirche im Neuen Testament. GNT 10 (Göttingen: Vandenhoeck & Ruprecht, 1993), pp. 21–26. E. P. Sanders (Jesus and Judaism [1985]) disagrees with most contemporary Christian New Testament scholars when they argue that the main reasons for Jesus' death was either his messianic self-consciousness (his "self-claim") or his opposition to and conflict with the Torah. He sees the major reasons that led to the opposition of Jesus as being his criticism of the temple, his negation of one particular part of the law ("let the dead bury the dead"), and in his associating with the "sinners" (not the amme ha-arets, but the "wicked"). Although he admits that the religious and the political realms cannot be separated (p. 296), he tends to emphasize the political aspects for Jesus crucifixion and he considers the Roman authorities to be the major agitators (p. 293). Whatever the historical details may have been, the religious question, the struggle for the right understanding of "God", was certainly at stake in Jesus' view of reality. For a first orientation about the different religious parties and their views during the time of Jesus—i.e., the High Priests, the chief priests, the Levites, the Sadducees, the Pharisees, the Essenes (Qumran), the scribes, the Zealots, the various apocalyptic groups, the Romans—I would suggest the respective articles in the TDNT, the IDB, the TRE, The Anchor Bible Dictionary, and, of course, Bill., especially vol. IV/1 and 2, and vol. II, pp. 494–519.

exercises constituted the true worship of God. Those who could not participate in such cultic practices and those who did not know the law, belonged to the "ignorant" and "unclean" whose acceptability before God was questioned.

Besides knowing the Torah and practicing the cult, God's favor and salvation was for many also tied to the performance of good works. These did not only include the study of the law and the observance of the cult, but also the works of charity like feeding the hungry, helping the poor and the stranger, burying the dead, consoling the sad, and visiting the sick and the prisoner. For doing these things, God would reward them. There was therefore a close relationship between what persons did on earth and what would be done for them in heaven. This thinking was conducive to developing an attitude of self-righteousness among those who were sure that their good works were more numerous than their bad works. At the same time, it led to a soteriological uncertainty for those who were unsure, and it meant rejection for the marginal groups like fishermen, publicans, lepers, sinners, and prostitutes, who under those conditions would have no hope of inheriting the kingdom of God.

For some God was a quietist who was not active in human history, while for others he was actively engaged in the militant opposition against the Roman occupation forces. God therefore tended to become functionalized for political programs that either counseled withdrawal from or involvement in the affairs of the world.

Others saw God's main interest and activity to lie in the future. They had no hope for "this world". Therefore one could only long for its passing, and wait for the "new" world, the "world to come", and one would be busily engaged in trying to develop apocalyptic timetables for the passing of this world and the arrival of the world "to come".

This description is somewhat of a stereotype, and it does not properly reflect the complex historical situation or the diversity of Jewish belief and practice. Yet we need to be aware of the historical context in order to appreciate the fact that Jesus' death was not an accident of history, that he did not die of old age, and that his execution was not the result of a judicial error. A major reason for the opposition against him can be explained by the common struggle for the right understanding of God and its implications for the concrete shaping of human life. Of course there were the more immediate reasons of political expediency, and one should also not forget the fact that every institution and its leadership try to protect their self-interest and try to assure their survival. Yet the question of God, who he is, how he relates to the world, and what he demands, cannot be eliminated if one wants to understand the opposition to Jesus.

Many of the above emphases were in tension and even in contradiction with Jesus' own understanding of God and with his subsequent vision of reality. When he envisioned the restoration of Israel—for instance by calling the "twelve" to represent the twelve tribes of Israel—it would include all of Israel, including those who were religiously or morally suspect. And when he was confronted with the needs of Gentiles, he did not exclude them from his ministry. His radical emphasis that love for God manifests itself ultimately in the love of one's enemies (Matt 5:43–48) was given concrete visibility in his ministry. Although he did not categorically reject or negate the Torah and the cult as such, it was certainly surprising to see with what sovereign authority he ignored, relativized, and even negated law and cult when they stood in the way of his dominating passion to love God and to restore human life.

He claimed that God was present in his ministry of healing, forgiveness, and reconciliation. This God was a loving father (he called him "Abba") who would relativize all customs, traditions, laws and cultic rules in order to make his grace real and concrete to people. Jesus therefore relativized the law and the cult and claimed that the Sabbath was made for man, not man for the Sabbath (Mark 2:27). Related to the conviction that God as creator of the world loves his creation, Jesus negated the distinction between the holy and the profane and associated with people, even called people into his immediate community, who were considered religiously unclean and morally suspect. His relationship to God was marked by an immediacy and personal quality which arose out of the experience that God was near as father ("Abba"), and that one could communicate with him in prayer without the mediation of law and cult. He also associated with Gentiles and refused to create a closed and elitist community.

This led to a seemingly irreconcilable conflict between Jesus and the religious groups of his day. They were not willing to surrender or even modify their understanding of God. To them Jesus was a blasphemer and one who led the people astray, and who, therefore, in the name of their God deserved capital punishment.

Jesus, on the other hand, remained true to his understanding of God. He did it in a nonviolent manner and therefore did not resist his arrest and death sentence.

Yet on "Good Friday" it was unclear whose understanding of God was right. Does not Moses say in the Torah:

> The Lord your God will raise up for you a prophet like me from among you, from your brethren—him you shall heed—just as you desired of the Lord your God at Horeb on the day of the assembly. . . . And the Lord said to me, ". . . I will raise up for them a prophet like you from among their brethren; and I will put my words in his mouth, and he shall speak to them all that I command him. . . . *But the prophet who presumes to speak a word in my name which I have not commanded him to speak, or who speaks in the name of other gods, that same prophet shall die.*" And if you say in your heart, "How may we know the word which the Lord has not spoken?"—when a prophet speaks in the name of the Lord, if *the word does not come to pass or come true, that is a word which the Lord has not spoken*; the prophet has spoken it presumptuously, you need not be afraid of him. (Deut 18:15–22, emphases mine).

Any simplistic view of salvation history or of God confirming his will in history could come to the conclusion that the understanding of God held by Jesus' opponents was validated by a divine verdict in history. Did they not win in the struggle with Jesus? And God certainly did not interfere on Jesus' behalf! Yes, this understanding of God had even won the hearts and minds of his male disciples. They fled!

The change, the transfiguration of reality, came on "Easter Day". By raising Jesus from the dead God established once and for all time that his nature corresponds to Jesus' understanding and praxis, not to that of his opponents. Through the resurrection appearances the proper understanding of God was re-created in the hearts of the disciples. Those who had doubted that God was with Jesus in his passion and death became convinced by God himself that he had shared his life with the dead Jesus.

The resurrection of the crucified Christ is therefore fundamental for our understanding of God. God is not a "bookkeeper" who evaluates human worth according to a person's deeds. God cannot be known simply by studying the law. God cannot be pleased by cultic and religious exercises. Rather, God is a father who welcomes all people as his creatures into a living relationship with himself. His acceptance is unconditional, and it becomes real in the obedience of faith. Because God is love and as such comes to his creation, therefore the focus is upon those who live at the margin of society. In the historical context of Jesus' ministry the immediate interest was to restore the outsiders to Israel, but by implication, the love of God is directed to all people. Within this living and dynamic relationship of faith, the study of the Torah, cultic practices, and ethical obedience assume an important role in order to express worship, educate faith, and relate faith to all areas of life. But apart from the living, personal and unconditional acceptance by God himself, the Torah, the cult, and human deeds lose their life, and become shells of death.

INTIMATIONS OF TRINITY

With the resurrection of Christ the symbol "God" became inherently linked to the name of Jesus and to the effective power of the Holy Spirit.

This interrelationship between God, Jesus, and the Spirit was already evident in Jesus' ministry.[5] On the one hand, Jesus grounded his own authority in God, and he did his work in the power of the Spirit: ". . . if it is by the finger [Matthew: "spirit"] of God that I cast out demons, then the kingdom of God has come upon you" (Luke 11:20 = Matt 12:28). He did not speak of his own "reign", but it was the future "reign of God" that came near and was even present in his ministry. He did not do his own will, but the dominating passion of his life was to accomplish the will of God. He did not proclaim himself, he represented God as the liberating and saving reality. He did not call people to faith

---

5. For details see: Wolfgang Schrage, "Theologie und Christologie bei Paulus und Jesus auf dem Hintergrund der modernen Gottesfrage," *EvTh* 36 (1976, pp. 121–154), pp. 135–151.

in himself, but in his presence people experienced faith in God, or they experienced wholeness, which Jesus then interpreted to be faith in God. He did not grant his own forgiveness, but the forgiveness of God. He did not pray to himself, but to God. The Gospel of John has clearly formulated this relational-reality:

> And Jesus cried out and said, "He who believes in me, believes not in me but in him who sent me. And he who sees me sees him who sent me. . . . I have not spoken on my own authority; the Father who sent me has himself given me commandment what to say and what to speak. And I know that his commandment is eternal life. What I say, therefore, I say as the Father has bidden me." (12:44f.49f.; compare also the Q-saying Luke 10:16/Matt 10:40).

Yet, on the other hand, the coming of the "reign of God" and its presence in the power of the Spirit was inherently linked with the person and the ministry of Jesus. The parables are language-events because in their telling Jesus brought the "reign of God" near to people. He drove out demons, healed the sick, and proclaimed liberation to the captives—all manifestations showing that in and through his ministry the "reign of God" was in their midst (Luke 17:21).

After Easter the interlocking of God's activity with the work of the Holy Spirit and the resurrection of Christ was formulated in the pre-Pauline tradition: ". . . the gospel concerning his Son, who was descended from David according to the flesh and designated Son of God in power according to the *Spirit of holiness* by his *resurrection from the dead*, Jesus Christ our Lord" (Rom 1:3f., emphasis mine).[6] This tradition is continued by the apostle Paul who can use "God" and "Christ" interchangeably, without dissolving their distinction, or relativizing their difference. The activity of God and the activity of Christ are interrelated, and yet it is "Christ" who died for our sins, not "God", and ultimately it is "God" who will be all in all, not "Christ".[7]

This "trinitarian" tendency also became evident when the early Christians spoke of their activities, performed in the power of the Spirit (exorcisms, baptism, forgiveness, preaching, teaching, healing, prayer, worship), as being executed in "the name of Jesus".[8] Later this led to even more explicit "trinitarian"

---

6. Compare further: Rom 8:11, 10:9. For details see: Wolfgang Schrage, "Theologie und Christologie bei Paulus und Jesus auf dem Hintergrund der modernen Gottesfrage," *EvTh* 36 (1976, pp.121–154), pp. 122–124.

7. For details see Wolfgang Schrage, "Theologie und Christologie bei Paulus und Jesus auf dem Hintergrund der modernen Gottesfrage," *EvTh* 36 (1976, pp. 121–154), pp. 124–129.

8. The trinitarian intention is clear: ". . . be filled with the Spirit, . . ., always and for everything giving thanks in the name of our Lord Jesus Christ to God the Father" (Eph 5:18–20); "Whoever receives one such child in my name receives me; and whoever receives me, receives not me, but him who sent me" (Mark 9:37); "And Peter said to them,

formulations: "Go therefore and make disciples of all nations, baptizing them in the name of the Father and of the Son and of the Holy Spirit" (Matt 28:19). "The grace of the Lord Jesus Christ and the love of God and the fellowship of the Holy Spirit be with you all" (2 Cor 13:14).[9]

The resurrection of Christ, therefore, implies a trinitarian understanding of God. The reality created and manifested in and by the resurrection led inexorably to the doctrine of the Trinity in the post-New Testament period.[10] For the Christian "'Father, Son, and Holy Spirit' in fact occupies . . . the place occupied in Israel by 'Yahweh' or, later 'Lord'. . . ."[11]

GOD AS A RELATIONAL REALITY

A theological problem of long standing is how we can think God's trinitarian nature as the distinctively Christian understanding of God without surrendering the unity of the Godhead on the one hand, and the universal sovereignty of the one God on the other. The focus on the resurrection of Christ as an act of God may be of help in addressing this problem. It would suggest that we should refuse to start our thinking of God with any given idea of deity or transcendence or metaphysics or ontology.[12] Rather, for the Christian, God is the One who has acted in correspondence with his being when he raised the crucified Jesus from the dead. All reflection about the nature and being of God must therefore accept the normativity of the resurrection of the crucified Christ to determine the content of the word "God".

'Repent, and be baptized every one of you in the name of Jesus Christ for the forgiveness of your sins; and you shall receive the gift of the Holy Spirit" (Acts 2:38); "But to all who received him, who believed in his name, he gave power to become children of God" (John 1:12).

9. Compare further: Rom 14:17f., 15:30; 1 Cor 2:2–5, 12:4–6; 2 Cor 1:21f., 3:3; Phil 3:3; 1 Thess 5:18–20; Col 1:6–8; Eph 1:11–14.17, 2:18–22, 3:2–7.14–17, 4:4–6, 5:18–20; Jude 20f.; Col 1:6–8; Titus 3:4–6.

10. A brief but excellent sketch of this development is provided by Robert Jenson, "The Triune God," in: Carl E. Braaten and Robert W. Jenson, eds., *Christian Dogmatics*, vol. 1 (Philadelphia: Fortress, 1984, pp. 79–191), pp. 115–161; similar in: Robert W. Jenson, *The Triune Identity. God according to the Gospel* (Philadelphia: Fortress, 1982), pp. 61–131.

11. Robert W. Jenson, "The Triune God," in: Carl E. Braaten and Robert W. Jenson, eds., *Christian Dogmatics*, vol. 1 (1984), p. 92, compare pp. 96, 99; Robert W. Jenson, *The Triune Identity* (1982), pp. 2–13, 21.

12. Such an emphasis in approach and methodology is, of course, the great legacy of Martin Luther's "theology of the cross". In our time this approach has been given eminence by Karl Barth and those, like Eberhard Jüngel und Jürgen Moltmann, who have followed this theological method. The methodological problem implied in determining the starting point and the ultimate reference point for the doctrine of God is well summarized by Bertold Klappert, "Tendenzen der Gotteslehre in der Gegenwart," *EvTh* 35 (1975), pp. 189–208.

This would suggest that we think of God's being as a relationship of "Father", "Son", and "Holy Spirit". God reveals himself as the "Father" of the "Son" by raising Jesus from the dead, and this "fatherhood" is extended to his creation by making the event of the death and resurrection of Jesus Christ an event "for us". God is the "Son" in that in the life, death, and resurrection of Jesus he has revealed himself as unconditional and uncompromising love. God is the "Holy Spirit" in that the power of the resurrection of the crucified Christ is made available to all creation and is effectively shared with those who believe.

By raising the crucified Christ from the dead, God has revealed that humanity is not strange to his being, and more so, he has opened his very being to the estranging power of sin. Thereby God, in his very being, has bridged the gulf between God and humanity, between heaven and earth, between transcendence and immanence.[13] He is not far, but near; and this nearness is not qualified by morality and fear but by unconditional love and grace. He indeed *is* love. His being consists in sharing his rich life with his creation, and making it possible for all human beings to know him through faith.

This emphasis that God was really in Christ also suggests that we must resist any kind of modalism that seeks a deity beyond its manifestations as Father, Son, and Holy Spirit. At the same time it shows the inadequacy of the different sorts of subordination or adoptionism that tend to relativize the deity of Christ. Indeed, as Rahner and Jüngel have emphasized, the immanent trinity *is* the economic trinity.[14]

GOD AS A PERSONAL REALITY

Since it is Jesus who was raised from the dead and who was exalted to "the right hand of God", therefore God must be understood as a personal reality. Not only Jesus himself can call God "Abba", but those who believe in him are drawn

---

13. This distinctively Christian understanding of God is developed in contemporary theology by Eberhard Jüngel, *The Doctrine of the Trinity. God's Being is in Becoming* (Grand Rapids, Mich.: Eerdmans, 1976); Eberhard Jüngel, *God as the Mystery of the World. On the Foundation of the Theology of the Crucified One in the Dispute between Theism and Atheism* (Grand Rapids, Mich.: Eerdmans, 1983); Jürgen Moltmann, *The Crucified God. The Cross of Christ as the Foundation and Criticism of Christian Theology* (London: SCM, 1974), ch. 6; Jürgen Moltmann, *The Trinity and the Kingdom of God* (London: SCM, 1981); Robert Jenson, "The Triune God," in: Carl E. Braaten and Robert W. Jenson, eds., *Christian Dogmatics*, vol. 1 (1984, pp. 79–191), pp. 115–191; Robert W. Jenson, *The Triune Identity* (1982), chapts. 3–5; Wolfhart Pannenberg, *Systematic Theology*, vol. 1 (Grand Rapids, Mich.: Eerdmans, 1991) chapts. 5–6, vol. 2 (1994), chapt. 10.

14. Karl Rahner, *The Trinity* (London: Burns & Oates, 1970), pp. 22f., 101–103; Eberhard Jüngel, "Das Verhältnis von 'ökonomischer' und 'immanenter' Trinität. Erwägungen über eine biblische Begründung der Trinitätslehre—im Anschluss an und in Auseinandersetzung mit Karl Rahners Lehre vom dreifaltigen Gott als transzendenten Urgrund der Heilsgeschichte," *ZThK* 72 (1975), pp. 353–364.

into this personal relationship through the ministry of the Holy Spirit: ". . . because you are sons, God has sent the *Spirit* of his *Son* into our hearts, crying, '*Abba! Father!*' " (Gal 4:6, emphasis mine; compare Rom 8:15). Within this relational reality God is not dissolved into our *humanum*; he remains over-against-us, and as such he can be addressed by our prayers, he can say something new, and he can speak "into our hearts". This human face of God is explicated when the risen and exalted Christ is referred to as our "advocate with the Father" (1 John 2:1).

GOD AND DEATH

On the basis of the resurrection of the crucified Christ the church believes that the living God has shared his life with the dead Jesus, thereby revealing himself as "the God . . . who gives life to the dead and calls into existence the things that do not exist" (Rom 4:17).

This means, firstly, that God's being cannot be regarded as being aloof from the power of death. Under the influence of Greek thinking, Christian theology has always had problems in thinking of God and death together.[15] On the basis of the resurrection of the crucified Christ it must be maintained that God exposed his very being to the estranging power of death, yet without ceasing to be God. Using the analogy of a bee that dies when it has stung someone, and paraphrasing the apostle Paul's words in 1 Corinthians 15:54f., we may ask rhetorically: "O death, where is your deadly sting? O death, where is that sting which spells an end to life, and already poisons our existence?"—to which the answer of faith sounds: "The sting of death has been sunk into the heart of God. God himself has struggled with death and removed its ultimate threat. That has become revealed in the resurrection of Jesus." God has thereby negated the ultimate negation. The resurrection reveals that the life of God is stronger than the estranging power of death. The resurrection of Jesus means the ultimate death of death.

This means, secondly, that in the process of a history that is decisively marked and overshadowed by the reality of death, in which every human being must die, and in which the estranging power of death is already at work in the quenching of life, history is confronted with a new dimension of reality. A

---

15. For details see: Robert Jenson, "The Triune God," in: Carl E. Braaten and Robert W. Jenson, eds., *Christian Dogmatics*, vol. 1 (1984, pp. 79–191), pp. 115–134; Robert Jenson, *The Triune Identity* (1982), pp. 57–92; Eberhard Jüngel, "Vom Tod des lebendigen Gottes. Ein Plakat," *ZThK* 65 (1968), pp. 93–116; Eberhard Jüngel, "Welcher Gott ist tot? Zum Wiederaufleben des Gesprächs über Gott," *EK* 2 (1969), pp. 127–132; Eberhard Jüngel, "Das dunkle Wort vom 'Tode Gottes'," *EK* 2 (1969), pp. 133–138, 198–202; Eberhard Jüngel, *God as the Mystery of the World* (1983), parts II and V; Jürgen Moltmann, *The Crucified God* (1974), pp. 87–92, 267–270; Jürgen Moltmann, *The Trinity and the Kingdom of God* (1981), § II/1.

reality that is stronger than death and therefore can relativize its dehumanizing power.

It means, thirdly, that the resurrection of the crucified Christ provides the basis for the hope that not death, but God, will determine our ultimate destiny, and that in light of that promise we can resist the encroaching and estranging power of death that is at work in history now.

THE HUMANITY OF GOD

The resurrection of Jesus Christ authorizes us, furthermore, to call God a *human God*. In taking up the life of Jesus into himself, God has shown that humanity is not strange or secondary to his nature, but that humanity is part of his nature. Some excellent formulations from the pen of Karl Barth illustrate that point:

> We have seen that there is . . . an inner divine correspondence and similarity between the being of the man Jesus for God and His being for His fellows. This correspondence and similarity consists in the fact that the man Jesus in His being for man repeats and reflects the inner being or essence of God and this confirms His being for God. . . . The humanity of Jesus is not merely the repetition and reflection of His divinity, or of God's controlling will; it is the repetition and reflection of God Himself, no more and no less.[16]

> The Godhead of the true God is not a prison whose walls have first to be broken through if He is to elect and do what He has elected and done in becoming man. . . . He is the Lord over life and death. He does not become a stranger to Himself when in His Son He also goes into a far country. He does not become another when in Jesus Christ He also becomes and is man.[17]

> . . . es gibt zwar eine Gottlosigkeit des Menschen, es gibt aber laut des Wortes von der Versöhnung keine Menschenlosigkeit Gottes. . . .[18]

---

16. *Church Dogmatics* III/2 (1960), p. 219.

17. *Church Dogmatics* IV/2 (1958), p. 84.

18. *Die Kirchliche Dogmatik* IV/3,1 (1959), p. 133. We have cited this in German because the English translation (*Church Dogmatics* IV/3,1 [1961], p. 119) fails to render the theological significance of this formulation. Literally the text says that the human being can become "god-less", but that according to the message of reconciliation, God cannot become "human-less", that humanity is therefore a constitutive part of God's nature. Compare also Barth's brief essay "The Humanity of God," (1956) in: *The Humanity of God* (Richmond: John Knox Press, [10]1972), pp. 35–65.

On that basis we can live our life under the promise and therefore in the confidence and hope that God is always with us, leading, guiding, and prodding us, even when we are not aware of it. Our fate is linked to the very being of God himself.

THE SUFFERING OF GOD

We have to go a step further and speak not only of the humanity of God, but also of the suffering of God.[19] In raising Jesus from the dead, God defines his Godhood in correspondence with the life and death of Jesus. "Jesus" or "Jesus Christ" are therefore not abstract religious or theological symbols that are open for a wide range of content. They are inherently linked to the story of Jesus of Nazareth, who lived a certain kind of life, and who, as a consequence of that life, accepted suffering and death. By raising Jesus from the dead, God reveals his identification with that particular life.

For Christian theology it has always been a problem to think of Jesus' suffering in relation to the being of God. Although it is fairly clear that Jesus during his life experienced opposition, rejection, pain, and suffering, including the agony of feeling forsaken by God (Mark 15:34.37), we can detect tendencies as early as the New Testament period to sublimate that essential element of his life. While in the Gospels of Mark and Matthew Jesus cries: "My God, my God, why hast thou forsaken me?" (Mark 15:34, par. Matt 27:46), in the Lukan and in the Johannine Passion story this cry of dereliction does not occur. In Luke Jesus dies with the more pious expression on his lips: "Father, into thy hands I commit my spirit!" (23:46), and in the Gospel of John he climaxes his life with the shout of victory: "It is finished!" (19:30).

These attempts to avoid the suggestion that God and Jesus as the Son of God actually suffered, flourish even more in the second century and later. Tertullian (approx. 150–220) in his *Treatise against Praxeas* (approx. C.E. 200) accuses the Monarchians of blasphemy and says in that context:

> Let us be content with saying that Christ died, the Son of the Father; and let this suffice, because the Scriptures have told us so much. . . . Now, although when two substances are alleged to be in Christ—namely, the divine and the human—it plainly follows that the divine nature is immortal, and that which is human is mortal. . . . In short, since he says that it was Christ (that is, the Anointed One) that died, he shows us that that which

---

19. Compare: Jürgen Moltmann, *The Crucified God* (1974), pp. 267–291; Jürgen Moltmann, *The Trinity and the Kingdom of God. The Doctrine of God* (London: SCM, 1981), part II (pp. 21–60); Hans Küng, *The Incarnation of God. An Introduction to Hegel's Theological Thought as Prolegomena to a Future Christology* (Edinburgh: T. & T. Clark, 1987), pp. 518–525; Paul Fiddes, *The Creative Suffering of God* (Oxford: Clarendon Press, 1988).

died was the nature which was anointed; in a word, the flesh. . . . we do not maintain that He died after the divine nature, but only after the human. . . . the Father was not associated in suffering with the Son. . . . (Chap. 29)

You have Him exclaiming in the midst of His passion: "My God, my God, why hast Thou forsaken me?" Either, then, the Son suffered, being "forsaken" by the Father, and the Father consequently suffered nothing, inasmuch as He forsook the Son; or else, if it was the Father who suffered, then to what God was it that He addressed His cry? But this was the voice of flesh and soul, that is to say, of man—not of the Word and Spirit, that is to say, not of God; and it was uttered so as to prove the impassibility of God, who "forsook" His Son, so far as He handed over His human substance to the suffering of death. (Chap. 30)[20]

We may further recall two representative credal formulations that have maintained their authority and influence up to the present day. The Protestant Westminster Confession of Faith (1646) defines the nature of God as follows:

There is but one only living and true God, who is infinite in being and perfection, a most pure spirit, invisible, without body, parts, or passions, immutable, immense, eternal, incomprehensible, almighty, most wise, most holy, most free, most absolute, . . . and is alone in and unto himself all sufficient, not standing in need of any creatures which he has made. . . .[21]

The Roman Catholic Dogmatic Constitution of the Catholic Faith, formulated at the First Vatican Council (1870), reads:

The holy, Catholic, Apostolic Roman Church believes and confesses that there is one true and living God, Creator and Lord of heaven and earth, almighty, eternal, immense, incomprehensible, infinite in intelligence, in will, and in all perfection, who, as being one, sole, absolutely simple and immutable spiritual substance, is to be declared as really and essentially distinct from the world, of supreme beatitude in and from himself, and ineffably exalted above all things which exist, or are conceivable, except himself.[22]

---

20. The citations are taken from *The Ante-Nicene Fathers*, Vol. III (Grand Rapids, Mich.: Eerdmans, reprinted 1980), pp. 625–627.

21. Cited from J. H. Leith, ed., *Creeds of the Churches*, (Richmond: John Knox Press, rev. ed. 1973), p. 197.

22. Cited from P. Schaff, *The Creeds of Christendom*, 3 vols. (New York: Harper and Brothers, 1877), vol. II, p. 239.

Are these formulations not fairly representative of the popular Christian understanding of God? God is then seen, firstly, as an objective spiritual being who lives essentially in and for himself. As such, he has, secondly, all power and all knowledge. He is, thirdly, essentially different from and independent of his creation, and finally, he cannot suffer, because perfection and unchangeability exclude suffering. This God is so imprisoned in his holiness that he cannot look at sin. He lives in such splendid isolation that the suffering and agony of the world would never reach him.

With this in mind, let us listen to a contemporary poem by Vinicio Aguilar, arising out of the struggle for human dignity in Central America:

> Where was god, daddy; where, where, where,
> when the commissioners
>   broke the fence,
>   burnt the farm,
>   destroyed the harvest,
>   killed the pigs,
>   raped Imelda,
>   drank our rum?
>
> HE WAS UP THERE, boy.
>
> Where was god, daddy; where, where, where,
> when because we complained
>   the state judge came and fined us
>   the bailiff came to arrest us
>   and even the priest came to insult us?
>
> HE WAS UP THERE, boy.
>
> Well then daddy; we must now tell him plainly
> that he must come down sometimes
> to be with us.
> You can see how we are, daddy,
> with no fields sown, no farm, no pigs, nothing, and he
> as if nothing had happened. It isn't right, you know, daddy.
> If he's really up there
> let him come down
> Let him come down to taste this cruel hunger with us
> let him come down and sweat
> in the maize-fields, come down to be imprisoned,
> let him come down and spew on the rich man
> who throws the stone and hides his hand,
>   on the venal judge,
>   on the unworthy priest,

and on the bailiffs and commissioners
who rob and kill
the peasants;
because I certainly don't want to tell my son when he asks
me one day:

HE WAS UP THERE, boy.[23]

And can we not all join in? Was God absent when Jesus struggled in the desert of temptation and in the Garden of Gethsemane? Was God absent when Jesus died on the cross? Was God absent in the persecution and execution of 5,000 Anabaptists who wanted to be true to their voice of conscience? Was God absent in Auschwitz and Buchenwald and Dachau? Was God absent in Hiroshima and Vietnam? Is God absent in the Sahel Zone? Is God absent in our cancer wards and our torture cells? If he were, then we cannot expect a healing, consoling, liberating, or reconciling word from him when we walk through the valleys of shadow and death.

By raising the crucified Jesus from the dead, God has declared once and for all times—to all who want to hear!—that he was present in the sufferings and death of his Son. Even though Jesus may have felt forsaken, God was there. There was no victim in Buchenwald in whose agony God himself did not share. There is no degrading of human dignity which is not at the same time causing scars to God's being.

The Bible says: "God is love" (1 John 4:8). God's love implies suffering. This is evident in surveying the history of God with his people. Because of his personal identification with the suffering of his people in Egypt and at the waters of Babylon he plans for their liberation. Is God not present in the agony of Job, and does he not find him, even when Job has had enough and wants to bury himself in the dust of the earth—"thou wilt seek me, but I shall not be" (7:21)? God suffers because he loves. Where there is love, suffering is not far away. The more one loves the more intensive is the suffering because love participates in the fate of the ones who are loved.

And yet, it must be said with equal emphasis that suffering is not identical with God. God is not without suffering, but he is "more" than suffering. The statement "God suffers" cannot be turned around to mean "suffering is God". Suffering must not be given an eternal dignity by the confession that God is a suffering God. God suffers because he loves and shares his life with his creation. Every act of injustice, every cry of pain, every shout of despair causes a suffering moment within God himself.

23. Cited from: Julia Esquivel Velasquez, "A letter from Central America . . .," *IRM* LXVI (July, 1977, pp. 248–252), pp. 249f.

But hope grounded in the resurrection of Christ, also affirms that the day will come when "he will wipe away every tear from their eyes, and death shall be no more, neither shall there be mourning nor crying nor pain any more . . ." (Rev 21:4). God's suffering therefore arises from his loving identification with his creation. Because he is love, he cannot force us to do what he wants us to do. Love pleads and begs—"We beg you on behalf of Christ, be reconciled to God" (2 Cor 5:20)—but love cannot rape. But this same love turns into suffering for the victims of injustice and hatred, for the poor and hungry and naked; and it turns into wrath for the selfish and rich and powerful who keep the poor poor and the hungry hungry, who use their power to dominate and exploit their fellow human beings, who, even if it is done under the halo of religious commitment, absolutize their understanding of faith and thereby become modern-day "Sadducees", "Pharisees", and "Romans" who crucify Jesus again and again.

The suffering of God on the one hand assures God's identification with all who suffer, but on the other hand, because it is the living God who suffers, it promises an ultimate end to all suffering. Those who have been drawn into that knowledge through faith in Christ will already engage themselves by trying to create analogies to God's love and God's justice.

THE RELATIVITY OF GOD'S HIDDENNESS

We note, finally, that the resurrection of Jesus Christ manifests that God is a God who reveals himself, who becomes active in human history, who brings light into darkness, who creates life out of death. God, in other words, is ultimately not a hidden God.

The hiddenness of God is an existential and a theological problem of the greatest magnitude.[24] It is related to our topic of discussion, because the risen Christ does not leave behind the cross and the life that led up to it. The shame of the cross is not dissolved into the glory of the resurrection. Rather, it is the crucified Christ that has been raised from the dead, and his identifying marks are the marks of his crucifixion (John 20:20; Luke 24:39). The God who raised Jesus from the dead remains hidden in the Crucified One, in history, and in our human experience.

Another aspect of God's hiddenness as it relates to our discussion is the fact that the risen Christ seemingly appeared only to believers or to people who in

---

24. Compare: Gerhard Ebeling, *Dogmatik des Christlichen Glaubens* (1979), Bd. 1, pp. 254–257, Bd. 2, pp. 243–249, 438–442, Bd. 3, pp. 485–491; Eberhard Jüngel, "Quae supra nos, nihil ad nos. Eine Kurzformel der Lehre vom verborgenen Gott—im Anschluss an Luther interpretiert," *EvTh* 32 (1972), pp. 197–240; Hans Friedrich Geisser, "Zur Hermeneutik der Verborgenheit Gottes," in: Hans Friedrich Geisser/Walter Moster, eds., *Wirkungen hermeneutischer Theologie*. Eine Zürcher Festgabe zum 70. Geburtstag Gerhard Ebelings (Zürich: Theologischer Verlag, 1983), pp. 155–167.

the encounter with the risen Christ became believers. Apparently there were no disinterested observers of the resurrection; there were no neutral and objective witnesses of that event. This difficulty has been felt from the beginning. But while the New Testament writings respect this mystery, the extracanonical Gospel of Peter gives details about the actual resurrection of Jesus itself, how Christ, accompanied by two men from heaven, walks out of the tomb, how this event was observed by the soldiers whose task it was to guard the tomb, and how this demonstrative evidence led to faith in Jesus as the Son of God.[25] A similar apologetic interest can be discerned in the attempt of some modern theologians who try to verify the resurrection of Christ by emphasizing the historical veracity of the empty tomb traditions.

Nevertheless, the resurrection affirms that the hiddenness of God is not an arbitrary hiding. Rather, as the New Testament suggests (Col 1:15; John 1:18; Heb 11:27; 1 Tim 6:16) it expresses God's holy otherness. Yet, God's holy otherness entails his radical being for his creation. His otherness, therefore, is light—"unapproachable light" (1 Tim 6:16), yes!—but not darkness! His holy otherness therefore does not imply separateness or disinterest. It simply means that God can only be known if a person recognizes God as God, on God's own terms. Such a recognition is not possible by a disinterested, neutral, and so-called "objective" act of reason, but it is only possible in the experience of obedient faith.

Where this obedient faith becomes an event, the hiddenness of God is in part broken through. Faith therefore confesses that the God who has taken Jesus into himself continues to share his life with his creation.

This is confirmed by the experience of the church through the ages and around the world; and it is confirmed in our own experience. The reality and quality of prayer, the experience of community, the participation in the sacraments, worship, but also the churches' engagement for the poor and disabled and exploited—all of it lives from the reality that God in the resurrection of Jesus Christ has opened himself towards history, and that human beings can respond to him in faith, prayer, and good works. The affirmation of the hiddenness of God is therefore part of the confession of faith in the living God: "Truly, thou art a God who *hidest thyself*, O God of Israel, the *Savior*" (Isa 45:15, emphasis mine).

CONCLUSION

I have tried to show that the resurrection of Christ is not only a christological, but also a theological event: it must shape our understanding of the nature and being of God. By raising the crucified Jesus from the dead, God affirmed and validated Jesus' understanding of God. At the same time God revealed him-

---

25. Gospel of Peter §§ 8–11 (§§ 28–49); see pp. 174f. above.

self as a God who is for us—a reality that can only be expressed in trinitarian language. This "being for us" finds its deepest expression in that the One who raised the crucified Jesus from the dead, has exposed his own being to suffering and death—yet without ceasing to be God. In the crucifixion of Jesus, God made himself vulnerable to the injustice and pain of creation. This includes a mystery that is contrary to all rationality, but this mystery is made partly accessible to those who accept God on his terms. For obedient faith the crucifixion includes a promise that is made known and made effective in the resurrection of Christ. The hiddenness of God is an aspect of his holiness and as such it participates in the promise that the God who is light and who is love is a God who is for us.

Chapter 12

All-encompassing Salvation

". . . if you confess with your lips that Jesus is Lord and believe in your heart that God raised him from the dead, you will be saved" (Rom 10:9); ". . . if while we were enemies we were reconciled to God by the death of his Son, much more, now that we are reconciled, shall we be saved by his life" (Rom 5:10). This interlocking between the universal Lordship of Christ and the reality of salvation is an important biblical emphasis that needs to be retrieved by Christian theology. There has been the tendency to focus the saving work of Christ exclusively on the atoning death of Jesus, or, as it is the case with some liberal and liberation theologians, on Jesus' life, Jesus' God consciousness, or Jesus' messianic consciousness. Such one-sided approaches need to be corrected by emphasizing the soteriological dignity of the resurrection and of the risen life of Christ.

We also need to note that the concept of "salvation" has become controversial. It is sometimes used to refer to "saving a person's soul". This would be misleading if by "soul" only part of a person's created being is meant. The New Testament emphasizes the "bodily" resurrection of Jesus Christ, and it qualifies this resurrection as a new beginning, containing a promise for the whole of creation. By emphasizing the "resurrection of the body", and not the "immortality of the soul", the early Christians wanted to say that human beings have to be understood as a unity of body, soul, and spirit, together with their interwovenness in society, nature, and history. It is this total *humanum* in its ecological context that is graced with the promise of salvation. Salvation includes the seed of newness and the promise of universality. The God "who gives life to the dead and calls into existence the things that do not exist" (Rom 4:17), is the God who "justifies the ungodly" (Rom 4:5). And this reality of salvation opens up into a future when "the creation itself will be set free from its bondage to decay and obtain the glorious liberty of the children of God" (Rom 8:21). Indeed, by analogy with the risen Christ being "the beginning, the first-born from the dead" (Col 1:18; compare 1 Cor 15:20.23; Acts 26:23), those who follow Christ are the ones "who have the first fruits of the Spirit" groaning "inwardly as" they "wait for adoptions as sons, the redemption of our bodies" (Rom 8:23). And since with "our bodies" we are woven into nature, history, and cosmos, this promise entails a universal thrust.

266

THE RESURRECTION AS THE PRESUPPOSITION FOR SALVATION

For the New Testament authors the resurrection of Jesus Christ is a necessary presupposition for salvation. The so-called passion predictions, in which the words of Jesus and the theological convictions of the earliest churches blend together, insist on the divine necessity of Jesus' death and resurrection: ". . . the Son of man *must* suffer many things, and be rejected . . . and be killed, and after three days rise again" (Mark 8:31, compare 9:31, 10:33f.). For Paul, saving faith has the content that Jesus Christ "was put to death for our trespasses and raised for our justification" (Rom 4:25, compare 2 Cor 5:15). Indeed, "if Christ has not been raised, then our preaching is in vain and your faith is in vain. . . . If Christ has not been raised, your faith is futile and you are still in your sins. Then those who have fallen asleep in Christ have perished" (1 Cor 15:14.17f.). A number of theological concepts elaborate this fundamental conviction.

Risen "on the Third Day"

There is, first of all, the confession that Christ was raised from the dead "on the third day".[1] This is not a chronological statement. It is a theological assertion, pointing to the soteriological significance of the resurrection of the crucified Christ. In Jewish thinking the reference to the "third day" had an important soteriological thrust. According to Hosea 6:2, for instance, God would restore the sick nation on the third day; Jonah was delivered from the belly of the fish after three days and three nights (Jonah 1:17); Moses met God on Mount Sinai on the third day (Exod 19:16). The Midrash Rabbah refers to these and other Old Testament texts (Midrash Rabbah Genesis 56:1), and affirms that "The Holy One, blessed be He, never leaves the righteous in distress more than three days" (Midrash Rabbah Genesis 91:7), and: "Israel are never left in dire distress more than three days" (Midrash Rabbah Esther 9:2).[2] Lehmann summarizes his investigation of these and similar texts:

> The third day brings the turn to the new and the better. God's mercy and justice creates a new "time" of salvation, of life, of victory. The third day brings a matter of decisive importance to a final and history-creating solution by a saving act of God.[3]

---

1. Compare: 1 Cor 15:4; Acts 10:40; Mark 8:31 (par. Matt 16:21; Luke 9:22), 9:31 (par. Matt 17:23), 10:34 (par. Matt 20:19; Luke 18:33); Matt 27:63; Luke 24:7.46. These and other texts that make reference to the "three days" are analyzed in Karl Lehmann, *Auferweckt am dritten Tag nach der Schrift. Früheste Christologie, Bekenntnisbildung und Schriftauslegung im Lichte von 1 Kor 15,3–5.* Quaestiones Disputatae 38 (Freiburg: Herder, 1968), pp. 159–176. The following thoughts are indebted to this book.

2. See Karl Lehmann, *Auferweckt am dritten Tag nach der Schrift* (1968), pp. 176–181, pp. 205–230, pp. 262–281.

3. *Auferweckt am dritten Tag nach der Schrift* (1968), p. 181 (my translation); similar summary statements are found on p. 264 and p. 280.

This religio-historical background suggests that the confession that Jesus Christ was raised "on the third day" means that God himself has accepted the life and death of Jesus, and by raising him from the dead, God has acted in a significant way for the salvation of his creation.

The Resurrection as Exaltation

Secondly, we recall again the interpretation of the resurrection as exaltation: "The God of our fathers raised Jesus whom you killed by hanging him on a tree. God exalted him at his right hand as Leader and Savior, to give repentance to Israel and forgiveness of sins" (Acts 5:30f.). On the basis of his "exaltation" the early Christians believed Christ to be present in their midst in the power of the Spirit. They sang hymns to him and praised him as savior of humankind, and as Lord of the universe (Phil 2:6–11; Col 1:15–20; 1 Tim 3:16; 1 Pet 3:22). They celebrated his presence in the Lord's Supper—"This is my body. . . . This cup is the new covenant . . ." (1 Cor 11:24f.)—and they invoked him to visit them now and to speed up his return: "Our Lord, come!" (1 Cor 16:22; Didache 10:6; Rev 22:20).[4] Their mission was carried on in the conviction that "all authority in heaven and on earth" had been given to the risen Christ, and that he would be with them "always, to the close of the age" (Matt 28:18–20). They believed that as the exalted Lord he was their advocate with God (1 John 2:1: "We have an advocate with the Father, Jesus Christ . . ."); and that as the living Lord—being the High Priest "for ever" (Heb 5:6, 6:20; 7:17)—he always made intercessions for his followers (Heb 7:25).

Preaching "to the Spirits in Prison"

We note thirdly that 1 Peter relates the death and resurrection of Jesus Christ to the preaching of the gospel "to the spirits in prison" (3:18–20), and "even to the dead" (4:6). Many matters related to the theological symbol of "Christ's descent into hell" and to these texts are controversial.[5] Nevertheless, whatever the

---

4. The Aramaic background to μαράνα θά (marana tha) can suggest an indicative understanding ("our Lord comes" or "our Lord has come") or it can be understood as an imperative ("our Lord, come!"). The interpretation suggested here is the most likely one. See: Karl Georg Kuhn, "μαράναθά," (maranatha), in: *TDNT* IV (1967 [1942]), pp. 466–472; Werner Kramer, *Christ, Lord, Son of God*. SBT 50 (London: SCM, 1966), pp. 99–107; Hans Conzelmann, *1 Corinthians. A Commentary on the First Epistle to the Corinthians*. Hermeneia (Philadelphia: Fortress Press, 1975), pp. 300f.

5. It is controversial, for instance, whether the symbol of "Christ's descent into hell" (Apostle's Creed: *"descendit ad inferna"* [= realm of the dead]) is anchored in these texts or in extra-Christian narratives like Genesis 6:1–6 and Ethiopic Enoch 10–16, 19, 21 (for details see: Norbert Brox, *Der erste Petrusbrief*. EKK, xxi [Zürich: Benziger Verlag, Neukirchen-Vluyn: Neukirchener Verlag, ²1986], pp. 171–175). It is also controversial whether the "spirits" in 1 Peter 3:19 and the "dead" in 1 Peter 4:6 refer to the same or to different people (compare: ibid, pp. 171–174, 196–199). It has also been de-

exegetical and religio-historical difficulties may be, it is clear that the significance of the resurrection of the crucified Christ includes the promise of salvation for the dead.[6] This means, of course, that Christ is "Lord both of the dead
and of the living" (Rom 14:9), and that therefore nothing, not even death, "will
be able to separate us from the love of God in Christ Jesus our Lord" (Rom
8:38f.). But at the same time it reminds us that we are woven into the process
of the history of successive generations. The resurrection of Christ provides the
theological basis for our hope that salvation includes the generations that have
gone before us, and at the same time and with the same intensity it reminds us
of our responsibility for future generations so that they also may be able to hear
the gospel and enjoy its fruits.[7]

These traditional theological symbols—risen "on the third day", "exalted to
the right hand of God", "descent into hell"—remind us that the Christian faith
from its beginning saw an inner connection between the resurrection of the crucified Christ and the Christian experience and understanding of salvation. More
precisely: the resurrection of Christ is confessed to be the necessary basis and
the content of salvation.

FORGIVENESS AND DISCIPLESHIP

The risen Christ frees believers from the burdens and failures of the past and
thereby lays the foundation for a new beginning. That is the experience and assurance of salvation. We have seen that the disciples' faith faltered and failed

---

bated whether these texts serve to interpret the soteriological depth and significance of
Christ's *death* (so Jeremias, Pannenberg, Moltmann, and, traditionally, Reformed theology) or of his resurrection (so, traditionally, Eastern Orthodoxy and Lutheran theology [but not Luther himself]). As to the theological question of whether we have here
a symbolic interpretation of Christ's death or his resurrection, I think that such an alternative does not do justice to the intention of the texts. It seems to me that both the
New Testament message in general and the texts in 1 Peter in particular see the Christ-
event in its unity of death (life) and resurrection as the basis for salvation. While 1 Peter
3:18 begins that "Christ . . . died for our sins once for all", it immediately interprets this
statement in its inherent relation to the resurrection: ". . . being put to death in the flesh
but made alive in the spirit." And it is "in the spirit", i.e. in the power of the resurrection, that "he went and preached to the spirits in prison." For a general orientation see:
Ernst Koch, "Höllenfahrt Christi," in: *TRE* 15 (1986), pp. 455–461 (lit.!); Joachim
Jeremias, "Zwischen Karfreitag und Ostern. Descensus und Ascensus in der
Karfreitagstheologie des Neuen Testamentes," in: Joachim Jeremias, *ABBA. Studien zur
neutestamentlichen Theologie und Zeitgeschichte* (Göttingen: Vandenhoeck & Ruprecht,
1966), pp. 323–331; Wolfhart Pannenberg, *Jesus—God and Man* (1968), pp. 269–274;
Jürgen Moltmann, *The Way of Jesus Christ* (1990), pp. 189–192.

6. Whether the "spirits" of 3:19 and the "dead" of 4:6 refer to the same or to different groups of people is theologically of little significance. Important is that the soteriological work of Christ includes all people, the living and the dead.

7. This is emphasized by Jürgen Moltmann, *The Way of Jesus Christ* (1990), p. 192.

during the passion of our Lord. They forsook him. Only some female friends accompanied him to the cross. Peter went further than the others, but he also failed when the test came. Fear was not the only reason why the disciples forsook Jesus; they had begun to doubt the veracity, validity, and theology of his mission. They were no longer sure that God was with him. How could God be on the side of a loser? The cross did not only mean death for Jesus, but it also signified a crisis for the disciples' faith and theology.

The resurrection of Jesus from the dead led to the rebirth of the disciples' faith in Jesus, and thus to a new fellowship with him. After the crisis of the cross, God himself took the initiative and offered reconciliation and forgiveness to them. He wanted to restore the broken relationship and heal the shattered trust. The risen Christ therefore "breathed on" the gathered community of men and women, "and said to them, 'Receive the Holy Spirit. If you forgive the sins of any, they are forgiven; if you retain the sins of any, they are retained' " (John 20:22f.). Since we discussed the structure of resurrection faith in the previous part, we only need to outline briefly some elements of the experience of salvation that stand out in the biblical resurrection narratives.

There is first of all the experience of forgiveness which becomes exemplified in Peter's encounter with the risen Christ and in the meal motif of the Easter narratives.

All four gospels tell the story of how Peter denied being a follower of Jesus while Jesus was being investigated before the Jewish religious authorities (Mark 14:53f.66–72; Matt 26:57f.69–75; Luke 22:54–62; John 18:15–18.25–27). Despite tensions and differences in these accounts, there must have been a historical event that gave rise to them. During the night following the capture of Jesus, and at the same time as the investigation had commenced against Jesus, Peter denied that he had personal association with the prisoner. He denied his life relationship with the same Jesus who had called him to be one of his closest followers and friends.

It is furthermore unquestioned that the same Peter occupied a leading role in the Jerusalem church and its mission. He experienced one of the first resurrection appearances (1 Cor 15:5; Luke 24:34). His leadership role in the early church is reflected in the lists of apostles (Mark 3:16; Matt 10:2; Luke 6:14; Acts 1:13), and in the fact that he generally functions as the spokesman of the disciples. Also the first half of the book of Acts witnesses to his leading role; and when Paul made his first visit to Jerusalem he mainly went to see Peter (Gal 1:18f.).

Between Peter's denial of Jesus and his leadership role in the earliest church, his decisive encounter with the risen Christ took place. This encounter meant for him the restoration of a broken relationship, the experience of forgiveness, and a commissioning to a new task. This is focused in the beautiful story of encounter between Peter and the risen Christ in John 21:15–17. The reference to the denial is clearly intended by the threefold repetition of question and answer, echoing the threefold denial of Peter. As he did on the occasion of the first call to discipleship by the shore of the lake of Galilee, so Jesus again takes the initiative by inviting Peter to renew his relationship to him: "Simon, do you love me?" It is possible that in response to that expression of grace—not as a presupposition for it!—Peter became aware of the tragedy of his denial, which may have moved him to the confession: "Depart from me, for I am a sinful man, O Lord." This is told in Luke 5:4b-6.8 which was originally probably an Easter narrative (compare the parallel resurrection story in John 21:1–7). But where sin is great, grace is even more overwhelming (Rom 5:20). Forgiveness becomes real as the relationship with Jesus is restored. That such a relationship can never be conceived solely in terms of a private religious experience is seen in the call to service: "Tend my sheep."

A further illustration of the motif of forgiveness is found in those resurrection stories where the encounter with the risen Lord takes place within the context of a meal: John 21:9.12f.; Luke 24:30f.; Mark 16:14; Acts 10:40f. "The fact that the risen Lord ate with His disciples who had forsaken Him . . . means the readmission of the disciples into the old fellowship, and is a visible sign of His forgiveness."[8] To understand the theological significance of the meal motif we have to realize that table fellowship was of immense religious and sociological significance in the ancient Near East. Individuals understood themselves as social beings whose identity and survival depended upon their acceptance by others. At the meal table such human fellowship became concrete. To eat with someone implied a close relationship to that person. A Pharisee would therefore be very cautious as to whom he would invite to a meal, so that he would not have to have table fellowship with someone who was religiously less qualified than he was.

Here we may also recall the important role which the meal played in Old Testament literature. In Genesis 18 the Lord appears to Abraham and makes important promises in the context of a meal. The covenant between God and humanity is sealed by a covenant meal on Mount Sinai (Exod 24:9–11). The covenants between Laban and Jacob (Gen 31:54), Abimilech and Isaac (Gen 26:30), and between Joshua and the Hivites (Josh 9:14) are confirmed by a meal where God is thought of as being present as the invisible witness. The cooperation between Israel and Jethro (Exod 18:12), Gaal and the men of Shechem (Judg 9:26f.), and between Abram and the king of Sodom (Gen 14:17–24) are celebrated with a meal. When a king is elected, the people celebrate at a meal with him (1 Kgs 1:25.41; 1 Sam 11:15; compare 1 Sam 9:22f.). The meal is used to give concrete expression to the granting of forgiveness and mercy. David displays kindness to Mephibosheth, son of Jonathan, with the words: "you shall eat at my table always" (2 Sam 9:7.10.11.13). On his deathbed David instructs Solomon: "deal loyally with the sons of Barzillai the Gileadite, and let them be among those who eat at your table" (1 Kgs 2:7). The king of Babylon, Evil-merodach shows mercy to Jehoiachin, king of Judah; consequently "every day

---

8. Joachim Jeremias, *The Eucharistic Words of Jesus* (Oxford: Blackwell, 1955), p. 136[2].

of his life he dined regularly at the king's table" (2 Kgs 25:29; compare Jer 52:33).

These examples may suffice to illustrate that at a meal table a close personal fellowship in the presence of God is experienced. Thus the meal motif in the resurrection narratives are a concrete expression of the new beginning which the risen Christ wants to make with the disciples who had forsaken him.

When we today confess that God raised Jesus from the dead then we are not only making a statement about something that happened long ago, but we are entering a divine reality in which the resurrection power of God becomes real in the experience of forgiveness.

Secondly, the experience of forgiveness must be related to Christian discipleship so that it remains clear that "life in Christ" is grounded in the resurrection of the crucified Christ, and therefore cannot be reduced to a private and individualistic religious experience.[9] Although there has been considerable hesitancy in Protestant theology to interrelate the resurrection and discipleship,[10] the identity and content of the Christian faith is at stake at this point. Since it was the crucified Jesus who was raised from the dead, theology must resist any attempt to make grace cheap. At the same time, Christian discipleship needs the reality of the resurrection so that its liberating manifestation of the gospel is not reduced to sterile moralism.[11]

It must, thirdly, become clear that salvation is not a static but a dynamic reality. Faith participates in the promise of salvation and anticipates its fulfill-

---

9. Here it is not possible to develop the content of Christian discipleship. Compare: Eduard Schweizer, *Lordship and Discipleship*. SBT 28 (London: SCM, 1960); Eduard Schweizer, "Discipleship and Church," in: *The Beginnings of the Church in the New Testament* (Edinburgh: Saint Andrew Press, 1970), pp. 85–104; Athol Gill, *Life on the Road. The Gospel Basis for a Messianic Lifestyle* (Scottdale, Pa.: Herald Press, 1992 [1989]); Athol Gill, *The Fringes of Freedom. Following Jesus, Living Together, Working for Justice* (Homebush West: Lancer, 1990); Ferdinand Hahn, "Pre-Easter Discipleship," in: *The Beginnings of the Church in the New Testament* (Edinburgh: Saint Andrew Press, 1970), pp. 9–39; Martin Hengel, *The Charismatic Leader and His Followers* (Edinburgh: Clark, 1981); August Strobel, "Discipleship in the Light of the Easter-event," in: *The Beginnings of the Church in the New Testament* (Edinburgh: Saint Andrew Press, 1970), pp. 40–84; Segundo Galilea, *Following Jesus* (Maryknoll, N.Y.: Orbis, 1981); Reiner Strunk, *Nachfolge Christi. Erinnerungen an eine evangelische Provokation* (München: Kaiser, 1981).

10. This hesitancy is lamented by Karl Barth (*Church Dogmatics* IV/2 [Edinburgh: T. & T. Clark, 1958], pp. 533–553.), Dietrich Bonhoeffer (*The Cost of Discipleship* [New York: MacMillan, 1963 (1937)], chapter 1 on "Costly Grace"), Jürgen Moltmann ("Einführung," in: Jürgen Moltmann, ed., *Nachfolge und Bergpredigt* [München: Kaiser, ²1982, pp. 7–11] pp. 8f.; *The Way of Jesus Christ. Christology in Messianic Dimensions* [London: SCM, 1990], pp. 116–119), and Reiner Strunk (*Nachfolge Christi. Erinnerungen an eine evangelische Provokation* [München: Kaiser, 1981], pp. 174, 189f.).

11. More details in: Thorwald Lorenzen, "Resurrection and Discipleship," in: *Festschrift Günter Wagner*. Ed. by Faculty of Baptist Theological Seminary, Rüschlikon/Switzerland. International Theological Studies: Contributions of Baptist Scholars, Vol. 1 (Bern: Peter Lang, 1994), pp. 87–100; see also pp. 231–235 above.

ment. The earliest Christians did not understand the resurrection of Jesus to be an isolated event, an event completed and frozen into the past. In speaking of the resurrection they used language that made it quite explicit that the resurrection of Jesus had implications for the understanding of their own future and the future of the world.

At this point we must theologically appreciate the religio-historical observation that the "resurrection language" of the early Christians was adopted from an apocalyptic understanding of history.[12] Here we cannot discuss the difficult problem how determinative an apocalyptic worldview was for the shaping of early Christian theology. Suffice it to say that when in the context of an apocalyptic worldview the early Christians were confronted with the reality and experience of the resurrection of Jesus Christ, they interpreted that to mean the beginning of the end. This comes to expression not only in the formula that Jesus Christ is "the beginning, the first-born from the dead" (Col 1:18; compare 1 Cor 15:20.23; Rom 8:29; Acts 26:23; Rev 1:5), but also in the somewhat strange narrative Matthew 27:52f.: ". . . the tombs also were opened, and many bodies of the saints who had fallen asleep were raised, and coming out of the tombs after his resurrection they went into the holy city and appeared to many." This text is best understood in the context of the resurrection message, expressing the conviction that the resurrection of Jesus was the beginning of the general resurrection.

With the resurrection of Jesus our own future is determined and promised. The resurrection of Jesus Christ is therefore the ground and basis for our own resurrection. The God who raised Jesus from the dead and has taken him into his presence will do the same for all who believe in him. The resurrection of Jesus is God's down payment granting us certainty that our future lies in his hands.

This conviction stands also behind the many texts that explicitly state that Jesus' resurrection implies the resurrection of all believers: "If the Spirit of him who raised Jesus from the dead dwells in you, he who raised Christ Jesus from the dead will give life to your mortal bodies also through his Spirit which dwells in you" (Rom 8:11); and: ". . . God raised the Lord and will also raise us up by his power" (1 Cor 6:14; compare further 2 Cor 4:14 and 1 Cor 15:1–34).

In 1 Corinthians 15:1–28 Paul develops a vision of the relationship of the resurrection of Jesus Christ to the future of the world. He first insists on the historical reality of the resurrection of Jesus Christ (vv. 1–20). And yet, in speaking of Jesus' resurrection Paul already points to its openness towards the future. While all the surrounding verbs are in the aorist tense, describing a completed action in the past—"Christ died . . . was buried . . . appeared"—"he has been raised" (v. 4) is in the perfect passive tense. The passive describes that God is the acting subject in the resurrection; the perfect tense indicates that the resurrection is an

---

12. Compare: Wolfhart Pannenberg, *Jesus—God and Man* (1968), pp. 74–88; Jürgen Moltmann, *Theology of Hope* (1967), pp. 190–197; Walter Kreck, *Die Zukunft des Gekommenen. Grundprobleme der Eschatologie* (München: Kaiser, 1966), pp. 199–213.

event of the past with consequences for the future! Christ is the "first fruits" (v. 23); his resurrection is theologically and chronologically the first! Then, in the unknown future—"at his coming" (v. 23)—follow "those who belong to Christ" (v. 23). This means that the resurrection is certain, but it also means that it is not yet. Jesus has been raised, the believers will be raised. "Then comes the τέλος (telos) . . ." (v. 24). If we could translate τέλος (telos) with "rest" then Paul is speaking here of the general resurrection of all dead.[13] But this translation is probably incorrect because we have no other texts where τέλος (telos) means "rest", and at no other place does Paul speak of a general resurrection. The phrase must therefore be translated "then comes the end."[14] The end is when God will be "all in all," when God's rule will be direct and sovereign over all his creation. The time in between, i.e., between the resurrection of Jesus Christ and the end, will be marked by struggle and conflict. It will be an existence under the cross, sustained by the hope which is based on the resurrection of Jesus Christ. It is the time when Christ and his followers struggle against "every rule and every authority and power" (v. 24), and, yes, even against the great enemy "death" itself (v. 26).

The disciple of Christ lives in the hope that ultimately God will triumph over the forces of estrangement, enmity, and death. Faith in Christ entails the conviction that ultimately the oppressors will not triumph over their victims. Christian existence is sustained by the hope that the Risen Christ gives a purpose to history that can serve as a basis for hope in the midst of the experienced ambiguity of life. This hope is not wishful thinking. It is grounded in the resurrection of Jesus Christ. The same God who raised Jesus from the dead will reserve the final word in history for himself. The certainty of that final word is anticipated in the life of faith.

LIBERATION AND JUSTICE

The resurrection of the crucified Christ also compels us to avoid a one-sided and reduced view of salvation. Salvation is concrete and it begins here and now. A holistic view of salvation must therefore include a commitment to liberation[15] and a passion for justice.

---

13. Hans Lietzmann, *An die Korinther I-II*, HNT, 9. 4. von Werner Georg Kümmel ergänzte Auflage (Tübingen: Mohr, 1949), p. 80; against Lietzmann's view, the comment by Werner Georg Kümmel in the appendix on p. 193.

14. Hans Conzelmann, *I Corinthians* (1975), pp. 270f.; Gerhard Delling, "τέλος κτλ.," (telos ktl.) in: *TDNT* VIII (1972), p. 55.

15. Compare Part I, chapter 4 above. This is not the place to discuss theologies of liberation. It must be emphasized, however, that the majority of liberation theologians consider the Christ-event to be the necessary basis, presupposition, and content for their understanding of salvation. Salvation for them is not reduced to liberation, but it includes liberation. Compare: Gustavo Gutiérrez, *A Theology of Liberation. History, Politics, and Salvation* (Maryknoll, N.Y.: Orbis, rev. ed. 1988), chapt. 9; Hans Kessler, *Reduzierte Erlösung? Zum Erlösungsverständnis der Befreiungstheologie* (Freiburg: Herder, 1987).

Freedom as Liberation

With the resurrection of Jesus Christ, God has begun to liberate his world from the enslaving chains of law, sin, and death. Those who confess that God raised Jesus from the dead are the same who proclaim: "For freedom Christ has set us free" (Gal 5:1)! This freedom is not simply there. It needs to be claimed, it needs to be asserted, it needs to be enacted. Freedom becomes actual in the process of liberation. The believer therefore leans forward into the future, tuning with all creation into the longing for liberation from the powers of estrangement (Rom 8:18–25). The resurrection of Jesus Christ has set a process into motion, a process of liberation, to which every believer is called to contribute. This process of liberation is the concrete outworking of God's resurrection activity in our history. The liberating activity becomes manifest in the various areas of life.

The New Testament speaks of liberation from the power of sin. Sin is a power before it is an act. Paul therefore prefers to speak of "sin" in the singular. It is a power which determines human beings at the core of their existence and estranges them from their true selves, from their fellow human beings, from nature, from history, and from God. It makes human persons slaves (Rom 6:16–23) who cannot do the right that they recognize and want to do (Rom 7:18). More so: even in our most noble and religious strivings human beings remain sinners who are motivated by a strong desire towards self-aggrandizement and selfishness.

It is important to recognize, however, that sin does not only determine us in our hearts, our wills, and our consciences. Sin also becomes objectified in structures of evil and injustice. Paul, in the context of his worldview, spoke of "elemental spirits of the universe" (Gal 4:3), of "beings that by nature are no gods" (Gal 4:8). In Ephesians 6:12 we read of "principalities", of "powers", of "world rulers of this present darkness", and of "spiritual hosts of wickedness in the heavenly places". These "beings" or "spirits" were understood to be personal powers that laid claim on the conscience of people. The people tried to be in good standing with such powers by practicing religious rites, keeping feast days, and observing ceremonial laws. Christ was experienced as liberation from the claims that these "spirits" and "powers" had upon the people.

If we want to tune into the liberating message of the resurrection of Christ we must locate and analyze the structures that estrange people from each other and from God today. We must read the signs of the times and interpret our reality in light of the gospel by locating the structures that dehumanize our human existence. Do not our confrontations with economic, political, and cultural structures often cause a fear of lostness; of being caught in a system with "no exit"? The reason, for instance, that one-fourth of humankind lives in abject poverty, lacking cultural identity, and seeing no hope for a better future, is not to be explained by the assertion that the poor of our world are lazy. No, they are victims of an unjust economic world order which favors the rich and powerful, and disadvantages the poor and oppressed. Also the disrespect in our treatment of nature, giving more importance to economic profit than to a responsible stewardship of natural resources may lead to a destruction of the very "garden" which sustains us.

An understanding of salvation that is grounded in the liberating message of the resurrection of Christ must include the dynamic impulse to be liberated from those structures that dehumanize human life. The modern struggle for the implementation of human rights belongs into the Christian doctrine of salvation. The struggle for liberation from servitude, oppression, racism, and apartheid is an integral part of a person's faith in the risen Christ. When God shares his life with his creation, he does not only want to save a person's soul, but he wants to save the person's life. Belief in the resurrection of Christ therefore means liberation from all forces that estrange us from our true *humanum*. For the Christian it is imperative, however, that the ends and the means cohere in the process of liberation. The means by which the process of liberation is fueled must be shaped by the content of the gospel, Jesus Christ.

A further dimension of liberation is that the risen Christ begins to liberate the believer from legalism and dogmatism, the subtle manifestations of law. Legalism and dogmatism are the inherent temptation of every religious insight and experience. A religious experience has such an overwhelming claim of authenticity and veracity on a person, that religious believers and the religious institutions that they create tend to objectify and universalize such convictions. Instead of formulating their insight as an appeal or invitation and leaving the other person free to decide for or against it, they make it into a law, demanding the obedience of others. But the letter of the law always kills; it is the personal spirit which creates life!

We need to remind ourselves constantly that religious legalism and dogmatism were major forces in the opposition to, and the elimination of, Jesus. And anyone who is only vaguely familiar with the history of the church and who is engaged in church life today knows of the destructive power of legalism and dogmatism. Where does the danger lie? It does not lie in the fact that human persons seek for meaning in life, and then commit themselves at points where they have discovered an integrating vision to their lives. Commitment, obedience, and enthusiasm entail the promise of virtue. Every religious commitment, including the Christian faith, includes the seed of absolutism and implies a universal claim. The answer to legalism and dogmatism is neither relativism nor pluralism. It is also natural that one's faith in God expresses itself in certain doctrines, moral behavior, and in personal and community structures. Such doctrines and structures can serve as channels and manifestations of God's grace. But they are channels and manifestations of a reality; they are not identical with the reality from which they derive and to which they point. The demonic temptation is that doctrines and structures cease to be servants of the reality which expresses itself in and through them, and that they themselves replace that reality by claiming identity with the reality which gave rise to them. Then God no longer stands over against such doctrines and structures, constantly judging and reforming them, but the structures themselves claim divinity and infallibility. The deity of God is denied by forgetting that God alone is true (Rom 3:4) and that all human work remains sinful. The danger lies in replacing Jesus Christ as the ground and content of faith by certain structures and doctrines. If one then challenges such structures or doctrines then this is perceived as challenging God himself. The revolutionary Christian insight into reality is that religious devotion must never be addressed to historical, human, or earthly objects—be they as noble as the church, tradition, or the Bible—but only to the personal and living God himself!

A commitment to the risen Christ implies therefore a careful avoidance of all legalism and dogmatism. In raising Jesus from the dead God declared an end to the "law" as the object of our ultimate concern. Faith is grounded in and derives its content from the living personal reality of Christ. If that living and personal reality is replaced by something not living and not personal then the whole reality of faith becomes deformed. The risen Christ therefore protects the personal and liberating identity of Christian faith.

A third dimension of liberation is the liberation from the ultimate threat of death. The resurrection of Jesus Christ means the death of death: "For we know that Christ being raised from the dead will never die again; death no longer has dominion over him" (Rom 6:9). Jesus Christ therefore is "the resurrection and the life" (John 11:25). By raising Jesus from the dead God has demonstrated his victory over death and its estranging power.

The believer participates in that victory over death: "he who believes in me, though he die, yet shall he live, and whoever lives and believes in me shall never die" (John 11:25f.; compare John 5:24). Faith in the risen Christ liberates believers from the strangling anxiety of death, and at the same time makes them to servants of life who are engaged in a struggle against the many manifestations of death.

Death, as the Old Testament most eloquently reminds us, is more than the completion of one's earthly life. Death starts to spread its odor in the midst of life. It isolates human beings from the relationships which give and sustain life: from God, from their fellow human beings, from nature, and from history. The dead cannot praise God, and they cannot love their neighbor. Such isolation becomes most clearly visible in the physical death of a person. But the forces of isolation from the sources of life are already there in the midst of life. Injustice, exploitation, racism, and loneliness are messengers and instruments of death. In fighting them, the believer and the church are instruments of life and thus display that they have tuned in to the resurrection activity of God.

We mention finally that faith in the resurrection of Jesus implies a liberation from the illusion that we can live without God. Human beings can do much. Indeed, humanity has accomplished much. And because that is so, we are in constant danger of overestimating our own abilities. It is an illusion when modern humanity thinks that it can live without God, although many claim to do so. It is an illusion when we think that we can solve our own problems and at the same time deny the resources of faith.

The resurrection of Jesus as an act of God reminds us that it is only God himself who can ultimately and radically deal with the estranging forces of sin, law, and death.

The Promise of Justice

By raising the crucified Christ from the dead, God reveals and enacts, as part of his healing and saving activity, his passion for justice. To confess that God raised Jesus from the dead implies therefore that God's activity cannot be frozen into the past, nor should the word "God" be used to validate the ever present status quo. With the resurrection of the crucified Christ, God manifests himself as the One whose passion it is to change the world in the direction of justice. Faith in the risen Christ therefore makes the believer and the believing community sensitive to the recognition of injustice, and at the same time it provides the resources for a concrete commitment to justice and its implementation. Faith in the resurrection of Christ carries within itself the promise and the conviction that history needs to be changed and that history can be changed in the direction of justice.

What seems to be obvious is still somewhat controversial in the thinking and practice of Christians and churches. In our discussion of the various approaches to the resurrection we have become aware of the danger of freezing the resurrection of Christ into a past event which as such would then be primarily accessible to the instruments of reason; we have also met those theological views that tend to reduce the effect of the resurrection to a personal experience of faith, or to the ongoing worship life of the church. It is therefore necessary to retrieve the biblical conviction that God's passion for justice and the believers' commitment to tune into that passion are an inherent dimension of resurrection faith.

The God who raised Jesus from the dead is the God of Abraham, Isaac and Jacob. Resurrection faith relates therefore to the Jewish resurrection hope and its inherent linkage to the question of God's covenant faithfulness and the fulfillment of ultimate justice.

It is one thing to die, as Abraham, Isaac, David, and Job did, "in a good old age . . . and full of years" (Gen 25:8, 35:29; 1 Chr 29:28; Job 42:17). They will be "gathered to their people". Death for them was the end of life. It was accepted as the necessary consequence of the finitude of life. When, after a life of toil and labor, the time had arrived to die, then this had to be endured. There was always a strangeness associated with death, because God was considered to be the God of life, and death meant estrangement or even separation from God.[16] One was not sure what would happen after one's death. An existence in a nebulous and shadowy underworld (in *Sheol*), far away from God, was imagined: "The dead do not praise the Lord" (Ps 115:17, compare Ps 6:5, Ps 88).[17] Yet, death as the more or less natural end of life was deemed inevitable.

---

16. Compare Gerhard von Rad, *Old Testament Theology*, vol. 1: The Theology of Israel's Historical Traditions (Edinburgh: Oliver and Boyd, 1962), pp. 387–391.

17. For details see: Hans Walter Wolff, *Anthropology of the Old Testament* (London: SCM, 1974), chapter XII (pp. 99–118); Eberhard Jüngel, *Death. The Riddle and the Mystery* (Edinburgh: Saint Andrew Press, 1975), pp. 61–80.

But then there was the reality of death as the apparent and often untimely negation of life. It gave rise to the questions about God's faithfulness and God's justice: "Is thy steadfast love declared in the grave . . .?" (Ps 88:11). Can God's faithfulness and his justice be limited or even annulled by the power of death? Will death and its messengers in the long run be able to laugh in the face of God?

> Not to us, O Lord, not to us,
> but to thy name give glory,
> for the sake of thy steadfast love
> and thy faithfulness!
> Why should the nations say,
> "Where is their God?" (Ps 115:1f.)

In this correlation with experienced reality, the promise of faith began to take shape that "his steadfast love" and "the faithfulness of the Lord endures forever" (Ps 118:1–4; Ps 117:2). Given the conviction that God is the creator and sustainer of life, the answer to the problem of an untimely death could only be that God's relationship with human beings cannot be limited by the barrier of death.[18]

The problem was intensified when death was the obvious consequence of injustice. If God is not only the creator of heaven and earth, but also the sovereign master over history, how can it be that often the righteous suffer and the wicked prosper (Jer 12:1; Ps 73:3–14)? If God is God, how can it be that those who engage themselves for upholding the law and who have no other passion than to do God's will are being persecuted, tortured, and killed without seeing the cause of justice succeed? Indeed, the question must have arisen whether it is worthwhile at all to do what is right, if persecution, torture, and cruel death are the consequence. It was in response to such an experienced reality, and the questions related to it, that the implications of faith with regard to the ultimate fulfillment of justice and the future resurrection began to be formulated. God will not allow his relationship to his people to be broken! He will not allow the wicked to triumph ultimately! The Psalmist, after a long complaint against the prosperity of the wicked, comes to the conclusion that the relationship with God will prove stronger:

> When my soul was embittered,
> when I was pricked in heart,
> I was stupid and ignorant,
> I was like a beast toward thee.
> Nevertheless I am continually with thee;

---

18. This growing conviction is well portrayed by Hans Walter Wolff, *Anthropology of the Old Testament* (1974), pp. 107–110.

> thou dost hold my right hand.
> Thou dost guide me with thy counsel,
> and afterward thou wilt receive me to glory. . . .
> My flesh and my heart may fail,
> but God is the strength of my heart
> and my portion for ever (Ps 73:21–26).

God will be true to himself. He will fulfill his promises. His faithfulness, and his steadfast love will ultimately triumph. This conviction led to an explicit resurrection faith in the post-exilic period.

A late text in Isaiah 26:7–21 (probably coming from the period of around 300 B.C.E.) reflects a situation when the people of God experienced injustice (vv. 7f.21), war (v. 12), and oppression (v. 13). They longed for justice and peace. In that context there arose the hope for an ultimate justice. Faith began to find words to formulate such a hope. The wicked will die; "they will not live; they are shades, they will not arise" (v. 14). But the righteous, those who have suffered for their faith, those who have experienced injustice, they now hear the promise of the triumph of justice: "Your dead shall live, their bodies shall rise" (v. 19).

In another important text that reflects the period of persecution and oppression under Antiochus IV Epiphanes (176–164 B.C.E.), Daniel 12:1f., the author wants to encourage his hearers to remain firm in their commitment to God and to his Torah. This encouragement is grounded in the faithfulness of God. Israel's guardian angel Michael will protect them; and he, God himself, will make sure that "your people shall be delivered. . . . And many of those who sleep in the dust of the earth shall awake, some to everlasting life, and some to shame and everlasting contempt."

Also related to the period of oppression and persecution under Antiochus IV Epiphanes is the moving narrative in 2 Maccabees 7. Antiochus had oppressed the people with demands of tribute, he burned and plundered Jerusalem, and persecuted men, women, and children who resisted his authority.[19] He entered and pillaged the temple in Jerusalem. He forbade Jewish temple activities, he erected a heathen altar in the Jewish temple, and he made Jewish people eat pork. A number of Jews forsook their traditional ways and "joined with the Gentiles and sold themselves to do evil" (1 Macc 1:15, compare 1:43). "But many in Israel stood firm and were resolved in their hearts not to eat unclean food. They chose to die rather than be defiled by food or to profane the holy covenant; and they did die" (1 Macc 1:62f.). To this latter group there belonged also "seven brothers and their mother" (2 Macc 7:1). They "were arrested and were being compelled by the king, under torture with whips and cords, to partake of unlawful swine's flesh" (v. 1). However, each one of them endured terrible torture and cruel death, rather than compromise their confession to God.

---

19. A rich source of historical information is 1 Maccabees 1:10–7:50.

How were they sustained in their protest against the king and in their witness to their God? They were sustained by their faith that the "Lord God is watching over us and in truth has compassion on us" (v. 6), and that this their God would bring about ultimate justice. The oppressors, the persecutors, and the perpetrators of injustice will not escape the judgment of God (vv. 31.34f.), for them there "will be no resurrection to life" (v.14), but they, the faithful ones, will be raised up to "an everlasting renewal of life" (v. 9, compare vv. 11.14.23.29).

We may therefore say that in pre-Christian Jewish history resurrection faith was formulated in situations of conflict, persecution, and oppression. Two motifs were determinative: there was, firstly, God's faithfulness to his covenant with his people. It contained the promises that this covenant faithfulness cannot be canceled out by apparent injustice and by the reality of death. An implication of this was, secondly, the conviction that it is worthwhile to be faithful to God's law and God's will. If this faithfulness is not rewarded on earth, then there must be an equalizing justice on the other side of death, in a final judgment. This is necessary, because otherwise oppressors would indeed ultimately triumph over their victims. In the face of an experience of injustice, therefore, the question of justice was raised and it found an answer in the promise that ultimately, through the resurrection of the dead, God himself would establish justice.[20] God would ultimately be true to himself and to his promises. His faithfulness and steadfast love, often hidden under the experience of injustice, would ultimately triumph. This promise of ultimate justice was the foundation on which the commitment for justice during life on earth, even when it meant persecution and death, was considered worthwhile.

Jesus tuned into that tradition. He had only one passion in his life, and that was to let God be God. He wanted to give concrete expression to the first commandment. Like the mother and her seven sons, Jesus wanted to do God's will. His understanding of God, however, differed from that of the Maccabees. For him God was the "father" who loved all people; for him God's will cannot be identified with the words of the Torah and with a radical obedience of the cult; for him violence was unacceptable as a means to pursue God's will. Nevertheless, as was the case with the Maccabean martyrs, Jesus was also opposed, arrested, tortured, sentenced, and killed in direct consequence of the vision of God that he "fleshed out" with his life.

The cross therefore raises a number of questions related to our discussion of justice. Did not Jesus' death mean that God himself had been refuted? All that Jesus said and did, he did as a representative of the βασιλεία τοῦ θεοῦ (basileia tou theou)! It was therefore not only his own moral and spiritual con-

---

20. There are other texts—for example Hosea 6:1–3 and Ezekiel 37:1–14—that do not directly refer to a resurrection from the dead, but which use resurrection language to refer to the life-giving power of God that supplies hope, and releases the promise for justice in situations of injustice, oppression, and despair.

victions that were at stake in his life; it was God himself, or at least Jesus' representation of God. Was Jesus' death not history's verdict that Jesus' understanding of God was wrong, and that the theology and practice of Pilate and Caiaphas were right?

And how should Jesus' own life be interpreted in the light of his death? Was it not a grand illusion in the flow of history that love for one's enemy, commitment to the marginalized, and nonviolence can actually be lived? Was it not an unrealistic dream, that the ground of history, God, is a God who loves sinners and publicans and Gentiles and lepers? That he is a God who sees and hears, and therefore knows, the pain of the oppressed, and who longs for their liberation? That he is a God who does not predestine and fate the poor, but who gives them resources of faith that help them to analyze and understand their situation as the result of injustice, so that they may be empowered to begin shaping their own future? Was Jesus' passion for God and with it his healing, saving, and liberating commitment to the marginalized people worthwhile? Has not history, and with it the God of history, spoken their verdict against Jesus? Should not Pilate and Caiaphas rather than Jesus inform our faith in God?

And what about the religious and political establishment? They used violence, arrest, and crucifixion, to get rid of Jesus. In their view it was socially and politically expedient that one person may have to be sacrificed in order to preserve political order and prevent social unrest. Is expediency of greater value in the process of history than truth? Is truth the measure of the law, or is law the manifestation of truth? Did not history itself proclaim the religious and political establishment as victors in their struggle for truth with Jesus?

And what does the cross say about the people with whom Jesus shared his life, to whom he tried to minister the riches of God's grace, and whom he tried to remind of the inherent dignity that God had granted to them? Was his commitment to the poor and oppressed a grand illusion? His healing of the leper, his words of hope, his granting of forgiveness, his promise of a future—was all of this an insignificant footnote in a history that is marked by a social Darwinism in which only the fit can survive and only the strong can be free?

The answer to these questions was given with the resurrection of the crucified Christ from the dead. The resurrection is not merely God's validation of Jesus' life and death. It is certainly not the anticipation of revenge that God will deal out to the oppressor. It is God's protest against injustice, the injustice inflicted upon Jesus and against those to whom he ministered; and it is God's promise that his justice will ultimately triumph. With the resurrection of Jesus, God commits himself to the cause of justice and its implementation. The believer's and the church's commitment to justice stands therefore under the rainbow of the divine promise that ultimately truth and love will triumph because the God who revealed himself in the resurrection of the crucified Christ is the ground and the telos of history.

This conviction has led the early Christians to seek the presence of the risen Christ not only in the preaching of the word and in the administration of the sacraments but also in the poor and the oppressed. This is so clearly spelled out in the New Testament that it can only be considered a serious indictment of the self-interest and the cultural captivity of North Atlantic theology that this has not been given the theological status that it deserves.

If faith can only remain Christian if it is tied to Jesus Christ, then the question arises where Christ can be found in our world. In Matthew 25:31–46 (compare also Mark 9:36f. par.) faith makes the challenging confession that by feeding the hungry, in welcoming the stranger, by clothing the naked, by visiting the sick and the prisoners, one was in fact, whether one knew and acknowledged it or not, ministering to Jesus Christ. He, the crucified and risen Christ, was therefore considered to be present in the poor and oppressed. Christian faith thereby properly recognized that the God who has always been partial to the stranger, the slave, the orphan, and the widow, has manifested this partiality by raising the crucified Jesus from the dead. When faith therefore seeks to remain tied to Jesus Christ, it must also seek him in the poor and oppressed. Faith in him must take on the concrete form of showing solidarity with them. Refusing to do so would not only be a denial of justice; it would also be a denial of Christ.[21]

We need to distinguish two dimensions of the same reality. There are firstly those Christians who have power and money and expertise. They are called by Christ to engage themselves for the dismantling of injustice and the establishment of justice. The Christians and the Christian churches in the North Atlantic countries, for instance, must be deeply troubled about the structural violence and injustice which our economic and political imperialism has brought and still brings to the nations and peoples in the "South".

Then there is, secondly, the dimension of justice which inspires and empowers those who are poor and oppressed, telling them that God has neither fated nor forgotten them. With that promise spoken into their hearts and minds they can begin to understand that their situation and their existence are not fated, but that their predicament is the result of structures that can be changed. They can have their consciousness raised and take life into their own hands and thus actively join God in his passion for justice and liberation.[22] In all of this we must not forget, however, that for Christian ethics the means must correspond to the end. It is for that reason that nonviolence must be the determining motivation for Christian activity in the world.

---

21. It is this dimension of faith which has been rightly retrieved by those churches and theologians that have shown a special sensitivity to the theological place of the poor and oppressed; compare Gustavo Gutiérrez, *A Theology of Liberation. History, Politics, and Salvation*. Rev. ed. with a new introduction (Maryknoll, N.Y.: Orbis Books, 1988), pp. 112–116; Jon Sobrino, S. J., *Christology at the Crossroads. A Latin American Approach* (Maryknoll, N.Y.: Orbis Books, 1978), pp. 195–198, 204–209, and further: chapters 7 and 8 (pp. 236–272).

22. Compare: Gustavo Gutiérrez, *A Theology of Liberation. History, Politics, and Salvation* (1988), pp. 57, 67f., 69f., 153–156; Paulo Freire, *Pedagogy of the Oppressed* (New York: The Seabury Press, 1970).

We have seen, then, that the indicative of salvation includes the imperative of justice. Salvation without justice is reduced and distorted; justice apart from the context of salvation lacks motivation and content. Yet the question must be faced: in light of the apparent triumph of injustice is it worthwhile to engage oneself for justice? Resurrection faith answers "Yes"! An inherent part of faith in the risen Christ is the eschatological promise of the final establishment of justice. The resurrection of Christ is the theological ground for the worth-whileness of the believer's engagement for justice. The believer cannot ratio-nally prove that Jesus has been raised from the dead, but through the praxis of discipleship believers and the believing community can demonstrate that Jesus has been raised from the dead! This does not mean that the truth of the resur-rection is established by our praxis. It does mean, however, that the truth of the resurrection has persuaded and convinced us and has thereby made us witnesses to the resurrection of the crucified Christ.

SALVATION, NATURE, AND THE COSMOS

Christ's salvation does not only include the believer and the church. It en-compasses all of reality. We must therefore also speak of the cosmological and ecological significance of the resurrection. When the Aramaic-speaking Jewish Christians acclaimed the risen Christ as Lord of history and called upon him to come and fulfill his plans in and with the world—"Our Lord, Come!" (1 Cor 16:22; Rev 22:20)—and when in the Greek-speaking Hellenistic and Hellenistic Jewish Christian churches the *Kyrios* title was used to emphasize the universal reign of the risen Christ over all creation (Phil 2:11), then they confessed that all ungodly and estranging powers of the universe including Satan, the antichrist, and death had been defeated (1 Cor 15:24–27; Col 2:10; 1 John 3:8; Rev 13). Therefore they could be freed from the demands of the powers of estrangement (Col 2:14f.; Gal 4:3–7), and enjoy the liberty of the children of God (John 8:36; Gal 4:3–7).

This confidence was grounded in the experience of the resurrection of the crucified Christ. On the basis of that experience the resurrection was inter-preted in relation to the whole process of creation (Rom 4:17) and redemption (1 Cor 15:28). Christ was confessed as the mediator of creation (1 Cor 8:5f.; Col 1:16; Heb 1:2f.10; John 1:3; Rev 3:14), who through his soteriological work on the cross had reconciled all things to God (2 Cor 5:19; Col 1:20; Eph 1:9f.).[23] His mediatorship does not only refer to the original act of creation, but it includes his continuing and sustaining influence on the process of cre-

---

23. Compare: Allan D. Galloway, *The Cosmic Christ* (London: Nisbet, 1951), part I (pp. 3–56); George A. Maloney, S. J., *The Cosmic Christ. From Paul to Teilhard* (New York: Sheed and Ward, 1968), chapters I–III (pp. 17–98); Jürgen Moltmann, *The Way of Jesus Christ. Christology in Messianic Dimensions* (London: SCM, 1990), pp. 280–286.

ation, his present significance for the "holding together of all things" (Col 1:17),[24] and the promise of being the pioneer for the new creation when "all things" will be united "in him, things in heaven and things on earth" (Eph 1:9f.).[25] The church, which derives its identity and mission from Jesus Christ, is therefore commissioned "to preach the gospel to the whole creation" (Mark 16:15, compare Col 1:23).

Recent philosophical and theological reflections have called for a paradigm shift in our perception of reality.[26] Since the Reformation in the 16th century, the Enlightenment in the 17th and 18th centuries, and especially since the scientific, technological, and industrial revolution, together with economic and political imperialism and colonialism in the 19th century, we have perceived and interpreted reality primarily in historical categories. The focus was on humanity and progress. People began to realize that history can be shaped and changed; and that in shaping history, people could fashion their own identity and determine their own future. Too long, it was felt, had people resigned themselves to the unchangeable laws of nature. Too long had people accepted blindly the authority of traditional institutions, like state, crown, and church. The time had come not to be determined by history, not to be puppets on the stage of history, but to create and change history. The time had come to accept and assert responsibility for one's own future. History came to be understood in terms of advance and progress. Instead of being passive objects in the historical process, men and women assumed the role of being active subjects of history. Thus historical consciousness went hand in hand with the process of human emancipation from which we have all tremendously profited.

Nevertheless, there is also a negative side to this historical consciousness that can no longer be overlooked. The rational attempt to objectify nature, and with it the human will to define and to act, has not only produced the triumph of science, and the technological and industrial revolution. It has not only made the "North Atlantic" nations the richest and most powerful part of the world. But it has also been the reason for the ecology crisis, and it has pro-

---

24. Note the references to the present significance of Christ as the mediator of creation: 1 Corinthians 8:6: ". . . for us there is . . . one Lord, Jesus Christ, through whom are all things and through whom we exist." Hebrews 1:3: ". . . upholding the universe by his word of power"; John 1:5: "The light shines in the darkness . . ." (in relation to John 1:3).

25. This inclusive understanding of Christ as "Ground of Creation", as "Evolution's Driving Force" and as "Redeemer of Evolution" is developed by Jürgen Moltmann, *The Way of Jesus Christ* (1990), pp. 286–305.

26. See: Hans Küng and David Tracy, eds., *Paradigm Change in Theology* (Edinburgh: T&T Clark, 1989); also: David Tracy, Nicholas Lash, "Editorial Reflections," in: David Tracy and Nicholas Lash, eds., *Cosmology and Theology*. Concilium 166 (6/1983) (Edinburgh: T. & T. Clark; New York: Seabury, 1983), pp. 87–92; Odil Hannes Steck, *World and Environment*. Biblical Encounter Series (Nashville: Abingdon, 1980), pp. 27–42; Jürgen Moltmann, *God in Creation. An Ecological Doctrine of Creation*. The Gifford Lectures 1984–1985 (London: SCM, 1985), chapter II, §§ 1–3 (pp. 20–52).

duced a world economic order in which two-thirds of the world are fated to poverty and dependence. The problem lies not with nature. It is a human problem. By desacralizing nature and by placing the human being in the center of reality, we have created the presupposition for controlling and exploiting nature.

This domination by historical consciousness is now being called into question. We are beginning to apprehend that our emphasis on history was not only motivated by a desire to understand, but also by the human will to define and to rule. History provided the possibility of progress. It was the field in which to create our world and to extend our influence. And this fascination with history has blinded us to the ecological context, which in fact is more basic for our life and our survival than history.[27] Every time in our daily life when we witness that in situations of conflict economic considerations are given priority over ecological concerns, we have a further illustration that we have not yet fully grasped the ecological dimensions of human existence. Most people still think that they can take an objective stance over against nature, and from there define and use it for their purposes. In recent years, however, there have been experiences and insights that have given rise to the need for deeper and more comprehensive theological reflections.[28] We have become conscious of the ambiguity of historical progress. We can no longer overlook the *ecological crisis*. We realize today that it is not possible to separate nature and history.[29] History and nature are essentially interrelated. Indeed the whole of nature and the cosmos is part of a continuing and ever changing evolutionary process. We as human beings are, on the one hand, ontologically woven into this evolutionary process. We are therefore bound to, and dependent upon, nature and the cosmos. Human life apart from nature and cosmos is not possible. On the other hand, we are also historical beings, and as such we can adopt an attitude towards nature and cosmos, and we can take a stand over against them. We can destroy or restore nature. We are beginning to understand, however, that our historical consciousness in recent centuries has repressed our inherent dependence on nature, and the results of this repression comes to the surface in the present ecology crisis. This real-

---

27. ". . . the fact is that the rediscovery of 'history' by contemporary theology has not been matched by a parallel rediscovery of 'nature'." (David Tracy, Nicholas Lash, "Editorial Reflections," in: David Tracy and Nicholas Lash, eds., *Cosmology and Theology*. Concilium 166 [6/1983, pp. 87–92], p. 89). Compare: George S. Hendry, *Theology of Nature* (Philadelphia: Westminster, 1980), chapt. 1 (pp. 11–30); Jürgen Moltmann, *The Way of Jesus Christ* (1990), pp. 246f.

28. Hans Küng lists the results of an international conference on the question: "What characterizes today's crisis?" in: "A New Basic Model for Theology: Divergences and Convergences," in: Hans Küng and David Tracy, eds., *Paradigm Change in Theology* (1989, pp. 439–452), pp. 445–447.

29. Compare, for instance: Gordon D. Kaufmann, "A Problem for Theology: the Concept of Nature," *HThR* 65 (1972), pp. 337–366; Jürgen Moltmann, *The Way of Jesus Christ* (1990), pp. 246f.

ization, that we are not only historical beings but also natural beings, calls for theological reflection.[30]

That Christ and nature are interwoven is so evident that it does not need any detailed discussion here. He was "born of woman" (Gal 4:4), he had a human body, his ministry was limited by time and space, and he lived an active life in which he met opposition, and received affirmation. In his proclamation he freely used the images of nature and cosmos: rain and sun, birds and flowers, trees and their fruit, sheep and goats. As a consequence of his understanding of God and his vision of life he was arrested, tried, and executed. When he was raised from the dead, the early Christians confessed in a variety of ways that his resurrection was, both and at the same time, an exaltation into the presence of God and a "bodily" resurrection. They wanted to counter any suspicion that in Jesus Christ only his "soul" or his "spirit" was raised, while his "body" would be doomed to nothingness. For this very reason, the earliest Christians rejected the idea of the "immortality of the soul", and they affirmed instead the "resurrection of the body".[31] Although they had great difficulty in finding language that would adequately express the resurrection of Jesus Christ, they resisted any attempt to spiritualize their Christology. The ongoing church tuned into this emphasis when it confessed Jesus Christ not only as truly divine, but also as truly human.[32] Any reduction in his humanity would automatically reduce his divinity, and vice versa.[33] Jesus Christ was not only part of history, but he was also ontologically woven into the fabric of nature and cosmos.

---

30. In contemporary theology it has been especially Jürgen Moltmann who has taken up this challenge and related the resources of Christian faith to the challenges of our time: *God in Creation* (1985); *The Way of Jesus Christ* (1990).

31. The Apostle's Creed states: "I believe in . . . the resurrection of the body." In contemporary theology, Willi Marxsen speaks of the purpose or the cause of Jesus (*die Sache Jesu*), that lives on in and through the proclamation of the witnesses: "The Resurrection of Jesus as a Historical and Theological Problem," in: C. F. D. Moule, ed., *The Significance of the Message of the Resurrection of Faith in Jesus Christ*. Studies in Biblical Theology, 2nd Series, 8 (London: SCM, 1968, pp. 15–50), p. 38; *The Resurrection of Jesus of Nazareth* (Philadelphia: Fortress, 1970), pp. 147f. This is inadequate, because it removes the christological basis from the reality of the resurrection, and reduces Jesus to a moral example or moral teacher. (Compare the discussion of Marxsen's view by Gerhard Friedrich, "Die Auferweckung Jesu, eine Tat Gottes oder ein Interpretament der Jünger?" *KuD* 17 [1971], pp. 153–187).

32. At Chalcedon (451 C.E.) the church confessed that Jesus Christ "is perfect both in deity and also in human-ness; this selfsame one is true God and true human being. . . . He is of the same essence as God as far as his deity is concerned, and of the same essence as we ourselves, as far as his human-ness is concerned" (adapted from John H. Leith, ed., *Creeds of the Churches* [Richmond, Va.: John Knox Press, rev. ed. 1973], pp. 35f.). Controversial at that time was not Christ's deity, but his humanity! Teilhard de Chardin muses about a "third" nature of Christ (in addition to the divine and the human natures). He means by it "the 'cosmic' function of Christ in the universe." (George A. Maloney, S.J., *The Cosmic Christ* [1968], p. 201, compare pp. 201–203).

33. This is the intention of the Chalcedonian definition (451 C.E.) when it explains: ". . . this one and only Christ, Son, Lord, only-begotten, in two natures, without con-

As we have noted earlier in our discussion we must avoid two extremes. We must not spiritualize the resurrection of Jesus by denying the New Testament emphasis on the "bodily" resurrection, and we must not relativize the novum of the resurrection by placing the resurrection of Jesus in the same category as the resurrection narratives of Lazarus (John 11:38–44) or of Jairus's daughter (Mark 5:21–24a. 35–43) or of the widow's son at Nain (Luke 7:11–15). This is obviously also the intention of the biblical authors. The gospel narratives underline the "bodilyness" of the appearances of the risen Christ, and at the same time they insist that it is a special "bodilyness"—the risen Christ can walk through closed doors and seems to transcend the limitations of time and space.

Paul addresses this problem of continuity and discontinuity of the resurrection body with nature in his long discourse on the resurrection in 1 Corinthians 15:35–58. He clearly distinguishes between the resurrection of Jesus Christ and the resurrection of believers. Jesus Christ is the necessary ground and content for the resurrection of believers (1 Cor 15:3–8.12–21). Nevertheless, given that theological basis, Paul's description of the nature of the resurrection applies to both Christ and to believers.[34]

On the one hand he insists that the resurrection constitutes a novum. There is no natural continuity between the earthly body and the risen body. This discontinuity is described by contrasting metaphors:

> What is sown is perishable,
>   what is raised is imperishable.
> It is sown in dishonour,
>   it is raised in glory.
> It is sown in weakness,
>   it is raised in power.
> It is sown a physical body,
>   it is raised a spiritual body (vv. 42–44).

This reasoning climaxes in the assertion that "flesh and blood cannot inherit the kingdom of God" (v. 50).

On the other hand he argues that the resurrection is real (1 Cor 15:12–19), that it is related to Jesus' resurrection (1 Cor 15:3–8), and that it is a "bodily" resurrection (v. 35: σῶμα [sōma]). Therefore, within the discontinuity, the novum character, there is also continuity. The continuity, however, does not consist in an observable, predictable, and empirically verifiable natural

---

fusing the two natures (ἀσυγχύτως [asynchytōs]), without transmuting one nature into the other (ἀτρέπτως [atreptōs]), without dividing them into two separate categories (ἀδιαιρέτως [adairetōs]), without contrasting them according to area or function (ἀχωρίστως [achōristōs]) . . ." (adapted from John H. Leith, ed., *Creeds of the Churches* [rev. ed. 1973], p. 36).

34. The same can be seen in Romans 8:11 and 1 Corinthians 6:14; it applies also for 2 Corinthians 5:1–5.

process. Paul distinguishes between "flesh" (σάρξ [sarx]) and "body" (σῶμα [sōma]). "Flesh" here refers to the earthly existence of species (v. 39). However, when he speaks of "body" in its new existence, he associates it with the concept of "glory" (δόξα [doxa]: vv. 40f.43). "Glory" designates here the divine reality of the risen body.[35] Continuity is given by the active faithfulness of God. The text insists, however, that this God-given continuity does not eradicate every relationship to that which has gone before. Nature provides analogies to the continuity in the process of transfiguration: "a bare kernel" is sown, "perhaps of wheat or of some other grain"; but this "bare kernel" is not identical with the "body". It is "God" who "gives it a body as he has chosen" (vv. 37f.).[36] This body is a "spiritual body" (v. 44), and the continuity consists in the fact that "God gives . . . to each kind of seed its own body" (v. 38).

The "change" of which Paul speaks (vv. 51f.) is therefore a transfiguration from an earthly existence to an existence that is given by God. The nature of that existence escapes our rational capacities. It can only be affirmed in the categories of faith and promise. Continuity and discontinuity are held together in the affirmation that it was the crucified Christ (continuity) who has been raised from the dead (discontinuity).

The great difference that makes talk about continuity and discontinuity necessary, is the Christian claim that with the resurrection of Jesus Christ eternity has broken into time, and the divine life has broken the ultimate power of death. Death will be no more. Life, light, and love will determine reality because God will be God (1 Cor 15:28; Rev 21:3f.6f., 22:1–5). While the present life is lived within the parameters of time and space, and is delimited by death, the resurrection of Christ has revealed the foundations for a new reality: He "will never die again; death no longer has dominion over him" (Rom 6:9). Both the natural death to which all creatures are subject, and the unnatural death of the tortured and oppressed and exploited have their limit in the resurrection of Christ.

---

35. In Philippians 3:20f. Paul says that "the Lord Jesus Christ . . . will change our lowly body to be like his glorious body" (literally: "his body [σῶμα, sōma] of glory [δόξα, doxa]"). At this point we may also mention Mark 9:2–8 in which the church's experience of the resurrection is clearly reflected. Jesus was "transfigured . . . and his garments became glistening, intensely white, as no fuller on earth could bleach them." Elijah and Moses are seen, who were known to exist in heavenly glory, and then God speaks: "This is my beloved Son; listen to him." Also in Stephen's vision of Christ at the right hand of God, and in Luke's accounts of Paul's call, we can see that the motif of divine glory is central (Acts 7:55, 9:3, 22:6.9.11, 26:13). The same idea is reflected in Jesus' reply to the Sadducees about the risen life in the kingdom of God: ". . . when they rise from the dead, they neither marry nor are given in marriage, but are like angels in heaven" (Mark 12:18–27).

36. Compare also 2 Corinthians 4:16–5:10 where Paul encourages believers by saying "that if the earthly tent we live in is destroyed, we have a building from God, a house not made with hands, eternal in the heavens" (5:1, compare 5:5).

Both our experience that as human beings we are interwoven with nature and cosmos, and the message that Christ is indeed the cosmic redeemer, has consequences then for our appreciation and interpretation of nature and cosmos. Through the resurrection of Christ, nature and cosmos participate in the promise of salvation. This leads us to the following conclusions.

It means, firstly, that the "body" (σῶμα [sōma] rather than σάρξ [sarx])—that is, the whole existence of body, soul, and spirit, with all their manifold relationships to humanity, to nature, and history, and to God—is not negated.[37] It is not left behind. It is transfigured into a new form of existence. Since the "body" cannot be abstracted from its interwovenness with nature and cosmos, nature and cosmos are also graced with the promise of newness. Whatever this newness entails, the old is not denied, destroyed, and negated. It is transfigured. This promise of newness becomes real and effective in the present in that we recognize the dignity of nature and cosmos and accept responsibility for them. Just as the promise of human salvation does not negate the dignity and responsibility of our life on earth here and now, so also the promise that nature and cosmos participate in salvation does not relativize, but rather affirms their dignity and our responsibility for them.

By emphasizing the cosmic dimension of the saving work of Christ, we resist, secondly, a theological dualism. Allan D. Galloway says correctly:

> Unless one is prepared to accept the type of dualism which condemns the whole physical order as being not of God and interprets redemption simply as release from the physical order, then one is forced to raise the question of cosmic redemption not in contrast with, but as an implicate of the idea of personal redemption. Physical nature cannot be treated as an indifferent factor—as the mere stage and setting of the drama of personal redemption. It must either be condemned as in itself evil or else it must be brought within the scope of the redemptive act.[38]

The resurrection of Christ must therefore not be reduced to the plane of history, anthropology, and ecclesiology. The theological confession that God raised Christ from the dead and therefore chose to have his own being determined by the Crucified One, compels us to think of the cosmological significance of the resurrection.

Theologians have been hesitant at this point. They have feared that the emphasis on humanity, on sin, on human salvation, and on God's dealing with

---

37. Paul reflects this view when he writes to the Thessalonians: "May the God of peace himself sanctify you wholly; and may your spirit and soul and body be kept sound [in wholeness] and blameless at the coming of our Lord Jesus Christ" (1 Thess 5:23).

38. *The Cosmic Christ* (1951), p. 205; this text was also quoted by Joseph Sittler in his famous address at the WCC Assembly in New Delhi 1961: "Called to Unity," *SEAJT* 3 (1962, pp. 6–15), p. 7.

history might thereby be neglected, and that this would result in a mythologi-cal, triumphant, or speculative christology.[39]

Such a concern for a relevant christology should be appreciated. Indeed, no christology can be true to the biblical intention that is not also relevant to the fundamental needs of humanity here and now. But that is exactly the reason why a shift of emphasis is needed. We have to realize that nature and the cosmos pro-vide the context in which human life takes place. All talk about creation, sin, and salvation is therefore "hanging in the air" if they are not related to a theo-logical appreciation of nature and the cosmos. Cosmic redemption is God's re-sponse to a cosmic estrangement. This estrangement becomes manifest in the ecological crisis today. On an even deeper level it is also seen in the deep-seated unwillingness to recognize the seriousness of the problem and in the subsequent laziness to take the necessary steps and accept the necessary conflicts to do some-thing about it. Karl Barth summarizes this dimension of sin well:

> . . . sin has not merely the heroic form of pride but also, in complete an-tithesis yet profound correspondence, the quite unheroic and trivial form of sloth. In other words, it has the form, not only of evil action, but also of evil inaction; not only of the rash arrogance which is forbidden and reprehensible, but also of the tardiness and failure which are equally for-bidden and reprehensible.[40]

Thirdly, this promise that the whole cosmos will be saved is anticipated by life in the Spirit. The promise releases hope within the believer, and this hope activates the believer to anticipate this ultimate reconciliation by making it real and present now. Dietrich Bonhoeffer makes the helpful distinction between the "ultimate" and the "penultimate".[41] The salvation that God has established through Jesus Christ means that God has related himself to this world. In this

---

39. Compare for instance: Wilhelm Andersen, "Jesus Christus und der Kosmos. Missionstheologische Überlegungen zu Neu-Delhi," *EvTh* 23 (1963, pp. 471–493), pp. 483–486. This scepticism is sometimes traced back to the pre-Colossian hymn (Col 1:15–20), because this hymn, while speaking of creation and reconciliation, fails to give any reason for the need of reconciliation; it does not mention the fall, sin, or evil.

40. *Church Dogmatics* IV/2 (1958), p. 403. He then notes that in "Protestantism, and perhaps in Western Christianity generally, there is a temptation to overlook this aspect of the matter and to underestimate its importance." (Loc. cit.). The original German text is even more expressive when it interprets "Trägheit" ("sloth") with "Schläfrigkeit, Faulheit, Schwerfälligkeit, Rückständigkeit" ("sluggishness, indolence, slowness or in-ertia"): *Die Kirchliche Dogmatik* IV/2 (1955), p. 452; *Church Dogmatics* IV/2 (1958), p. 403. Compare the important essay by Sandra Postel on the various psychological at-tempts to "deny" the seriousness of the crisis. She alludes to a possible epitaph for hu-manity with the inscription: "they saw it coming but hadn't the wit to stop it happening." ("Denial in the Decisive Decade," in: Lester R. Brown et al., *State of the World 1992*. A Worldwatch Institute Report on Progress Toward a Sustainable Society [New York/London: W. W. Norton 1992, pp. 3–8], p. 8).

41. *Ethics*, ed. by Eberhard Bethge (London: SCM, 1955), pp. 79–100.

relatedness God remains God and the world remains world. God neither deifies the world, nor does he destroy the penultimate reality of the world. His passion is to save it. Christian life, therefore, "is participation in the encounter of Christ with the world."[42] It is "the dawning of the ultimate in me; it is the life of Jesus Christ in me."[43] The penultimate becomes the preparing of the way of the Lord:

> The hungry man needs bread and the homeless man needs a roof; the dispossessed need justice and the lonely need fellowship; the undisciplined need order and the slave needs freedom. To allow the hungry man to remain hungry would be blasphemy against God and one's neighbour. . . . It is for the love of Christ, which belongs as much to the hungry man as to myself, that I share my bread with him and that I share my dwelling with the homeless. . . . To provide the hungry man with bread is to prepare the way for the coming of grace.[44]

Today this active and concrete anticipation must include responsibility for nature as God's creation: "The earth is the Lord's and the fullness thereof, the world and those who dwell therein" (Ps 24:1). We saw that the ecological crisis is the result of human mismanagement, and this mismanagement is the consequence of a deep-seated self-will. For that very reason, the healing process must also include a change of human consciousness and with it a modification of human action. The gospel addresses therefore human persons to make them aware of their relational existence, to accept responsibility for it, and to cause a change from an attitude of "having" to an attitude of "being".

It is important to remember, as a fourth point, that it was the crucified body of Christ which was raised from the dead. For Christian theologians it is therefore not possible simply to engage in an intellectual discussion about the possibility and intelligibility of a resurrection. The resurrection of Christ is God's protest against the estranging forces of sin, and it is the revelation that in Christ God has dealt with these forces and thereby freed the believer to celebrate life. This implies a corresponding responsibility. The thrust of the resurrection of the crucified Christ is to reveal and to enact God's saving passion for his world. This passion was manifest in the life of Jesus, it was given soteriological depth in his death, and it was effectively revealed through his resurrection. This passion is a mixture of love and struggle. It manifests the concrete partiality of God for the brokenness of his creation. At the same time, it is a protest against any kind of social Darwinism, imperialism or exploitation. The reference to the crucified Christ should caution us against any attempt to identify the risen Christ with an evolutionary principle that may be inherent to the process of nature and

---

42. *Ethics* (1955), p. 91.
43. *Ethics* (1955), p. 99.
44. *Ethics* (1955), p. 95.

the cosmos, or to see "Christ" as the ultimate fulfillment, as the *telos*, of the process of evolution. That would mean that the process of evolution reveals who Christ is. "Christ" would then stand for those natural forces that determine the process of evolution, and that have been victorious in the process of selection. We easily overlook the fact that the process of evolution has also an underside involving the victims of the process of selection. In his discussion with Teilhard de Chardin and Karl Rahner, Jürgen Moltmann argues convincingly that Christ is not the inherent principle, the Omega Point, or the ultimate *telos*, but the necessary redeemer of evolution.[45]

The challenge is, finally, to turn away from seeing nature as an object, and to discover nature as creation with its own rights. We need to learn not only to be concerned with human rights, but also with the rights of nature.[46] This concern has a very utilitarian motivation. Apart from a functioning ecology human survival is not possible. We need to retrieve the tradition marked by names like Francis of Assisi (1181/82–1226) and Albert Schweitzer (1875–1965)[47] and today

---

45. Jürgen Moltmann, *The Way of Jesus Christ* (1990), pp. 292–301. Moltmann problematizes the christological visions of Teilhard de Chardin and Karl Rahner in that they fail to give an adequate place to the destructive power of sin and evil, and, more importantly, that they overlook the victims in the process of evolution. Evolution is carried forward on the principle of the "survival of the fittest", while Christ identifies with those who are excluded from this process of selection.

46. This concern has been discussed within the context of the United Nations for the last 20 years; compare *The Global Partnership for Environment and Development. A Guide to Agenda 21—Post Rio Edition* (New York: United Nations, 1993). Rights of nature were also a matter of debate at the General Assembly of the World Alliance of Reformed Churches (in Seoul, August 1989), and at the World Convocation of the World Council of Churches on "Justice, Peace, and Integrity of Creation" (Seoul, March 1990). Compare the texts, and the contributions by Lukas Vischer ("Vorwort", "Rolle und Beitrag der Kirchen"), Jürgen Moltmann/Elizabeth Giesser ("Menschenrechte, Rechte der Menschheit und Rechte der Natur"), Peter Saladin/Christoph Zenger ("Rechte künftiger Generationen"), Jörg Leimbacher ("Die Rechte der Natur"), Christian Link ("Rechte der Schöpfung—Theologische Perspektiven"), in: "Rechte künftiger Generationen—Rechte der Natur," *EvTh* 50 (1990), pp. 433–477. Further: Jürgen Moltmann, "Human Rights, the Rights of Humanity and the Rights of Nature," in: Hans Küng and Jürgen Moltmann, eds., *The Ethics of World Religions and Human Rights.* Concilium 1990/2 (London: SCM; Philadelphia: Trinity Press International, 1990), pp. 120–135.

47. Albert Schweitzer describes the moment when he discovered the principle that became central for his understanding and interpretation of reality: "Late on the third day, at the very moment when, at sunset, we were making our way through a herd of hippopotamuses, there flashed upon my mind, unforeseen and unsought, the phrase, 'Reverence for Life.' The iron door had yielded: the path in the thicket had become visible. Now I had found my way to the idea in which world- and life-affirmation and ethics are contained side by side! Now I knew that the world-view of ethical world- and life affirmation, together with its ideals of civilization, is founded in thought." (*My Life & Thought. An Autobiography* [London: Allen & Unwin, 1948], pp. 185f., compare pp. 185–190, 235, 267, 269). This discovery is unfolded in Schweitzer's *The Philosophy of Civilization* (New York: MacMillan, 1959 [1923]).

by Rupert Sheldrake[48] that sees nature as friend and partner and considers a "reverence for life" including all living things to be essential for the survival of human civilization.[49] Faith in Christ therefore cannot only free us from our self-orientation and thus make a community of human brothers and sisters possible (compare Gal 3:26–28), but it can also be the foundation on which a partnership relation with nature can be restored. When the Priestly writer designated the human pair as the "image of God" and gave them "dominion" over nature (Gen 1:26–31) then this was not meant in terms of domination, definition, control, and exploitation. Rather, humanity was entrusted with the privilege and responsibility of representing God on the earth and caring for the earth within the parameters that God had set. "Dominion" has to be understood in terms of responsible care and providing food, work, and shelter for the human population.[50]

CONCLUSION

The resurrection of the crucified Christ reminds us that salvation must not be reduced to any part of God's creation, be it humanity or be it the church. Salvation is God's act in Jesus Christ and therefore it encompasses all of reality. Our focus on the resurrection has helped us to retrieve the theological significance of nature and cosmos. The God, apart from whom nothing can exist, who constantly protects, sustains and renews his creation (Ps 104:29f.) is none other than the Father of our Lord Jesus Christ.

We saw that it is not enough to qualify salvation merely with reference to the death of Jesus—that "Christ died for our sins." Without questioning or relativizing the necessity and significance of Jesus' death, we must say that his death alone—isolated from his life and resurrection—cannot be the sufficient basis for our salvation. Any theory of atonement in which the constitutive and

---

48. Compare: *The Presence of the Past, Morphic Resonance and the Habits of Nature* (New York: Vintage Books, 1989), *The Rebirth of Nature: The Greening of Science and God* (New York: Doubleday/Bantam, 1991).

49. Compare the prophetic vision of peace and harmony between humanity and its environment in Isaiah 11:6–9 and Ezekiel 34:25. George S. Hendry outlines in three chapters "The Mystery of Nature", "The Religion of Nature", and "The Philosophy of Nature" (George S. Hendry, *Theology of Nature* [1980], chapters 2–4 [pp. 33–94]).

50. Compare also Gen 2:15 (J); Ps 104:14f.23. Odil Hannes Steck comments upon the creation narrative of *P*: "The limitations laid down in Genesis 1 show that for *P* the possibility of an exploitation of the earth to the point of the exhaustion of its resources, or the contingency that autocratic man might poison and destroy living space on earth, is not remotely considered in this authorization. The subjection of the earth is only so that man may be supplied with useful plants [for food and nourishment]—and in addition the passage presupposes a permanent and completely sufficient supply of wild vegetation for the nourishment of wild animals, birds, and creeping things (1:30)." (*World and Environment* [1980], p. 107 [words in brackets added for clarification], compare further pp. 102–108, 190–203).

necessary role of Jesus' life and resurrection is not clearly spelled out, is not in harmony with the New Testament witness to Christian faith.

Furthermore, the resurrection must not be interpreted as eliminating the offense of the cross. It must not make the cross appear to be a tragic mistake or an accident of history which God consequently rectified by raising Jesus from the dead. The cross was not a flaw in the pattern of the universe which God then remedied. No, in our theological thinking it must remain central that it was and is the Crucified One who is risen and who has entered the presence of God.

The resurrection is, thirdly, not merely of noetic significance, informing us of the significance of Jesus' life and death. No, Jesus himself is risen and has thereby been established as the ground and content of our salvation. Thus Karl Barth, for instance, emphasizes again and again that besides the cross, the resurrection "is an autonomous, new act of God. It is not, therefore, the noetic converse" of the cross.[51] The fact that the risen Christ appeared to the disciples must not be interpreted in terms of a subjective vision. But it is the way in which the divine reality of the resurrection is communicated under the limitations of time and space.

We saw, finally, that the resurrection of the crucified Christ becomes concrete in that the process of history is being changed in the direction of justice. This has a very personal aspect in the experience of forgiveness. The experience of forgiveness is interrelated with a life of obedient discipleship through which Christ is experienced and made known as the crucified One, and in which the ultimate victory of the crucified Christ is anticipated. The life of obedient discipleship is motivated by the pledge that God will be faithful to his promises, and that therefore obedience to his will is worthwhile.

The resurrection of Jesus Christ is an act of God for us. It is not simply a declaration that Jesus' perception of God and the world was right and that he is now accepted by God. It is not only the demonstration that his opponents were wrong. It is not merely the manifestation that God can and does raise people from the dead. It is all this—and yet more! In raising Jesus from the dead, God has made Jesus become potentially real to us. He has not merely validated him as a great and pious man of the past, but he has received Jesus into his own being and thus given him eternal dignity and thereby made it possible for Jesus to become a personal reality to every one who is prepared to follow him. We have tried to show that when Christian faith confesses Jesus Christ to be the savior, then the salvation which has its foundation in him is not only grounded in his life and death, but also in his resurrection. The resurrection is a necessary part of the salvation event, because it alone universalizes the resources of salvation and also makes them available on the stage of history, it alone protects salvation against moral sterility, and it alone safeguards faith against the temptation of privatization and individualization. The resurrection ensures that salvation is celebration, and because it is the resurrection of the crucified One, it assures us that this celebration does not bypass those who are in need, rather it insists on including them.

---

51. Karl Barth, *Church Dogmatics* IV/1 (1956), p. 304.

Chapter 13

The Church and Its Mission

The understanding of the church is controversial today. On the one hand, even interested people experience a certain tiredness when they consider their relationship to the church. Jesus, "yes"; the church, "no"! Faith in God, "yes"; engagement in a church, "no"! Church-related events like "Billy Graham Crusades", a "visit of the Pope", or the "Kirchentag" in Germany are crowded by over 100,000 people, many of whom have a critical attitude towards the church. Parachurch groups, ecumenical movements like the "Fokolar" movement, and monastic communities like the Taizé Community in France are seen by many as the last hope for Christians who feel disillusioned with the church. On the other hand, the institutional structures of the churches struggle for survival and feel that the only way to maintain their identity is to follow conservative, restrictive, and expansionist policies. Identity seems to be more important than relevance. Creative and critical people are marginalized. Problems and endless debates about women's ordination, the place of homosexuals in the church, and the responsibility of the church in and to the world sap the energy of Christians. Can our focus on the resurrection of the crucified Christ help us to understand and interpret this situation, and open perspectives for the future?

It is not only the church but also its mission that is viewed with great suspicion today. On the one hand there are the more conservative churches which place great emphasis on evangelism and mission, but who have often failed to critically evaluate the cultural captivity of their missionary message and methods. On the other hand there is, especially in more academic theological circles, a growing tendency towards a religious pluralism that is critical of traditional missionary activities, but at the same time tends to relativize the questions of truth and justice.[1] Can our focus on the resurrection of the crucified Christ throw some light on this controversy?

Our basic thesis is that every reality seeks to create corresponding historical forms, structures, and institutions. The identity, authenticity, and credibility of

---

1. I have addressed this problem in an article: "Baptists and the Challenge of Religious Pluralism," *RExp* 89 (Winter 1992), pp. 49–69.

such structures remain dependent on the reality in which they are grounded. The community structure that corresponds to the resurrection of the crucified Christ is the church. The church is the social dimension of faith in Christ. Against the powerful "Western" individualism it must be asserted that the church as the intentional community of believers is necessary for faith in Christ. The critical but decisive question is, however, whether the church reflects and manifests its own identity in the resurrection of the crucified Christ.

THE ORIGIN OF THE CHURCH

One of the unsolved questions in New Testament and historical scholarship is when, where, and how the Christian church came into being. Is the traditional opinion correct, that Jesus, before his death, founded the church?[2] Did the post-Easter community actualize the intention of the historical Jesus? Did the risen Christ found the church? Was the church—as a community and a movement separate from Judaism—a distortion of Jesus' intentions? Although it is not possible here to develop an ecclesiology, we do need to point out that both the resurrection of Jesus and the institution of the church would be misunderstood if their inner relationship is not adequately recognized.[3]

Jesus gathered disciples around himself and thus founded and shaped a reform community within Judaism. He called the "twelve" (Mark 3:14) to symbolize that he wanted to call the twelve tribes of Israel (Matt 19:28), i.e., all of Israel,[4] back to a living relationship with their God. Their aim was to go "to the lost sheep of the house of Israel" (Matt 10:6, compare 15:24) and proclaim that

---

2. In 1910 Pope Pius X composed an oath which the clergy of the Roman Catholic Church had to swear. The third article reads: "And with firm faith, I equally believe that the Church, the guardian and teacher of the revealed Word, was directly founded by the real and historical Christ himself, as he dwelt with us, and that she was built upon Peter, the prince of the Apostolic hierarchy and his successors forever." ("Pius X's Oath against Modernism," in: Philip Schaff, *The Creeds of Christendom with a History and Critical Notes*. Bibliotheca Symbolica Ecclesiae Universalis. Vol. II: The Greek and Latin Creeds with Translations [New York: Harper & Brothers, 1877, pp. 613–615], p. 613).

3. For a discussion of problems raised here, consult: Hans Küng, *The Church* (New York: Sheed and Ward, 1967), pp. 54–79; Jürgen Moltmann, *The Church in the Power of the Spirit. A Contribution to Messianic Ecclesiology* (London: SCM, 1977), pp. 66–132. For the more recent results of New Testament scholarship see: Jürgen Roloff, *Die Kirche im Neuen Testament* (Göttingen: Vandenhoeck and Ruprecht, 1993), chapts. I and II.

4. This is illustrated with the parable of the "lost sheep" (Luke 15:4–7/Matt 18:12–14). God undertakes everything possible to lead every erring sheep back to the fold! The critical, indeed revolutionary, thrust of calling the "twelve" becomes clear when we realize that the "twelve" tribes of Israel did not exist any more during the time of Jesus. Only the northern tribes of Judah and Benjamin, and perhaps part of the tribe of Levi were left. Jesus' vision is therefore not focused on cementing the empirical status quo, but on gathering a "new" Israel.

the "time is fulfilled, and the kingdom of God is at hand; repent, and believe in the gospel" (Mark 1:15). This message went hand in hand with actual demonstrations that the living and loving rule of God was present in human history through Jesus and his disciples: healing the sick, casting out demons, relativizing law and cult. Jesus and his disciples did not feel themselves bound to the traditional orthodox and legalistic interpretations of faith in God. They questioned the absolute authority of cultic rules, like fasting and Sabbath observance. And when Gentiles entered their radius of ministry they did not neglect them.[5] Can this group of disciples, whom Jesus called and commissioned, be called "church?"

In one sense one may say: "yes". They were an intentional community of people worshipping and serving God. The disciples were commissioned by Jesus and they were given clearly defined tasks of preaching and ministry. Their community ethos was shaped by values that were different from the world around them (Mark 10:42–45). In their community Jesus was the unquestioned teacher and leader, and perhaps Peter fulfilled some kind of "speaker's" role. They ate and served together, and Jesus had taught them a community prayer (Luke 11:2–4, par. Matt 6:9–13). Toward the end of his life, when it became increasingly clear that Israel's leadership would reject Jesus' invitation to open themselves to the kingly reign of God, Jesus celebrated with his closest friends a meal during which he realistically interpreted the imminent threat upon his life and indicated his willingness to lay down his life for "the many". As such he would provide the foundation for them to continue their mission of announcing and demonstrating the nearness of the βασιλεία τοῦ θεοῦ (basileia tou theou).[6]

Yet, on further reflection, one must say: "no". It is quite certain that Jesus did not intend to leave the bounds of Judaism and start a new religion. This happened after Easter. By opposing, capturing, and executing Jesus, it became quite clear that Israel's religious and political leadership rejected Jesus' new understanding of God. This rejection persisted when God infused a new reality into the world by raising Jesus from the dead. Jesus himself did not start a separate movement, as the Essenes or the Pharisees did. He did not call for faith in himself,[7] and the disciples did not meet "in his name". The religious and cultic structures (the Lord's Prayer, the "farewell" meal) on their own would be

---

5. Consider the stories of the centurion at Capernaum (Matt 8:5–10.13, par. Luke 7:1–9 and John 4:46–53), and the Syro-Phoenician woman (Mark 7:24–30); and words like: "I tell you, many will come from east and west and sit at the table with Abraham, Isaac, and Jacob in the kingdom of heaven" (Matt 8:11).

6. The social structure of the Jesus-Community is summarized by Gerhard Lohfink, *Jesus and Community. The Social Dimension of Christian Faith* (Philadelphia: Fortress / New York: Paulist, 1984), pp. 7–73; Jürgen Roloff, *Die Kirche im Neuen Testament*. GNT 10 (Göttingen: Vandenhoeck & Ruprecht, 1993), pp. 37–57.

7. In the Synoptic gospels there is only one text that speaks of faith in Jesus (Matt 18:6), which, however, is clearly an editorial interpretation of the Marcan source (Mark 9:42). After Easter the language of faith "in Jesus Christ" virtually explodes, as can be clearly seen in Pauline and Johannine theology.

insufficient to guarantee and shape an ongoing community. There were no sacraments. As far as we know, Jesus did not baptize,[8] and he formulated no doctrines to express the identity of this "Jesus community". The most one may say is that Jesus incarnated in his words (parables), deeds (fellowship with outsiders), lifestyle (intentional servant community), and spirituality (calling God "Abba") an understanding of God which was so new that contemporary Judaism could not contain it without revising its own understanding of temple, law, and cult. In that sense one may speak not only of an implicit Christology, but also of an implicit ecclesiology. In Jesus' life and ministry the seed for a church was sown. His new and revolutionary understanding of God with its consequences for the world contained an inherent promise for the future. But—and this must be clearly recognized—if the crucifixion of Jesus were to have been the end, then there would have been no Christian church. Hans Küng comments: "For all the New Testament writers the Church is conditioned by the death and resurrection of Christ. Not until Jesus is risen from the dead do the first Christians speak of a 'Church'. The Church . . . is therefore a post-Easter phenomenon."[9]

After Easter, in retrospect, the early Christians began to realize that already during Jesus' life on earth he had laid certain foundations—a community meal, a prayer, a messianic lifestyle, a new understanding of God and the implied critique of law and cult—on which they could now build. But this realization would not have come apart from the experiences of Easter.

There is one text, however—Matthew 16:17–19—that seems to stand against this view:

> And Jesus answered him, "Blessed are you, Simon Bar-Jona! For flesh and blood has not revealed this to you, but my Father who is in heaven. And I tell you, you are Peter [Πέτρος (Petros)/kepha = "stone"], and on this rock [πέτρα (petra)/kepha = "rock"] I will build my church [ἐκκλησία (ekklēsia)], and the powers of death shall not prevail against it. I will give you the keys of the kingdom of heaven, and whatever you bind on earth shall be bound in heaven, and whatever you loose on earth shall be loosed in heaven."

This text and Matthew 18:17 are the only texts in the gospels where the word "church" (ἐκκλησία [ekklēsia]) is mentioned, while in the literature which directly reflects the situation after Easter (e.g., the Book of Acts and the Epistles)

---

8. The only indication to the contrary, John 3:22.26, 4:1, is relativized in the same context, 4:2. The unanswered question is, however, whether and why the disciples baptized, while Jesus did not. Those disciples may have been followers of John the Baptist; and then, under Jesus' leadership, they may have continued John's baptism, or a modification of it. However, that was certainly not a Christian Baptism. It was not performed in the name of Jesus, and it did not presuppose the events of Good Friday, Easter, and Pentecost.

9. Hans Küng, *The Church* (1967), p. 73.

"church" is used often. The instructions contained in Matthew 18 are most likely a reflection of the situation in the Matthean church. These two texts provide typical illustrations for the fact that the gospel writers were not primarily interested in writing a biography of Jesus. Their intention was to interrelate their own situation with the story of Jesus, and to interpret their situation in light of that story. Therefore, the horizon of Jesus' life flows together with the horizon of the churches in whose context the gospels were written. For the Matthean community "Peter" had become the guarantor of their theological continuity with Jesus, and at the same time he symbolized for them what a true disciple of Jesus should be like. The following arguments support the view that Matthew 16:17–19 is a gathering of motifs that reflect the situation after Easter.[10]

Matthew 16:17f. describes a scene at Caesarea Philippi, how Simon, in response to his messianic confession, is given the name of "Peter"—meaning "stone" (Aramaic: kepha; Greek transliteration: Κηφᾶς [Kēphas]; Greek translation: Πέτρος [Petros]). Nevertheless, when one looks where the other gospels place this name-giving event, then it becomes quite clear that the specific occasion was no longer remembered when the gospels were composed. In Mark it is referred to at the calling of the twelve (3:16). In John it is predicted (future tense!) at Simon's first encounter with Jesus (1:42), but then it is no longer mentioned in the fourth Gospel. If, in addition, one considers that in the oldest gospel traditions Simon Peter is always addressed as "Simon",[11] then the most plausible explanation seems to be that Simon was called "Peter" as result of his encounter with the risen Lord.[12] With the passing of time the name of honor became part of the normal name "Simon Peter", and the exact occasion as to when Simon received the name "Peter" was lost. Consequently, the motifs in Matthew 16:17–19 are best understood as reflecting the Easter encounter of Simon—the same event that is referred to in 1 Corinthians 15:5, Luke 24:34, and John 21:15–17. In the Matthean church this decisive encounter was placed within the earthly life of Jesus for theological reasons. The church wanted to relate its identity figure "Simon Peter" not merely to their experience of the risen Christ, but, through Peter, to the historical Jesus.[13]

---

10. For exegetical details and for different scholarly opinions consult Ulrich Luz, *Das Evangelium nach Matthäus*. 2. Teilband, Mt 8–17. EKK I/2 (Zürich: Benziger Verlag/Neukirchen Vluyn: Neukirchener Verlag, 1990), pp. 452–483; the problems related to the origin, use and meaning of Πέτρος (Petros)/kepha/stone and πέτρα (petra)/kepha/rock are discussed by Peter Lampe, "Das Spiel mit dem Petrusnamen—Matt. XVI.18," *NTS* 25 (1979), pp. 227–245.

11. The only exception, Luke 22:34, is clearly a Lukan editorial comment, as a comparison with Mark 14:29 shows. "Simon" was a common Jewish name.

12. For details see: Erich Dinkler, "Petrus, Apostel," in: *RGG* 5 (³1961), cols. 247–249.

13. A similar tendency can be observed in the Johannine community with the Beloved Disciple. For the Lucan writings and for the Pastoral epistles it is the apostle Paul who serves as the identity and authority figure, for the Epistle of James it is Jesus' brother James. The same phenomenon can be observed with the Teacher of Righteousness in the Qumran community.

If the historical Jesus had said the words contained in Matthew 16:17–19 then it is inconceivable to think why the other gospels do not report such an important event; especially in light of the fact that in none of the gospels do we meet a marked anti-Petrine tendency.[14]

The most convincing explanation about the church's origin is that the seeds were sown with Jesus and his community of friends. These seeds began to bud and blossom with the resurrection appearances of Jesus Christ to Mary Magdalene, to Peter, to Paul, and possibly to others. The theological ground and content of the church is Jesus Christ—his life, death, and resurrection. The historical actualization of the church begins with the Easter event and then gradually takes shape as the communities of faith seek to find their identity and express their faith in the various geographical and cultural settings. At first, this community still operated within the bounds of Judaism, but soon, especially under the influence of Stephen and Paul, it became clear that the gospel of the radical grace of God could not be tied to religious and legal requirements like circumcision or refraining from fellowship with Gentiles (compare the controversies implied in Galatians 2). Thus, what was implicitly there in the ministry of Jesus, now becomes explicit: the Christian church as a movement distinct from Judaism and with the divine imperative to preach the gospel to all nations.

What does this historical result mean for our understanding of Jesus Christ and the church? It means that when we speak about the resurrection of Jesus Christ we are also speaking about the church. Christ and church are related, but the priority must be observed. It was not the church that created Jesus, but it was Christ who created the church. This means that the church has its identity in him. It is *his* church; the church is on *his* mission. The crucified and risen Christ must be the criterion for everything the church tries to be and do. Theologically speaking: ecclesiology must be an aspect of christology; christology must not be dissolved into ecclesiology.

THE CALL TO MISSION

We saw earlier that the resurrection of Jesus was understood as the "beginning of the end", and that Christian existence here and now is an existence "under the cross", serving humanity in the name of Jesus. These observations suggest a close link between the resurrection of Jesus and the mission of the church. The resurrection narratives, the confessions of those who experienced the risen Christ, and the apostolic office as such, show that the reality of the resurrection becomes historically manifest in the mission of the church.

---

14. Any supposed anti-Petrine tendency in the Gospel of Mark is clearly relativized by Mark 16:7!

The Resurrection Narratives

The resurrection narratives from all four gospels testify to the interrelationship between the resurrection of Jesus and Christian mission:

> . . . Jesus came and said to them, "All authority in heaven and on earth has been given to me. Go therefore and make disciples of all nations, baptizing them in the name of the Father and of the Son and of the Holy Spirit, teaching them to observe all that I have commanded you; and lo, I am with you always, to the close of the age" (Matt 28:19f.)

> . . . . he appeared to the eleven themselves as they sat at table; and he upbraided them for their unbelief and hardness of heart, because they had not believed those who saw him after he had risen. And he said to them, "Go into all the world and preach the Gospel to the whole creation . . ." (Mark 16:15).

> [The risen Christ] said to them, "Thus it is written, that the Christ should suffer and on the third day rise from the dead, and that repentance and forgiveness of sins should be preached in his name to all nations, beginning from Jerusalem. You are witnesses of these things. And behold, I send the promise of my Father upon you; but stay in the city, until you are clothed with power from on high" (Luke 24:46–49).

> ". . . you shall receive power when the Holy Spirit has come upon you; and you shall be my witnesses in Jerusalem and in all Judea and Samaria and to the end of the earth" (Acts 1:8).

> [The risen] Jesus said to them again, "Peace be with you. As the Father has sent me, even so I send you." And when he had said this, he breathed on them, and said to them, "Receive the Holy Spirit. If you forgive the sins of any, they are forgiven; if you retain the sins of any, they are retained" (John 20:21).

Exegetical and theological differences between these texts cannot be discussed here, but a number of recurring motifs highlight and interpret the interrelationship between the resurrection of Christ and Christian mission.

There is, first of all, the emphasis that it is the risen Christ who, after the crucifixion, takes the initiative by appearing to the disciples and addressing them. In the pre-Matthean tradition the resurrection is understood as exaltation to heaven[15] where Jesus is installed to cosmic rulership: "all authority in heaven

---

15. The evangelist may suggest a modification by saying "and coming toward them (προσελθών [proselthōn]) Jesus spoke to them saying . . ." (v. 18a). This may indicate that for Matthew Jesus does not appear from heaven, but is present on the earth.

and on earth has been given to me" (Matt 28:18). According to Daniel 7:13f. it is at the end of time when the Son of man shall be given "dominion and glory and kingdom, that all peoples, nations, and languages should serve him." That promise has been fulfilled proleptically in and with the resurrection of Jesus. It is important to note, however, that Jesus is not only Lord of all the peoples of the earth, but of all of creation, of the universe, of the cosmos. Christian mission can therefore not be limited to the spiritual and social needs of people; it must also include ecological concerns.

Secondly, the call to mission is part of the saving and liberating power of the gospel. The risen Christ does not reveal himself as a giver of law, but as a giver of life. The Johannine account makes this explicit: "Peace be with you" (John 20:19) are the first words of the risen Christ to the community of men and women (in the Johannine narrative Mary is among them!). In theological terminology this means that the imperative to mission is grounded in the indicative of salvation. The first reaction to the risen Lord is therefore joy (John 20:20; Luke 24:41).

Thirdly, the content and norm of the mission that is implied in the resurrection of Christ is Jesus. The disciple must therefore be taught "to observe all that I have commanded you" (Matt 28:20). This does not make the hermeneutical task of translating the Christian message into one's respective culture superfluous. But Jesus must remain the norm. Christian faith must maintain its essential continuity with Jesus if it is not to be dissolved into personal or ecclesiastical self-interest.

Fourthly, the mission of the church must correspond to the universal Lordship of Christ. The disciples are to "go into all the world and preach the gospel to the whole creation" (Mark 16:15). They are to "make disciples of all nations" (Matt 28:19). They are his "witnesses in Jerusalem and in all Judea and Samaria and to the end of the earth" (Acts 1:8). Christian mission therefore has a universal thrust. Through the resurrection the particularity of Jesus' earthly existence and his mission to the Jews has been extended to all people. The God of "Abraham, Isaac and Jacob" is the "creator of heaven and earth", and therefore his saving passion is directed to all people and to all of creation.

A fifth point is that the narratives emphasize the identity of the risen Lord as the crucified One (John 20:20; Luke 24:39), that he "ate before them" (Luke 24:41f.; John 21:9.12f.), and that the mission of those who follow him will be accompanied by signs and wonders (Mark 16:17). These references underline that the mission of the church addresses the concrete needs of people. This aim at concreteness is illustrated by the reference to signs and wonders. It does not mean, of course, that we today must search for first-century demons in order then to cast them out; to catch poisonous snakes and test God's presence and power by handling them; to drink poison and see whether God will save us from its effect; to seek the gifts of tongues in order to find an empirical verification for the existence of God. Our task is, rather, to determine the demons that dehumanize us today and then fearlessly unmask them; to handle the snakes of militarism, oppression, and consumerism which seem to have so much power that no one is willing to stand in their way; to drink the poison of identifying with the tortured and oppressed; and to find ever new "tongues" to proclaim the riches of the gospel.

We note further, as a sixth point, that the aim of the church's mission is to "make disciples of all nations, baptizing them in the name of the Father and the Son and the Holy Spirit, teaching them to observe all that I have commanded you" (Matt 28:19f.), and to preach "repentance and forgiveness of sins" (Luke 24:47; similar John 20:23). Thus the reality of the resurrection reaches its aim when, through faith in Christ, Christ becomes the determining and integrating center of peoples lives. Thereby God reclaims a little of his creation, and people are drawn into the liberating and saving passion of God for his creation.

As a seventh point we observe that the means of mission are determined by the fact that the risen Lord identifies himself as the crucified One: "he showed them his hands and his side" (John 20:20, compare 20:25–28; Luke 24:39). In light of the terrible mistakes that the churches have committed when they adopted methods and means of imperialism and colonialism in their attempts to "save souls", it must be insisted that the means of mission must be consistent with the content of faith. There can be no coercion in the name of Jesus. The missionary can only come in the form of a beggar: "we beg you [δεόμεθα (deometha)] on behalf of Christ, be reconciled to God" (2 Cor 5:20).

We further observe, as an eighth point, that Matthew makes clear that responsible mission implies a certain self-limitation of God. Although "all authority in heaven and on earth has been given" to the risen Christ, it is the church that is called to mission: "Go therefore. . . ." This does not only mean that the church can be a missionary community in the sense that it has the inner motivation, strength, and consolation for that difficult task; rather, the church must be on mission if and as long as Jesus is its Lord. The Lordship of Jesus is at stake in the existence of the church. Jesus' Lordship, which the church affirms and confesses, must become real on earth, as it is in heaven. His Lordship is not complete, his intentions have not yet been fulfilled, until he reigns on earth. And the only witness to and instrument of that mission is the church. The very essence of the church, the very reason for its being, is to make itself available to the risen Lord to win his world back to himself. The self-limitation of God makes the obedience, freedom, and dignity of the church possible. The texts can therefore say that in and through the mission of the church Christ himself can minister to his creation: "If you forgive the sins of any, they are forgiven; if you retain the sins of any, they are retained" (John 20:23; compare Matt 16:19, 18:18).

At the same time, we note as a ninth point, that the risen Lord promises to provide the sustaining spirituality for the task of mission: "and lo, I am with you always, to the close of the age" (Matt 28:20). The risen Christ will be with them in the power of the Holy Spirit (Luke 24:49; Acts 1:8; John 20:22).

We finally remind ourselves that faith is a relational reality and therefore it creates a community, the church. The resurrection narratives show the awareness of this by grounding communal structures in the message of the risen Lord. The community is grounded in the reality of a trinitarian God (Matt 28:19), believers are baptized as a public confession of their faith (Matt 28:19; Mark 16:16), and the structures of the life of faith must be related to the content of Jesus' life (Matt 28:20; Luke 24:44–48).

Paul's Call to Mission

The close relationship between the resurrection of Jesus Christ and the call to mission is also confirmed by the personal testimony of the apostle Paul. Even before his encounter with the risen Christ, Paul was a very religious man. God was the determining reality of his life. Being a good Pharisee (Phil 3:5; compare Gal 1:14), he believed that God had revealed himself in the Torah and its authentic interpretations ("the traditions of my fathers" [Gal 1:14]). To him worship of God implied obedience to the law and the practice of the cult, and "as to righteousness under the law" he considered himself "blameless" (Phil 3:6). Hand in hand with these religious convictions went a certain religious elitism which he considered divinely ordained — "circumcised on the eighth day, of the people of Israel, of the tribe of Benjamin, a Hebrew born of Hebrews" (Phil 3:5; compare 2 Cor 11:22; Rom 11:1). Günter Bornkamm comments: "These accumulations of terms convey not only his own Jewish descent as a matter of race but also his people's unique religious standing in the world."[16]

When Paul met Christians who did not only proclaim that the crucified Jesus was the Messiah, but who, in consequence of that conviction, relativized the authority of law and cult,[17] the main pillars of Judaism, this to him could only mean blasphemy and heresy. Worship to God in that context implied for him: "I persecuted the church of God violently and tried to destroy it" (Gal 1:13; compare Phil 3:6). Does not the law say: "a hanged man is accursed by God" (Deut 21:23)? And how can people who "speak words against this holy place and the law" and who believe that Jesus of Nazareth "will change the customs which Moses delivered to us" (Acts 6:13f.) still be worshippers of the one, true and only God, the God of Israel?

Then came his encounter with the risen Christ![18] In this encounter, Christ himself convinced Paul that God is not revealed in law and cult, but in Jesus

---

16. Günter Bornkamm, *Paul* (New York: Harper and Row, 1971), p. 4.

17. It is a consensus among critical New Testament scholars that from the earliest days onwards there were Christians who exercised their new found faith within the bounds of Judaism—thus keeping law and cult and not engaging in mission to the Gentiles—and Christians who felt that faith in Christ implied a break with Judaism and an openness to the Gentiles. It was mainly these latter Christians to whom Paul refers; compare: Walter Schmithals, *Paul and James*. SBT 46 (London: SCM, 1965), chapt. I; Ernst Haenchen, *The Acts of the Apostles. A Commentary* (Oxford: Blackwell, 1971), commentary on 6:1–8:3.

18. Compare pp. 135–139 above.

Christ (Gal 1:16). Consequently, it was not his traditional understanding of God that was right, but the Christian view which he had opposed so violently. His unenlightened zeal (Rom 10:2) dissolved, when he came to know "the light of the knowledge of the glory of God in the face of Christ" (2 Cor 4:6). His experience of Christ meant for Paul the end of the ultimate authority of the law (Rom 10:4). His religious devotion was no longer fed by and focused on the law, but Christ became the determining center of his existence. In Phil 3:7–11 Paul contrasts his existence under the law with his newly found faith in Christ:

> But whatever gain I had, I counted as loss for the sake of Christ. Indeed I count everything as loss because of the surpassing worth of knowing Christ Jesus my Lord. For his sake I have suffered the loss of all things, and count them as refuse, in order that I may gain Christ and be found in him, not having a righteousness of my own, based on law, but that which is through faith in Christ, the righteousness from God that depends on faith; that I may know him and the power of his resurrection, and may share his sufferings, becoming like him in his death, that if possible I may attain the resurrection from the dead.

If Christ relativizes law and cult, then this must also imply the elimination of religious elitism for Israel. In Christ there is "neither Jew nor Greek" (Gal 3:28). This, together with the conviction that through the resurrection Jesus Christ was revealed as the universal savior, meant that Paul interpreted his encounter with the risen Christ as a call to mission among the Gentiles: ". . . when he who set me apart before I was born, and had called me through his grace, was pleased to reveal his Son to me, in order that I might preach him among the Gentiles" (Gal 1:15f.). His encounter with the risen Christ implied a divine "obligation both to Greeks and to barbarians, both to the wise and to the foolish" (Rom 1:14). He experienced his call as a divine "necessity" laid upon him, so much so, that he could only think of an eschatological curse if he were not to be obedient to God's call: "Woe to me if I do not preach the gospel!" (1 Cor 9:16).

The point is clear. Just as Jesus expressed his relationship with God by going to the marginalized people—the publicans and lepers and fishermen and women and children so that the grace of God might become an event to those who were considered godless—so Paul, when he encountered God in Christ, became a missionary to the Gentiles.

Peter's Call to Mission

The interrelationship between the reality of the resurrection and the call to mission became also manifest in the life of the apostle Peter. With regard to Peter it is much more difficult to make historically accurate statements because from Peter we have no primary sources, and the reports about Peter's life and ministry are not without tensions and difficulties.

It is generally agreed that Peter belonged to the foundational witnesses of the resurrection. He was the first to whom the risen Christ appeared in Galilee: 1 Cor 15:5 mentions the appearance to him first; and in its present context Luke 24:34 guards the primacy of Peter's encounter with the risen Christ over against the encounter of the risen Christ with the disciples on the road to Emmaus; also John 21:1–14 (compare Luke 5:4b–6.8) contains an older tradition which spoke of a first appearance before Peter on the lake of Galilee.[19] Peter's prominent place in the Easter events is also confirmed by John 21:15–17 and Mark 16:7, as well as indirectly by Matthew 16:18f. and Luke 22:31f., both of which originally belonged to the Easter tradition.

It is furthermore clear that the encounter of Peter with the risen Lord meant a call to a missionary existence: "Peter, who in accordance with the early Christian view did not yet distinguish between sending and gathering, had a twofold task—he was the leader of the Church and he was the most influential missionary."[20] Although Peter was without doubt a missionary from the beginning, in the first few years after his call he was also the prominent leader in the church in Jerusalem.[21] There Paul visited him shortly after his call to pay homage to him (Gal 1:18). But 14 years later at the apostolic council in Jerusalem (48 C.E.) Paul's delegation is met by three pillars of the Jerusalem church—James, Peter, and John—and Paul mentions James before Peter (Gal 2:9). It is therefore likely that in Jerusalem James had become the leader,[22] while Peter specialized more in leading the Jewish Christian mission activities (compare Gal 2:8f.).

Again, what was true for Paul, is also true for Peter. The risen Lord calls those to whom he appears to engage in mission. "The first Easter witness . . . was *eo ipso* a missionary."[23] Although this mission was not separate from his leadership role in Jerusalem, and it was mainly directed to Jewish people, Peter adopted a very open attitude toward Gentiles (compare Gal 2:11–14; Acts 8:25, 10:1–48) and therefore was in full agreement with Paul's mission to the Gentiles.

James, the Brother of Jesus

In the list of resurrection appearances we also find James, the brother of Jesus (1 Cor 15:7). Although, as far as we know, he was not a follower of the historical Jesus, in consequence of the resurrection appearance he became a believer,

---

19. For details substantiating this view see: Thorwald Lorenzen, *Der Lieblingsjünger im Johannesevangelium* (1971), §7.

20. Ferdinand Hahn, *Mission in the New Testament* SBT 47 (London: SCM, 1965), p. 48.

21. Although Acts 1–11 is Luke's composition, the dominant role of Peter clearly shines through.

22. This is suggested by Gal 2:12, but also by Acts 12:17, 15:2–21, 21:18.

23. Heinrich Kasting, *Die Anfänge der urchristlichen Mission. Eine historische Untersuchung.* BEvTh, 55 (München: Kaiser, 1969), p. 86 (my translation).

and in due course he became the dominant leader in the Jewish Christian church in Jerusalem.[24] When Paul in about 48 C.E. visited Jerusalem for his important meeting with the three "pillars"—James, Peter, and John—James seems to have been the *primus inter pares* in Jerusalem (Gal 2:9). Several years later (about 56 C.E.) James had emerged as the sole leader in the Jerusalem church (Acts 21:18). Although James was most likely a conservative Jewish Christian leader, he agreed to Paul's mission to the Gentiles without requiring circumcision (Gal 2:9f.); indeed, Luke presents him as a defender of Paul's mission to the Gentiles (Acts 15:13–21). We may therefore safely conclude that James also understood his call as a call to mission, although for him personally this meant mission to the Jewish community. The circumstances forced him to become primarily concerned with protecting the unity of the church and the survival of the Jewish Christian church in Jerusalem. Although he tried to live the Christian faith within the bounds of Judaism, the Sadducees accused him of transgressing the law. They brought a charge against him, the Sanhedrin condemned him and he was delivered up to be stoned; thus he belonged to the first Christian leaders who were killed for their faith.[25]

The Apostolic Office

What is true for Paul, Peter, and James in particular, is true for the apostolic office in general. A pre-Pauline tradition speaks of a resurrection appearance to the "twelve" and "to all the apostles" (1 Cor 15:5.7). With the formation of the "twelve" after Easter, the intention of Jesus for the restoration of all Israel is renewed. Soon, however, this circle is enlarged to "all the apostles" whose function it was to make God's salvation known to all people.

It would be false to say that everyone who saw the risen Lord became an apostle. That would already be difficult to maintain with reference to the 500 brethren who are reported to have experienced an encounter with the risen Lord (1 Cor 15:6). But it is possible that every apostle had the experience of an encounter with the risen Christ. This remains doubtful with regard to Andronicus and Junia (a woman!) whom Paul counts among the apostles (Rom 16:7), but about whom we have no further information.

A problem is that Luke seems to have a very different concept of apostleship. According to him an apostle must be someone who had known and accompanied the historical Jesus "beginning from the baptism of John until the day when he was taken up from us" (Acts 1:21f.). Paul, therefore, for Luke is not officially an apostle. In Acts 14:4 and 14 he is referred to as apostle, but

---

24. For details see the interesting article by Martin Hengel, "Jakobus der Herrenbruder—der erste 'Papst'?" in: *Glaube und Eschatologie*. Festschrift für Werner Kümmel zum 80. Geburtstag, Hg. von Erich Grässer und Otto Merk. Tübingen: Mohr, 1985, pp. 71–104. Further: W. A. Beardslee, "James," in: *IDB* II (1962), pp. 791–794.
25. This is reliably reported by the Jewish historian Josephus in: *Jewish Antiquities*, Book XX, §§ 197–203.

there "apostle" is probably a more general description of a representative of a church.[26] But there is a wide consensus of opinion that Luke is more interested in affirming the theological continuity of the gospel tradition and the church with Jesus, than giving an account of the origin of the apostolic office.

It is probably best to follow Paul's lead and suppose that all apostles had seen the risen Lord, or at least had intentionally identified with Peter's encounter of the risen Christ. In 1 Cor 9:1 Paul defends his apostleship—"Am I not an apostle?"—by claiming to be a witness of the resurrection appearances of Jesus: "Have I not seen Jesus our Lord?" Paul therefore presupposes that "having seen the Lord" is the decisive criterion for being an apostle. In 1 Cor 15:7 Paul speaks of "all the apostles" as a distinct group who had all encountered the risen Lord. He himself was brought into that group because "last of all" Jesus appeared also to him. Indeed there is no evidence that the early Christian group of apostles included others after Paul—e.g. Timothy and Titus—who were not direct witnesses of the risen Christ.

For our investigation it is important that the apostolic office is grounded in the resurrection of the crucified Christ and that therefore a missionary orientation and an existential involvement with Christ is the essential content of the apostolic office. Karl Heinrich Rengstorf comments about the first: "This missionary element is something which radically distinguishes the NT apostolate from the Jewish שָׁלִיחַ (šālîaḥ) institution."[27] And Jürgen Roloff comments on the second point:

> . . . the whole existence of the apostle is the explication of the gospel, because it is the commission of the risen One who determines and shapes the apostle's life. Paul draws the attention of the Corinthian Christians to his sufferings (2 Cor 4:7–18), to his weakness (12:9f.), his patience (12:12), and his being a servant of all (4:5): thereby he demonstrates to them the structure of the gospel which is grounded in the way of Jesus, and therefore is in fact the structure of the cross. On that basis he can demand: "Become imitators of me!" (1 Cor 4:16; 11:11), "become as I am!" (Gal 4:12). Ultimately the whole apology of the apostolic office in 2 Cor 2:14–7:4 rests on this correspondence between the apostle and the gospel: By explicating his own behavior and conduct the apostle makes the structure of the gospel visible.[28]

We may conclude therefore that "for the apostle of Jesus Christ Christophany and call to mission belong together in the same way as it was with theophany

---

26. Jürgen Roloff ascribes Acts 14:4 and 14 to a non-Lukan source: "Apostel/Apostolat/Apostolizität I," in: *TRE* III (1978, pp. 430–445), p. 435 and p. 443.

27. Karl Heinrich Rengstorf, "ἀπόστολος," (apostolos) in *TDNT* I (1964 [1933], pp. 407–445), p. 432.

28. Jürgen Roloff, "Apostel/Apostolat/Apostolizitäat I," in: *TRE* III (1978, pp. 430–445), p. 439 (my translation).

and call to mission for the Old Testament prophets."[29] In the encounter with the risen Christ the apostles become authorized and empowered to continue the mission which Jesus of Nazareth had commenced on earth.[30] An encounter with the risen Christ means being drawn into the passion of God for his world.

Consequences

From the texts that we have examined it has become obvious that the reality of Easter did not only manifest the beginning of the church, but at the same time it defined the nature of the church as witness to and participant in God's mission to the world. Although it is not possible here to develop a theology of mission, we must try to sketch what consequences our investigation may have for our modern understanding and praxis of mission.

It has become clear, firstly, that a confession of the resurrection of Jesus Christ implies the acceptance of the call and commitment to mission. The risen Lord sends those who believe in him! The basis for this can be clarified on several levels.

On the christological level the call to universal Christian mission is implied in the realization that the resurrection of Jesus Christ is his exaltation and installation to cosmic rulership. Mission is then the historical actualization of that rulership on earth. In its worship the church can already celebrate the cosmic rulership of Christ (compare the early Christian hymns Col 1:15–20; Phil 2:6–11; 1 Tim 3:16). Nevertheless, that cosmic rulership is not yet historically manifest. In actual fact Christ is, so far, only Lord of the church. But the church is only obedient to its Lord insofar as it understands itself as being sent to implement the concrete realization of that Lordship in the world.[31]

On the theological level we arrive at the same conclusion when we understand that the God "who gives life to the dead" (Rom 4:17) is the same God "who justifies the ungodly" (Rom 4:5). This means that "God is love." Love is not one attribute of God among others, it is *the* attribute. Love is not simply the

---

29. Ibid., pp. 437f. (my translation).

30. For the relationship of the call to mission by the risen Lord to the ministry of the historical Jesus, see Heinrich Kasting, *Die Anfänge der urchristlichen Mission* (1969), pp. 124–126; Ferdinand Hahn, *Mission in the New Testament* (1965), pp. 26–46; Martin Hengel, "Die Ursprünge der christlichen Mission," *NTS* 18 (1971, pp. 16–38), pp. 35–37.

31. This can be illustrated by a careful exegesis of Colossians 1:15–29, noting especially the difference in christology between the pre-Colossian hymn and the author of the epistle. The hymn confesses Christ as "the head of the body" (v. 18: in the hymn "body" refers to the cosmos) who has performed reconciliation of all things "through the blood of the cross" (v. 20). The author of Colossians interprets from this that in actuality the Lordship of Christ so far only extends to the church ("the head of the body, the church" [v.18]). So far the mystery of salvation has been made manifest only to the saints (v. 26). The saints must let their lives be shaped by the gospel (v. 23) and proclaim the gospel "to every creature under heaven" (v. 23). The potential Lordship of Christ seeks to become actual in the mission of the church.

content of his action as distinct from his being; it is God's very being, his nature, his essence. This denotes essentially two things. It means, firstly, that God is not static. He is not an isolated being that exists in and for himself. His very nature is his being "for us". The mission of the church to all the world is therefore grounded in God's very nature. And secondly: God *is* in being on the way to liberate and save his creation. The creating God is the saving God. When we confess that Jesus has been raised from the dead, we are giving expression to the conviction that he has become part of God's being. For us this means that every follower of Jesus is drawn into God's passion to heal the world. That is the reason why the apostle Paul grounds both the event of reconciliation and the ministry of reconciliation in God himself and insists that both belong together (2 Cor 5:18–20).

Christianity is mission because it is grounded in the *missio dei*! Any Christian self-understanding that is not at its center moved by this missionary concern is deficient.

Secondly, it is the crucified and risen Christ himself who calls the church to mission. This should counteract any ecclesiastical triumphalism on one hand, and any discouraged resignation on the other. Mission is not primarily the expanding of denominational influence. Mission means tuning into the passion of Christ to make this world whole. It is the church's privilege and responsibility to manifest its faith in Christ by being obedient and faithful in his service.

The content of the church's missionary message and mission program can be no other than Jesus Christ crucified and risen. In Christ, God has identified himself with all people and he wants all people to become whole so as to enjoy their life as God has intended it for them. For the experience of that wholeness people need to be invited to faith in God. Such faith belongs to their human destiny. At the same time, one needs to work for social and environmental conditions in which people can live a life of human dignity. Believers are also to be integrated into a meaningful Christian community. Such a community will not be a religious club, but it will function in such a way that it serves the missionary task of the church. As Christ served people so the church of Christ will be a servant church: "If I then, your Lord and Teacher, have washed your feet, you also ought to wash one another's feet" (John 13:14).

Since Christ is one, and since the call to mission is his call, an ecumenical longing must accompany all missionary activity. The church should be one, and one in purpose—even as the Father and the Son are one (John 17:21). If this oneness is really intended by God—and there is no doubt that biblical and theological reflection point in that direction—then we must display an ecumenical concern on earth. The church will lack in credibility and effectiveness as long as we do not make clear to the world that we know whom we believe! Mission boards and missionaries are challenged today to examine whether in their mission it is really Christ who is honored and proclaimed, and not a certain church tradition.

We observe, thirdly, that mission grounded in the resurrection of Jesus Christ must express God's concern for all creation. It must be a universal mission. In and with the resurrection of Jesus, God has intensified the process to win the world back to himself. The church tunes into this universal passion of God. The fact that the church has confessed its belief in the "bodily" resurrection of Jesus is also of importance in this connection. It is not Jesus' spirit or his soul, but his whole existence that is taken up into God. This in itself speaks against a Christian mission which is only interested in saving "souls". A person cannot be separated into body and soul, or into body, soul, and spirit. A person is a unit and as such part of a society and of the environment. Thus the saving message of God's love for humanity must address human beings in the wholeness of their existence. It must include humanity's spiritual and material well-being as well as humanity's relationships and environment.

It is one of those unfortunate facts which erodes the credibility of the church that in this critical time of human history, when humankind is threatened with war, hunger, and the destruction of the environment, that the church spends a large amount of its time, money, and energy in debating such theological issues as "salvation" or "humanization". Both slogans are misleading and properly interpreted mean exactly the same. The issue for the church cannot be evangelism or social action and environmental concern, but the "or" must be replaced by an "and". Mission tries to make God's love real and concrete by witnessing to the wholeness of the salvation and liberation that faith in Christ brings. This does not mean that for functional reasons the church may not specialize in evangelism, if there are other organizations who meet the other needs. But such possible functional limitation must never blind us towards the universal task of mission.

We note, fourthly, that Christ himself through the Holy Spirit will provide the empowering motivation and sustenance in and for the task of mission. Mission in our time is a very difficult task. The needs are great. At the same time there is great uncertainty, even in church pews, yes, even in the hearts of missionaries, whether God is real, and whether it is morally justified to preach the Christian message to people of other faiths. This uncertainty has led to a spiritual dearth and denominational ideology as far as the missionary task of the church is concerned. In this difficult time a new search for the living reality of God himself, a new willingness to repent, may bring the required insights and motivation.

This brings us to the concluding observation that faith in the resurrection of Jesus Christ implies a certain understanding of missionary existence in and through which Christ is revealed as crucified and risen. What we mean can again be clarified with a few brief references to Paul's epistles. In 2 Corinthians 1:3–11 Paul speaks about the afflictions which have come to him as result of his missionary service: "we were so utterly, unbearably crushed that we despaired of life itself" (v. 8). He interprets this as sharing "abundantly in Christ's sufferings" (v. 5). Similarly in 2 Corinthians 4:7–15 Paul interprets the difficulties in his missionary existence christologically: "always carrying in the body the death of Jesus" (v. 10). And again in Galatians 6:17: "I bear on my body the marks of Jesus." Paul interprets his life of hardship, which is the direct result of his missionary existence, as participating in the sufferings of Christ. He who is a fellow worker with God (1 Cor 3:9) shares in God's passion for the world.

However, in accepting the cross, he also experienced the resurrection power of God. He learned to rely "on God who raises the dead" (2 Cor 1:9), "so that the life of Jesus may be manifested in our mortal flesh" (2 Cor 4:11). Paul interpreted his own life in analogy to the life of Jesus: "For he was crucified in weakness, but lives by the power of God. For we are weak in him, but in dealing with you we shall live with him by the power of God" (2 Cor 13:4). The cross and resurrection of Jesus Christ became an existential reality in the apostle's own existence. The crucifixion and resurrection of Jesus Christ are the theological basis for the apostle's testimony:

> We are afflicted in every way, but not crushed;
> perplexed, but not driven to despair,
> persecuted, but not forsaken,
> struck down, but not destroyed.
>
> (2 Cor 4:8f.)

> We are treated as impostors, and yet are true;
> as unknown, and yet well known;
> as dying, and behold we live;
> as punished, and yet not killed;
> —as sorrowful, yet always rejoicing;
> as poor, yet making many rich;
> as having nothing, and yet possessing everything.
>
> (2 Cor 6:8b, 10)

The existence of the missionary and the structure of the mission-oriented church acquire therefore kerygmatic significance. Just as Jeremiah and Jesus and Paul verified their message with their existence—they did not only preach a certain message, but they incarnated that message in and with their lives—so the church and its missionaries today are not only called to preach the gospel of the crucified and risen Christ, but also to give a concrete manifestation of that gospel in their lives and structures. Jesus did not just proclaim that God loves sinners, but he demonstrated the reality of that proclamation by having close communion with publicans and sinners. The missionary Christian today must accept the challenge of trying to participate in restoring the credibility of the Christian church. There must be a new commitment to holiness, to uncompromising justice, and to love for all humans, especially for those who lie bruised in the side streets of life.

THE SHAPE OF THE CHURCH

The shape of the church must reflect what the church is and to whom it belongs. It must become evident that the crucified and risen Christ is the founder and the shaper of the church; that the church is his "body", through whom he wants to encounter the world as savior and liberator. Christology must determine ecclesiology, not vice versa. This calls for some structural consequences that have been implied in our discussion.

Firstly, the church tunes into the resurrection of the crucified Christ by being the church "for others" (Bonhoeffer) and "with others" (Moltmann).[32] Jesus manifested his divinity—his sinlessness!—by having fellowship and showing solidarity with "publicans and sinners". The apostle Paul makes the "unbeliever" and the "person of the street" (the ἄπιστος [apistos] and the ἰδιώτης [idiōtēs]) the criteria for the validity of the church's structures and activities (1 Cor 14:16.23–25). The church distinguishes itself from a sect or from a religious club by being open to the outsider. Like a ship—often used to symbolize the church—the church is not meant to anchor in a safe harbor, but to fulfill its function in the stormy seas of life.

Secondly, a mission-oriented church takes the Reformation insight of the priesthood of all believers seriously, and is therefore interested in mobilizing all believers for the task and privilege of mission. This means that the church must be a fellowship in which the gifts of the members are discovered and developed. The realization that mission in the world can only be effectively accomplished by those who live and work in the world must be internalized. There must be a refocusing of the church's interest away from the clergy towards the "ordinary" believer. The latter must be motivated, inspired, and trained for the task of mission.

Thirdly, in its mission the church must display the same concern and partiality for the disadvantaged as Jesus manifested in his own life. Especially in so-called Christian countries the church must be aware of the constant temptation to become functionalized to serve as the religious validation of the status quo. The separation of church and state must be the presupposition for the church's critical relationship in societal affairs.

Fourthly, if the church is to fulfill its call to mission it must be open and willing to change. A fast-moving and increasingly pluralistic world cannot be met

---

32. In an "outline for a book", Dietrich Bonhoeffer said in August 1944, that in analogy to Jesus, whose being is a being for others, the "Church is the Church only when it exists for others." (In: Eberhard Bethge, ed. *Letters and Papers from Prison* [London: SCM, ³1967], pp. 208–211); compare Dietrich Bonhoeffer, *Ethics*, ed. Eberhard Bethge (London: SCM, 1955), pp. 194–196: "Deputyship, and therefore also responsibility, lies only in the complete surrender of one's life to the other man." (pp. 195f.); in his interpretation of the beatitudes, Bonhoeffer says: "The disciple-community does not shake off sorrow as though it were no concern of its own, but willingly bears it. And in this way they show how close are the bonds which bind them to the rest of humanity." (*The Cost of Discipleship* [New York: MacMillan, 1963], p. 122). Ernst Lange portrays the development of the theme "the church as the church for others" in Bonhoeffer's theological pilgrimage: "Kirche für andere. Dietrich Bonhoeffer's Beitrag zur Frage einer verantwortbaren Gestalt der Kirche in der Gegenwart," *EvTh* 27 (1966/1967), pp. 513–546. Jürgen Moltmann, *Theology of Play*, trans. Reinhard Ulrich (New York: Harper and Row, 1972), pp. 70f.

at the points of its real needs by a church who is always looking backwards trying to preserve a "Christian" ethos. If God really is present through the ministry of his Spirit—as the church has been confessing from the beginning—then
the church must continuously change to meet the needs of the time and thus
fulfill its mission.

Fifthly, we note that the church's leadership structures must reflect the christological identity of the church. Leaders must reflect the mind of Christ and
they must enable the church to be what is: the body of Christ. It must be clear
that church leaders are servants of Christ who can have no other passion than
enabling the church to create analogies to the story of Jesus. Ordination should
not set people apart for special privileges or special status. Rather, ordination
is the church's symbolic and prophetic act by which it recognizes that some
people are called to study, live, and speak the word of God as it is centered in
the crucified and risen Christ. Here we must again mention the fact that the first
appearance of the risen Christ was probably to Mary Magdalene, a woman,[33]
that in earliest Christianity many (house) churches were led by women,[34] that
in the Gospel of John the apostolic group included Mary (John 20:18–22), and
that also Paul knows of at least one female apostle (Rom 16:7). It would be
ironical if it were not so tragic that many churches who would with gusto affirm the resurrection of Christ continue to deny ordination to women.

THE "GATHERED COMMUNITY" AND THE SACRAMENTS

The fact that resurrection narratives speak of appearances to individuals
(Mary, Peter, Paul, James) and to groups (the "twelve", all the apostles, the five
hundred brethren) shows the early Christian awareness that Christian life must
be lived in community. This community regularly gathers for fellowship and
worship (1 Cor 11:17f.20.33f., 14:23; Acts 2:44). In the context of these gatherings the presence of the risen Christ was celebrated with prayer, hymns, teaching, and preaching. The longing for Christ's presence and for the fulfillment of
his future issued into the invocation "our Lord, come!" (1 Cor 16:22, Rev 22:20).
It was in the context of these "gathered communities" that the sacraments of
baptism and the Lord's supper became formative for the Christian churches.

We have already seen that the call to mission, grounded in the resurrection
of the crucified Christ, included the command to baptize disciples "in (εἰς [eis])
the name of the Father and of the Son and of the Holy Spirit," (Matt 28:19, compare Mark 16:16). Since, as far as we know, Jesus did not baptize those who
followed him, and since the baptismal texts of the early Christian churches

---

33. Compare pp. 140f. above.
34. Specific mention is made of Phoebe (Rom 16:1), Nympha (Col 4:15), Lydia (Acts
16:14f.40), Mary, the mother of John Mark (Acts 12:12), and Priscilla, who is often
mentioned before Aquila (Rom 16:3.5a; Acts 18:18.26; 2 Tim 4:19).

clearly presuppose the death and resurrection of Christ, the most likely genesis of Christian baptism is the post-Easter community, which baptized new converts into the reality of the resurrection of the crucified One.[35] Historically, the
practice of baptism was probably taken over from John's baptism to which Jesus
had also submitted. The Christian content was given with its essential relation
to the name of "Jesus" or of "Christ". In baptism believers publicly place themselves under the liberating Lordship of Christ. Thereby they celebrate being
part of the eschatological community of God's people. They gratefully hear the
promise of Christ's continuing presence in their lives through the ministry of
the Holy Spirit, they commit themselves to the way of discipleship, they become an intentional part of a community in which social barriers are relativized
(Gal 3:27f.), and they participate in the mission of the church to be the "body"
through which Christ wants to encounter the world.

Also the second major sacrament of the church, the Lord's Supper (so called
in 1 Cor 11:20), is theologically grounded in the resurrection of the crucified
Christ. It has, of course, a strong rooting in Israel's history and in the life of
Jesus. Jesus practiced table fellowship with "publicans and sinners", and,
shortly before his arrest, he had a communal farewell meal with his disciples,
which in its form took up elements of the passover meal. This meal-tradition
relates the Lord's Supper to the liberating history of God with his people and
with his creation.[36] However, the Eucharist as the "Lord's Supper", in which
Christ is present, and on whom the community feeds by faith, is a post-Easter
phenomenon. Here, at the Lord's table, the community of believers remembers
its Lord, worships him, and anticipates his future.

The theological importance of the Lord's Supper and its interlocking with
the resurrection of Christ is also reflected in two of the resurrection narratives
of the Gospels. In the Lukan narrative about the two disciples on the road to
Emmaus (Luke 24:13–35) it is at the meal table that the disciples recognize
Jesus as the risen Christ. And the meal is portrayed in Lord's Supper terminology: "When he was at table with them, he took the bread and blessed, and broke
it, and gave it to them" (v. 30).[37] With this story the church confesses that it is
not the knowledge of the historical Jesus and his mighty words and deeds (vv.
14.19), not the historical knowledge of the crucifixion (v. 20), not the knowledge of the scriptures (v. 27), not even the historical reports about the empty

---

35. A recent statement on an emerging ecumenical doctrine of baptism is the Faith
and Order statement on "Baptism," in: *Baptism, Eucharist and Ministry*. Faith and Order
Paper No. 111 (Geneva: WCC, 1982), pp. 2–7.

36. Compare: Jürgen Moltmann, *The Church in the Power of the Spirit. A Contribution
to Messianic Ecclesiology* (London: SCM, 1977), chapt. V/4; A recent statement on an
emerging ecumenical doctrine of the Lord's Supper is the Faith and Order statement on
"Eucharist", in: *Baptism, Eucharist and Ministry*. Faith and Order Paper No. 111
(Geneva: WCC, 1982), pp. 9–17.

37. Compare the language of the Lord's Supper tradition in Mark 14:22, par. Matt
26:26, Luke 22:19; 1 Cor 11:23f.

tomb and the vision of the heavenly messengers (vv. 22–24), that was sufficient to remove their sadness (v. 17) and create faith in the risen Christ. It was at the table, where, although the disciples invited the stranger, the stranger immediately assumes the role as host, "their eyes were opened and they recognized him" (v. 31). The story continues: "and he vanished out of their sight" (v. 31). What does this mean? The story wants to say that it is not enough to know all the available facts about Jesus—his life, his death, the empty tomb, the messianic promises in the Old Testament; God alone can help them to recognize Jesus as the risen Christ ("their eyes were opened"), and the reality of the risen Christ remains present in the intentional communion of Christians with each other and with their Lord, ever again symbolized in the Lord's Supper. Although he vanished, his presence will be remembered "in the breaking of the bread."

Another text which reflects this connection of the Lord's Supper with the resurrection is the fragment of a resurrection narrative contained in John 21:9.12f. It is part of a longer narrative, John 21:1–14, which is probably a conflation of two appearance stories: one, connected with a miraculous catch of fish, before Peter and some other disciples (vv. 1–7, par. Luke 5:4b–6.8), and one, connected with a meal, before some disciples (vv. 9.12f).[38] The meal episode in vv. 9 and 12f. is probably a fragment of an appearance story which circulated originally independently of the other. It portrays the appearance of Christ to some disciples at a meal of fish. The risen Lord assumes the role of host, and the story is told in eucharistic terminology: "Jesus came and took the bread and gave it to them, and so with the fish" (v. 13).

We may therefore say, in conclusion, that the sacraments of baptism and the Lord's Supper are both grounded in the reality of the resurrection of the crucified Christ. They are therefore to be understood primarily as christological, and only as such also as ecclesiological, sacraments. In the celebration of baptism and the Lord's Supper it is Christ who shares the riches of his life with those who follow him. Baptism is performed once in the believer's life, to confess and celebrate the beginning of the way of discipleship; while the Lord's Supper is celebrated again and again to feed on Christ in faith, to live under the promise of his future, and to become aware of the fact that although the Christian life tries to form analogies to the intentions of Jesus, it is not a way of legalism or dogmatism. It is a way in which Jesus Christ is constantly remembered through the ministry of the Holy Spirit, and this remembrance brings the resources of Christ's life, death, and resurrection into the present and thereby releases hope for the future.

It is important to remember this relationship of the sacraments to the resurrection. Thereby they become dynamic sacraments. No longer can they be used to validate the status quo or to cement elitism in the church. But they are the sacraments of the people of God whose only orientation is the crucified and

---

38. Compare: Thorwald Lorenzen, *Der Lieblingsjünger im Johannesevangelium* (1971), pp. 60–69 (I/§7).

risen Christ, and who are therefore uncomfortable with the status quo. Beginning with baptism and with the continuing inspiration and motivation of the Lord's Supper they are leaning into the future, celebrating and actively anticipating the day when Christ shall complete his resurrection.

CONCLUSION

Again we have seen that the New Testament texts do not allow us to view the resurrection of Christ as an isolated event. It cannot be frozen into the past. It cannot simply be observed and described. It has created a new reality, and part of this new reality is the church. The church is "the body of Christ", it is the community through which Christ wants to encounter the world as savior and liberator. Just as we use our bodies to meet the world around us, so the church is the "body of Christ" in that it makes room so that through its ministry Christ can share his life with the world. This christological orientation must have consequences for all that the church is and does. Every aspect of the church's being and ministry must be measured by this criterion, whether it is the crucified and risen Christ who is becoming manifest in the church's existence and ministry.

Conclusion

We have come to the end of an essay in which we have tried to understand the resurrection of Jesus Christ. We have sought to do so in the context of contemporary theology and in the context of the world in which we live (Part I). Priority has been given, however, to the primary sources because we wanted to understand the resurrection, as far as it is possible, on its own terms.

With the New Testament and with the church through the ages we have designated the resurrection of the crucified Christ as the foundational event for the Christian faith and the Christian church (Part II). This implies, of course, that faith in the risen Christ has consequences, not only for the nature of faith (Part III), but also for the ground and content of faith. In Part IV we have described some of those consequences which are directly related to our discussion of the resurrection. Within the limited space available it was not possible to develop a christology, a doctrine of God, a soteriology, and an ecclesiology. All that we could do is to indicate what consequences our understanding of the resurrection has for other dimensions of faith. That, however, needed to be done in order to do justice to the "open" nature of the resurrection. In our discussion we have limited ourselves to those themes that are immediately evident in the reading of the biblical resurrection texts.

We saw that the resurrection is the hermeneutical key for properly understanding the meaning of Jesus' life and death. At the same time it is the theological basis for Christian hope because it affirms the new life of the risen Christ in the trinitarian being of God. This has consequences for the being of God and for our understanding of God. For Christians the word "God" must be exegeted with reference to the resurrection of the crucified Christ. The fact that through the resurrection the crucified Christ was given universal Lordship implies the all-encompassing nature of salvation. Jesus incarnated an understanding of God as "Savior, who desires all men to be saved and to come to the knowledge of the truth" (1 Tim 2:3f.). Even more than that, salvation must not be limited to humanity. It must include ecological and cosmological dimensions. God the creator seeks to redeem his creation through the saving and liberating work of Christ. Just as Jesus staked his life on this understanding of God, and therefore went to the margins in order to heal what is broken and save what is lost, so the risen Christ extends the soteriological work of Jesus' life and death to include all of reality. And since it was the crucified Christ who was raised from the dead, salvation must have a special thrust for those who are fated to the underside of history. This has also consequences for the

319

nature of the church and its call to mission. Since both the church and its mission are grounded in the resurrection of the crucified Christ, the task that is inherent to its identity is to witness in a credible way to God's passion for the world and as such to participate in the *missio dei* to liberate and save his creation.

Bibliography

(For translations I have included the original date of publication or the date of the publication from which the translation was made in brackets.)

Aguilar, Vinicio. "Where was God, daddy. . . ," in: Julia Esquivel Velasquez, "A letter from Central America. . . ," *IRM* LXVI (July, 1977, pp. 248–252), pp. 249f.

Aland, Kurt. "Neue Neutestamentliche Papyri II," *NTS* 12 (1965–66), pp. 193–210.

_____. "Die Bedeutung des P^{75} für den Text des Neuen Testaments. Ein Beitrag zur Frage der 'Western non-interpolations'," in: *Studien zur Überlieferung des Neuen Testaments und seines Textes*. Arbeiten zur Neutestamentlichen Forschung II. Berlin: Walter de Gruyter, 1967, pp. 155–172.

Albertz, R./Westermann, C. "*Ruah*, Geist," in: *THAT* II (1976), cols. 726–753.

Alsup, John E. *The Post-Resurrection Appearance Stories of the Gospel Tradition: A History-of-Tradition Analysis with Text-Synopsis*. Stuttgart: Calwer, 1975.

Althaus, Paul. *Fact and Faith in the Kerygma of Today*. Trans. David Cairns. Philadelphia: Muhlenberg Press, 1959 (1958).

_____. *The So-Called Kerygma and the Historical Jesus*. Trans. David Cairns. Edinburgh: Oliver & Boyd, 1959 (1958).

Andersen, Wilhelm. "Jesus Christus und der Kosmos. Missionstheologische Überlegungen zu Neu-Delhi," *EvTh* 23 (1963), pp. 471–493.

The Ante-Nicene Fathers. Vol. III. Grand Rapids, Mich.: Eerdmans, reprinted 1980.

Austin, J. L. *How to Do Things with Words*. The William James Lectures delivered at Harvard University in 1955. Cambridge, Mass.: Harvard University Press, 1962.

Baptism, Eucharist and Ministry. Faith and Order Paper No. 111. Geneva: WCC, 1982.

"The Barmen Theological Declaration," (1934), in: J. H. Leith, ed., *Creeds of the Churches* (Richmond: Knox, rev. ed. 1973), pp. 517–522; a newer translation in *JTSA* 47 (June 1984), pp. 78–81.

Barth, Karl. *The Epistle to the Romans*. Trans. Edwyn C. Hoskyns. London: Oxford University Press, 1933 (^{6}1928).

_____. *The Resurrection of the Dead*. Trans. H. J. Stenning. London: Hodder & Stoughton, 1933 (1924).

_____. "Gospel and Law," (1935), in: *Community, State, and Church. Three Essays*. Gloucester, Mass.: Peter Smith, 1968, pp. 71–100.

_____. "Church and State," (1938), in: *Community, State, and Church. Three Essays*. Gloucester, Mass.: Peter Smith, 1968, pp. 101–148.

_____. *Die Kirchliche Dogmatik*, Bd. I: Die Lehre vom Wort Gottes. Prolegomena zur Kirchlichen Dogmatik, 1. Halbband. Zürich: EVZ Verlag, 1964 (1932); Bd. III: Die Lehre von der Schöpfung, Teil 2. Zollikon-Zürich: Evangelischer Verlag, 1948; Bd. IV: Die Lehre von der Versöhnung, Teil 1. Zollikon-Zürich: Evangelischer Verlag, 1953; Teil 2. Zollikon-Zürich: Evangelischer Verlag, 1955; Teil 3, 1.Hälfte. Zollikon-Zürich: Evangelischer Verlag, 1959.

_____. *Church Dogmatics*, Vol. I: The Doctrine of the Word of God, Part 1. Eds. G. W. Bromiley and T. F. Torrance, trans. G. W. Bromiley. Edinburgh: T. & T. Clark, 1975 (1932); Part 2. Eds. G. W. Bromiley and T. F. Torrance, trans. G. T. Thomson and H. Knight. Edinburgh: T. & T. Clark, 1956 (1938). *Church Dogmatics*, Vol. III: The Doctrine of Creation, Part 1. Eds. G. W. Bromiley and T. F. Torrance, trans. J. W. Edwards, O. Bussey, H. Knight. Edinburgh: T. & T. Clark, 1958 (1945); Part 2. Eds. G. W. Bromiley and T. F. Torrance, trans. H. Knight, G. W. Bromiley, J. K. S. Reid, R. H. Fuller. Edinburgh: T. & T. Clark, 1960 (1948). *Church Dogmatics*, Vol. IV: The Doctrine of Reconciliation, Part 1. Eds. G. W. Bromiley and T. F. Torrance, trans. G. W. Bromiley. New York: Scribner's Sons, 1956 (1953); Part 2. Eds. G. W. Bromiley and T. F. Torrance, trans. G. W. Bromiley. Edinburgh: T. & T. Clark, 1958 (1955); Part 3, 1st half. Eds. G. W. Bromiley and T. F. Torrance, trans. G. W. Bromiley. Edinburgh: T. & T. Clark, 1961 (1959); Part 3, 2nd half. Eds. G. W. Bromiley and T. F. Torrance, trans. G. W. Bromiley. Edinburgh: T. & T. Clark, 1962 (1959). Part 4. Eds. G. W. Bromiley and T. F. Torrance, trans. G. W. Bromiley. Edinburgh: T. & T. Clark, 1969 (1967).

_____. "The Humanity of God," (1956). Trans. John Newton Thomas. In: *The Humanity of God*. Richmond: John Knox Press, 1972, pp. 35–65.

Barth, Karl and Bultmann, Rudolf. *Letters 1922–1966*. Ed. Bernd Jaspert, trans. and ed. Geoffrey W. Bromiley. Grand Rapids, Mich.: Eerdmans, 1981 (1971).

Bartsch, Hans Werner. "Inhalt und Funktion des urchristlichen Osterglaubens," in: Hildegard Temporini und Wolfgang Haase, Hg., *Aufstieg und Niedergang der Römischen Welt. Geschichte und Kultur Roms im Spiegel der Neueren Forschung*, II.25.1: *Religion (Vorkonstantinisches Christentum: Leben und Umwelt Jesu; Neues Testament [Kanonische Schriften und Apokryphen])*. Hg. Wolfgang Haase. Berlin, New York: Walter de Gruyter, 1982, pp. 794–890.

Bater, R. Robert. "Towards a More Biblical View of the Resurrection," *Interp* 23 (1969), pp. 47–65.

Batey, Richard, ed. *New Testament Issues*. London: SCM, 1970.

Batstone, David. *From Conquest to Struggle. Jesus of Nazareth in Latin America*. Albany, N.Y.: State University of New York Press, 1991.

Baumgärtel, Friedrich; Bieder, Werner; Sjöberg, Erik. "Πνεῦμα κτλ. [Pneuma ktl.] Spirit in the OT," in: *TDNT* VI (1968 [1959]), pp. 359–389.

Bayer, Hans F. *Jesus' Predictions of Vindication and Resurrection. The provenance, meaning and correlation of the Synoptic predictions*. WUNT, 2. Reihe, 20. Tübingen: Mohr, 1986.

Beardslee, W. A. "James," in: *IDB* II (1962), pp. 791–794.

Beare, F. W. *A Commentary on the Epistle to the Philippians*. London: Black, 1959.

Bender, Harold S. " 'Walking in the Resurrection' —the Anabaptist Doctrine of Regeneration and Discipleship," *MennQR* 35 (1961), pp. 96–110.

Berger, Klaus. *Die Auferstehung des Propheten und die Erhöhung des Menschensohnes. Traditionsgeschichtliche Untersuchungen zur Deutung des Geschickes Jesu in frühchristlichen Texten*. StUNT, 13. Göttingen: Vandenhoeck & Ruprecht, 1976.

_____. "Geist, Heiliger Geist, Geistesgaben III. Neues Testament," in: *TRE* XII (1984), pp. 178–196.

Berkhof, Hendrikus. *The Doctrine of the Holy Spirit*. Richmond: John Knox, 1977 (1964).

Bertram, Georg. "συνεργός κτλ.," [synergos ktl.] *TDNT* VII (1971 [1964]), pp. 871–876.

Betz, Hans Dieter. "The Origin and Nature of Christian Faith According to the Emmaus Legend (Luke 24:13–32)," *Interp* 23 (1969), pp. 32–46.

Betz, Otto. "Probleme des Prozesses Jesu," in: Hildegard Temporini und Wolfgang Haase, Hg., *Aufstieg und Niedergang der Römischen Welt. Geschichte und Kultur Roms im Spiegel der Neueren Forschung*, II.25.1: *Religion (Vorkonstantinisches Christentum: Leben und Umwelt Jesu; Neues Testament [Kanonische Schriften und Apokryphen])*. Hg. Wolfgang Haase. Berlin, New York: Walter de Gruyter, 1982, pp. 565–647.

Blank, Josef. *Krisis. Untersuchungen zur johanneischen Christologie und Eschatologie*. Freiburg: Lambertus Verlag, 1964.

_____. *Paulus und Jesus. Eine theologische Grundlegung*. München: Kösel, 1968.

Blass, F. and Debrunner, A. *A Greek Grammar of the New Testament and Other Early Christian Literature*. Trans. and ed. Robert W. Funk. Chicago: Chicago University Press, 1961.

Bobrinskoy, Boris. "The power of the resurrection," in: *Jesus Christ—the Life of the World. An Orthodox contribution to the Vancouver theme*. Ion Bria, ed. Geneva: WCC, 1982, pp. 102–105.

Boff, Clodovis. *Theology and Praxis. Epistemological Foundations*. Trans. Robert R. Barr. Maryknoll, N.Y.: Orbis Books, 1987 (1978).

Bonhoeffer, Dietrich. *The Cost of Discipleship*. Trans. R. H. Fuller. New York: MacMillan, 1963 (1937).

_____. *Ethics*. Ed. Eberhard Bethge. Trans. Neville Horton Smith. London: SCM, 1955 (1949).

_____. *Letters and Papers from Prison*. Ed. Eberhard Bethge. Trans. R. H. Fuller. London: SCM, ³1967 (1951).

Bornkamm, Günter. *Jesus of Nazareth*. Trans. Irene and Fraser McLuskey. London: Hodder & Stoughton, 1960 (1956).

_____. *Paul*. Trans. D. M. G. Stalker. New York: Harper and Row, 1971 (1969).

Braaten, C. E. and Harrisville, Roy A., eds., *The Historical Jesus and the Kerygmatic Christ. Essays on the New Quest of the Historical Jesus*. Trans. C. E. Braaten and Roy A. Harrisville. New York/Nashville: Abingdon, 1964,

Brandenburger, Egon. "Pistis und Soteria. Zum Verstehenshorizont von 'Glaube' im Urchristentum," *ZThK* 85 (1988), pp. 165–198.

Braun, Herbert. *Spätjüdisch-häretischer und frühchristlicher Radikalismus. Jesus von Nazareth und die essenische Qumransekte*. BHTh 24/I & II. 2 vols. Tübingen: Mohr, 1957.

_____. *Qumran und das Neue Testament*. Band II. Tübingen: Mohr, 1966.

Broer, Ingo. "Zur heutigen Diskussion der Grabesgeschichte," *BiLe* 10 (1969), pp. 40–52.

_____. "Zur historischen Frage nach der Auferstehung Jesu," *AnzKG* 80 (1971), pp. 424–434.

_____. *Die Urgemeinde und das Grab Jesu. Eine Analyse der Grablegungsgeschichte im Neuen Testament*. StANT, XXXI. München: Kösel, 1972.

_____. " 'Seid stets bereit, jedem Rede und Antwort zu stehen, der nach der Hoffnung fragt, die euch erfüllt" (1 Petr 3,15). Das Leere Grab und die Erscheinungen Jesu im Lichte der historischen Kritik," in: Ingo Broer/Jürgen Werbick, eds., *"Der Herr ist wahrhaft erschienen" (Lk 24,34). Biblische und systematische Beiträge zur Entstehung des Osterglaubens*. SBS 134. Stuttgart: Verlag Katholisches Bibelwerk, 1988, pp. 29–61.

Broer, Ingo/Werbick, Jürgen, eds., *"Der Herr ist wahrhaft erschienen" (Lk 24,34).* *Biblische und systematische Beiträge zur Entstehung des Osterglaubens.* SBS 134. Stuttgart: Verlag Katholisches Bibelwerk, 1988.

Brown, C. and Bartels, K. H. "Remember, Remembrance," *NIDNT* 3 (1978 [1971]), pp. 230–247.

Brown, Raymond E. *The Gospel According to John (xiii–xxi).* The Anchor Bible, 29A. Garden City, N.Y.: Doubleday, 1970.

———. *The Virginal Conception and Bodily Resurrection of Jesus.* New York: Paulist, 1973 (London: Geoffrey Chapman, 1974).

Brown, Robert McAfee. *Theology in a New Key. Responding to Liberation Themes.* Philadelphia: Westminster, 1978.

———. *Spirituality and Liberation. Overcoming the Great Fallacy.* Philadelphia: Westminster, 1988.

Brox, Norbert. *Der erste Petrusbrief.* EKK, xxi. Zürich: Benziger Verlag, Neukirchen-Vluyn: Neukirchener Verlag, ²1986.

Brunner, Emil. *The Christian Doctrine of God. Dogmatics:* Vol. 1. Trans. Olive Wyon. Philadelphia: Westminster, 1950 (1946).

Bulgakov, Sergei. "Meditations on the Joy of the Resurrection," (1938), in: Alexander Schmemann, ed., *Ultimate Questions. An Anthology of Modern Russian Religious Thought.* Crestwood, N.Y.: St. Vladimir's Seminary Press, 1977, pp. 299–309.

Bultmann, Rudolf. "Karl Barth, *The Resurrection of the Dead,*" (1926), in: *Faith and Understanding,* Vol. 1. Ed. Robert W. Funk, trans. L. P. Smith. London: SCM, 1969, pp. 66–94.

———. *The History of the Synoptic Tradition.* Trans. John Marsh. Oxford: Blackwell, 1963 (1931).

———. "New Testament and Mythology," (1941). Trans. Reginald H. Fuller. In: Hans Werner Bartsch, ed., *Kerygma and Myth: A Theological Debate.* New York: Harper & Row, 1961 (1953), pp. 1–44.

———. "Is Exegesis without Presuppositions Possible?" (1957), in: Schubert M. Ogden, ed. and trans., *Existence and Faith: Shorter Writings of Rudolf Bultmann.* London: Hodder and Stoughton, 1961, pp. 289–296.

———. *Jesus Christ and Mythology.* New York: Scribner's Sons, 1958.

———. "The Primitive Christian Kerygma and the Historical Jesus," (1959), in: Carl E. Braaten and Roy A. Harrisville, eds., *The Historical Jesus and the Kerygmatic Christ: Essays on the New Quest of the Historical Jesus.* Trans. Carl E. Braaten and Roy A. Harrisville. New York/Nashville: Abingdon, 1964, pp. 15–42.

———. "Bultmann Replies to His Critics," trans. Reginald H. Fuller. In: Hans Werner Bartsch, ed., *Kerygma and Myth: A Theological Debate.* New York: Harper & Row, 1961 (1953), pp. 191–211.

———. "A Reply to the Theses of J. Schniewind," trans. Reginald H. Fuller. In: Hans Werner Bartsch, ed., *Kerygma and Myth: A Theological Debate.* New York: Harper & Row, 1961 (1953), pp. 102–123.

Burkholder, J. Lawrence. "The Anabaptist Vision of Discipleship," in: *The Recovery of the Anabaptist Vision. A Sixteenth Anniversary Tribute To Harold S. Bender.* Ed. Guy F. Hershberger. Scottdale, Pa.: Herald Press, 1957, pp. 135–151.

Burton, Ernest De Witt. *A Critical and Exegetical Commentary on the Epistle to the Galatians.* ICC. Edinburgh: T. & T. Clark, 1921.

Bussmann, Claus. *Themen der paulinischen Missionspredigt auf dem Hintergrund der spätjüdisch-hellenistischen Missionsliteratur.* Europäische Hochschulschriften XXIII/3. Bern: Lang, 1971.

Campenhausen, Hans von. "The Events of Easter and the Empty Tomb," in: *Tradition and Life in the Church. Essays and Lectures in Church History.* Trans. A. V. Littledale. Philadelphia: Fortress, 1968 (1960), pp. 42–89.

Carnley, Peter, "The Poverty of Historical Scepticism," in: S. W. Sykes and J. P. Clayton, eds., *Christ, Faith and History.* Cambridge: University Press, 1972, pp. 165–189.

_____. *The Structure of Resurrection Belief.* Oxford: Clarendon Press, 1987.

Charles, R. H. *Critical History of the Doctrine of a Future Life in Israel, in Judaism, and Christianity.* Jowett Lectures 1898–99. London: Black, 1899.

Childs, Brevard S. *Memory and Tradition in Israel.* Studies in Biblical Theology. London: SCM, 1962.

Coenen, L. and Trites, A. A. "Witness, Testimony," *NIDNT* 3 (1978 [1971]), pp. 1038–1051.

Collingwood, R. G. *The Idea of History.* Oxford: Clarendon Press, 1946.

Collins, John J. Daniel. *A Commentary on the Book of Daniel.* Minneapolis: Fortress Press, 1993.

Comblin, José. *The Holy Spirit and Liberation.* Trans. Paul Burns. Maryknoll, N.Y.: Orbis Books, 1989 (1987).

Conzelmann, Hans. "Auferstehung Christi. I. Im NT," in: *RGG* 1 (^{3}1957), pp. 698–700.

_____. *The Theology of St. Luke.* Trans. Geoffrey Buswell. London: Faber and Faber, 1960 (1954).

_____. *1 Corinthians. A Commentary on the First Epistle to the Corinthians.* Trans. James W. Leitch. Hermeneia. Philadelphia: Fortress, 1975 (1969).

Costas, Orlando E. *Christ Outside the Gate. Mission Beyond Christendom.* Maryknoll, N.Y.: Orbis Books, 1982.

Crossan, John Dominic. "Empty Tomb and Absent Lord (Mark 16:1–8)," in: Werner H. Kelber, ed., *The Passion in Mark. Studies on Mark 14–16.* Philadelphia: Fortress, 1976, pp. 135–152.

Cupitt, Don. *Christ and the Hiddenness of God.* Philadelphia: Westminster, 1971.

_____. "The Resurrection: A Disagreement: A Correspondence with C. F. D Moule," *Theology. A Monthly Review* 75, No. 628 (October 1972), pp. 507–519.

Cushman, Robert E. "Christology or Ecclesiology? A Critical Examination of the Christology of John Knox," *ReL* 27 (Autumn 1958, No. 4), pp. 515–526.

Dalferth, Ingolf U. "Theologischer Realismus und realistische Theologie bei Karl Barth," *EvTh* 46 (1986), pp. 402–422.

_____. "Der Mythos vom inkarnierten Gott und das Thema der Christologie," *ZThK* 84 (1987), pp. 320–344.

Dauer, Anton. "Lk 24,12—ein Produkt lukanischer Redaktion," in: F. van Segbroeck, C. M. Tuckett, G. van Belle, J. Verheyden, eds. *The Four Gospels 1992. Festschrift Frans Neirynck.* Vol. II. Leuven: University Press, 1992, pp. 1697–1716.

Davies, W. D. *Paul and Rabbinic Judaism. Some Rabbinic Elements in Pauline Theology.* Philadelphia: Fortress, ^{4}1980 (1948).

Delling, Gerhard. "The Significance of the Resurrection of Jesus for Faith in Jesus Christ," in: C. F. D. Moule, ed., *The Significance of the Message of the Resurrection for Faith in Jesus Christ.* Trans. R. A. Wilson Studies in Biblical Theology, 2nd Series, 8. London: SCM, 1968 (1966), pp. 77–104.

_____. "τελος κτλ.," [telos ktl.] in: *TDNT* VIII (1972 [1969]), pp. 49–87.

Denck, Hans (John). "Whether God is the Cause of Evil," (1526), in: George Hunston Williams and Angel M. Mergal, eds., *Spiritual and Anabaptist Writers.* The Library of Christian Classics XXV. Philadelphia: Westminster, 1957, pp. 88–111.

Dinkler, Erich. "Petrus, Apostel," in: *RGG* 5 (³1961), cols. 247–249.

Dodd, C. H. *The Founder of Christianity.* New York: Macmillan, 1970.

Driver, John. *Community and Commitment.* Scottdale, Pa.: Herald Press, 1976.

Dunn, James D. G. *Jesus and the Spirit. A Study of the Religious and Charismatic Experience of Jesus and the First Christians as Reflected in the New Testament.* London: SCM; Philadelphia: Westminster, 1975.

_____. *The Evidence for Jesus. The Impact of Scholarship on Our Understanding of How Christianity Began.* London: SCM, 1985.

_____. *Jesus, Paul and the Law. Studies in Mark and Galatians.* London: SPCK, 1990.

Dussel, Enrique. *Ethics and Community.* Trans. Robert R. Barr. Maryknoll, N.Y.: Orbis Books, 1988 (1986).

Ebeling, Gerhard. "Jesus and Faith," (1958), in: *Word and Faith.* Trans. James W. Leitch. Philadelphia: Fortress, 1963 (1960), pp. 201–246.

_____. "Word of God and Hermeneutics," (1959), in: *Word and Faith.* Trans. James W. Leitch. Philadelphia: Fortress, 1963 (1960), pp. 305–332.

_____. *Dogmatik des Christlichen Glaubens.* 3 vols. Tübingen: Mohr, 1979.

_____. "Karl Barths Ringen mit Luther," in: *Lutherstudien,* Band III: Begriffsuntersuchungen—Textinterpretationen—Wirkungsgeschichtliches. Tübingen: Mohr, 1985, pp. 428–573.

_____. "Über die Reformation hinaus? Zur Luther-Kritik Karl Barths," *ZThK.* B 6 (1986), pp. 33–75.

Eising, H. "Zakar," in: *ThWAT* 2 (1977), pp. 571–593.

Farmer, W. R., Moule, C. F. D., Niebuhr, R. R., eds., *Christian History and Interpretation: Studies Presented to John Knox.* Cambridge: University Press, 1967.

Fascher, Erich. "Johannes 16:32. Eine Studie zur Geschichte der Schriftauslegung und zur Traditionsgeschichte des Urchristentums," *ZNW* 39 (1940), pp. 171–230.

Fiddes, Paul. *The Creative Suffering of God.* Oxford: Clarendon Press, 1988.

Fiedler, Peter. "Vorösterliche Vorgaben für den Osterglauben," in: Ingo Broer/Jürgen Werbick, eds., *"Der Herr ist wahrhaft erschienen" (Lk 24,34). Biblische und systematische Beiträge zur Entstehung des Osterglaubens.* SBS 134. Stuttgart: Verlag Katholisches Bibelwerk, 1988, pp. 9–28.

Fischer, Karl Martin. *Das Ostergeschehen.* Göttingen: Vandenhoeck & Ruprecht, ²1980 (1978).

Florovsky, Georges. "The Resurrection of Life," *HDSB* I (1952), pp. 5–26.

_____. *Creation and Redemption.* Vol. III in the Collected Works. Belmont, Mass.: Nordland Publishing Company, 1976.

Fohrer, Georg and Lohse, Eduard. "Ζιών, Ἱερουσαλήμ, κτλ.," [Ziōn, Ierousalēm, ktl.] *TDNT* VII (1971 [1964], pp. 292–338.

Freire, Paulo. *Pedagogy of the Oppressed.* Trans. Myra Bergman Ramos. A Continuum Book. New York: The Seabury Press, 1970 (1968).

Friedmann, R. *The Theology of Anabaptistm. An Interpretation.* Scottdale, Pa.: Herald Press, 1973.

Friedrich, Gerhard. "Die Auferweckung Jesu, eine Tat Gottes oder ein Interpretament der Jünger?" *KuD* 17 (1971), pp. 153–187.

Fuchs, Ernst. "What is a 'Language-event'. A Letter," (1960), in: *Studies of the Historical Jesus.* Trans. Andrew Scobie. Naperville, Ill.: Allenson, 1964, pp. 207–212.

_____. "The Essence of the Language-event and Christology," (1962), in: *Studies of the Historical Jesus.* Trans. Andrew Scobie. Naperville: Allenson, 1964, pp. 213–228.

Fuchs, Ernst and Künneth, Walter. *Die Auferstehung Jesu Christi von den Toten.*

Dokumentation eines Streitgesprächs. Nach einer Tonbandaufzeichnung hg. von Christian Möller. Neukirchen-Vluyn: Neukirchener Verlag, 1973.

Fuller, Daniel P. *Easter Faith and History.* Grand Rapids, Mich.: Eerdmans, 1965.

_____. "The Resurrection of Jesus and the Historical Method," *JBR* 34 (1966), pp. 18–24.

Fuller, Reginald H. *The Formation of the Resurrection Narratives.* New York: Macmillan/London: Collier-Macmillan, 1971 (London: SPCK, 1972).

Gadamer, Hans-Georg. *Truth and Method.* Trans. and ed. Garrett Barden and John Cumming from the second edition (1965). London: Sheed and Ward, 1975 (1960).

Galilea, Segundo. *Following Jesus.* Trans. Sister Helen Phillips. Maryknoll, N.Y.: Orbis, 1981 (1974/75).

Galloway, Allan D. *The Cosmic Christ.* London: Nisbet, 1951.

Galvin, John P. "Resurrection as *Theologia crucis Jesu*: The Foundational Christology of Rudolf Pesch," *TS* 38 (1977), pp. 513–525.

_____. "The Origin of Faith in the Resurrection of Jesus: Two Recent Perspectives," *TS* 49 (1988), pp. 25–44.

Geisser, Hans Friedrich. "Zur Hermeneutik der Verborgenheit Gottes," in: Hans Friedrich Geisser/Walter Moster, eds., *Wirkungen hermeneutischer Theologie.* Eine Zürcher Festgabe zum 70. Geburtstag Gerhard Ebelings. Zürich: Theologischer Verlag, 1983, pp. 155–167.

Geyer, Hans-Georg. "The Resurrection of Jesus Christ: A Survey of the Debate in Present Day Theology," in: C. F. D. Moule, ed., *The Significance of the Message of the Resurrection for Faith in Jesus Christ.* Trans. R. A. Wilson. Studies in Biblical Theology, 2nd Series, 8. London: SCM, 1968 (1966), pp. 105–135.

Gilkey, Langdon. *Naming the Whirlwind. The Renewal of God-Language.* Indianapolis/New York: Bobbs-Merrill, 1969.

Gill, Athol. *The Fringes of Freedom. Following Jesus, Living Together, Working for Justice.* Homebush West: Lancer, 1990.

_____. *Life on the Road. The Gospel Basis for a Messianic Lifestyle* (Scottdale, Pa.: Herald Press, 1992 (1989).

Gnilka, Joachim. *Das Evangelium nach Markus. 2. Teilband Mk 8.27–16.20.* Neukirchen: Neukirchener Verlag, Zürich: Benziger Verlag, 1979.

Goppelt, Leonhard. *Theology of the New Testament.* Vol. 1. Ed. Jürgen Roloff, trans. John E. Alsup. Grand Rapids, Mich.: Eerdmans, 1981 (1975).

Goppelt, Leonhard; Thielicke, Helmut and Müller-Schwefe, Hans-Rudolf. *The Easter Message Today. Three Essays.* Trans. Salvator Attanasio and Darrell Likens Guder. With an Introduction by Markus Barth. New York: Thomas Nelson & Sons, 1964.

Gózdz, Krzysztof. *Jesus Christus als Sinn der Geschichte bei Wolfhart Pannenberg.* Eichstätter Studien, Neue Folge 25. Regensburg: Friedrich Pustet, 1988.

Grass, Hans. *Ostergeschehen und Osterberichte.* Göttingen: Vandenhoeck & Ruprecht, ⁴1970 (1956).

Grebel, Conrad. "Letters to Thomas Müntzer," in: George Hunston Williams and Angel M. Mergal, eds., *Spiritual and Anabaptist Writers.* The Library of Christian Classics XXV. Philadelphia: Westminster, 1957, pp. 73–85.

Grenz, Stanley J. *Reason for Hope. The Systematic Theology of Wolfhart Pannenberg.* New York/Oxford: Oxford University Press, 1990.

Griffin, David R. *A Process Christology.* Philadelphia: Westminster, 1973.

Gutiérrez, Gustavo. *We Drink from Our Own Wells: The Spiritual Journey of a People.* Trans. Matthew J. O'Connell. Maryknoll, N.Y.: Orbis, 1984 (1983).

_____. *A Theology of Liberation. History, Politics, and Salvation*. Rev. Edition with a New Introduction. Trans. and ed. Sister Caridad Inda and John Eagleson. Maryknoll, N.Y.: Orbis Books, 1988 (1971).

Güttgemanns, Erhardt. *Der leidende Apostel und sein Herr. Studien zur paulinischen Christologie*. Göttingen: Vandenhoeck & Ruprecht, 1966.

Habermas, Jürgen. *Knowledge and Human Interest*. Trans. Jeremy J. Shapiro. Boston: Beacon Press, 1971 (1968).

Haenchen, Ernst. *The Acts of the Apostles. A Commentary*. Trans. Bernard Noble, Gerald Shinn, Hugh Anderson, R. McL. Wilson. Oxford: Blackwell, 1971 (⁵1965).

Hahn, Ferdinand. *Mission in the New Testament*. Trans. Frank Clarke. SBT 47. London: SCM, 1965 (1963).

_____. "Pre-Easter Discipleship," in: *The Beginnings of the Church in the New Testament*. Trans. Iain and Ute Nicol. Edinburgh: Saint Andrew Press, 1970 (1967), pp. 9–39.

_____. "Methodologische Überlegungen zur Rückfrage nach Jesus," in: Karl Kertelge, ed., *Rückfrage nach Jesus. Zur Methodik und Bedeutung der Frage nach dem historischen Jesus*. Freiburg/Basel/Wien: Herder, 1974, pp. 11–77.

_____. "Das biblische Verständnis des Heiligen Geistes. Soteriologische Funktion und 'Personalität' des Heiligen Geistes," in: Claus Heitmann/Heribert Mühlen, eds., *Erfahrung und Theologie des Heiligen Geistes*. Hamburg: Agentur des Rauhen Hauses, München: Kösel, 1974, pp. 131–147.

_____. "Work, Do, Accomplish," in: *NIDNT* 3 (1978 [1971]), pp. 1147–1159.

Harakas, Stanley Samuel, "Resurrection and Ethics in Chrysostom," *Ex Auditu* 9 (1993), pp. 77–95.

Harvey, Van A. *The Historian and the Believer: The Morality of Historical Knowledge and Christian Belief*. Philadelphia: Westminster, 1966.

Hendry, George S. *The Holy Spirit in Christian Theology*. Revised and enlarged edition. London: SCM; Philadelphia: Westminster, 1965.

_____. *Theology of Nature*. Philadelphia: Westminster, 1980.

Hengel, Martin. "Maria Magdalena und die Frauen als Zeugen," in: Otto Betz, Martin Hengel, Peter Schmidt, eds., *Abraham unser Vater. Juden und Christen im Gespräch über die Bibel*. Festschrift für Otto Michel zum 60. Geburtstag. Leiden/Köln: Brill, 1963, pp. 243–256.

_____. "Die Ursprünge der christlichen Mission," *NTS* 18 (1971), pp. 16–38.

_____. "Ist der Osterglaube noch zu retten?" *TQ* 153 (1973), pp. 252–269.

_____. *Judaism and Hellenism. Studies in Their Encounter in Palestine during the Early Hellenistic Period*. Trans. John Bowden. Vols. 1 and 2. Philadelphia: Fortress, 1974 (1973).

_____. *The Charismatic Leader and His Followers*. Trans. James C. G. Greig. Ed. John Riches. Edinburgh: Clark, 1981 (1968).

_____. "Jakobus der Herrenbruder—der erste 'Papst'?" in: *Glaube und Eschatologie*. Festschrift für Werner Kümmel zum 80. Geburtstag, Hg. von Erich Grässer und Otto Merk. Tübingen: Mohr, 1985, pp. 71–104.

Hennecke, Edgar. *New Testament Apocrypha*, Vol. 1: *Gospels and Related Writings*. Ed. by Wilhelm Schneemelcher. English translation ed. by R. McL. Wilson, Vol. I: The Gospels and Related Writings (Philadelphia: Westminster, 1963 [1959]).

Henry, Carl F. H. *God, Revelation and Authority*, Vols. 1–6. Waco, Tex.: Word Books, 1976–1983.

Hermisson, Hans-Jürgen and Lohse, Eduard. *Faith.* Trans. Douglas W. Stott. Biblical Encounter Series. Nashville: Abingdon, 1981 (1978).

Herodotus. With an English Translation by A. D. Godley. In four Volumes. Vol. 2, Books 3 and 4. The Loeb Classical Library. Cambridge, Mass.: Harvard University Press, 1963.

Heron, Alasdair I. C. *A Century of Protestant Theology.* Guildford: Lutterworth, 1980.

_____. *The Holy Spirit.* Philadelphia: Westminster, 1983.

Hershberger, Guy F., ed. *The Recovery of the Anabaptist Vision. A Sixteenth Anniversary Tribute To Harold S. Bender.* Scottdale, Pa.: Herald Press, 1957.

Herzog, Frederick. *God-Walk. Liberation Shaping Dogmatics.* Maryknoll, N.Y.: Orbis Books, 1988.

Hick, John, ed., *The Myth of God Incarnate.* London: SCM, 1977.

Hoffmann, Paul. *Die Toten in Christus. Eine religionsgeschichtliche und exegetische Untersuchung zur paulinischen Eschatologie.* Münster: Aschendorff, 1966.

Hoskyns, Edwyn Clement/Dayey, Francis Noel. *Crucifixion—Resurrection. The Pattern of the Theology and Ethics of the New Testament.* Ed. with a Biographical Introduction by Gordon S. Wakefield. London: SPCK, 1983.

Hubmaier, Balthasar. "Eighteen Theses," (1524), in: W. R. Estep, ed., *Anabaptist Beginnings* (1523–1533). A Source Book. Nieuwkoop: B. De Graaf, 1976, pp. 23–26.

Hübner, Hans. "Kreuz und Auferstehung im Neuen Testament," *ThR 54* (1989), pp. 262–306 and 57 (1992), pp. 58–82.

Hunsinger, George. *How to Read Karl Barth. The Shape of His Theology.* New York/Oxford: Oxford University Press, 1991.

Jenson, Robert W. *The Triune Identity. God according to the Gospel.* Philadelphia: Fortress, 1982.

_____. "The Triune God," in: Carl E. Braaten and Robert W. Jenson, eds., *Christian Dogmatics*, Vol. 1. Philadelphia: Fortress, 1984, pp. 79–191.

Jeremias, Joachim. *Heiligengräber in Jesu Umwelt (Mt. 23,29; Lk. 11,47). Eine Untersuchung zur Volksreligion der Zeit Jesu.* Göttingen: Vandenhoeck & Ruprecht, 1958.

_____. *The Eucharistic Words of Jesus.* Trans. Arnold Ehrhardt. Oxford: Blackwell, 1955 (1935).

_____. "Zwischen Karfreitag und Ostern. Descensus und Ascensus in der Karfreitagstheologie des Neuen Testamentes," in: Joachim Jeremias, *ABBA. Studien zur neutestamentlichen Theologie und Zeitgeschichte.* Göttingen: Vandenhoeck & Ruprecht, 1966, pp. 323–331.

_____. *New Testament Theology. The Proclamation of Jesus.* Trans. John Bowden. New York: Charles Scribner's Sons, 1971 (1971).

Jeremias, Jörg. "Theophany in the OT," in: *IDB* Supplementary Volume (1976), pp. 896–898.

_____. *Theophanie. Die Geschichte einer alttestamentlichen Gattung.* WMANT 10 Neukirchen-Vluyn: Neukirchener Verlag, 1965.

Josephus, Flavius. *Jewish Antiquities.* In ten vols. Trans. Louis H. Feldman. The Loeb Classical Library. Cambridge, Mass.: Harvard University Press, 1965.

Jüngel, Eberhard. "Vom Tod des lebendigen Gottes. Ein Plakat," *ZThK 65* (1968), pp. 93–116.

_____. "Welcher Gott ist tot? Zum Wiederaufleben des Gesprächs über Gott," *EK 2* (1969), pp. 127–132.

_____. "Das dunkle Wort vom 'Tode Gottes'," *EK 2* (1969), pp. 133–138, 198–202.

_____. "Quae supra nos, nihil ad nos. Eine Kurzformel der Lehre vom verborgenen Gott—im Anschluss an Luther interpretiert," *EvTh* 32 (1972), pp. 197–240.

_____. *Death. The Riddle and the Mystery*. Trans. Iain and Ute Nicol. Edinburgh: Saint Andrew Press, 1975 (1971).

_____. *The Doctrine of the Trinity. God's Being is in Becoming*. Trans. Horton Harris. Grand Rapids, Mich.: Eerdmans, 1976 (1965).

_____. *God as the Mystery of the World. On the Foundation of the Theology of the Crucified One in the Dispute between Theism and Atheism*. Trans. Darrell L. Guder. Grand Rapids, Mich.: Eerdmans, 1983 (1977).

_____. "Das Verhältnis von 'ökonomischer' und 'immanenter' Trinität. Erwägungen über eine biblische Begründung der Trinitätslehre—im Anschluss an und in Auseinandersetzung mit Karl Rahners Lehre vom dreifaltigen Gott als transzendenten Urgrund der Heilsgeschichte," *ZThK* 72 (1975), pp. 353–364.

_____. "Zum Verhältnis von Kirche und Staat nach Karl Barth," *ZThK*. B 6 (1986), pp. 76–135.

Käsemann, Ernst. "Geist und Geistesgaben im NT," in: *RGG* 2 (³1958), cols. 1272–1279.

_____. "The Problem of the Historical Jesus," in: *Essays on New Testament Themes*. Trans. W. J. Montague. SBT 41. Naperville, Ill.: Allenson, 1964 (1960), pp. 15–47.

Kasting, Heinrich. *Die Anfänge der urchristlichen Mission. Eine historische Untersuchung*. BEvTh, 55. München: Kaiser, 1969.

Kaufmann, Gordon D. "A Problem for Theology: the Concept of Nature," *HThR* 65 (1972), pp. 337–366.

Keller, Carl A. "Enthusiastisches Transzendenzerleben in den nichtchristlichen Religionen," in: Claus Heitmann/Heribert Mühlen, eds., *Erfahrung und Theologie des Heiligen Geistes*. Hamburg: Agentur des Rauhen Hauses, München: Kösel, 1974, pp. 49–63.

Kendall, Daniel, S.J. and O'Collins, Gerald, S.J., "The Uniqueness of the Easter Appearances," *CBQ* 54 (1992), pp. 287–307.

Kessler, Hans. *Reduzierte Erlösung? Zum Erlösungsverständnis der Befreiungstheologie*. Freiburg: Herder, 1987.

_____. *Sucht den Lebenden nicht bei den Toten. Die Auferstehung Jesu Christi in biblischer, fundamentaltheologischer und systematischer Sicht*. Düsseldorf: Patmos, ²1987 (1985).

Kienzler, Klaus. *Logik der Auferstehung. Eine Untersuchung zu Rudolf Bultmann, Gerhard Ebeling und Wolfhart Pannenberg*. Freiburg/Basel/Wien: Herder, 1976.

Klaassen, Walter, ed., *Anabaptism in Outline. Selected Primary Sources*. Kitchener, Ont.: Herald Press, 1981.

Klappert, Bertold. (ed.), *Diskussion um Kreuz und Auferstehung*. Wuppertal: Aussaat, 1967.

_____. *Die Auferweckung des Gekreuzigten. Der Ansatz der Christologie Karl Barths im Zusammenhang der Christologie der Gegenwart*. Neukirchen-Vluyn: Neukirchener Verlag, 1971.

_____. "Tendenzen der Gotteslehre in der Gegenwart," *EvTh* 35 (1975), pp. 189–208.

_____. "Die Rechts-, Freiheits- und Befreiungsgeschichte Gottes mit dem Menschen. Erwägungen zum Verständnis der Auferstehung in Karl Barths Versöhnungslehre (KD IV/1–3)," *EvTh* 49 (1989), 460–478.

Klinger, Georges. "La doctrine de la Croix et de la Résurrection de Rudolf Bultmann en confrontation avec la théologie de l'Eglise d'Orient," *Ist*. 25 (1980), pp. 176–211.

Knox, John. *Jesus: Lord and Christ: A Trilogy Comprising "The Man Christ Jesus,"*

(1941) *"Christ the Lord,"* (1945) *"On the Meaning of Christ,"* (1947), New York: Harper & Brothers, 1958.

_____. *Criticism and Faith.* New York/Nashville: Abingdon-Cokesbury, 1952.

_____. *The Church and the Reality of Christ.* New York: Harper & Row, 1962.

_____. *The Humanity and Divinity of Christ: A Study of Pattern in Christology.* Cambridge: University Press, 1967.

Koch, Ernst. "Höllenfahrt Christi," in: *TRE* 15 (1986), pp. 455–461.

Kramer, Werner. *Christ, Lord, Son of God.* Trans. Brian Hardy. SBT 50. London: SCM, 1966 (1963).

Kraus, Hans-Joachim. *Heiliger Geist. Gottes befreiende Gegenwart.* München: Kösel, 1986.

Kreck, Walter. *Die Zukunft des Gekommenen. Grundprobleme der Eschatologie.* München: Kaiser, ²1966.

Kremer, Jacob. *Die Osterevangelien—Geschichten um Geschichte.* Stuttgart: Katholisches Bibelwerk, ²1981 (1977).

_____. "Die Auferstehung Jesu Christi," in: *Handbuch der Fundamental-Theologie. 2: Traktat Offenbarung.* Freiburg: Herder, 1985, pp. 175–196.

Krötke, Wolf. "Gott und Mensch als 'Partner'. Zur Bedeutung einer zentralen Kategorie in Karl Barths Kirchlicher Dogmatik," *ZThK.* B6 (1986), pp. 158–175.

Kuhn, Karl Georg. "μαραναθά," (maranatha) in: *TDNT* IV (1967 [1942]), pp. 466–472.

Kümmel, Werner Georg. *The Theology of the New Testament According to Its Major Witnesses, Jesus—Paul—John.* Trans. John E. Steely. Nashville: Abingdon, 1973 (1969).

Küng, Hans. *The Incarnation of God. An Introduction to Hegel's Theological Thought as Prolegomena to a Future Christology.* Trans. John R. Stephenson. Edinburgh: T. & T. Clark, 1987 (1970).

_____. *The Church.* Trans. Ray and Rosaleen Ockenden. New York: Sheed and Ward, 1967 (1967).

_____. *Eternal Life?* Trans. Edward Quinn. London: Collins, 1984 (1982).

_____. *On Being a Christian.* Trans. Edward Quinn. Garden City, N.Y.: Doubleday & Company, 1976 (1974).

_____. "A New Basic Model for Theology: Divergences and Convergences," in: Hans Küng and David Tracy, eds., *Paradigm Change in Theology. A Symposium for the Future.* Trans. Margaret Köhl. Edinburgh: Clark, 1989, pp. 439–452.

Küng, Hans and Tracy, David, eds. *Paradigm Change in Theology. A Symposium for the Future.* Trans. Margaret Köhl. Edinburgh: Clark, 1989 (1989).

Künkel, Christoph. *Totus Christus. Die Theologie Georges V. Florovskys.* Göttingen: Vandenhoeck & Ruprecht, 1991.

Künneth, Walter. *The Theology of the Resurrection.* Trans. James W. Leitch. St. Louis, Mo.: Concordia, 1965 (1933, new ed. 1951).

_____. *Entscheidung heute. Jesu Auferstehung—Brennpunkt der theologischen Diskussion.* Hamburg: Friedrich Wittig, 1966.

Kuntz, J. Kenneth. *The Self-revelation of God.* Philadelphia: Westminster, 1967.

Ladd, George Eldon. "The Resurrection of Jesus Christ," in: Carl F. H. Henry, ed., *Christian Faith and Modern Theology. Contemporary Evangelical Thought.* New York: Channel, 1964, pp. 263–284.

_____. *I Believe in the Resurrection of Jesus.* London: Hodder and Stoughton, 1975.

Lampe, Peter. "Das Spiel mit dem Petrusnamen—Matt. XVI.18," *NTS* 25 (1979), pp. 227–245.

Lange, Ernst. "Kirche für andere. Dietrich Bonhoeffer's Beitrag zur Frage einer verantwortbaren Gestalt der Kirche in der Gegenwart," *EvTh* 27 (1967), pp. 513–546.

Lapide, Pinchas. *The Resurrection of Jesus. A Jewish Perspective.* Introduction by Carl E. Braaten. Trans. Wilhelm C. Linss. Minneapolis: Augsburg Publishing House, 1983 (1977).

Lehmann, Karl. *Auferweckt am dritten Tag nach der Schrift. Früheste Christologie, Bekenntnisbildung und Schriftauslegung im Lichte von 1 Kor. 15, 3–5.* Quaestiones Disputatae 38. Freiburg/Basel/Wien: Herder, 1968.

_____. "Die Erscheinungen des Herrn. Thesen zur hermeneutisch—theologischen Struktur der Ostererzählungen," in: H. Feld und J. Nolle, Hrsg., *Wort Gottes in der Zeit.* Festschrift K. H. Schelkle zum 65. Geburtstag (Düsseldorf: Patmos, 1973), pp. 361–377.

Leimbacher, Jörg. "Die Rechte der Natur," *EvTh* 50 (1990), pp. 450–459.

Leith, John H. ed. *Creeds of the Churches.* Rev. ed. Richmond: John Knox Press, 1973.

Lietzmann, Hans. *An die Korinther I-II.* HNT, 9. 4. von Werner Georg Kümmel ergänzte Auflage. Tübingen: Mohr, 1949.

Lindars, Barnabas. "Jesus Risen: Bodily Resurrection But No Empty Tomb," *Theol* 89 (1986), pp. 90–96.

Link, Christian. *Schöpfung. Schöpfungstheologie in reformatorischer Tradition.* HSTh 7/1. Gütersloh: Mohn, 1991.

_____. *Schöpfung. Schöpfungstheologie angesichts der Herausforderungen des 20. Jahrhunderts.* HSTh 7/2. Gütersloh: Mohn, 1991.

_____. "Rechte der Schöpfung—Theologische Perspektiven," *EvTh* 50 (1990), pp. 459–468.

Littell, Franklin H. "The Discipline of Discipleship in the Free Church Tradition," *MennQR* 35 (1961), pp. 111–119.

Lochmann, Jan Milic. *Reconciliation and Liberation. Challenging a One-Dimensional View of Salvation.* Trans. David Lewis. Belfast, Dublin, Ottawa: Christian Journals Limited; Philadelphia: Fortress, 1980 (1977).

Lohfink, Gerhard. *Die Himmelfahrt Jesu. Untersuchungen zu den Himmelfahrts-und Erhöhungstexten bei Lukas.* StANT, XXVI. München: Kösel, 1971.

_____. "Der Ablauf der Osterereignisse und die Anfänge der Urgemeinde," *ThQ* 160 (1980), pp. 162–176; also in: Gerhard Lohfink. *Studien zum Neuen Testament.* SBAB, 5. Stuttgart: Katholisches Bibelwerk, 1989, pp. 149–167.

_____. *Jesus and Community. The Social Dimension of Christian Faith.* Trans. John P. Galvin. Philadelphia: Fortress / New York: Paulist, 1984 (1982).

Lorenzen, Thorwald. *Der Lieblingsjünger im Johannesevangelium. Eine redaktionsgeschichtliche Studie.* SBS 55. Stuttgart: Katholisches Bibelwerk, 1971.

_____. "Ist der Auferstandene in Galiläa erschienen? Bemerkungen zu einem Aufsatz von B. Steinseifer," *ZNW* 64 (1973), pp. 209–221.

_____. "The Meaning of the Death of Jesus Christ," in: *ABQ* IV (March, 1985), pp. 3–34.

_____. "Baptists and the Challenge of Religious Pluralism," *RExp* 89 (Winter 1992), pp. 49–69.

_____. "The Crucified Christ as Lord of the Church. Theological Reflections on 1 Corinthians 11-14," to be published in a *Festschrift* for Dr. Athol Gill.

_____. "Resurrection and Discipleship," in: *Festschrift Günter Wagner.* Ed. by Faculty of Baptist Theological Seminary, Rüschlikon/Switzerland. International Theological Studies: Contributions of Baptist Scholars, Vol. 1. Bern: Peter Lang, 1994, pp. 87–100.

Lossky, N. O. "The Resurrection of the Body," *AThR* 31 (1949), pp. 71–82.

Lossky, Vladimir. *Orthodox Theology: An Introduction.* Trans. Ian and Ihita Kesarkodi-Watson. Crestwood, N.Y.: St. Vladimir's Seminary Press, 1978.

Lucian. With an English translation by A. M. Harmon. Vol. 5. The Loeb Classical Library. Cambridge, Mass.: Harvard University Press, 1962.

Lüdemann, Gerd. *Die Auferstehung Jesu. Historie, Erfahrung, Theologie.* Göttingen: Vandenhoeck & Ruprecht, 1994.

Lührmann, Dieter. *Das Offenbarungsverständnis bei Paulus und in Paulinischen Gemeinden.* WMANT 16. Neukirchen-Vluyn: Neukirchener Verlag, 1965.

_____. *Glaube im frühen Christentum.* Gütersloh: Gerd Mohn, 1976.

_____. *Der Brief an die Galater.* Zürcher Bibelkommentare NT 7. Zürich: Theologischer Verlag, 1978.

Luz, Ulrich. *Das Evangelium nach Matthäus.* 2. Teilband, Mt 8–17. EKK I/2. Zürich: Benziger Verlag / Neukirchen Vluyn: Neukirchener Verlag, 1990.

Mahoney, Robert. *Two Disciples at the Tomb: The Background and Message of John 20:1–10.* Theologie und Wirklichkeit, Vol.6. Bern: Lang, 1974.

Maloney, George A., S. J. *The Cosmic Christ. From Paul to Teilhard.* New York: Sheed and Ward, 1968.

Mantzaridis, Georges I. *The Deification of Man. St Gregory Palamas and the Orthodox Tradition.* Trans. from the Greek by Liadain Sherarrd; with a foreword by Bishop Kallistos of Diokleia. Crestwood, N.Y.: St. Vladimir's Seminary Press, 1984.

Marxsen, Willi. "The Resurrection of Jesus as a Historical and Theological Problem," in: C. F. D. Moule, ed., *The Significance of the Message of the Resurrection for Faith in Jesus Christ.* Trans. Dorothea M. Barton. Studies in Biblical Theology, 2nd Series, 8. London: SCM, 1968 (1966), pp. 15–50.

_____. *The Resurrection of Jesus of Nazareth.* Trans. Margaret Kohl. Philadelphia: Fortress, 1970 (1968).

_____. *Der Evangelist Markus. Studien zur Redaktionsgeschichte des Evangeliums.* Göttingen: Vandenhoeck & Ruprecht, ²1959.

McDonald, J. I. H. *The Resurrection. Narrative and Belief.* London: SPCK, 1989.

McGrath, Alister E. *The Making of Modern German Christology: From the Enlightenment to Pannenberg.* Oxford: Basil Blackwell, 1986.

McKenzie, John L. *A Theology of the Old Testament.* Garden City, N.Y.: Doubleday Image Books, 1974.

Metallinos, Georgios D. "Betrachtung des Menschen im Lichte der Auferstehung," in: *Begegnung mit der Orthodoxie. Vorträge vom "Seminar für Orthodoxe Liturgie und Spiritualität", Frankfurt 1985.* München: Kloster des Hl. Hiob von Pocaev, 1986, pp. 67–83.

Metz, Johann Baptist. *Faith in History and Society. Toward a Practical Fundamental Theology.* Trans. David Smith. London: Burns and Oates, 1980 (1977).

Metzger, Bruce. *A Textual Commentary on the Greek New Testament.* London: United Bible Societies, 1971.

Meyendorff, John. *Byzantine Theology. Historical Trends and Doctrinal Themes.* London & Oxford: Mowbrays, 1974.

_____. *Christ in Eastern Christian Thought.* Crestwood, N.Y.: St. Vladimir's Seminary Press, 1987.

_____. "New Life in Christ: Salvation in Orthodox Theology," *TS* 50 (1989), pp. 481–499.

Meyer, Ben. *The Aims of Jesus.* London: SCM, 1979.

Michaelis, Wilhelm. "Ὁράω κτλ., (horaō ktl.),"in: *TDNT* V (1967 [1954]) pp. 315–381.

Moltmann, Jürgen. "Verkündigung als Problem der Exegese," (1963), in: *Perspektiven der Theologie. Gesammelte Aufsätze*. München: Kaiser, 1968, pp. 113–127.

_____. "Theology in the World of Modern Science," (1966), in: *Hope and Planning*. Trans. Margaret Clarkson. New York: Harper & Row, 1971 (1968), pp. 200–223.

_____. "Antwort auf die Kritik der Theologie der Hoffnung," in: Wolf-Dieter Marsch, ed., *Diskussion über die "Theologie der Hoffnung" von Jürgen Moltmann*. München: Kaiser, 1967, pp. 201–238.

_____. *Theology of Hope. On the Ground and the Implications of a Christian Eschatology*. Trans. James Leitch. London: SCM, 1967 (1964).

_____. "Gott in der Revolution," (1968), in: Ernst Feil and Rudolf Weth, eds., *Diskussion zur "Theologie der Revolution"*. München: Kaiser, Mainz: Matthias Grünewald, ²1970, pp. 65–81.

_____. "God and Resurrection. Resurrection Faith in the Forum of the Question of Theodicy," (1968), in: *Hope and Planning*. Trans. Margaret Clarkson. New York: Harper & Row, 1971 (1968), pp. 31–55.

_____. *Theology of Play*. Trans. Reinhard Ulrich. New York: Harper and Row, 1972 (1971). In England published under *Theology and Joy*. With an extended introduction by David E. Jenkins. Trans. Reinhard Ulrich. London: SCM, 1973 (1971).

_____. "The Hope of Resurrection and the Practice of Liberation," (1972), in: *The Future of Creation*. Trans. Margaret Kohl. London: SCM, 1979 (1977), pp. 97–114.

_____. *The Crucified God. The Cross of Christ as the Foundation and Criticism of Christian Theology*. Trans. R. A. Wilson and John Bowden. London: SCM, 1974 (1973).

_____. *The Church in the Power of the Spirit. A Contribution to Messianic Ecclesiology*. Trans. Margaret Kohl. London: SCM, 1977 (1975).

_____. *Experiences of God*. Trans. Margaret Kohl. London: SCM, 1980 (1979).

_____. "Theological Proposals toward the Resolution of the Filioque Controversy," in: Lukas Vischer, ed., *Spirit of God, Spirit of Christ*. Ecumenical Reflections on the *Filioque* Controversy. Faith and Order Paper No. 103. Geneva: WCC, London: SPCK, 1981, pp. 164–173.

_____. *The Trinity and the Kingdom of God. The Doctrine of God*. Trans. Margaret Kohl. London: SCM, 1981 (1980).

_____. "Einführung," in: Jürgen Moltmann, ed., *Nachfolge und Bergpredigt*. München: Kaiser, ²1982, pp. 7–11.

_____. *On Human Dignity. Political Theology and Ethics*. Trans. M. Douglas Meeks. London: SCM, 1984.

_____. "Political Theology and Political Hermeneutic of the Gospel," in: *On Human Dignity, Political Theology and Ethics*. Trans. M. Douglas Meeks. London: SCM, 1984, pp. 97–112.

_____. *God in Creation. An Ecological Doctrine of Creation*. Trans. Margaret Kohl. The Gifford Lectures 1984–1985. London: SCM, 1985 (1985).

_____. *Theology Today. Two Contributions Towards Making Theology Present*. Trans. John Bowden. London: SCM, 1988 (1988).

_____. "The Course of Theology in the Twentieth Century," in: *Theology Today. Two Contributions Towards Making Theology Present*. Trans. John Bowden. London: SCM, 1988 (1988), pp. 1–51.

_____. "Mediating Theology Today," in: *Theology Today. Two Contributions Towards Making Theology Present*. Trans. John Bowden. London: SCM, 1988 (1988), pp. 53–99.

_____. "Human Rights, the Rights of Humanity and the Rights of Nature," in: Hans Küng and Jürgen Moltmann, eds., *The Ethics of World Religions and Human Rights*. Concilium 1990/2. London: SCM; Philadelphia: Trinity Press International, 1990, pp. 120–135.

_____. *The Way of Jesus Christ. Christology in Messianic Dimensions*. Trans. Margaret Kohl. London: SCM, 1990 (1989).

_____. *The Spirit of Life. A Universal Affirmation*. Trans. Margaret Kohl. London: SCM, 1992 (1991).

Moltmann, Jürgen and Giesser, Elizabeth. "Menschenrechte, Rechte der Menschheit und Rechte der Natur," *EvTh* 50 (1990), pp. 437–444.

Morse, Christopher. *The Logic of Promise in Moltmann's Theology*. Philadelphia: Fortress, 1979.

Moule, C. F. D., ed., *The Significance of the Message of the Resurrection for Faith in Jesus Christ*. Studies in Biblical Theology, Second Series 8. Trans. Dorothea M. Barton and R. A. Wilson. London: SCM, 1968 (1966).

Moule, C. F. D. and Cupitt, Don. "The Resurrection: A Disagreement," *Theology. A Monthly Review* 75, No. 628 (October 1972), pp. 507–519.

Mühlen, Heribert. "Soziale Geisteserfahrung als Antwort auf eine einseitige Gotteslehre," in: Claus Heitmann / Heribert Mühlen, eds., *Erfahrung und Theologie des Heiligen Geistes*. Hamburg: Agentur des Rauhen Hauses, München: Kösel, 1974, pp. 253–272.

Nauck, Wolfgang. "Die Bedeutung des leeren Grabes für den Glauben an den Auferstandenen," *ZNW* 47 (1956), pp. 243–267.

Nestle-Aland, *Novum Testamentum Graece*. Stuttgart: Deutsche Bibelstiftung, 26. neu bearbeitete Auflage, 1979 and 27. revidierte Auflage, 1993.

Nicholson, Oliver. "Holy Sepulcher, Church of the," in: David Noel Freedman, ed., *The Anchor Bible Dictionary* 3 (1992), pp. 258–260.

Nickelsburg, George W. E. *Resurrection, Immortality, and Eternal Life in Intertestamental Judaism*. HThSt XXVI. Cambridge: Harvard University Press, 1972.

Niebuhr, Richard R. *Resurrection and Historical Reason. A Study of Theological Method*. New York: Charles Scribner's Sons, 1957.

Nützel, Johannès M. "Zum Schicksal der eschatologischen Propheten," *BZ* 20 (1976), pp. 59–94.

O'Collins, Gerald, S. J. *Interpreting Jesus*. Introducing Catholic Theology. London: Geoffrey Chapman/Ramsey, N.J.: Paulist Press, 1983.

_____. *Jesus Risen*. London: Darton, Longman and Todd, 1987.

O'Collins, Gerald S. J. and Daniel Kendall, S. J., "Mary Magdalene as major witness to Jesus' resurrection," *TS* 48 (1987), pp. 631–646.

Oepke, Albrecht. "ἀνίστημι κτλ.," (anhistēmi ktl.) in: *TDNT* I (1964 [1933]), pp. 368–372.

_____. "ἐγείρω κτλ.," (egeirō) in: *TDNT* II (1964 [1935]), pp. 333–339.

Ohlig, Karl-Heinz. *Fundamentalchristologie—Im Spannungsfeld von Christentum und Kultur*. München: Kösel Verlag, 1986.

Ott, Heinrich. "The Historical Jesus and the Ontology of History," (1960) in: C. E. Braaten and Roy A. Harrisville, eds., *The Historical Jesus and the Kerygmatic Christ. Essays on the New Quest of the Historical Jesus*. Trans. C. E. Braaten and Roy A. Harrisville. New York/Nashville: Abingdon, 1964, pp. 142–171.

Pannenberg, Wolfhart. "Redemptive Event and History," (1959), in: *Basic Questions in*

Theology: Collected Essays, Vol. 1. Trans. George H. Kehm. Philadelphia: Fortress, 1970 (1967), pp. 15–80.

_____. "Dogmatic Theses on the Doctrine of Revelation," (1960), in: Wolfhart Pannenberg, ed., *Revelation as History*. Trans. David Granskou. London: Macmillan, 1968 (1961), pp. 123–158.

_____. "Introduction," (1960), in: Wolfhart Pannenberg, ed., *Revelation as History*. Trans. David Granskou. London: Macmillan, 1968 (1961), pp. 1–21.

_____. "Types of Atheism and Their Theological Significance," (1960), in: *Basic Questions in Theology: Collected Essays*, Vol. 2. Trans. George H. Kehm. Philadelphia: Fortress, 1971 (1967), pp. 184–200.

_____. "Insight and Faith," (1963), in: *Basic Questions in Theology: Collected Essays*, Vol. 2. Trans. George H. Kehm, Philadelphia: Fortress, 1971 (1967), pp. 28–45.

_____. "On Historical and Theological Hermeneutic," (1964), in: *Basic Questions in Theology: Collected Essays*, Vol. 1. Trans. George H. Kehm. Philadelphia: Fortress, 1970 (1967), pp. 137–181.

_____. "Did Jesus really rise from the dead?" (1965), in: Richard Batey, ed., *New Testament Issues*. London: SCM, 1970, pp. 102–117.

_____. "Faith and Reason," (1965), in: *Basic Questions in Theology: Collected Essays*, Vol. 2. Trans. George H. Kehm, Philadelphia: Fortress, 1971 (1967), pp. 46–64.

_____. "The Revelation of God in Jesus of Nazareth," (1965), in: James M. Robinson and John B. Cobb, Jr., eds., *Theology as History*. New Frontiers in Theology. Discussions among Continental and American Theologians, Vol. 3. New York: Harper and Row, 1967, pp. 101–133.

_____. "Response to the Discussion," in: James M. Robinson and John B. Cobb, Jr., eds., *Theology as History*. New Frontiers in Theology. Discussions among Continental and American Theologians, Vol. 3. New York: Harper and Row, 1967, pp. 221–276.

_____. "Dogmatische Erwägungen zur Auferstehung Jesu," (1968), in: *Grundfragen Systematischer Theologie. Gesammelte Aufsätze*, Vol. 2. Göttingen: Vandenhoeck & Ruprecht, 1980, pp. 160–173 (also in *KuD* 14 [1968], pp. 105–118).

_____. *Jesus—God and Man*. Trans. Lewis L. Wilkins and Duane A. Priebe. Philadelphia: Westminster, 1968 (1964).

_____. *What Is Man? Contemporary Anthropology in Theological Perspective*. Trans. Duane A. Priebe. Philadelphia: Fortress, 1970 (1962).

_____. "Christologie und Theologie," (1975) in: *Grundfragen Systematischer Theologie. Gesammelte Aufsätze*, Vol. 2. Göttingen: Vandenhoeck & Ruprecht, 1980, pp. 129–145 (also in *KuD* 21 [1975], pp. 159–175).

_____. "Response to the Debate," in: *Did Jesus Rise From The Dead? The Resurrection Debate*. Gary R. Habermas and Anthony G. N. Flew, eds. San Francisco: Harper & Row, 1987, pp. 125–135.

_____. *Systematische Theologie*. Göttingen: Vandenhoeck & Ruprecht. Bd. I (1988), Bd. II (1991), Bd. III (1993).

_____. *Systematic Theology*. Grand Rapids, Mich.: Eerdmans. Trans. Geoffrey W. Bromiley. Vol. 1 (1991 [1988]), Vol. 2 (1994 [1991]).

_____. "Die Auferstehung Jesu—Historie und Theologie," *ZThK* 91 (1994), pp. 318–328.

Papandreou, Damaskinos. "Christologie und Soteriologie im Verständnis der Kirchenväter," in: *Orthodoxie und Ökumene. Gesammelte Aufsätze von Damaskinos Papandreou*. Ed. by Wilhelm Schneemelcher. Stuttgart: Kohlhammer, 1986, pp. 58–70.

Perkins, Pheme. *Resurrection: New Testament Witness and Contemporary Reflection.* London: Chapman, 1984.

Pesch, Rudolf. "Zur Entstehung des Glaubens an die Auferstehung Jesu. Ein Vorschlag zur Diskussion," *ThQ* 153 (1973), pp. 201—228.

_____. "Materialien und Bemerkungen zu Entstehung und Sinn des Osterglaubens," in: Anton Vögtle/Rudolf Pesch, *Wie kam es zum Osterglauben?* Düsseldorf: Patmos Verlag, 1975, pp. 133–184.

_____. *Das Markusevangelium, II. Teil, Kommentar zu Kap. 8,27–16:20.* HthK. Freiburg: Herder, 1977.

Philostratus. *The Life of Apollonius of Tyana.* With an English Translation by F. C. Conybeare. Vol. 2. The Loeb Classical Library. Cambridge, Mass.: Harvard University Press, 1950.

Pomazansky, Protopresbyter Michael. *Orthodox Dogmatic Theology. A Concise Exposition.* Trans. by Hieromonk Seraphim Rose. Platina, Ca.: Saint Herman of Alaska Brotherhood, 1984.

The Pontifical Biblical Commission. "The Interpretation of the Bible in the Church. With a Preface by Joseph Cardinal Ratzinger," (November 1993), in: *Catholic International* (March 1994), pp.109–147.

Pope John Paul II. "Priestly Ordination" ("*Ordinatio sacerdotalis*"). "Apostolic Letter on Ordination and Women of Pope John Paul II of May 30, 1994," *Origins* 24/4 (9 June 1994), pp. 49, 51f.

Pope Pius X. "Pius X's Oath against Modernism," in: Philip Schaff, *The Creeds of Christendom with a History and Critical Notes.* Bibliotheca Symbolica Ecclesiae Universalis. Vol. II: The Greek and Latin Creeds with Translations. New York: Harper & Brothers, 1877, pp. 613–615.

Postel, Sandra. "Denial in the Decisive Decade," in: Lester R. Brown et. al. *State of the World 1992.* A Worldwatch Institute Report on Progress Toward a Sustainable Society (New York/London: W. W. Norton, 1992), pp. 3–8.

Rad, Gerhard von. *Old Testament Theology.* 2 vols. Trans. D. M. G. Stalker. Edinburgh: Oliver and Boyd, vol. I, 1962 (1957), vol. II. 1965 (1960).

_____. "Offene Fragen im Umkreis einer Theologie des Alten Testaments," *ThLZ* 88 (1963), pp. 401–416.

_____. *God at Work in Israel.* Trans. John H. Marks. Nashville: Abingdon, 1980 (1974).

Rahner, K. "Current Problems in Christology," in: *Theological Investigations*, Vol.1: God, Christ, Mary and Grace. Trans. Cornelius Ernst. London: Darton, Longman and Todd, 1961 (1954), pp. 149–200.

_____. *The Trinity.* Trans. Joseph Donceel. London: Burns & Oates, 1970 (1967).

_____. *Foundations of the Christian Faith. An Introduction to the Idea of Christianity.* Trans. William V. Dych. London: Darton Longman & Todd, 1978 (1976).

Rahner, K., Schmitt, J., Bulst, W. "Resurrection of Christ," in: *Encyclopedia of Theology. The Concise Sacramentum Mundi.* London: Burns and Oates, 1975, pp. 1430–1442.

Rengstorf, Karl Heinrich. "ἀπόστολος," (apostolos) in *TDNT* I (1964 [1933]), pp. 407–445.

_____. *Die Auferstehung Jesu. Form, Art und Sinn der urchristlichen Osterbotschaft.* Witten/Ruhr: Luther Verlag, 1967.

Ricoeur, Paul. "The Hermeneutics of Testimony," (1979), in: *Essays on Biblical Interpretation.* Ed. with an introduction by Lewis S. Mudge. Trans. David Stewart and Charles E. Reagan. Philadelphia: Fortress, 1980, pp. 119–154.

Ritschl, Dietrich. "Historical Development and Implications of the Filioque Controversy," in: Lukas Vischer, ed., *Spirit of God, Spirit of Christ.* Ecumenical

Reflections on the *Filioque* Controversy. Faith and Order Paper No. 103. Geneva: WCC, London: SPCK, 1981, pp. 46–65.

Robinson, James M. "Revelation as Word and as History," in: James M. Robinson and John B. Cobb, Jr., eds., *Theology as History*. New Frontiers in Theology. Discussions among Continental and American Theologians, Vol. 3. New York: Harper and Row, 1967, pp. 1–100.

Robinson, James M. and Cobb, John B. Jr., eds., *Theology as History*. New Frontiers in Theology. Discussions among Continental and American Theologians, Vol. 3. New York: Harper and Row, 1967.

Roloff, Jürgen. "Apostel/Apostolat/Apostolizität I," in: *TRE* III (1978), pp. 430–445.

_____. *Die Kirche im Neuen Testament*. GNT 10. Göttingen: Vandenhoeck & Ruprecht, 1993.

Rowley, H. H. *The Faith of Israel: Aspects of Old Testament Thought*. London: SCM, 1961 (1956).

Ruckstuhl, Eugen und Pfammatter, Josef. *Die Auferstehung Jesu Christi. Heilsgeschichtliche Tatsache und Brennpunkt des Glaubens*. München: Rex Verlag, 1968.

Rumpeltes, Hans. "Bibliographie (bis 1973—about the resurrection)," in: Hildegard Temporini und Wolfgang Haase, Hg., *Aufstieg und Niedergang der Römischen Welt. Geschichte und Kultur Roms im Spiegel der Neueren Forschung*, II.25.1: *Religion (Vorkonstantinisches Christentum: Leben und Umwelt Jesu; Neues Testament [Kanonische Schriften und Apokryphen])*. Hg. Wolfgang Haase. Berlin/New York: Walter de Gruyter, 1982, pp. 844–890.

Sacred Congregation for the Doctrine of the Faith. "On the Question of the Admission of Women to the Ministerial Priesthood" ("*Inter insigniores*"), Declaration of Oct. 15, 1976 of the Sacred Congregation for the Doctrine of the Faith (U.S. Catholic Conference Edition with Commentary [Washington, D.C., 1977]); *AAS* 69 (1977), pp. 98–116.

Saladin, Peter and Zenger, Christoph. "Rechte künftiger Generationen," *EvTh* 50 (1990), pp. 444–450.

Sanders, E. P. *Jesus and Judaism*. London: SCM, 1985.

Schaff, Philip. *The Creeds of Christendom*. 3 vols. New York: Harper and Brothers, 1877.

Schenke, Ludger. *Auferstehungsverkündigung und leeres Grab. Eine traditions-geschichtliche Untersuchung von Mk 16,1–8*. SBS 33. Stuttgart: Katholisches Bibelwerk, 1968.

Schillebeeckx, Edward. *Christ. The Christian Experience in the Modern World*. Trans. John Bowden. London: SCM Press, 1980 (1977).

_____. *Interim Report on the Books Jesus & Christ*. Trans. John Bowden. New York: Crossroad, 1981 (1978).

_____. *Jesus. An Experiment in Christology*. Trans. Hubert Hoskins. New York: Crossroad, 1987 (1979; 1974).

Schlier, Heinrich. *Der Brief and die Galater*. KEK. Göttingen: Vandenhoeck & Ruprecht, ¹¹1951.

_____. *Über die Auferstehung Jesu Christi*. Kriterien 10. Einsiedeln: Johannes Verlag, 1968.

Schmid, Hans Heinrich. "Ekstatische und charismatische Geistwirkungen im Alten Testament," in: Claus Heitmann/Heribert Mühlen, eds., *Erfahrung und Theologie des Heiligen Geistes*. Hamburg: Agentur des Rauhen Hauses; München: Kösel, 1974, pp. 83–100.

Schmidt, Werner H.; Schäfer, Peter. "Geist/Heiliger Geist/Geistesgaben I und II," in: *TRE* XII (1984), pp. 170–178.

Schmithals, Walter. *Paul and James.* Trans. Dorothea M. Barton. SBT, 46. London: SCM, 1965 (1963).

Schottroff, Willy. *'Gedenken' im Alten Orient und im Alten Testament. Die Wurzel ZAKAR im semitischen Sprachkreis.* WMANT 15. Neukirchen-Vluyn: Neukirchener Verlag, 1964.

Schrage, Wolfgang. "Theologie und Christologie bei Paulus und Jesus auf dem Hintergrund der modernen Gottesfrage," *EvTh* 36 (1976), pp. 121–154.

_____. "Das Verständnis des Todes Jesu im Neuen Testament," in: Fritz Vierig, ed., *Das Kreuz Jesu Christi als Grund des Heils.* Gütersloh: Mohn, 1967, pp. 49–89.

Schreiber, Johannes. "Die Bestattung Jesu. Redaktionsgeschichtliche Beobachtungen zu Mk 15:42–47 par," *ZNW* 72 (1981), pp. 141–177.

Schubert, Kurt. "Die Entwicklung der Auferstehungslehre von der nachexilischen bis zur frührabbinischen Zeit," *BZ NF* 6 (1962), pp. 177–214.

Schürer, Emil. *The History of the Jewish People in the Age of Jesus Christ* (175 B.C.–A.D. 135). A New English Version, revised and edited by Geza Vermes, Fergus Millar, Matthew Black. Vol. II. Edinburgh: Clark, 1979 [1885]).

Schüssler Fiorenza, Elisabeth. *In Memory of Her. A Feminist Theological Reconstruction of Christian Origins.* London: SCM, 1983.

Schüssler Fiorenza, Francis. *Foundational Theology. Jesus and the Church.* New York: Crossroad, 1986.

Schweitzer, Albert. *The Quest of the Historical Jesus: A Critical Study of Its Progress from Reimarus to Wrede.* Trans. W. Montgomery. London: Adam & Charles Black, 1948 (1906).

_____. *My Life & Thought. An Autobiography.* Trans. C. T. Campion. London: Allen & Unwin, 1948 (1931).

_____. *The Philosophy of Civilization.* Trans. C. T. Campion. New York: MacMillan, 1959 (1923).

Schweizer, Eduard. "πνεῦμα κτλ. [pneuma ktl.] The New Testament," in: *TDNT* VI (1968 [1959]), pp. 396–455.

_____. *Lordship and Discipleship.* SBT 28. London: SCM, 1960 (1955).

_____. "Discipleship and Church," in: *The Beginnings of the Church in the New Testament.* Trans. Iain and Ute Nicol. Edinburgh: Saint Andrew Press, 1970 (1967), pp. 85–104.

_____. "σῶμα κτλ.," (sōma ktl.) in: *TDNT* VII (1971 [1964]), pp. 1024–1094.

_____. *The Good News According to Mark.* Trans. Donald H. Madvig. Richmond: Knox, 1970 (1967).

_____. *Jesus.* Trans. David E. Green. London: SCM, 1971 (1968).

_____. A Review of Klaus Berger's book, *Die Auferstehung des Propheten und die Erhöhung des Menschensohnes* (1976), *ThLZ* 103 (1978), pp. 876–878.

_____. *The Holy Spirit.* Trans. Reginald H. and Ilse Fuller. Philadelphia: Fortress, 1980 (1978).

Schwertner, Siegfried M. *Abkürzungsverzeichnis.* 2., überarbeitete und erweiterte Auflage. *Theologische Realenzyklopädie.* New York/Berlin: Walter de Gruyter, 1994.

Segundo, Juan Luis. *Liberation of Theology.* Trans. John Drury. Maryknoll, N.Y.: Orbis Books, 1976 (1975).

Senn, Frank C. "Berdyaev, Orthodoxy, and the Theology of Hope," *JESt* 7 (1970), pp. 455–475.

Sheldrake, Rupert. *The Presence of the Past. Morphic Resonance and the Habits of Nature.* New York: Vintage Books, 1989.

_____. *The Rebirth of Nature: The Greening of Science and God.* New York: Doubleday/Bantam, 1991.

Sittler, Joseph. "Called to Unity," *SEAJT* 3 (1962), pp. 6–15.

Sobrino, Jon, S.J. *Christology at the Crossroads. A Latin American Approach.* Trans. by John Drury. Maryknoll, N.Y.: Orbis Books, 1978 (1976).

_____. *The True Church and the Poor.* Trans. Matthew J. O'Connell. London: SCM, 1985 (1981).

_____. *Jesus in Latin America.* Maryknoll, N.Y.: Orbis Books, 1987 (1982).

_____. *Spirituality of Liberation: Toward Political Holiness.* Trans. Robert R, Barr Maryknoll, N.Y.: Orbis Books, 1988.

_____. "The Greatest Love," *Sojourners* (April 1990), pp. 16–21.

Stackhouse, Max L. *Apologia. Contextualization, Globalization, and Mission in Theological Education.* Grand Rapids, Mich.: Eerdmans, 1988.

Staniloae, Dumitru. *Orthodoxe Dogmatik.* Trans. by Hermann Pitters. Foreword by Jürgen Moltmann. Öth, 15. II. Band. Zürich: Benziger Verlag / Gütersloh: Gerd Mohn, 1990.

Steck, Odil Hannes. *World and Environment.* Biblical Encounter Series. Nashville: Abingdon, 1980 (1978).

Stemberger, Günter. *Der Leib der Auferstehung. Studien zur Anthropologie und Eschatologie des palästinischen Judentums im neutestamentlichen Zeitalter (ca. 170 v. Chr.—100 n. Chr.).* AnBib 56. Rome: Biblical Institute Press, 1972.

Strack, Hermann L. and Billerbeck, Paul. *Kommentar zum Neuen Testament aus Talmud und Midrasch.* Band III: Die Briefe des Neuen Testaments und die Offenbarung Johannis erläutert aus Talmud und Midrasch. München: Beck, 1926; Band IV: Exkurse zu einzelnen Stellen des Neuen Testaments. Abhandlungen zur neutestamentlichen Theologie und Archäologie, zweiter Teil. München: Beck, 1928.

Strathmann, H. "μάρτυς κτλ.," (martus ktl.) *TDNT* IV (1967 [1942]), pp. 474–514.

Strauss, David Friedrich. *The Old Faith and the New: A Confession.* Trans. Mathilde Blind. New York: Henry Holt & Co., 1873 (1872).

_____. *The Life of Jesus Critically Examined.* Ed. Peter C. Hodgson, trans. George Eliot. Philadelphia: Fortress, 1972 (⁴1840).

Strobel, August. "Discipleship in the Light of the Easter-event," in: *The Beginnings of the Church in the New Testament.* Trans. Iain and Ute Nicol. Edinburgh: Saint Andrew Press, 1970 (1967), pp. 40–84.

Strunk, Reiner. *Nachfolge Christi. Erinnerungen an eine evangelische Provokation.* München: Kaiser, 1981.

Stuhlmacher, Peter. "Das Bekenntnis zur Auferweckung Jesu von den Toten und die Biblische Theologie," *ZThK* 70 (1973), pp. 365–403.

_____. "Kritischer müssten mir die Historisch-Kritischen sein!" *TQ* 153 (1973), pp. 244–251.

_____. "The Resurrection of Jesus and the Resurrection of the Dead," *Ex Auditu* 9 (1993), pp. 45–56.

Tarazi, Paul N. "Witnessing the Dynamics of Salvation," *SVSQ* 22 (1978), pp. 179–191.

Terrien, Samuel. *The Elusive Presence.* Toward a New Biblical Theology. Religious Perspectives, 26. New York: Harper & Row, 1978.

Tertullian. *Treatise against Praxeas. The Ante Nicene Fathers.* Trans. of *The Writings of the Fathers down to A.D. 305.* The Rev. Alexander Roberts and James Donaldson, eds. Vol. III: Latin Christianity: Its Founder, Tertullian. Grand Rapids, Michigan: Eerdmans, reprinted 1980, pp. 597–627.

Thiselton, Anthony C. *New Horizons in Hermeneutics*. London: Harper Collins Publishers, 1992.

Tholin, Richard. "The Holy Spirit and Liberation Movements: The Response of the Church," in: Dow Kirkpatrik, ed., *The Holy Spirit*. Nashville: Tidings, 1974, pp. 40–75.

Thüsing, Wilhelm. *Erhöhungsvorstellung und Parusieerwartung in der ältesten nachösterlichen Christologie*. SBS 42. Stuttgart: Katholisches Bibelwerk, 1969.

_____. "Neutestamentliche Zugangswege zu einer transzendental-dialogischen Christologie," in: Karl Rahner—Wilhelm Thüsing, *Christologie—Systematisch und Exegetisch. Arbeitsgrundlagen für eine interdisziplinäre Vorlesung*. Freiburg/Basel/Wien: Herder, 1972, pp. 79–303.

_____. *Die Neutestamentlichen Theologien und Jesus Christus. I: Kriterien aufgrund der Rückfrage nach Jesus und des Glaubens an seine Auferweckung*. Düsseldorf: Patmos, 1981.

Tillich, Paul. *Dynamics of Faith*. New York: Harper & Row, 1957; also found in: Carl Heinz Ratschow, ed., *Paul Tillich, Main Works/Hauptwerke*, Vol. 5. Berlin/New York: De Gruyter, 1988, pp. 231–290.

Torrance, Thomas F. *Space, Time and Resurrection*. Grand Rapids, Mich.: Eerdmans, 1976.

Tracy, David. *Blessed Rage for Order: The New Pluralism in Theology*. A Crossroad Book. New York: Seabury, 1975.

_____. *The Analogical Imagination. Christian Theology and the Culture of Pluralism*. London: SCM, 1981.

Tracy, David and Lash, Nicholas, eds. *Cosmology and Theology*. Concilium 166 (6/1983). Edinburgh: T. & T. Clark; New York: Seabury, 1983.

Trites, Allison A. *The New Testament Concept of Witness*. Cambridge: University Press, 1977.

Troeltsch, Ernst. "Historical and Dogmatic Method in Theology," (1898), in: *Religion in History*. With an Introduction by James Luther Adams. Trans. James Luther Adams and Walter F. Bense. Fortress Texts in Modern Theology. Minneapolis: Fortress, 1991, pp. 11–32.

Tupper, E. Frank. *The Theology of Wolfhart Pannenberg*. Philadelphia: Westminster, 1973.

United Nations. "Weltcharta für die Natur beschlossen und feierlich verkündet durch die Generalversammlung der Vereinten Nationen am 28. Oktober 1982," *EvTh* 50 (1990), pp. 472–477.

_____. *The Global Partnership for Environment and Development. A Guide to Agenda 21—Post Rio Edition*. New York: United Nations, 1993.

Vassiliades, Nicilaos P. "The Mystery of Death," *GOTR* 29 (Spring 1984/1), pp. 269–282.

Verweyen, Hansjürgen. "Die Sache mit den Ostererscheinungen," in: Ingo Broer/Jürgen Werbick, eds., *"Der Herr ist wahrhaft erschienen" (Lk 24,34). Biblische und systematische Beiträge zur Entstehung des Osterglaubens*. SBS 134. Stuttgart: Verlag Katholisches Bibelwerk, 1988, pp. 63–80.

Vischer, Lukas, ed. *Spirit of God, Spirit of Christ*. Ecumenical Reflections on the *Filioque* Controversy. Faith and Order Paper No. 103. Geneva: WCC, London: SPCK, 1981.

_____. "Vorwort zu 'Rechte künftiger Generationen—Rechte der Natur'," *EvTh* 50 (1990), pp. 433–436.

_____. "Rolle und Beitrag der Kirchen," *EvTh* 50 (1990), pp. 468–471.

Vögtle, Anton. "Wie kam es zum Osterglauben?" in: Anton Vögtle/Rudolf Pesch, *Wie kam es zum Osterglauben?* Düsseldorf: Patmos Verlag, 1975, pp. 9–131.

_____. *Die Dynamik des Anfangs. Leben und Fragen der jungen Kirche.* Freiburg/Basel/Wien: Herder, 1988.

Walter, Nikolaus. " 'Historischer Jesus' und Osterglaube. Ein Diskussionsbeitrag zur Christologie," *ThLZ* 101 (5, 1976), cols. 321–338.

Wanke, Joachim. " '. . . wie sie ihn beim Brotbrechen erkannten'. Zur Auslegung der Emmauserzählung Lk 24,13–35," *BZ* 18 (1974), pp. 180–192.

Ware, Bishop Kallistos. *The Orthodox Way.* London & Oxford: Mowbray, 1979.

Ware, Timothy. *The Orthodox Church.* Hammondsworth: Penguin Books, 1963.

Weiser, Alfons/Pöhlmann, Horst G. "Himmelfahrt Christi," *TRE* 15 (1986), pp. 330–341.

Wenger, John C. "Grace and Discipleship in Anabaptism," *MennQR* 35 (1961), pp. 50–69.

Wengst, Klaus. *Ostern—Ein wirkliches Gleichnis, eine wahre Geschichte. Zum neutestamentlichen Zeugnis von der Auferweckung Jesu.* München: Kaiser, 1991.

Wenz, Günther. "Ostern als Urdatum des Christentums. Zu Wolfhart Pannenbergs Theologie der Auferweckung Jesu," in: Ingo Broer/Jürgen Werbick, eds., *"Der Herr ist wahrhaft erschienen" (Lk 24,34). Biblische und systematische Beiträge zur Entstehung des Osterglaubens.* SBS 134. Stuttgart: Verlag Katholisches Bibelwerk, 1988, pp. 133–157.

Westermann, Claus. "The Way of Promise through the Old Testament," (1963), in: Bernhard W. Anderson, ed., *The Old Testament and Christian Faith. A Theological Discussion.* Trans. Lloyd Gaston and Bernhard W. Anderson. New York: Harper & Row, 1963, pp. 200–224.

_____. "Das Alte Testament und die Menschenrechte," in Jörg Baur, ed., *Zum Thema Menschenrechte. Theologische Versuche und Entwürfe.* Stuttgart: Calwer Verlag, 1977, pp. 5–18.

_____. "Geist im Alten Testament," *EvTh* 41 (1981), pp. 223–230.

Wilckens, Ulrich. "Der Ursprung der Überlieferung der Erscheinungen des Auferstandenen. Zur traditionsgeschichtlichen Analyse von 1. Kor. 15,1–11," in: Wilfried Joest and Wolfhart Pannenberg, eds., *Dogma und Denkstrukturen.* Göttingen: Vandenhoeck & Ruprecht, 1963, pp. 56–95.

_____. "The Tradition-history of the Resurrection of Jesus," in: C. F. D. Moule, ed., *The Significance of the Message of the Resurrection for Faith in Jesus Christ.* Trans. R. A. Wilson. Studies in Biblical Theology, 2nd Series, 8. London: SCM, 1968 (1966), pp. 51–76.

_____. *Die Missionsreden der Apostelgeschichte. Form- und traditionsgeschichtliche Untersuchungen.* WMANT 5. Neukirchen-Vluyn: Neukirchener Verlag, 3. überarbeitete und erweiterte Auflage 1974.

_____. *Resurrection: Biblical Testimony to the Resurrection. An Historical Examination and Explanation.* Trans. A. M. Stewart. Atlanta: John Knox, 1978 (1970).

Wildberger, Hans. "'Glauben' im Alten Testament," *ZThK* 65 (1968), pp. 129–159.

_____. "Fest, sicher," in: *THAT* I (1971), cols. 177–209.

Williams, Rowan. *Resurrection. Interpreting the Easter Gospel.* London: Darton, Longman & Todd, 1982.

Winger, J. Michael. "When Did the Women Visit the Tomb? Sources for Some Temporal Clauses in the Synoptic Gospels," *NTS* 40 (1994), pp. 284–288.

Wolff, Hans Walter. *Anthropology of the Old Testament.* Trans. Margaret Kohl. London: SCM, 1974 (1973).

Wright, G. Ernest. *God Who Acts. Biblical Theology as Recital.* SBT, 8. London: SCM, 1952.

Zahrnt, Heinz. *The Historical Jesus.* Trans. J. S. Bowden. New York: Harper and Row, 1963 (1960).

Zimmerli, Walther. "Promise and Fulfillment," (1952), in: Claus Westermann, ed., *Essays on Old Testament Hermeneutics.* Trans. and ed. James Luther Mays. Atlanta: John Knox Press, 1963 (1960), pp. 89–122.

_____. *Old Testament Theology in Outline.* Trans. David E. Green. Atlanta: John Knox Press, 1978 (1972).

Author and Subject Index

Scripture Index